T0207111

Lecture Notes in Computer Science 11970

More information about this series at http://www.springer.com/series/7409

Asbjørn Følstad · Theo Araujo ·
Symeon Papadopoulos · Effie Lai-Chong Law ·
Ole-Christoffer Granmo · Ewa Luger ·
Petter Bae Brandtzaeg (Eds.)

Chatbot Research and Design

Third International Workshop, CONVERSATIONS 2019
Amsterdam, The Netherlands, November 19–20, 2019
Revised Selected Papers

 Springer

Editors
Asbjørn Følstad (ID)
SINTEF
Oslo, Norway

Symeon Papadopoulos (ID)
CERTH-ITI
Thessaloniki, Greece

Ole-Christoffer Granmo (ID)
University of Agder
Grimstad, Norway

Petter Bae Brandtzaeg (ID)
University of Oslo
Oslo, Norway

Theo Araujo (ID)
University of Amsterdam
Amsterdam, The Netherlands

Effie Lai-Chong Law (ID)
University of Leicester
Leicester, UK

Ewa Luger (ID)
University of Edinburgh
Edinburgh, UK

ISSN 0302-9743   ISSN 1611-3349 (electronic)
Lecture Notes in Computer Science
ISBN 978-3-030-39539-1   ISBN 978-3-030-39540-7 (eBook)
https://doi.org/10.1007/978-3-030-39540-7

LNCS Sublibrary: SL3 – Information Systems and Applications, incl. Internet/Web, and HCI

This Springer imprint is published by the registered company Springer Nature Switzerland AG
The registered company address is: Gewerbestrasse 11, 6330 Cham, Switzerland

Preface

Introduction

Chatbots are conversational agents that allow the user access to information and services through natural language dialogue, including text and voice. Research on chatbots has advanced substantially in recent years, both in exploring the developments regarding their design and underlying technology, especially artificial intelligence and machine learning, and in advancing our knowledge about how people use and experience these agents. In addition, the ever-increasing usage of chatbots by people from many walks of life requires us to consider its societal impact and ethical implications. Chatbots are maturing for application areas including education, health, and information services, and may be designed for individual users or for supporting collaboration. They are an important emerging technology with potential to empower citizens to engage in societal issues, customers to obtain information and help from service providers, patients to get critical health-related information or advice, or professionals to get easy access to knowledge or resources for decision-making.

Within this evolving field, it is critical for researchers and practitioners to share findings and experiences, and to discuss challenges and future directions. In particular, we need meeting places that facilitate cross-disciplinary exchange, given the multifaceted challenges of the field of chatbot research, and their potential for societal impact.

These goals motivated us to organize the third international workshop on chatbot research and practice – CONVERSATIONS 2019 which was held during November 19–20, 2019, at the University of Amsterdam, the Netherlands. Chatbot researchers were invited to share empirical, theoretical, and design results through full and position papers. 50 participants with different backgrounds, including informatics, interaction design, media and communication science, as well as psychology and social sciences, registered for the workshop, reflecting the cross-disciplinary character of this area of interest.

Chatbot research spans a broad range of topics, including user and communication studies, user experience and design, development platforms and frameworks, chatbots in networked collaboration, chatbots for all, and ethics and privacy. On the basis of the results from the two previous CONVERSATIONS workshops, we outlined a set of research challenges to guide the workshop contributions and output in terms of the papers submitted and of group and plenary collaboration.

Paper Invitation, Review, and Revision

We invited researchers within the emerging field of chatbot research to submit papers on novel results from their work. In total, 31 papers were submitted to the workshop; 28 full papers and 3 position papers. A rigorous single-blind review process was conducted. All papers were reviewed by three reviewers with relevant expertise providing detailed feedback to the authors. The reviewers were Program Committee members and workshop organizers.

18 of the papers were accepted as full papers, 10 following requests for minor revision and 8 with requests for major revision. The revised papers were thoroughly checked to ensure they met the quality standard.

For submissions authored by one or more of the workshop organizers, the entire review and decision-making process was led by other organizers without the authoring organizer being involved or given insight.

Workshop Outcomes

The full papers in these proceedings are structured according to three topics within basic chatbot research – user and communication studies, user experience and design, and chatbots for collaboration – as well as two key chatbot application areas – customer service and education. The papers provide valuable new insight into these topics.

Under the topic of User and Communication Studies, Müller et al. applied qualitative comparative analysis to understand user resistance to chatbots for medication, an approach which may be relevant also for user studies in other application domains. Jalota et al. presented an approach to assess chatbots that serve as user interfaces to knowledge repositories, such as the DBpedia chatbot, and Ischen et al. reported on a study of user perceptions of chatbots in commercial contexts, with particular concern for how human-likeness in such chatbots affect privacy perceptions.

User Experience and Design was addressed in four papers. Baez et al. presented an approach to a conversational paradigm in web browsing to particularly benefit visually impaired users but also of relevance to other use cases. Catania et al. reported on a study of users' experiences with a conversational agent for the cognitively impaired, providing rich insight into the variations of how chatbot interaction may be perceived. Contributing to our understanding of how to design for good user experiences in conversations, Liebrecht and Van Hooijdonk leveraged data from web care representatives, identifying conversational characteristics of particular importance. Finally, the question of gender in chatbot design was discussed by Feine et al. in a timely study of a large number of current chatbots.

Four papers concerned the increasingly relevant topic of Chatbots for Collaboration, that is, how chatbots may engage in collaborative relationships with users – individually or in groups. Nordberg et al. presented a study of how chatbots may be useful within online peer support groups, Väänäänen et al. investigated how chatbots may encourage and facilitate social participation, and McAllister et al. discussed the benefit of a chatbot to support therapists preparing for bibliotherapeutic counselling. Heyselaar and Bosse, addressed a precondition for such collaboration: users' perceptions of agency in chatbots and how this may be implicitly studied through a theory of mind task.

Several papers also addressed specific application areas, in particular Customer Service and Education. Within the customer service area, two papers addressed factors affecting chatbot uptake and use for this purpose: Van der Goot and Pilgrim explored the effect of age differences on perceptions of chatbot communication and Laban and Araujo reported on the relationship between service performance evaluation and perceptions of cooperation with the chatbot. The remaining two papers on chatbots for customer service, by Kvale et al. and by Følstad and Tylor, pointed towards the benefits of using chatbot dialogue data to understand and improve such chatbots. Within the education application area, von Wolff et al. presented a study on students' requirements for educational chatbots. Hobert and Berens reported on a field study where an educational chatbot had been applied throughout a full semester university course, and Tegos et al. presented a framework for chatbot applications in massive open online courses (MOOC).

While the immediate tangible outcomes of the workshop are the presented papers, the group and plenary discussions returned an overview of key challenges and directions within the main topics of the emerging field of chatbot research. As such, the discussions at the workshop, in addition to the presented papers, serve as a good basis for future collaborations within this field. We already look forward to continuing the sharing and discussions at CONVERSATIONS 2020 – to be announced.

November 2019

Asbjørn Følstad
Theo Araujo
Symeon Papadopoulos
Effie L.-C. Law
Ole-Christoffer Granmo
Ewa Luger
Petter Bae Brandtzaeg

Organization

General Chairs/Workshop Organizers

Asbjørn Følstad   SINTEF, Norway
Theo Araujo   University of Amsterdam, The Netherlands
Symeon Papadopoulos   Centre for Research and Technology Hellas, Greece
Effie L.-C. Law   University of Leicester, UK
Ole-Christoffer Granmo   University of Agder, Norway
Ewa Luger   University of Edinburgh, UK
Petter Bae Brandtzaeg   University of Oslo and SINTEF, Norway

Program Committee

Adam Tsakalidis   University of Warwick, UK
Ahmed Fadhil   University of Trento, Italy
Amela Karahasanovic   SINTEF, Norway
Ana Paula Chaves   Northern Arizona University, USA
Brahim Zarouali   University of Amsterdam, The Netherlands
Carolin Ischen   University of Amsterdam, The Netherlands
Christian Löw   University of Vienna, Austria
David Kuboň   Charles University in Prague, Czech Republic
Despoina Chatzakou   Centre for Research and Technology Hellas, Greece
Dmitry Ilvovsky   National Research University Higher School
                            of Economics, Russia
Eleni Metheniti   Saarland University, Germany
Federica Tazzi   Assist Digital, Italy
Frank Dignum   Umeå University, Sweden
Jordi Vallverdú   Universitat Autònoma de Barcelona, Spain
Juanan Pereira   Universidad del País Vasco/Euskal Herriko
                            Unibertsitatea, Spain
Konstantinos Boletsis   SINTEF, Norway
Lara S. G. Piccolo   The Open University, UK
Leigh Clark   Swansea University, UK
Lorenz Cuno Klopfenstein University of Urbino "Carlo Bo", Italy
Margot van der Goot   University of Amsterdam, The Netherlands
Marita Skjuve   SINTEF, Norway
Minha Lee   Technical University of Eindhoven, The Netherlands
Rricha Jalota   Paderborn University, Germany

Stefan Schaffer   DFKI – German Research Center for Artificial
                               Intelligence, Germany
Stefanos Vrochidis   Centre for Research and Technology Hellas, Greece
Suhas Govind Joshi   University of Oslo, Norway
Tom Feltwell   Northumbria University, UK

Contents

User and Communication Studies

Conversational Agents in Healthcare: Using QCA to Explain Patients' Resistance to Chatbots for Medication

Lea Müller$^{(\boxtimes)}$ ⓘⒹ, Jens Mattke ⒾⒹ, Christian Maier ⒾⒹ, and Tim Weitzel ⒾⒹ

University of Bamberg, Bamberg, Germany
lea.mueller@uni-bamberg.de

Abstract. Complete information is very important to the accuracy of diagnosis in healthcare. Therefore, the idea to use conversational agents recording relevant information and providing it to healthcare facilities is of rising interest. A promising use case of the involvement of conversational agents is medication, as this data is often fragmented or incomplete. The paper at hand examines the hindrances in the way of patients sharing their medication list with a chatbot. Basing on established theories and using fuzzy-set qualitative comparative analysis (QCA), we identify bundles of factors that influence patients lacking willingness to interact with a chatbot. Those typologies of patients can be used to address these hindrances specifically, providing useful insights for theory and healthcare facilities.

Keywords: Conversational agents · Qualitative comparative analysis · Status quo bias perspective

1 Introduction

Adherence to therapies and medication is a primary determinant of treatment success, as a poor adherence reduces the clinical benefits and in the long-term, the overall effectiveness of health systems [1]. When prescribed a medication, only 50% of patients stick to their medication plan [1], which imposes severe risks to patients health. Further, there is often missing a complete overview on the prescribed and dispensed medication, due to inconsistent information between different actors of the healthcare system [2]. For example, a patient gets prescriptions from his or her general practitioner and from a cardiologic specialist, without knowing from each other and buys more drugs on in the local pharmacy, leading to fragmented information on one's medication plan. As a result, the patient himself might be the only one who knows exactly which drugs he is actually taking [2], which makes it not surprising that adverse drug events, such as overdosing, drug-drug-interactions, or contraindications are a major safety issue for hospitalized patients [3].

To avoid this fragmentation of information and the assigned negative consequences for patients' treatment and health, many European countries try to establish eHealth strategies, aiming at providing an accurate, current medication list of a patient [4]. One

© Springer Nature Switzerland AG 2020
A. Følstad et al. (Eds.): CONVERSATIONS 2019, LNCS 11970, pp. 3–18, 2020.
https://doi.org/10.1007/978-3-030-39540-7_1

attempt is to integrate chatbots, recording the required information from the patient and making it available to physicians [2]. This would not only provide better information on the patients' medication list and plan, but could also help patients' to gain information on the medications and drugs concerning adverse effects, drug-drug-interactions or contraindications [2]. However, in the same vein, a patient's medical record including the medication list depicts very sensitive data [5], which makes it not surprising that many users resist to chatbots in healthcare and are unwilling to change their current situation to use a chatbot for medication [6]. This resistance impedes a widespread chatbot adoption and therefore, the avoidance of adverse drug events in healthcare facilities. Therefore, this study aims at examining patients' resistance to using a chatbot for medication.

To examine why individuals are unwilling to change their current situation for something new depicts the central tenet of the status quo bias perspective (SQBP) [7]. The SQBP offers a useful framework to explain resistance behavior on the individual level [8]. SQBP is well established to explain resistance behavior in information systems (IS) research [9] and other disciplines [10], which is why we draw on SQBP to get insights on patients' resistance to using a chatbot for medication. In deep, the SQBP offers six influencing factors causing individuals' unwillingness to change the current status quo for something new factors [7]: transition costs, uncertainty costs, loss aversion, sunk costs, anticipated regret, and decisional control. We align with recent insights from resistance research in the context of enterprise IS, which states that different individuals differ in their reasons for usage resistance [11]. Therefore, we follow these insights and suggest that there are multiple configurations of these six influencing factors of the SQBP shaping patients resistance to using a chatbot for medication. Thus, the aim of this study is to examine those configurations, thus sets of influencing factors, that when working together, lead to patients' resistance to using a chatbot for medication. Providing this knowledge respecting the variance in perceptions from individual to individual helps to address the reasons why patients resist using a chatbot for medication. Consequently, it helps to realize the assigned advantages in terms of the avoidance of adverse drug effects and availability of the medication data. Therefore, we ask the following research question:

What configurations of influencing factors lead to patients' resistance to using a chatbot for medication?

As stated above, to answer our research question, we base on SQBP and apply a configurational approach using fuzzy set qualitative comparative analysis (fsQCA). Thereby, we reveal four configurations of influencing factors leading to patients' resistance to using a chatbot for medication. We contribute to resistance research by showing that resistance cannot be explained by a single influencing factor but by conjunctions of factors, that are equifinal, meaning that there is more than one configuration yielding the same outcome and asymmetry, indicating that an influencing factor within a configuration can be more or less important varying from individual to individual. Further, we contribute to chatbot research in the domain of healthcare, as we present reasons to resist using a chatbot for medication, which helps healthcare facilities to address these reasons better in order to realize their chatbot project.

2   Theoretical Background

To answer our research question concerning the underlying reasons for patients to resist using a chatbot for medication, we need to integrate prior research on chatbots in healthcare and prior research about resistance to something new, including the status quo bias perspective (SQBP). Integrating all of them enables us to combine existing knowledge in order to explain patients' resistance to using a chatbot for medication.

2.1   Chatbots in Healthcare

Chatbots nowadays use natural language processes pattern matching and ontologies to steadily improve the user experience and their imitation of human-to-human conversation [12]. Whereas early chatbots like ELIZA had only rudimentary abilities to take part in conversations based on simple decision trees [13], today's chatbots can be defined as computer programs enabling a natural language communication between a human and a computer, basing on artificial intelligence [12]. To address the rising costs and the still increasing demand for employees in the field of healthcare [14], the application chatbots in healthcare to reduce costs and optimize personnel-intensive processes like diagnosis and medication is not new [15]. However, there are also specific challenges that need to be considered for the application of technology-based optimizations, especially for technology, which should be delivered directly to patients [16]. The privacy and security of personal health information is a critical concern for the implementation of health IT applications [17]. Even if patients value the possible benefits accruing from the use of personal health information, they face the tension between concerns about the privacy of their information and the need for personalization [17]. These specific challenges need to be considered for the application of chatbots in this sector, especially for scenarios of chatbot applications that directly affect patients, as a disregard of these factors can cause patients' rejection of the chatbot and their resistance to using the chatbot as intended by care providers and employees of healthcare facilities.

Prior research has examined some use cases for chatbots in healthcare [18]. So far, chatbots have been already used in a medical offices to perform the interviewing duties of an intake nurse [19] or physician [20] or as "Pharmabot", designed for the prescription and suggestion of medicine for children, as well as a source for information about the medication for their parents [15]. A fourth example is the usage of chatbots in the field of mental healthcare [21]. The concept combines natural language understanding with emotion recognition and thus enables psychiatric counseling. The case-based counseling response model is combined with an ethical judgment model and has been applied in the intervention of alcohol consumption habits of young adults [21]. However, all these studies have focused the adoption or usage of chatbots [18, 20], whereas the studies examining the resistance to using chatbots in healthcare remain very limited. However, as resistance is not just the opposite of usage, due to the causal asymmetry, meaning that the inverted factors for usage of chatbot do not necessarily lead to resistance, but there are new specific factors causing resistance [8]. Therefore, to address patients' resistance to using chatbots for medication we need to consult explicitly prior research on resistance, which is presented hereafter.

2.2   Resistance and the Status Quo Bias Perspective

Individuals' resistance to change or to use a new IS has been an established research stream in IS and psychology, covering resistance from different perspectives, as resistance can be expressed through behavior, affective or cognitive resistance or describe a disposition [8, 22–24]. As the aim of this study is to explain patients' resistance to using a chatbot for medication, we focus on the behavioral perspective of resistance [8], defining resistance as the negative behavioral response associated with change. To explain individuals' unwillingness to change, IS scholars [8, 9, 24, 25] and related research [10, 26–28] have widely referred to the status quo bias perspective (SQBP) [7], considering the costs or threats associated with a change to a new situation. According to SQBP, an individual's resistance to something new is influenced by the six influencing factors **transition costs, uncertainty costs, loss aversion, sunk costs, anticipated regret** and **decisional control** [7]. Thereby, individuals' decision to stick with their current situation, meaning that they follow an incumbent course of action, rather than deciding to change their situation and adopt a new course is biased by these factors, which leads to individuals maintaining the status quo. **Transition costs** are defined as the assessment of the time and effort required to adapt to a new situation [24]. **Uncertainty costs** are defined as the assessment of information search and analysis efforts for decision-making [7]. **Loss aversion** refers to the observation that individuals weigh costs higher than gains [29]. **Sunk costs** refer to an individual's *"desire to justify previous commitments to a course of action by making subsequent commitment"* [7 p. 37] and motivate individuals to keep the status quo.. **Anticipated regret** is defined as individuals' feeling that they will regret their decision for something new in the future [30]. When individuals are in the decision-making process for something new, they asses how they will feel about leaving the status quo and whether they will regret leaving the status quo. **Decisional control** refers to the freedom to *"make choices as making a decision enforces the individual's perception that he or she controls the situation"* [7, p. 40].

So far, SQBP mainly has been used to explain resistance to change in the context of implementations of IS in the organizational context [8, 9], but there is no research treating the resistance to using a chatbot for medication or connecting resistance research with automation in healthcare. Therefore, we adapt the provided influencing factors identified by SQBP to the context at hand where necessary. In line with the insights from prior research [7–9], we define **patients' resistance to using a chatbot for medication** as *patients' negative behavioral response to the change from their current form of consultation to using a chatbot for medication*. Further, we adapted the identified six influencing factors to our application context, where needed, as presented in Table 1.

2.3   Research Gaps

Drawing on the insights from above, we see that there are several research gaps to address, which we want to summarize again in short.

First, research on the application of chatbots was mainly concerned with the acceptance of chatbots treating influencing factors of adoption and usage of chatbots.

Table 1. Adaptation of influencing factors

Influence factor	Definition in the context of using a chatbot for medication
Transition costs	Patients' assessment of time and effort requires adapting to use a chatbot for medication
Uncertainty costs	Patients' assessment of information search and analysis efforts for patients' decision-making whether to use a chatbot for medication
Loss aversion	Patients' tendency to weigh the costs of using a chatbot for medication higher than the benefits of using a chatbot for medication
Sunk costs	Patients' assessment of the effort and time invested in establishing and following the current form of consultation
Anticipated regret	Patients' assessment that they will regret to use a chatbot for medication
Decisional control	Patients' assessment of the freedom whether to use a chatbot for medication

Research states that a *study of the causes of acceptance often tells us very little about the causes of failure* [31], as resistance is not the counterpart usage [8]. Those constructs are related in causal asymmetry, which means that negating the factors leading to the usage of a chatbot does not necessarily lead to resistance, but resistance has their own influencing factors, which are not the mirror opposites of factors leading to usage [31].

Second, resistance research treats mainly the examination of resistance to the implementation of a new IS in the organizational context [8, 11, 32], whereas insights on the resistance to private IS use, such as chatbots for medication are rare.

Third, recent research in the context of resistance to enterprise IS revealed, that different individuals resist different influencing factors [11]. This is in line with complexity theory [31, 33, 34], which states that (1) individuals' behavior is influenced by configurations of influencing factors [35, 36]. This means that patients do not evaluate each influencing factor of why they resist using a chatbot for medication in isolation, but they decide upon the complex interaction of the influencing factors, which in conjunction influence the behavior (conjunction causation). Furthermore, (2) there is no fixed set of influencing factors influencing patients, but that different patients might be influenced by different sets of influencing factors (equifinality). This is related to the fact that (3) influencing factors found to be causally related for one patient to explain resistance, may be irrelevant or even inversely related for other patients to explain resistance (asymmetry). In summary, theory and previous research suggest that an individual's resistance behavior is determined by configurations of interconnected relationships between influencing factors [37]. This perspective of complex pattern for individual's behavior generally confirmed in other disciplines [35, 36, 38, 39] and is initially confirmed with IS resistance research [11]. This suggests that there might be a certain typology of resistance behavior expressed through multiple configurations of influencing factors yielding and explaining patients' resistance behavior towards using chatbots for medication, which has not been treated so far.

3 Methodology

To address the revealed gaps, we base on a quantitative survey study analyzed with the configurational approach of fuzzy-set QCA to reveal configurations of factors leading to patients' resistance to using a chatbot for medication, as suggested by prior IS research [40–43]. The data collection and data analysis are presented in more detail below, including the used measures, the validity, and reliability of the measurement model and the validity of our results.

3.1 Data Collection

We used an online survey using Amazon Mechanical Turk (mTurk), which is a valid and established data collection approach [44], frequently applied in research to identify distinct types of individuals [45]. Our sampling strategy was to attract individuals from different countries who have consulted their physician within the past year, as we wanted them to be able to assess their current consultation form and treatment situation. We only accepted individuals who are aware of chatbots, meaning that we ask them with a little scenario at the beginning, whether they have heard of conversational agents before and if they could name an example where they got in touch with them. We provided information on what medication is and how the medication process works to explain the use case. We followed recommendations and used multiple screening questions to filter out individuals who did not understand our explanations [44]. In total 255 individuals participated in the survey, 44 participants were removed, as they did not pass the screening questions ensuring that the individuals understood the concept of chatbots for medication. We removed 15 participants as they failed the 'robot-questions' ("Please select the shown answer in the picture to assure that you are not a robot."). To ensure a high quality of the data, we included two attention tests [44]. The attention tests are questions embedded into other questions, asking to select a distinct value on a Likert-scale. In the first attention test, eight individuals did not select the correct value on the Likert-scale, and seven participants failed the second attention test. Overall, the low failure rate of the attention test indicates a high quality of the data sample. The final sample consists of 181 individuals. In line with sample size requirements for QCA studies [46], we need at least 30 participants, therefore the sample size is large enough. The demographics are displayed in Table 2.

We additionally tested for common method bias and applied Harman's single factor test, which indicates how much of the data is explained by only one factor [47, 48]. Harman's single factor test reveals that only 35% of the variance is explained by one factor, which is below the recommended 50% threshold.

3.2 Measures

Our measures are based on existing validated measures from previous research (see Appendix). To measure patients' resistance to using a chatbot for medication, we adapted three items [24] by changing the context to not using a chatbot for medication (Cronbach's alpha: $\alpha = 0.90$). For transition costs, we used two items used in previous resistance studies [24]. We adapted the items to our context by referring to the usage of

Table 2. Demographics

Demographics of 181 participants					
Country of residence [%]		**Gender [%]**		**Age [%] (Mean: 34.0; SD:10.7)**	
United Kingdom	5.3	Male	39.5	18-20	6.7
United States	76.8	Female	53.2	21-30	45.6
Canada	1.6	Other	7.4	31-40	25.6
Italy	2.1			41-51	13.9
India	1.6			51 - 60	7.2
Other	12.6			61 - 70	1.1
Highest education level [%]				**Frequency of medical consultation per year [%] (Mean: 2.9)**	
High School / GED	13.9			1	38.5
Some College	15.0			2	18.4
2-year College Degree	17.2			3	17.8
4-year College Degree	35.0			4	10.3
Master's Degree	13.9			5	4.6
Professional Degree	5.0			>5	10.3

a chatbot for medication instead of referring to cloud software ($\alpha = 0.84$). For uncertainty costs, we use three items [49] and adapted the items to our context ($\alpha = 0.87$). The same applies to our two items for measuring sunk costs [24] ($\alpha = 0.92$) and the two items measuring anticipated (action) regret [50] ($\alpha = 0.88$). For decisional control, we base on three items [51] ($\alpha = 0.79$). To measure loss aversion, we follow the recommendation of Lee and Joshi [9] to assess whether patients assign greater weight to costs rather than benefits when deciding on using a chatbot for medication. For this, we additionally measured perceived benefits using five items [52] and adapt the items to our context ($\alpha = 0.89$). We then compare the perceived costs, composed of transition costs and uncertainty costs, to perceived benefits. If the mean perceived costs outweigh the perceived benefits, then loss aversion is present. Otherwise, if the perceived benefits outweigh the mean perceived costs, then loss aversion is absent.

3.3 Measurement Model

To ensure *content validity* we only used items validated in previous research. All item loadings were higher than 0.707, which attests *indicator reliability* [53]. To test for construct reliability, we tested for the average variance extracted (AVE) and composite reliability. The AVE of each construct is higher than 0.50 and the CR for each construct is higher than 0.70, which attests *construct reliability*. We can ensure discriminant validity, as the square root of the AVE is higher than the corresponding correlations of the constructs [54] (see Table 3). Furthermore, we calculated the heterotrait-monotrait (HTMT) ratio, which is 0.72. This is lower than the absolute HTMT0.85 criterion [55] and therefore attests *discriminant validity*.

Table 3. Descriptive statistics and discriminant validity

		α	CR	AVE	Mean	SD	1	2	3	4	5	6	7
1	Transition costs	0.84	0.93	0.86	2.72	1.05	0.929						
2	Uncertainty costs	0.87	0.91	0.71	4.03	1.41	0.193	0.846					
3	Sunk Costs	0.92	0.96	0.93	4.41	1.68	0.091	0.279	0.964				
4	Regret	0.88	0.91	0.72	5.62	1.15	0.105	0.298	0.203	0.851			
5	Decisional control	0.79	0.88	0.70	5.23	1.10	-0.251	-0.182	0.084	0.119	0.839		
6	Resistance	0.90	0.94	0.83	4.47	1.42	0.265	0.527	0.317	0.415	-0.099	0.839	
7	Loss aversion	-	-	-	-2.01	1.80	0.592	0.617	0.246	0.283	-0.334	0.580	-

3.4   Data Analysis Using fsQCA

To analyze which configurations of the six SQBP influencing factors lead to patients' resistance to using a chatbot for medication, we take a configurational approach [37, 56] and use fuzzy-set qualitative comparative analysis (fsQCA). fsQCA primarily reveals sufficient configurations associated with an individual's resistance. Within this configuration, the influencing factors can either be present or absent. The data analysis consists of three steps. First, the **calibration**, transforming the scale values of the survey data into fuzzy sets using three qualitative anchors (value 1 for full non-membership; value 4 for the crossover point, value 7 for full membership) [37, 57]. Second, the analysis of **necessary influencing factors** that need to be present if patients resist using a chatbot for medication. To be considered as necessary, the influencing factor needs to exceed the recommended consistency threshold of 0.90 [58]. The consistency indicates the degree to which cases with the same influencing factors share the same outcome [59]. Third, the analysis of **sufficient configurations of influencing factors** examining bundles of influencing factors leading to patients' resistance to chatbots for medication. For all three steps, we used the fsQCA software 3.0 provided. To conduct the analysis, we first construct the truth table which lists all possible configurations of the influencing factors. Because we have six influencing factors, the truth table consists of 2k configurations, with k being the number of influencing factors. Thus, the truth table shows 64 possible configurations. Second, we apply a recommended frequency threshold (n = 2), consistency threshold (consistency = 0.85) and a PRI consistency threshold (PRI consistency = 0.75) to reduce the truth table to sufficient configurations. This means that all configurations that do not represent at least two observations, which have a lower consistency than 0.85 and a lower PRI consistency then 0.80 are excluded from further analyses. Third, we apply the Quine-Mc-Cluskey algorithm to minimize the sufficient configurations of influencing factors leading to an individual's resistance.

4   Results

The analysis of *necessary influencing factors* for patients' resistance to using a chatbot for medication reveals anticipated regret to be a necessary influencing factor (consistency > 0.96, coverage > 0.71). This means that every time patients resist using a chatbot for medication, they feel that they may regret their decision for it and aim at avoiding a potential feeling of regret. Yet, the sheer presence of anticipated regret does not necessarily lead to resistance behavior. Therefore, we analyze for *sufficient configurations of influencing factors*. We identified four sufficient configurations leading to patients' resistance to using a chatbot for medication (see Fig. 1). Black circles indicate the presence of an influencing factor, e.g. a black circle for uncertainty costs indicates that the patient perceives high uncertainty costs. Crossed out white circles indicate the absence of an influencing factor, blank spaces indicate a 'don't care situation'. For instance, a blank space for uncertainty costs means that in this sufficient configuration, uncertainty costs have a subordinated role because the patient can either assess to have uncertainty costs or assess not to have uncertainty costs. The overall solution consistency is 0.92 and the solution coverage is 0.68. Coverage thereby is a measure of the proportion of cases explained by the four sufficient configurations.

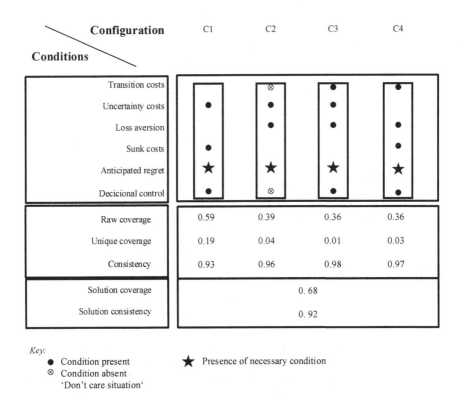

Fig. 1. Sufficient configurations leading to patients' resistance to using a chatbot

The first configuration (C1) indicates the presence of uncertainty costs, sunk costs and decisional control, as well as the necessary condition anticipated regret, whereas transition costs and loss aversion are outweighed by these factors. This indicated that this type of patient does not see a high effort to change to using a chatbot for medication and does not worry about the benefits a chatbot could bring. However, the uncertainty of whether it is the right decision to use a chatbot for medication and the strong feeling of anticipated regret, in terms of false medication if the chatbot makes a mistake or a misuse of private sensitive data, leads to resistance. The third and fourth configuration (C3, C4) match the SQBP, as all factors are present and sunk costs/uncertainty costs are outweighed by the other factors. The second configuration (C2) shows a type of patient who does not feel free in his or her decision in not using a chatbot for medication, and is resisting to using a chatbot for medication because he just cannot decide to do so. This type is aware of the benefits and does not see any transition costs. Further, together with the anticipated regret of misdiagnoses or data misuse, it outweighs the lack of transition costs.

5   Discussion

Despite the advantages of using a chatbot for medication in terms of data access and the avoidance of medication failure, many patients resist to using them [6]. This impedes the widespread adoption of chatbots for medication. This study bases on SQBP [7] examine patients' resistance to using a chatbot for medication respecting that patients might resist for different reasons, assessing influencing factors differently [11]. Based on a quantitative study, we identified four sufficient configurations of these influencing factors leading to patient's resistance to using a chatbot for medication with a fsQCA approach. Identifying these sufficient configurations, we contribute to existing research and provide guidance to practitioners, which both are presented in the following.

5.1   Theoretical Contribution

We contribute to the research stream of chatbots in healthcare, as we examine the resistance to using chatbots, enlarging recent insights focusing on the adoption or usage of chatbots [12]. Resistance is not the not just the opposite of usage, due to the causal asymmetry, meaning that the negated factors for usage do not necessarily lead to resistance, but there are new specific factors causing resistance [8]. To examine these factors, be based on SQBP [7] and adapted the influencing factors to the context at hand. Further, as resistance research in enterprise IS revealed, that different individuals resist different (patterns of) influencing factors [11] we take a configurational approach and examine what configurations of the six influencing factors from SQBP lead to resistance. Using a configurational approach, we reveal equifinality of patients' resistance to using a chatbot for medication [37, 56]. This means that a patient's resistance is not explained by one configuration of influencing factors. Contrary, there exist four sufficient configurations, which all lead to patient's resistance. Future research should, therefore, consider that individuals are heterogeneous and that resistance is grounded in different influencing factors. This means that there is no 'one-size-fits-all' intervention to reduce resistance. Promising future research thus needs to examine what different interventions are effective for each configuration. For instance, different interventions might be needed for the individuals experiencing uncertainty costs than for those experiencing transition costs.

Further, as shown above, we identified anticipated regret as a necessary condition of the resistance to using a chatbot for medication, indicating that the patients do not trust enough in chatbots to not being afraid of regretting using a chatbot for medication in the future. This echoes prior research showing that different levels of trust exist for the adoption of chatbots [60]. Whereas configurations C3 and C4 represent the existing knowledge presented by the SQBP [7, 8], configurations C1 and C2 add valuable knowledge. C2 probably wants to use a chatbot for medication but does not feel free in his decision to do so, because of missing opportunities and C1 is an example of the lack of trust causing the resistance to using a chatbot for medication as explained above. The identification of sufficient configurations thereby not only contributes to the research stream of chatbots in healthcare but also to resistant research, enlarging the limited existing research on the resistance to private IS, as prior research was mainly concerned with the examination of resistance to the implementation of a new IS in the organizational context [8, 11, 32].

5.2 Practical Contribution

With the identification of four sufficient configurations leading to patients' resistance to using a chatbot for medication, we provide useful insights for healthcare facilities willing to introduce such a chatbot. First, we see that all of the patients acknowledge the advantages of chatbots in medication, but assess the assorted costs and risks higher than the benefits. Strategically, this means that healthcare facilities should not be stressing the advantages but need to take care of patients' worries concerning the usage of a chatbot for medication. For example, the presence of uncertainty costs indicates, that the patients find it difficult make a well-grounded decision about using a chatbot for medication. Furthermore, the presence of sunk costs indicates, that the patients are worried to lose the connection to their physician. Here, healthcare facilities need to show, that the chatbot is not necessarily replacing the physician but supporting him or her in her diagnosis and the patient will still see his physician.

Further, we identified anticipated regret as a necessary condition, which seems plausible, as this indicates that the patients are worried that the chatbot might record or suggest the wrong things. The risk of data misuse or a false medication weighs heavy, as in the worst case this could threaten patients' lives. Here, healthcare facilities should stress the controlling mechanisms to increase trust, and compare results of the chatbots to normal consultations, as research indicates that these are not flawless as well [61].

5.3 Limitations and Future Research

In this paper, we use an individual perspective to explain why patients' resistance to using a chatbot for medication. Future research may also consider group effects, in terms of whether patients' are influencing each other in their perception of the chatbots for medication a resulting, in their resistance. Further, one could base on an explorative approach to identify further influencing factors on resistance to using a chatbot for medication, as well as the underlying mechanisms causing resistance generalizing the revealed insights to other use cases, as we focus only one. Also, with the sampling strategy of using MTurk for our data collection, we yield for a more diverse population. However, this is also just a sample and therefore restricted in terms of generalizability. Future research may want to reveal more diverse results for specific groups with the same healthcare system and then aggregate them to a broader picture.

Appendix

The Table below shows our constructs and measures we used in the questionnaire, as well as the loadings.

Construct and author	Adapted item	Loading
Benefits adapted from [52]	I think using a chatbot for medication is convenient	0.896
	I can improve my consultation by using a chatbot for medication	0.922
	I can save time by using a chatbot for medication	0.787
	Using a chatbot for medication enables me to inform the physician more quickly about my medical record than by talking to medical staff	0.877
	Using a chatbot for medication increases my productivity of the consultation	0.858
Transition costs adapted from [24]	Learning how to use a chatbot for medication would take much time	0.945
	Becoming skillful at using a chatbot for medication would be hard for me	0.914
Uncertainty costs adapted from [49]	It is hard to compare my current medication conducted by a 'real' physician with a medication conducted by a chatbot	0.786
	Even when I have all information about chatbots, comparing my current consultation conducted by a 'real' physician to a consultation with a chatbot for medication is difficult	0.869
	I would have to search a lot of information to decide whether to use a chatbot for medication	0.850
Sunk costs adapted from [24]	I have already invested a lot of time in the relationship with my physician during the consultation	0.963
	I have already invested a lot of time in establishing a good relationship with my physician (e.g. he knows all the details about me and memorizes them)	0.965

(*continued*)

(*continued*)

Construct and author	Adapted item	Loading
Anticipated regret adapted from [30]	If I decide to use a chatbot for medication and it turns out to be a failure, I will regret incurring a potentially large loss in terms of treatment	0.874
	If I decide to use a chatbot for medication and it turns out that the medication complicates my medical treatment, then I will regret not to consult a 'real' physician instead of the chatbot	0.882
Decisional control adapted from [51]	The decision whether to use a chatbot for medication gives me a chance to use my personal initiative or judgment	Removed
	The decision whether to use a chatbot for medication allows me to decide on my own	0.800
	The decision whether to use a chatbot for medication provides me autonomy in making the decision	0.886
	It was an easy decision to pick the best alternative	0.829
User resistance adapted from [8]	I will not comply with using a chatbot for medication	0.923
	I will not cooperate to use a chatbot for medication	0.909
	I oppose using a chatbot for medication	0.898
	I do not agree with the usage of a chatbot for medication	0.929

References

1. WHO: Adherence to long-term therapies: evidence for action. https://www.who.int/chp/knowledge/publications/adherence_full_report.pdf?ua=1
2. Tschanz, M., Dorner, T.L., Denecke, K.: eMedication Meets eHealth with the Electronic Medication Management Assistant (eMMA). eHealth (2017)
3. Lampert, M.L., Kraehenbuehl, S., Hug, B.L.: Drug-related problems: evaluation of a classification system in the daily practice of a Swiss University Hospital. Pharm. World Sci.: PWS **30**, 768–776 (2008)
4. Gall, W., Aly, A.-F., Sojer, R., Spahni, S., Ammenwerth, E.: The national e-medication approaches in Germany, Switzerland and Austria: a structured comparison. Int. J. Med. Inform. **93**, 14–25 (2016)
5. Kassirer, J.P.: Imperatives, expediency, and the new diagnosis. Diagnosis **1**, 11–12 (2014)
6. UserTesting: Will consumers trust healthcare chatbots?—UserTesting Blog. https://www.usertesting.com/blog/healthcare-chatbot-cx-index/
7. Samuelson, W., Zeckhauser, R.: Status quo bias in decision making. J. Risk Uncertainty **1**, 7–59 (1988)
8. Kim, H.-W., Kankanhalli, A.: Investigating user resistance to information systems implementation. A status quo bias perspective. MIS Q. **33**, 567–582 (2009)
9. Lee, K., Joshi, K.: Examining the use of status quo bias perspective in IS research: need for re-conceptualizing and incorporating biases. Inf. Syst. J. **27**, 733–752 (2017)

10. Fleming, S.M., Thomas, C.L., Dolan, R.J.: Overcoming status quo bias in the human brain. Proc. Natl. Acad. Sci. U.S.A. **107**, 6005–6009 (2010)
11. Klaus, T., Wingreen, S.C., Blanton, J.E.: Resistant groups in enterprise system implementations: a Q-methodology examination. J. Inf. Technol. **25**, 91–106 (2010)
12. Al-Ramahi, M., Noteboom, C.: A systematic analysis of patient portals adoption, acceptance and usage: the trajectory for triple aim? In: Hawaii International Conference on System Sciences 2018 (HICSS-51) (2018)
13. Schuetzler, R., Grimes, M., Giboney, J., Buckman, J.: Facilitating natural conversational agent interactions: lessons from a deception experiment. In: ICIS 2014 Proceedings (2014)
14. Statista: Health Care in Germany 2018-Statista. https://www.statista.com/study/46612/health-care-in-germany/
15. Comendador, B.E.V., Francisco, B.M.B., Medenilla, J.S., Mae, S.: Pharmabot: a pediatric generic medicine consultant chatbot. J. Autom. Control Eng. **3**, 137–140 (2015)
16. Lehto, T., Oinas-Kukkonen, H., Pätiälä, T., Saarelma, O.: Consumers' perception of a digital health check: an empirical investigation. In: ECIS 2012 Proceedings (2012)
17. Jena, R.: Sharing personal health information: personalization versus privacy. In: AMCIS 2015 Proceedings (2015)
18. Sherer, S.A.: Patients are not simply health IT users or consumers: the case for "e Healthicant" applications. CAIS **34**, 17 (2014)
19. Schuetzler, R.M., Grimes, G.M., Giboney, J.S.: An investigation of conversational agent relevance, presence, and engagement. In: AMCIS 2018 Proceedings (2018)
20. Denecke, K., Lutz Hochreutener, S., Pöpel, A., May, R.: Talking to ana. In: Kostkova, P., Grasso, F., Castillo, C., Mejova, Y., Bosman, A., Edelstein, M. (eds.) DH 2018, Proceedings of the 2018 International Conference on Digital Health: Lyon, France, 23–26 April 2018, pp. 85–89. The Association for Computing Machinery, New York (2018)
21. Oh, K.-J., Lee, D., Ko, B., Choi, H.-J.: A chatbot for psychiatric counseling in mental healthcare service based on emotional dialogue analysis and sentence generation. In: Proceedings of the 18th IEEE International Conference on Mobile Data Management, MDM 2017, Daejeon, South Korea, 29 May–1 June 2017, pp. 371–375. IEEE Computer Society, Los Alamitos (2017)
22. Laumer, S., Maier, C., Eckhardt, A., Weitzel, T.: User personality and resistance to mandatory information systems in organizations: a theoretical model and empirical test of dispositional resistance to change. J. Inf. Technol. **31**, 67–82 (2016)
23. Piderit, S.K.: Rethinking resistance and recognizing ambivalence: a multidimensional view of attitudes toward an organizational change. Acad. Manag. Rev. **25**, 783–794 (2000)
24. Polites, G.L., Karahanna, E.: Shackled to the status quo: the inhibiting effects of incumbent system habit, switching costs, and inertia on new system acceptance. MIS Q. **36**, 21–42 (2012)
25. Polites, G.L., Karahanna, E., Seligman, L.: Intention–behaviour misalignment at B2C websites: when the horse brings itself to water, will it drink? Eur. J. Inf. Syst. **27**, 22–45 (2017)
26. Fernandez, R., Rodrik, D.: Resistance to reform: status quo bias in the presence of individual-specific uncertainty. Am. Econ. Rev. **81**, 1146–1155 (1991)
27. Kahneman, D., Knetsch, J.L., Thaler, R.H.: Anomalies: the endowment effect, loss aversion, and status quo bias. J. Econ. Perspect. **5**, 193–206 (1991)
28. Mattke, J., Maier, C., Müller, L., Weitzel, T.: Bitcoin resistance behavior: a QCA study explaining why individuals resist bitcoin as a means of payment. In: ICIS 2018 Proceedings, San Francisco, CA (2018)
29. Kahneman, D., Tversky, A.: Prospect theory: an analysis of decision under risk. Econometrica **47**, 263–292 (1979)

30. Lankton, N., Luft, J.: Uncertainty and industry structure effects on managerial intuition about information technology real options. J. Manag. Inf. Syst. **25**, 203–240 (2008)
31. Woodside, A.G.: Embrace•perform•model: complexity theory, contrarian case analysis, and multiple realities. J. Bus. Res. **67**, 2495–2503 (2014)
32. Klaus, T., Blanton, J.E.: User resistance determinants and the psychological contract in enterprise system implementations. Eur. J. Inf. Syst. **19**, 625–636 (2010)
33. Fiss, P.C.: A set-theoretic approach to organizational configurations. Acad. Manag. Rev. **32**, 1180–1198 (2007)
34. Woodside, A.G.: Embracing the complexity turn in management research for modeling multiple realities. In: Woodside, A.G. (ed.) The Complexity Turn, pp. 1–19. Springer, Cham (2017). https://doi.org/10.1007/978-3-319-47028-3_1
35. Campbell, J.T., Sirmon, D.G., Schijven, M.: Fuzzy logic and the market: a configurational approach to investor perceptions of acquisition announcements. Acad. Manag. J. **59**, 163–187 (2016)
36. Pelli, D.G., Tillman, K.A.: The uncrowded window of object recognition. Nat. Neurosci. **11**, 1129 (2008)
37. Misangyi, V.F., Greckhamer, T., Furnari, S., Fiss, P.C., Crilly, D., Aguilera, R.: Embracing causal complexity: the emergence of a neo-configurational perspective. J. Manag. **43**, 255–282 (2017)
38. Spivack, A.J., Woodside, A.G.: Applying complexity theory for modeling human resource outcomes: antecedent configurations indicating perceived location autonomy and work environment choice. J. Bus. Res. **102**, 109–119 (2019)
39. Dwivedi, P., Joshi, A., Misangyi, V.F.: Gender-inclusive gatekeeping: how (mostly male) predecessors influence the success of female CEOs. Acad. Manag. J. **61**, 379–404 (2018)
40. Park, Y., Sawy, O.E., Fiss, P.: The role of business intelligence and communication technologies in organizational agility: a configurational approach. J. Assoc. Inf. Syst. **18**, 1 (2017)
41. Mattke, J., Müller, L., Maier, C.: Paid, owned and earned media: a qualitative comparative analysis revealing attributes influencing consumer's brand attitude in social media (2019). http://scholarspace.manoa.hawaii.edu/bitstream/10125/59520/1/0080.pdf
42. Müller, L., Mattke, J., Maier, C., Weitzel, T.: The curse of mobile marketing: a mixed methods study on individuals' switch to mobile ad blockers. In: ICIS 2017 Proceedings, p. 13 (2017)
43. Pflügner, K., Mattke, J., Maier, C.: Who is stressed by using ICTs? A qualitative comparison analysis with the big five personality traits to understand technostress. In: Proceedings of the 14th International Conference on Wirtschaftsinformatik, Siegen, Germany (2019)
44. Lowry, P.B., D'Arcy, J., Hammer, B., Moody, G.D.: "Cargo Cult" science in traditional organization and information systems survey research: a case for using nontraditional methods of data collection, including Mechanical Turk and online panels. J. Strat. Inf. Syst. **25**, 232–240 (2016)
45. Bennett, A.A., Gabriel, A.S., Calderwood, C., Dahling, J.J., Trougakos, J.P.: Better together? Examining profiles of employee recovery experiences. J. Appl. Psychol. **101**, 1635–1654 (2016)
46. Marx, A.: Towards More Robust Model Specification in QCA Results from a Methodological Experiment. American Sociological Association, Philadelphia, PA (2006)
47. Chin, W., Thatcher, J.B., Wright, R.T.: Assessing common method bias: problems with the ULMC technique. MIS Q. **36**, 1003–1019 (2012)
48. Podsakoff, P.M., MacKenzie, S.B., Lee, J.-Y., Podsakoff, N.P.: Common method biases in behavioral research: a critical review of the literature and recommended remedies. J. Appl. Psychol. **88**, 879 (2003)

49. Ray, S., Kim, S.S., Morris, J.G.: Research note—online users' switching costs: their nature and formation. Inf. Syst. Res. **23**, 197–213 (2012)
50. Lankton, N., McKnight, H.: Examining two expectation disconfirmation theory models: assimilation and asymmetry effects. J. Assoc. Inf. Syst. **13**, 88–115 (2012)
51. Morgeson, F.P., Humphrey, S.E.: The work design questionnaire (WDQ): developing and validating a comprehensive measure for assessing job design and the nature of work. J. Appl. Psychol. **91**, 1321 (2006)
52. Kim, D.J., Ferrin, D.L., Rao, H.R.: A trust-based consumer decision-making model in electronic commerce: the role of trust, perceived risk, and their antecedents. Decis. Support Syst. **44**, 544–564 (2008)
53. Carmines, E.G., Zeller, R.A.: Reliability and Validity Assessment. Sage Publ., Newbury Park (2008)
54. Fornell, C., Larcker, D.F.: Evaluating structural equation models with unobservable variables and measurement error. J. Mark. Res. **18**, 39–50 (1981)
55. Henseler, J., Ringle, C.M., Sarstedt, M.: A new criterion for assessing discriminant validity in variance-based structural equation modeling. J. Acad. Mark. Sci. **43**, 115–135 (2015). https://doi.org/10.1007/s11747-014-0403-8
56. El Sawy, O.A., Malhotra, A., Park, Y., Pavlou, P.A.: Research commentary—seeking the configurations of digital ecodynamics: it takes three to tango. Inf. Syst. Res. **21**, 835–848 (2010)
57. Fiss, P.C.: Building better causal theories: a fuzzy set approach to typologies in organization research. Acad. Manag. J. **54**, 393–420 (2011)
58. Schneider, C.Q., Wagemann, C.: Standards of good practice in qualitative comparative analysis (QCA) and fuzzy-sets. Comp. Sociol. **9**, 397–418 (2010)
59. Rihoux, B., Ragin, C.C.: Qualitative comparative analysis using fuzzy sets (fsQCA) (2009)
60. Müller, L., Mattke, J., Maier, C., Weitzel, T., Graser, H.: Chatbot acceptance. In: Joseph, D., van Slyke, C., Allen, J.P., Quesenberry, J., Wiesche, M. (eds.) Proceedings of the 2019 on Computers and People Research Conference - SIGMIS-CPR 2019, pp. 35–42. ACM Press, New York (2019)
61. Davenport, S., Goldberg, D., Millar, T.: How psychiatric disorders are missed during medical consultations. Lancet **330**, 439–441 (1987)

An Approach for Ex-Post-Facto Analysis of Knowledge Graph-Driven Chatbots – The DBpedia Chatbot

Rricha Jalota[1]([✉]) , Priyansh Trivedi[2], Gaurav Maheshwari[2],
Axel-Cyrille Ngonga Ngomo[1] , and Ricardo Usbeck[1,2]

[1] DICE Group, CS Department, Paderborn University, Paderborn, Germany
`rricha.jalota@upb.de`
[2] Fraunhofer IAIS, Dresden, Germany

Abstract. As chatbots are gaining popularity for simplifying access to information and community interaction, it is essential to examine whether these agents are serving their intended purpose and catering to the needs of their users. Therefore, we present an approach to perform an ex-post-facto analysis over the logs of knowledge base-driven dialogue systems. Using the DBpedia Chatbot as our case study, we inspect three aspects of the interactions, (i) user queries and feedback, (ii) the bot's response to these queries, and (iii) the overall flow of the conversations. We discuss key implications based on our findings. All the source code used for the analysis can be found at https://github.com/dice-group/ DBpedia-Chatlog-Analysis.

Keywords: Empirical study · Knowledge-driven chatbot · Intent clustering · Knowledge graph · Conversational AI

1   Introduction

Recent years have seen a resurgence [10] of chatbots. The solutions are now used by a large number of businesses, in the entertainment industry, and for curiosity-driven purposes. While some dialogue agents imitate customer-service behavior to carry out certain tasks (e.g., Siri, Alexa, pizza delivery/hotel reservation chatbots), others act as an interface to explore underlying knowledge bases or other structural databases. These latter kinds of chatbots provide unified, malleable access to information, potentially collected from a wide variety of heterogeneous data. Recently, these data-driven agents have attracted significant research interest leading to considerable enhancement in their capabilities [4]. However, only a few studies have investigated how the existing systems perform and have leveraged their findings. Therefore, in this study, we present a generalizable approach to examine how users interact with knowledge-driven chatbots and their expectations with these agents.

© Springer Nature Switzerland AG 2020
A. Følstad et al. (Eds.): CONVERSATIONS 2019, LNCS 11970, pp. 19–33, 2020.
https://doi.org/10.1007/978-3-030-39540-7_2

Here, we intend to analyze these conversations for understanding **(i) how users interact with knowledge-driven chatbots, (ii) whether the chatbots can sufficiently satisfy the expectations of the users, and (iii) the possible avenues for improving chatbot quality and subsequently the user experience.** To that end, we suggest three general analytical streams for investigating knowledge-driven chatbots. We run our analysis on a completely anonymized version of log files, broadly categorized in the following three classes:

- **Request Analysis:** We measure the intents, and complexity within user utterances to understand their perception towards the chatbot.
- **Response Analysis:** We characterize the common errors made by the chatbot as well as the reasons behind it.
- **Conversation Analysis:** We attempt to uncover common topics of conversation and inspect the use of anaphora in the conversations.

In particular, we investigate log files from the DBpedia Chatbot [4]. The log files provide domain-specific (here DBpedia-centered) information to enhance community interaction/engagement and answers factual questions on any topic using the DBpedia Knowledge Graph. Thus, this chatbot acts both as an agent that renders frequently asked questions (FAQs) and as an interface for knowledge-driven question answering, making it a unique case study. The DBpedia Chatbot has been running for around 26 months at the time of writing. During this period, it has been involved in over 9084 conversations. The findings from the ex-post-facto analysis of the DBpedia Chatbot suggest that while users do ask complex queries, they engage more in banter and simple questions. They also tend to use colloquial language, make spelling errors and feel reluctant to use appropriate casing or notation for proper nouns and abbreviations. This indicates that they anticipate intrinsic human-level comprehension from a machine, which in turn denotes the need for better natural language processing (NLP) tools or providing more intuition about the limiting cases of the chatbot.

We believe the analysis and findings from this case study will benefit all those genres of conversational interfaces that either engage in customer-service [18] or empower data-driven applications [15].

Our contributions in this paper are two-fold: (1) we propose retrospective data-driven approaches to inspect the performance and usage patterns of a knowledge-driven chatbot, and (2) based on the findings, we suggest solutions to improve DBpedia Chatbot's architecture and user-experience. The source code for our analysis of the DBpedia Chatbot[1] can be found online[2] along with the source code of the chatbot[3] itself. To ensure full compliance with the General Data Protection Regulation, we do not share or publish the dataset.

---

[1] http://chat.dbpedia.org.

[2] https://github.com/dice-group/DBpedia-Chatlog-Analysis.

[3] https://github.com/dbpedia/chatbot.

2   Related Work

In recent times, several new frameworks and approaches have been proposed to evaluate the usability of dialogue systems and the motivation behind their use. The evaluation of these systems can be carried out in experimental environments where a set of people examine a chatbot's performance for a certain time period and report their experience [14]. Or, they can be done in a completely natural setup where the chatbot interacts with the target audience and eventually, the log files, collected over a period of time, are studied [12,23]. Employing the natural evaluation setup, chatbot log files from a task-oriented chatbot of a telecommunications company were examined [2] to detect whether only conversations were sufficient to determine users' topics of interests and their level of satisfaction. For this purpose, conversations were characterized as sequences of events for network modeling and thereafter, network analysis techniques were applied. Conversation analysis techniques were also applied to a banking chatbot's log files [17]. In particular, the use of the intercoder reliability metric led to the discovery of multiple patterns of conversation breakdown. Various other experiments have also been conducted in experimental scenario-based settings to compare repair strategy [3] and user preferences in cases of unsuccessful interactions, and to improve the design of chatbots based on experiences of first-time users [13]. In contrast to the works mentioned above, which primarily examined domain-specific service-oriented chatbots, we carry out a global performance evaluation of a hybrid chatbot that is not only capable of delivering domain-specific information or engaging in banter but also acts as an interface to explore a large knowledge graph.

We perform a completely data-driven analysis and suggest three possible analytical steps for Knowledge Graph-driven Chatbots (see Sect. 5) to inspect various nuances of the usage-patterns and user-satisfaction of a goal-oriented chatbot.

3   Description of the DBpedia Chatbot

The open-source, open-access knowledge graph (KG) DBpedia [16], and its official community mailing list served as the heterogeneous data source for building the DBpedia-chatbot [4]. Developed for the purpose of enhancing community interactions in the DBpedia community, the chatbot is capable of interactively introducing users to the DBpedia KG, providing them with an intuitive interface to (1) query existing knowledge by the means of an underlying Knowledge Graph Question Answering (KGQA) [6] system, (2) answering queries regarding DBpedia service checks like *"Is lookup online?"*, and (3) information related to specific user chapters. The DBpedia Chatbot, hence, follows the pattern of task-oriented chatbots [2,14].

Upon receiving user input, the chatbot classifies the intent of input as either factual questions answerable via underlying KG, questions related to DBpedia community, or banter. The factual questions are answered using a combination of tools based on the question answering vocabulary - QANARY [5], and WolframAlpha,[4] while a rule-based system with pre-defined responses handles the DBpedia questions and the banter. The underlying system is trained by leveraging the existing FAQs, the DBpedia Discussion,[5] and DBpedia Developers mailing lists.[6] We refer interested readers to the DBpedia Blog[7] and the accompanying paper [4] on the abilities and the working mechanism of the chatbot.

4   Dataset

In this section, we introduce various statistical aspects of the chatbot's log dataset, which we subsequently analyze. The dataset is based on the anonymized[8] logs of the DBpedia Chatbot collected over two years and as of July 2019, contains 90,800 interactions. The chatbot was used by a total of 9084 users, with the most common channel being web (with 9078 users), followed by Slack and then Facebook Messenger. Every conversation in the dataset begins with the chatbot introducing itself and its capabilities to the user. The user then queries the chatbot, to which the chatbot responds with an answer and a feedback request. If the user submits feedback, the chatbot reacts to it accordingly. Otherwise, another dialogue begins if the user asks a new query. We present some preliminary characteristics of the dataset in Table 1, including:

- *Conversation length:* Number of interactions between a user and the chatbot.
- *User-request length:* The number of characters in a user utterance.
- *Feedback-asked:* The number of times the chatbot asks a user for feedback.
- *Feedback-received:* Amount of user responses to chatbot feedback requests.
- *Feedback-content:* The number of received positive and negative feedback.

Table 1. DBpedia Chatbot log data from Aug. 2017 to July 2019.

Characteristic	Measure	
Number of user-utterances	Absolute	30263
Conversation length	Avg.	10
	Max.	1661
User-request length	Avg.	113
	Max.	3389
Feedback	Feedback-asked	28953
	Feedback-received	7561
	Positive-feedback	3406
	Negative-feedback	4155

---

[4] http://products.wolframalpha.com/api/.

[5] https://sourceforge.net/p/dbpedia/mailman/dbpedia-discussion/.

[6] https://sourceforge.net/p/dbpedia/mailman/dbpedia-developers/.

[7] https://wiki.dbpedia.org/blog/meet-dbpedia-chatbot.

[8] No unique identifiers or demographics were collected by the DBpedia Chatbot.

5   Approach

In this section, we describe our proposed approach for analyzing various aspects of domain-specific, knowledge-driven chatbots. The goal of these analyses is (i) to understand the nature of user-requests: query-patterns and user-intentions; (ii) examine whether the chatbot can serve its purpose and satisfy user-requests; and (iii) get insights about the conversation flow to improve the chatbot's architecture. We divide our analysis, based on different aspects of the conversation, into three major categories, namely:

– **Request Analysis**: where we analyze a user's request based on the intent and complexity of the utterance. We propose to use either dependency parsing-based techniques or sentence embeddings to capture a query's intent and thereafter, applying an unsupervised clustering method for classifying the intent of the utterances. Furthermore, we present a rule-based dependency parsing approach for determining an utterance's complexity.
– **Response Analysis**: where we intend to identify common errors made by chatbot by analyzing common entity types in failed responses and length of conversations. We employ two different name entity recognition (NER) systems, namely spaCy and DBpedia Spotlight for identifying entity types.
– **Conversation Analysis**: where we identify common user topics. We propose to use DBpedia Spotlight to identify major conversation themes.

5.1   Request Analysis

In this section, we examine the manner in which users perceive and interact with a knowledge-driven chatbot, in particular the DBpedia Chatbot, to determine the important avenues of improvement. This is accomplished by identifying the **intent**, **complexity**, and **kind** (factual/non-factual) of user utterances.

Intent Analysis: The intent of a user utterance broadly refers to the desired outcome of a particular interaction with a chatbot. Our motivation is to check the coverage of a knowledge-driven chatbot. Due to the lack of ground truth data pertaining to queries' intent, we perform this experiment in an open-ended setting. This means, instead of classifying utterances into fixed classes, we use unsupervised clustering algorithms[9] to group user utterances and treat them as latent intents.

For better generalization, we first detect entity mentions (using DBpedia Spotlight [9]) and replace them with their corresponding schema type. For instance, a query, *"Who is Emmanuel Macron?"*, is first normalized to *"Who is Person?"* and then undergoes the transformation required for clustering.

That is, due to the variety of queries, we rely on two approaches: (1) extracting the verb-object pairs and vectorizing them through an embedding matrix, (2) utilizing sentence embeddings that capture the semantics of the entire utterance.

---

[9] Inspired by https://building.lang.ai/sorry-i-didnt-get-that-how-to-understand-what-your-users-want-a90c7ca18a8f.

(1) For extracting the candidate pair, i.e., the verb-object pair in the query, we employ the state-of-the-art Stanford's dependency parser [22]. User queries can lack either a verb or an object or both. If the `verb-object` pair is not found, we look for one of the following pairs: `noun-nmod`, `noun-nsubj/pron-nsubj`, `propn-nmod`, `nmod-case` or `noun-cop` in the order mentioned. This order was determined via a preliminary analysis over the dataset. Table 2 shows candidate pairs generated via dependency parsing on a few queries. These pairs are vectorized using fastText [21] subword vectors.

Table 2. Candidate pairs from dependency parsing

Query	Dependency relation	Candidate pair
give the German history	verb-object	(give, history)
What is the plot of Titanic?	noun-nmod	(Titanic, plot)
What is a computer?	pron-nsubj	(What, computer)
what about your breakfast	nmod-case	(breakfast, about)
Who is president of Country	propn-nmod	(president, Country)
now we want to be your friend	noun-cop	(friend, be)

(2) Taking into account that the dataset is replete with malformed queries, there are many utterances that do not fit the dependency relations described above. Thus, simply relying on candidate pairs is not sufficient for intent classification. In this regard, to capture a deeper insight, we employ Multilingual Universal Sentence Encoder [26] to encode user utterances and subsequently cluster the vectorized utterances based on their semantic similarity.

To cluster the vectors obtained via the two methods described above, we (1) reduce their dimensions (to 50) using Principal Component Analysis (PCA)[10] and (2) standardize them to obtain normally distributed data. From our observations, without standardization, the clustering algorithms did not perform well and categorized most of the data as noise.

We (3) applied t-Distributed Stochastic Neighbor Embedding (t-SNE) [19] as a preprocessing step to enhance the performance of the (4) density-based clustering performed via the Hierarchical Density-Based Spatial Clustering of Applications with Noise (HDBSCAN) [20] algorithm.[11]

As for the clustering algorithm itself, we chose HDBSCAN primarily because we found it to be faster on our dataset and superior at clustering data of varying

---

[10] Applied as a preprocessing step for t-SNE algorithm, see https://scikit-learn.org/stable/modules/generated/sklearn.manifold.TSNE.html.

[11] We refer the interested readers to also check https://stats.stackexchange.com/questions/263539/clustering-on-the-output-of-t-sne.

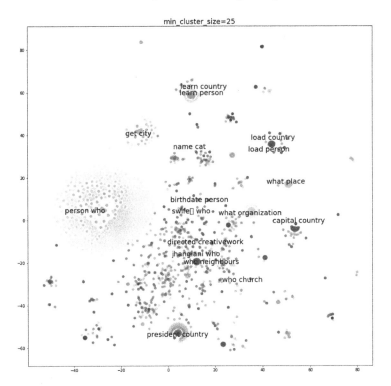

Fig. 1. Visualization of clusters obtained via HDBSCAN on the selected candidate-pair vector embeddings. Each cluster consists of at least 25 samples. The top 10 clusters out of a total of 35 have been labeled with their top terms.

densities. We also found that unlike other clustering algorithms that assume considerable domain knowledge, HDBSCAN has more intuitive parameters to make data-driven decisions. Figures 1 and 2 depict the results from both approaches.

Ex-post-facto research designs can be used if no requirements or experimental investigation strategies exist and noisy variables cannot be controlled. Thus, ex-post-facto designs only allow correlative statements on vast amounts of data. These vast amounts of data can be collected with little financial and personal effort using chatbot logs. By classifying utterances into well-defined categories, one could perform such a correlative analysis. However, this usually requires annotated data for the classification algorithm to generalize well.

Hence, we propose the above-described enhanced mechanism to automate the clustering of utterances based on semantic similarity and actionable word pairs, in the absence of labeled data. These clusters will guide our future research agenda to satisfy user information needs.

Complexity of Utterances: With the increasing research interest in developing solutions [1, 25] for complex question answering over knowledge-graphs, it is crucial to investigate the number of such questions that are actually asked

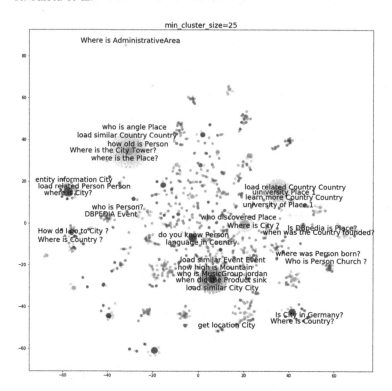

Fig. 2. Visualization of clusters obtained via HDBSCAN on sentence embeddings. Each cluster consists of at least 25 samples. The top 10 clusters out of a total of 33 have been labeled with their top terms.

by the users in real-world settings to such knowledge-graph driven interfaces. Since factual questions constitute a substantial part of interactions with knowledge graph-driven chatbots, we perform an experiment to better understand the nature of these questions.

This experiment is primarily based on a distinction of question complexity. A question is deemed to be complex if it contains a relative clause that modifies the noun or pronoun in it. An example of such an utterances is *"Can you give me the names of women born in the Country during the 19th century?"*. Contrarily, simple questions are devoid of any modifiers and follow a simple sentence structure, such as *"Who is Jimmy Wales?"*, *"When was Donald Trump born?"*.

This distinction closely follows the distinction in KGQA, where a question is defined to be simple if it is answerable via a single triple pattern. Existing literature in the field of KGQA [6] consists of different approaches specific to the aforementioned distinction of question complexity. Thus, estimating the distribution of simple and complex questions can guide the KGQA development.

To determine the complexity of a query, we examine its dependency parse tree. First, we look for a candidate relation pair and then check whether any of its child nodes (relation denoted by `(token-head)->child`) exhibit a clausal or nominal modifier. We then search for the following dependency relations: (obl-verb)-> amod or nmod or nummod, (nsubj-verb)->acl and (obj-verb)-> amod or mod or nummod to estimate the occurrence of complex utterances.

Using this approach, we estimate that only 3.3% of utterances given to DBpedia Chatbot were classified as complex questions, based on a sample set of 5,000 utterances.

Miscellaneous Analysis: Our goal through this analysis is to examine whether the users conform to the limitations of a chatbot even after being informed in advance. It is plausible that users perceive the capabilities of a chatbot to be analogous to Google Assistant, Apple Siri or Amazon Alexa.

Despite the fact that the DBpedia Chatbot is a domain specific dialog system that introduces its capabilities prior to the first user-utterance in every conversation, just like the other task-oriented chatbots [2,14], we notice several banter utterances from the user. To estimate the frequency of banter utterances, we manually inspect 2000 utterances, randomly sampled from the dataset. Through this, we find that about 12.6% are domain-agnostic, non-greeting utterances which we label as banter such as "united states president".

Moreover, an inspection of the language of utterances[12] suggests that users attempted to query the chatbot in their native languages; Russian, Arabic, German, Korean, Portuguese - naming a few, notwithstanding the language limitations of the chatbot.

5.2   Response Analysis

In the response analysis, we attempt to characterize common errors made by the knowledge-driven chatbots by investigating the requests corresponding to the responses that received negative feedback. We also attempt to discover the reason behind the chatbot's (in particular, the DBpedia Chatbot's) inability to answer those queries, using the following metrics:

Number of Failed Responses per Conversations: Approximately 6.9% of the chatbot's responses were marked as incorrect through the feedback form (optionally presented along with every response from the chatbot), indicating factual inaccuracy or general dissatisfaction for that response. Note that this estimation is not representative of all the cases where users experienced dissatisfaction, since responding to the feedback is optional.

Sustaining Conversations After Negative Feedback: Here, we intend to estimate the effect of erroneous response on the conversation by computing the average number of messages exchanged after the first negative feedback. In the case of the DBpedia Chatbot, we find that this number is approx. 7 (std. dev = 16.54). Together, these numbers, when compared with the average conversation length across all conversations, which is approx. 10, suggests that

---

[12] Using the python library **langdetect** https://pypi.org/project/langdetect/.

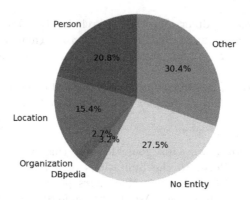

Fig. 3. Entity type distribution from 1000 manually annotated failed utterances.

users still interact with, and derive merit from the chatbot despite an erroneous response. This could be (partly) attributed to either the largely atomic nature of conversations (held by the DBpedia Chatbot) or to its ability to recover from failures using fallback mechanisms.

Entity Types in Utterances Prior to Negative Feedback: To gain an even deeper understanding of failing conversations, we manually annotate a subset of utterances with incorrect responses. We intend to characterize the utterances that caused a failure, to build targeted mechanisms to address these pitfalls. The distribution of manually annotated 1000 utterances has been reported in Fig. 3. A majority of 30.4% utterances, which have been marked as `Other`, consisted of entities like astronomical objects, movies, etc. (e.g. *"Is pluto a planet?"*).

We then compare the accuracy of DBpedia Spotlight [9] and pre-trained `spaCy NER` in spotting the person and location mentions that were identified above. The results of this experiment have been reported in Table 3. We find that while DBpedia Spotlight performs better than `spaCy NER` in our context, there is a need for using more robust entity detection and linking mechanism on noisy data. In hindsight, we also need better dialogue modules for utterances with no or uncommon entity types.

In general, the failure cases in other chat logs can also be examined by (i) calculating the number of failed responses in every conversation, (ii) checking the length of conversations after a negative feedback and (iii) inspecting the utterances prior to the negative feedback for domain-specific vulnerabilities (entity-types in our case).

Table 3. `spaCy-NER` and DBpedia Spotlight accuracy for detecting person and location mentions.

System	Person	Location
`spaCy-NER`	41.3%	42.2%
DBpedia Spotlight [4]	69.2%	46.1%

5.3   Conversation Analysis

Finally, we aim to uncover the common user topics that users ask a knowledge-driven chatbot and the use of anaphora in their conversations. This is to understand the potential improvements in the chatbot's architecture and the NLP tools used in the pipeline from the perspective of both knowledge-graph question answering and human-computer interaction.

For **extracting the topics**, we use DBpedia Spotlight [9] which provides us the underlying schema type for named entities. The schema-entity pair is obtained for every user-request. This enables us to measure the commonly-asked topics as indicated by the density of the schemas.

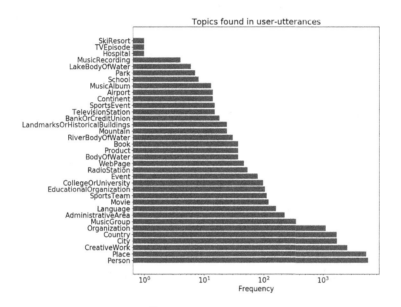

Fig. 4. Topics as identified by DBpedia Spotlight

Figure 4 suggests that a majority of user-queries were primarily concerned with `Person`, `Place` and `DBpedia` (categorized under `CreativeWork`). Referring to the same entity in a text is a commonly occurring linguistic phenomenon, typically referred to as **anaphora**. Detecting and resolving anaphora (or coreference resolution) is a crucial part of conversational agents, which requires keeping track of conversational context over time. We use the python library, `NeuralCoref` [13], which implements the state-of-the-art coreference resolution approaches [7,8], to estimate the frequency with which anaphora occurs in the data. We find that the library detects only 45 such instances out of 9084 conversations. We attribute this infrequent occurrence of the phenomenon to the nature of the DBpedia Chatbot

---

[13] https://github.com/huggingface/neuralcoref.

- of answering factual questions, and DBpedia service inquiries etc., which do not require multi-turn conversations. In contrast, a pizza delivery chatbot that collects required information through multiple rounds of disquisition with the user is more likely to see anaphora in user utterances more frequently.

In general, by fetching the schema to which an entity in utterance belongs, one can identify the topic of the utterances, which can be further used to enhance the backend engine of a chatbot. Additionally, to enhance the human-computer interface of a chatbot, one can inspect the log files for coreferences in queries.

6   Discussion

Based on our ex-post-facto analysis approach, which we applied to the DBpedia Chatbot, we summarize the key implications for future design of the DBpedia Chatbot:

- **Adding support for multilingualism:** In our analysis, we found several instances of user utterances in languages other than English, even though the interface clearly states English as the medium of conversation.
- **Smart Suggestions:** Upon manual inspection of a user query subset, we found several spelling errors, capitalization/casing errors, and other grammatical errors. To mitigate this, we suggest the use of auto-completion.
- **Detecting implicit feedback and out-of-scope queries:** As discussed in Sect. 5, the user perception of the chatbot often leads to out-of-scope questions, and sometimes, implicit feedback provided not via the feedback button but through utterances. It is imperative, thus, to be able to detect and subsequently handle these utterances explicitly. One promising approach for this is to utilize the automatic clustering discussed in Sect. 5.1.
- **Knowledge-based QA:** Most of the user utterances related to KGQA were simple, i.e., questions that are answerable by a single triple. Even though the underlying KGQA system reported very high performance in the simple QA setting [11], we found that the system often failed. The low performance suggests a need for a more robust question answering system. We also found that users expect the KGQA system to act as a search engine and thus the underlying question answering system also needs to support keyword queries.

Consequently, we can derive implications for general knowledge-driven conversational interfaces:

- **Multilingual Support:** (Knowledge-driven) chatbots must support multiple languages from the start, which could be accomplished by either using translation services or by using multilingual NLP tools in the pipeline.
- **Guide User Input:** Chatbots must account for imperfect user input by directing the user towards typing grammatically correct queries using auto-correcting, auto-completion or controlled natural language interfaces.
- **Guiding User Expectations:** Users can mistake simple conversational interfaces or KGQA systems for powerful general AI systems and end up in the uncanny valley. Thus, managing user expectations by detecting and reacting to out-of-scope user intents must be at the core of a chatbot [24].

– **Adding explainability:** Finally, we believe, extending the proposition of Ashktorab et al. [3] of adding explainability as a repair strategy to mitigate conversation breakdowns, will keep the users engaged and reduce the amount of negative feedback resulting from the frustration of unsuccessful queries.

7   Conclusion

In this work, we propose a threefold approach to conduct an ex-post-facto analysis on the user interaction logs of knowledge-driven chatbots. This analysis focuses on three broad perspectives, namely, (i) analysis of user-utterances, (ii) analysis of user-requests that received negative feedback, and (iii) an overall analysis of conversations. Our goal, through this work, is to identify the avenues for potential improvement through a data-driven method.

We substantiate the value of the analysis with experiments over the log files of the DBpedia Chatbot and report multiple findings, see Sect. 6. Broadly, we conclude that in the case of relatively open-ended chatbots, unsupervised clustering through universal sentence embeddings can effectively cluster user-utterances based on their semantic similarity, thereby signaling their intents. Through manual analysis over a subset of the logs, we find that entity mentions cannot be reliably detected through off-the-shelf solutions, and require the development and application of robust entity detection and linking approaches.

In our opinion, our approach has merit outside the narrow domain of the DBpedia Chatbot and can be generalized to other knowledge-driven chatbots. The implications from our findings can be incorporated in future chatbots for better user-experience. However, it is worth noting that, to extend these findings and their implications, other query logs must be examined with the proposed ex-post-facto approach.

Acknowledgments. This work has been supported by the Federal Ministry of Transport and Digital Infrastructure (BMVI) in the OPAL research project (grant no. 19F2028A) and LIMBO (no. 19F2029I) as well as by the German Federal Ministry of Education and Research (BMBF) within 'KMU-innovativ: Forschung für die zivile Sicherheit' in particular 'Forschung für die zivile Sicherheit' and the project SOLIDE (no. 13N14456).

References

1. Abujabal, A., Roy, R.S., Yahya, M., Weikum, G.: ComQA: a community-sourced dataset for complex factoid question answering with paraphrase clusters (2019)
2. Akhtar, M., Neidhardt, J., Werthner, H.: The potential of chatbots: analysis of chatbot conversations. In: CBI (2019)
3. Ashktorab, Z., Jain, M., Liao, Q.V., Weisz, J.D.: Resilient chatbots: repair strategy preferences for conversational breakdowns. In: CHI (2019)
4. Athreya, R.G., Ngomo, A.N., Usbeck, R.: Enhancing community interactions with data-driven chatbots-the dbpedia chatbot (2018)

5. Both, A., Diefenbach, D., Singh, K., Shekarpour, S., Cherix, D., Lange, C.: Qanary – a methodology for vocabulary-driven open question answering systems. In: Sack, H., Blomqvist, E., d'Aquin, M., Ghidini, C., Ponzetto, S.P., Lange, C. (eds.) ESWC 2016. LNCS, vol. 9678, pp. 625–641. Springer, Cham (2016). https://doi.org/10.1007/978-3-319-34129-3_38

6. Chakraborty, N., Lukovnikov, D., Maheshwari, G., Trivedi, P., Lehmann, J., Fischer, A.: Introduction to neural network based approaches for question answering over knowledge graphs. CoRR abs/1907.09361 (2019)

7. Clark, K., Manning, C.D.: Deep reinforcement learning for mention-ranking coreference models. In: EMNLP (2016)

8. Clark, K., Manning, C.D.: Improving coreference resolution by learning entity-level distributed representations (2016)

9. Daiber, J., Jakob, M., Hokamp, C., Mendes, P.N.: Improving efficiency and accuracy in multilingual entity extraction (2013)

10. Dale, R.: The return of the chatbots. Nat. Lang. Eng. **22**(5), 811–817 (2016)

11. Diefenbach, D., Migliatti, P.H., Qawasmeh, O., Lully, V., Singh, K., Maret, P.: QAnswer: a question answering prototype bridging the gap between a considerable part of the LOD cloud and end-users (2019)

12. Huang, J., Zhou, M., Yang, D.: Extracting chatbot knowledge from online discussion forums. In: IJCAI, vol. 7, pp. 423–428 (2007)

13. Jain, M., Kumar, P., Kota, R., Patel, S.N.: Evaluating and informing the design of chatbots. In: DIS (2018)

14. Jenkins, M.-C., Churchill, R., Cox, S., Smith, D.: Analysis of user interaction with service oriented chatbot systems. In: Jacko, J.A. (ed.) HCI 2007. LNCS, vol. 4552, pp. 76–83. Springer, Heidelberg (2007). https://doi.org/10.1007/978-3-540-73110-8_9

15. Keyner, S., Savenkov, V., Vakulenko, S.: Open data chatbot. In: Hitzler, P., et al. (eds.) ESWC 2019. LNCS, vol. 11762, pp. 111–115. Springer, Cham (2019). https://doi.org/10.1007/978-3-030-32327-1_22

16. Lehmann, J., et al.: DBpedia - a large-scale, multilingual knowledge base extracted from Wikipedia. Semant. Web **6**, 167–195 (2015)

17. Li, C., Chen, K., Chang, Y.: When there is no progress with a task-oriented chatbot: a conversation analysis (2019)

18. Lommatzsch, A., Katins, J.: An information retrieval-based approach for building intuitive chatbots for large knowledge bases (2019)

19. Van der Maaten, L., Hinton, G.: Visualizing data using t-SNE. J. Mach. Learn. Res. **9**(Nov), 2579–2605 (2008)

20. McInnes, L., Healy, J., Astels, S.: HDBSCAN: hierarchical density based clustering. J. Open Source Softw. **2**(11), 205 (2017)

21. Mikolov, T., Grave, E., Bojanowski, P., Puhrsch, C., Joulin, A.: Advances in pre-training distributed word representations. In: LREC (2018)

22. Qi, P., Dozat, T., Zhang, Y., Manning, C.D.: Universal dependency parsing from scratch (2018). https://nlp.stanford.edu/pubs/qi2018universal.pdf

23. Rivolli, A., Amaral, C., Guardão, L., de Sá, C.R., Soares, C.: KnowBots: discovering relevant patterns in chatbot dialogues. In: Kralj Novak, P., Šmuc, T., Džeroski, S. (eds.) DS 2019. LNCS (LNAI), vol. 11828, pp. 481–492. Springer, Cham (2019). https://doi.org/10.1007/978-3-030-33778-0_36

24. Skjuve, M., Haugstveit, I.M., Følstad, A., Brandtzaeg, P.B.: Help! is my chatbot falling into the uncanny valley? An empirical study of user experience in human-chatbot interaction. Hum. Technol. **15**, 30–54 (2019)
25. Vakulenko, S., Garcia, J.D.F., Polleres, A., de Rijke, M., Cochez, M.: Message passing for complex question answering over knowledge graphs (2019)
26. Yang, Y., et al.: Multilingual universal sentence encoder for semantic retrieval. CoRR abs/1907.04307 (2019)

Privacy Concerns in Chatbot Interactions

Carolin Ischen[(⊠)], Theo Araujo, Hilde Voorveld, Guda van Noort,
and Edith Smit

ASCoR, University of Amsterdam, 1001 NG Amsterdam, The Netherlands
{C.Ischen, T.B.Araujo, H.A.M.Voorveld, G.vanNoort,
E.G.Smit}@uva.nl

Abstract. Chatbots are increasingly used in a commercial context to make product- or service-related recommendations. By doing so, they collect personal information of the user, similar to other online services. While privacy concerns in an online (website-) context are widely studied, research in the context of chatbot-interaction is lacking. This study investigates the extent to which chatbots with human-like cues influence perceptions of anthropomorphism (i.e., attribution of human-like characteristics), privacy concerns, and consequently, information disclosure, attitudes and recommendation adherence. Findings show that a human-like chatbot leads to more information disclosure, and recommendation adherence mediated by higher perceived anthropomorphism and subsequently, lower privacy concerns in comparison to a machine-like chatbot. This result does not hold in comparison to a website; human-like chatbot and website were perceived as equally high in anthropomorphism. The results show the importance of both mediating concepts in regards to attitudinal and behavioral outcomes when interacting with chatbots.

Keywords: Chatbots · Anthropomorphism · Privacy concerns

1 Introduction

Through advances in artificial intelligence and machine learning, conversational agents in the form of text-based chatbots become more and more important for companies and brands to make product-, or service-related recommendations [18]. Chatbots interact with their users through natural language, and can provide guidance in a conversational manner [21, 42]. The conversational interaction in combination with human-like cues are crucial characteristics of such chatbots. Because of these characteristics, users might be more likely to attribute human-like characteristics to them (i.e., perceive them as anthropomorphic) [17, 27]. While this might lead users to appreciate the dialog and enjoy the interaction [10, 26], they also need to share personal information with the chatbot to receive a valuable recommendation. By doing so, the company that hosts the chatbot collects data of their users, who are possibly not aware of this data collection. In this regard, chatbots might also enhance privacy concerns users might have when interacting with digital technologies [15]. While we know from previous research that users are concerned about their online privacy when using websites [e.g., 8], also having downstream effects on e.g. self-disclosure [9], users' privacy concerns might differ for chatbots, especially when conveying a human-like appeal.

© Springer Nature Switzerland AG 2020
A. Følstad et al. (Eds.): CONVERSATIONS 2019, LNCS 11970, pp. 34–48, 2020.
https://doi.org/10.1007/978-3-030-39540-7_3

Therefore, this study investigates to what extent privacy concerns in chatbot interactions are related to users' attitudes and recommendation adherence, and furthermore, to what extent users feel comfortable sharing personal information with a human-like chatbot in comparison with a machine-like chatbot, or a website. The research question guiding this research is: To what extent do human-like characteristics of a chatbot influence perceived anthropomorphism, privacy concerns, and consequently, information disclosure, attitudes, and recommendation adherence?

Hereby, building on social response theory and previous research on informational privacy, this study aims to examine anthropomorphism and privacy concerns as sequential underlying mechanisms possibly explaining these outcomes. This study contributes to our understanding of chatbots in a digital communication environment in exploring how human-like attributes influence users' perceptions of the communication entity (chatbot and website) and their behavior when interacting with them. In examining the concept of privacy concerns, this study not only extends research in the field of human-machine-communication, but has societal implications. While the protection of online privacy is widely discussed, the acceptance of chatbots and related implications for privacy still need to be studied. It plays an increasingly important role to uncover whether and, if so, how human-like cues influence privacy concerns, and how aware users are that their data is being used. This specific context has to be addressed by companies using this technology as well as by policy makers to protect users' privacy.

2 Theoretical Background

2.1 Perceived Anthropomorphism

Anthropomorphism is the attribution of human-like characteristics to non-human entities [17]. This can be mindful, i.e. the conscious evaluation of humanness, as well as mindless, i.e. attributing human-like characteristics without realizing, such as being friendly or sociable [27]. Go and Sundar [20] differentiate three types of cues that can suggest humanness among chatbots (mindful as well as mindless). These are visual cues, such as the use of human-like figures; identity cues, such as human-associated names; and conversational cues, such as the mimicking of human language, i.e. acknowledging responses. The authors find effects of conversational cues on attitudes and behavioral intentions, and further, interaction effects for the three types of cues. A combination of the anthropomorphic cues as used in a human-like chatbot is expected to have the ability to influence mindless evaluations of humanness in particular, both in comparison to a machine-like chatbot without these anthropomorphic cues, and in comparison to a more traditional form of digital medium like an interactive website [2]. We do not expect differences between a machine-like chatbot and an interactive website. This is because both, website and machine-like chatbot include interactive elements (e.g., people have to disclose some personal information by answering questions) that might create a similar perception of anthropomorphism [26].

Subsequently, we examine three different outcomes. Firstly, level of comfort with information disclosure will be studied. Information disclosure in this context is the amount of true information customers reveal about themselves for a purchase decision online, e.g. providing personal details [9]. Level of comfort with information disclosure refers to user perceptions, i.e., to what extent they feel like having disclosed private or intimate information about themselves. Secondly, we will study attitudes towards the entity giving the recommendation, in this case the chatbot/website. The third outcome variable is recommendation adherence, i.e., the willingness to purchase the recommended product. We expect perceived anthropomorphism to positively influence all three outcome variables. In accordance with social response theory, stating that humans respond similarly to technology imbued with human-like characteristics as they respond to humans [30, 33], Go and Sundar [20] showed that attitudes and behavioral intentions can be influenced by the social connectedness induced by anthropomorphism. Secondly, based on brand relationship theory, users and brands can engage in relationships similar to interpersonal relationships, leading to positive brand responses [19, 31]. Similarly, interacting with a human-like chatbot created by a company can mimic interpersonal communication, positively influencing information disclosure, attitudes and recommendation adherence. Therefore, we propose the following hypothesis (H1):

> Receiving a product recommendation from a human-like chatbot leads to more (a) information disclosure, (b) positive attitudes towards the medium, and (c) recommendation adherence mediated by higher perceived anthropomorphism than receiving a product recommendation from a machine-like chatbot or an interactive website.

2.2 Privacy Concerns

Privacy concerns in a marketing context can be defined as "the degree to which a consumer is worried about the potential invasion of the right to prevent the disclosure of personal information to others" [3, 37]. To make recommendations, online services collect personal information. Personal information can amongst others be collected by direct requests to disclose this information. These direct requests might induce privacy concerns [39]. Previous research by Følstad et al. [18] showed that customers have a concern for privacy and security when it comes to interactions with chatbots, i.e. they have a need to be provided with a secure online service. As the conversation with a chatbot is a rather new phenomenon, users might be more aware of these direct requests, inducing more privacy concerns.

We expect privacy concerns to negatively influence information disclosure. While, as stated in the "privacy paradox", perceived privacy risks do not automatically translate into not disclosing information online [4, 14], several scholars found privacy concerns and information disclosure to be related [5]. For example, Dinev and Hart [15] found a negative relationship between privacy concerns and the willingness to provide personal information for internet-based transactions. Furthermore, privacy concerns are an important antecedent for the acceptance of mobile chatbots [16], and might thus be related to users' attitudes. Thirdly, users see privacy concerns as a reason to not shop online [23]. Hence, we expect privacy concerns to also negatively influence recommendation adherence. However, since we cannot formulate a direction of how human-like cues influence privacy concerns, we propose the following research question (RQ1):

Does receiving a product recommendation from a human-like chatbot lead to more, or less (a) information disclosure, (b) positive attitudes towards the medium, and (c) recommendation adherence mediated by higher privacy concerns than receiving a product recommendation from a machine-like chatbot or an interactive website?

2.3 Sequential Mediation of Perceived Anthropomorphism and Privacy Concerns

Lastly, we are interested in the relationship between perceived anthropomorphism and privacy concerns in a chatbot context. On the one hand, we argue that a chatbot that is perceived as highly anthropomorphic can enhance privacy concerns, when asking to disclose personal information. A human-like chatbot as a communication entity might be perceived as more personal and less anonymous, inducing more privacy concerns than a machine-like chatbot or a website [22, 35]. On the other hand, this feeling of communicating with an actual communication partner might also lead to less privacy concerns, because users might experience a closer connection to the human-like chatbot, increasing the willingness to use it as a companion [7]. Research in the health context showed that a chatbot was evaluated positively in comparison to e.g. search engines by adolescents, especially in regards to more sensitive questions [12]. Due to these contradictory findings, we propose a research question about the sequential mediating effects of perceived anthropomorphism and privacy concerns (RQ2):

Does receiving a product recommendation from a human-like chatbot lead to more, or less (a) information disclosure, (b) positive attitudes towards the medium, and (c) recommendation adherence sequentially mediated by perceived anthropomorphism and privacy concerns than receiving a product recommendation from a machine-like chatbot or an interactive website?

3   Method

3.1   Design and Sample

An experimental between-subjects design with three conditions (type of entity: human-like chatbot vs. machine-like chatbot vs. website) was implemented. Recruited through the Dutch online panel PanelClix, 231 participants took part in the study. Participants' age ranged from 18 to 73 ($M = 41.83$, $SD = 14.01$), 48.5% were female (51.5% male); 51.6% indicated to have a high educational level (38.9% middle, 9.5% low).

3.2   Procedure

Randomly assigned to the groups, participants interacted with either the website ($n_{website} = 73$), the machine-like ($n_{machine-like} = 85$), or the human-like ($n_{human-like} = 73$) chatbot to obtain a recommendation for the (fictitious) health insurance company "ZorgPlus" (engl. "CarePlus"). Several questions about demographics (i.e., age, gender, place of residence), preferences (i.e., current health insurance company, importance of customer service and travel behavior, budget), and two intrusive questions (i.e., legal residence in the Netherlands and number of sexual partners in the previous six-month) were asked, that participants could answer as they wish.

Afterwards, participants filled in a questionnaire measuring the dependent variables, mediators and control variables.

3.3 Stimuli

An interactive website was developed that gave a recommendation for a health insurance after participants filled in personal information.[1] Furthermore, two chatbots were created for this study using a conversational agent research toolkit for experimental research developed by Araujo [1]. The human-like version of the chatbot introduced itself with a name ("Sam"); displayed a visual of a cartoon-like customer service agent, similar to Verhagen et al. [36]; and used human conversational cues, i.e. acknowledged the responses of the participants (e.g. "gotcha", "I noted down your gender"). In the machine-like version, the chatbot did not carry a human-like name (it was called ChatbotX), similar to Araujo [2]; displayed a neutral visual of a dialog bubble, similar to Go and Sundar [20]; and only asked questions without acknowledging previous answers. An example of the human-like chatbot is given in Fig. 1.

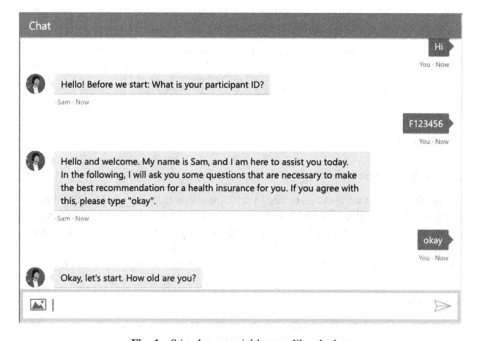

Fig. 1. Stimulus material human-like chatbot

---

[1] Similar to [26], conference presentation is available upon request to the first author.

3.4   Measurements

Mediators. We measured *mindless anthropomorphism* with four items on a 7-point-Likert-scale adapted from Kim and Sundar [27], e.g., "I perceived the chatbot/website as sociable" (1 = strongly disagree, 7 = strongly agree).[2] *Privacy concerns* were measured with four items on a 7-point-Likert-scale including "It bothers me that this chatbot asks me for this much personal information" (1 = strongly disagree, 7 = strongly agree) adapted from Xu et al. [40]. While the original scale was developed to measure privacy concerns as a trait, we adapted the measurement to assess privacy concerns in regards to the specific interaction participants engaged in.

Outcome Variables. *Level of comfort with information disclosure* was measured with four items adapted from Croes and Antheunis [11, 28], e.g. "I felt comfortable disclosing personal information during the interaction" (1 = strongly disagree, 7 = strongly agree). *Attitude towards the chatbot/website* was measured with items adapted from Becker-Olsen [6]. Five semantic differential scale items were used e.g "I think the chatbot/website is good/bad". To measure *recommendation adherence,* we used four items on a 7-point-Likert-scale adapted from Dabholkar and Sheng [13] including "Imagine you are considering a new health insurance: It is very likely that I would buy the recommended insurance" (1 = strongly disagree, 7 = strongly agree).

Control Variables. Besides age, gender, and education, we measured familiarity (with the chatbot/website, and with health insurances) with two items on a 7-point-Likert-scale adapted from Zhou, Yang and Hui [43]. Furthermore, we measured power usage [29], belief in machine heuristic [34], and enjoyment [23] as control variables. Scale reliabilities and mean values of the relevant scales are displayed in Table 1.

Table 1.   Scale reliability

Scale	Cr. Alpha	M	SD
Mindless anthropomorphism	.91	4.55	1.21
Privacy concerns	.91	4.20	1.28
Information disclosure	.89	4.24	1.15
Attitudes	.92	4.45	1.20
Recommendation adherence	.83	3.56	1.01
Familiarity medium	.83	4.76	1.39

3.5   Randomization Check

A randomization check showed that participants did not differ across groups in terms of *age, gender, education, power usage, enjoyment, belief in machine heuristic,* and

---

[2] Furthermore, we measured mindful anthropomorphism with three items on 7-point semantic differential scales [32]. A univariate analysis of variance showed no significant main effect of type of entity on mindful anthropomorphism ($F(2, 227) = 1.16$, p = .314).

familiarity with health insurances. Significant differences were found for *familiarity with the medium* ($F(2, 228) = 15.79$, $p < .001$). Participants were significantly less familiar with chatbots ($M_{machine-like} = 4.49$, $SD = 1.37$, $M_{human-like} = 4.36$, $SD = 1.40$) than with websites ($M_{websites} = 5.47$, $SD = 1.12$). Familiarity with the medium was included as a co-variate in the subsequent analyses.

4   Results

We performed serial multiple mediation analyses (model 6), using the PROCESS macro for IBM SPSS version 25 [24]. We used bootstrapping (5,000 bootstrap samples) to obtain bias-corrected 95% confidence intervals for the indirect effects of the independent variable *type of entity* on *information disclosure, attitudes,* and *recommendation adherence* through the mediators *mindless anthropomorphism* and *privacy concerns*. All paths for the full model are shown in Fig. 2 and the corresponding coefficients are displayed in Tables 2, 3 and 4. Separate path analyses were performed for the three dependent variables. The independent variable *type of entity* is multicategorical. We use the category *human-like chatbot* as the reference category, since we are primarily interested in the comparison human-like chatbot vs. machine-like chatbot, and human-like chatbot vs. website [25]. Additionally, we also compared machine-like chatbot and website using the category *machine-like chatbot* as the reference category.

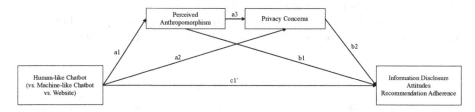

Fig. 2. Serial mediation model

4.1   Information Disclosure

Perceived Anthropomorphism and Information Disclosure. Firstly, we compared human-like chatbot to machine-like chatbot. As shown in Table 2, there is a significant direct effect of type of entity on mindless anthropomorphism (path a1). The human-like chatbot is perceived as higher in anthropomorphism than the machine-like chatbot. The specific indirect effect of type of entity on information disclosure through mindless anthropomorphism is significant (effect = −.20, $SE = .08$, $CI = −.37, −.06$), indicating that the human-like chatbot is perceived as higher in anthropomorphism than the machine-like chatbot, leading to more information disclosure. Secondly, comparing the human-like chatbot and the website, no significant effect on perceived anthropomorphism (path a1) is found, both are equally high in anthropomorphism. The specific indirect effect of type of entity on information disclosure through mindless anthropomorphism is not significant (effect = −.12, *SE* = .07, CI = −.28, .01), indicating no mediating effect of anthropomorphism. Additionally, we also compared machine-like chatbot and website, showing no significant effect on perceived anthropomorphism. The specific indirect effect of type of entity on information disclosure through mindless anthropomorphism is not significant (effect = .08, *SE* = .07, CI = −.06, .22).

Privacy Concerns and Information Disclosure. Firstly, we compared human-like chatbot to machine-like chatbot. There is no significant direct effect of type of entity on privacy concerns (path a2). The specific indirect effect on information disclosure through privacy concerns is not significant (effect = .07, *SE* = .07, CI = −.06, .21). Secondly, comparing the human-like chatbot and the website, no significant effect on privacy concerns (path a2) is found. The specific indirect effect on information disclosure through privacy concerns is also not significant (effect = .08, *SE* = .29, CI = −.29, .02). Thirdly, comparing machine-like chatbot and website, there is a significant direct effect on privacy concerns. Furthermore, the specific indirect effect of type of entity through privacy concerns is significant (effect = −.20, *SE* = .08, CI = −.36, −.06), indicating a mediating effect. The website induced higher privacy concerns than the machine-like chatbot, leading to less information disclosure.

Perceived Anthropomorphism, Privacy Concerns and Information Disclosure. Firstly, we tested a serial multiple mediation (including perceived anthropomorphism, and privacy concerns) comparing human-like chatbot and machine-like chatbot. The specific indirect effect of type of entity on information disclosure through both, mindless anthropomorphism and privacy concerns is significant (effect = −.04, *SE* = .02, CI = −.09, −.01). The human-like chatbot is perceived as higher in mindless anthropomorphism than the machine-like chatbot, leading to less privacy concerns, and consequently more information disclosure. Secondly, testing a serial multiple mediation comparing human-like chatbot and website, the specific indirect effect of type of entity on information disclosure through both, mindless anthropomorphism and privacy concerns is not significant (effect = −.03, *SE* = .02, CI = −.07, .001). Thirdly, testing a serial multiple mediation comparing machine-like chatbot and website, the specific indirect effect of type of entity on information disclosure through both, mindless anthropomorphism and privacy concerns is not significant (effect = .02, *SE* = .02, CI = −.01, .05).

Table 2. Path coefficients sequential mediation explaining information disclosure

	Human-like chatbot vs. machine-like chatbot	Human-like chatbot vs. website	Machine-like chatbot vs. website
a1	−.51** (.18)	−.32 (.19)	.20 (.18)
a2	−.20 (.20)	.37 (.21)	.56* (.20)
a3	−.24** (.07)	−.24** (.07)	−.24** (.07)
b1	.39*** (.05)	.39*** (.05)	.39*** (.05)
b2	−.35*** (.05)	−.35*** (.05)	−.35*** (.05)
c1'	−.10 (.13)	−.02 (.14)	.08 (.14)

*p = .05. **p < .005. ***p < .001; controlled for familiarity with medium

4.2 Attitudes

Perceived Anthropomorphism and Attitudes. The same type of analysis was conducted for attitudes as the outcome variable, as shown in Table 3. Firstly, we compared human-like chatbot and machine-like chatbot. The specific indirect effect through mindless anthropomorphism is significant (effect = −.33, SE = .11, CI = −.56, −.11), indicating that the human-like chatbot is perceived as higher in anthropomorphism than the machine-like chatbot, leading to more positive attitudes. When comparing the human-like chatbot and the website, the specific indirect effect through mindless anthropomorphism is not significant (effect = −.20, SE = .11, CI = −.43, .01). Lastly, comparing machine-like chatbot and website, the specific indirect effect through mindless anthropomorphism is also not significant (effect = .13, SE = .12, CI = −.10, .36).

Privacy Concerns and Attitudes. When comparing human-like chatbot and machine-like chatbot, the specific indirect effect through privacy concerns is not significant (effect = .01, SE = .02, CI = −.01, .06). The same holds for the comparison human-like chatbot and website (effect = −.02, SE = .03, CI = −.09, .02); and machine-like chatbot and website (effect = −.04, SE = .03, CI = −.11, .02).

Perceived Anthropomorphism, Privacy Concerns, and Attitudes. When testing a serial multiple mediation comparing human-like chatbot and machine-like chatbot, the specific indirect effect of type of entity on attitudes through both, mindless anthropomorphism and privacy concerns is not significant (effect = −.01, SE = .01, CI = −.03, .004). The same holds for the serial multiple mediation models comparing human-like chatbot and website (effect = −.01, SE = .01, CI = −.02, .003); and machine-like chatbot and website (effect = .003, SE = .004, CI = −.004, .03).

Table 3. Path coefficients sequential mediation explaining attitudes

	Human-like vs. machine-like	Human-like vs. website	Machine-like vs. website
a1	−.51** (.18)	−.32 (.19)	.20 (.18)
a2	−.20 (.20)	.37 (.21)	.56* (.20)
a3	−.24** (.07)	−.24** (.07)	−.24** (.07)
b1	.64*** (.05)	.64*** (.05)	.64*** (.05)
b2	−.07 (.05)	−.07 (.05)	−.07 (.05)
c1'	.15 (.14)	.10 (.15)	−.05 (.15)

*p = .05. **p < .005. ***p < .001; controlled for familiarity with medium

4.3 Recommendation Adherence

Perceived Anthropomorphism and Recommendation Adherence. We tested the models for recommendation adherence as the outcome variable, as shown in Table 4. Firstly, we compared human-like chatbot to machine-like chatbot. The specific indirect effect through mindless anthropomorphism is significant (effect = −.16, SE = .06,

CI = −.29, −.05), indicating that the human-like chatbot is perceived as higher in anthropomorphism than the machine-like chatbot, leading to more recommendation adherence. When comparing the human-like chatbot and the website, the specific indirect effect through mindless anthropomorphism is not significant (effect = −.10, SE = .06, CI = −.22, .01). Lastly, comparing machine-like chatbot and website, the specific indirect effect through mindless anthropomorphism is not significant (effect = .06, SE = .06, CI = −.05, .19).

Privacy Concerns and Recommendation Adherence. When comparing human-like chatbot and machine-like chatbot, the specific indirect effect through privacy concerns is not significant (effect = .03, SE = .03, CI = −.02, .09). When comparing the human-like chatbot and the website, the specific indirect effect through privacy concerns is not significant (effect = −.05, SE = .04, CI = −.13, .01). Comparing the machine-like chatbot and the website, the specific indirect effect through privacy concerns is significant (effect = −.07, SE = .04, CI = −.17, −.004). The website induces higher privacy concerns than the machine-like chatbot, leading to less recommendation adherence.

Perceived Anthropomorphism, Privacy Concerns, and Recommendation Adherence. When testing a serial multiple mediation comparing human-like chatbot and machine-like chatbot, the specific indirect effect of type of entity on information disclosure through both, mindless anthropomorphism and privacy concerns is significant (effect = −.02, SE = .01, CI = −.04, −.002). The human-like chatbot is perceived as higher in anthropomorphism than the machine-like chatbot, leading to less privacy concerns, and consequently more recommendation adherence. When testing the serial multiple mediation comparing the human-like chatbot and the website, the specific indirect effect of type of entity on information disclosure through both, mindless anthropomorphism and privacy concerns is not significant (effect = −.01, SE = .01, CI = −.03, .0008). The same holds for the comparison machine-like chatbot and website (effect = .01, SE = .01, CI = −.01, .02). A summary of the results is given in Table 5.

Table 4. Path coefficients sequential mediation explaining recommendation adherence

	Human-like vs. machine-like	Human-like vs. website	Machine-like vs. website
a1	−.51** (.18)	−.32 (.19)	.20 (.18)
a2	−.20 (.20)	.37 (.21)	.56* (.20)
a3	−.24** (.07)	−.24** (.07)	−.24** (.07)
b1	.32*** (.06)	.32*** (.06)	.32*** (.06)
b2	−.13** (.05)	−.13** (.05)	−.13** (.05)
c1'	.25 (.14)	.30 (.16)	.05 (.15)

*p = .05. **p < .005. ***p < .001; controlled for familiarity with medium

Table 5. Summary of results

Hypothesis/RQ	Human-like vs. machine like chatbot	Human-like chatbot vs. website	Machine-like chatbot vs. website
H1: Human-like chatbot → perceived anthropomorphism → information disclosure/attitudes/recommendation adherence	Supported. Human-like chatbot leads to more information disclosure, positive attitudes and recommendation adherence mediated by higher perceived anthropomorphism in comparison to machine-like chatbot	Not supported. Differences in anthropomorphism between human-like chatbot and website not significant	Differences in anthropomorphism between machine-like chatbot and website not significant
RQ1: Human-like chatbot → privacy concerns → information disclosure/attitudes/recommendation adherence	Not supported. Differences in privacy concerns between human-like chatbot and machine-like chatbot not significant	Not supported. Differences in privacy concerns between human-like chatbot and website not significant	Website induced higher privacy concerns than machine-like chatbot, leading to less information disclosure, and less recommendation adherence. No mediating effect on attitudes
RQ2: Human-like chatbot → perceived anthropomorphism → privacy concern → information disclosure/attitudes/recommendation adherence	Partially supported. Human-like chatbot leads to higher information disclosure, and recommendation adherence mediated by higher anthropomorphism and lower privacy concerns than machine-like chatbot. No mediating effect on attitudes	Not supported, no sequential mediation	No sequential mediation

5 Discussion and Conclusion

This study investigated the extent to which chatbots' human-like characteristics influence perceived anthropomorphism, users' privacy concerns, and consequently, information disclosure, attitudes, and recommendation adherence. Firstly, we showed that a chatbot using human-like cues leads to higher mindless anthropomorphism than a chatbot not using these cues. Thus, people indeed attribute human-like characteristics such as friendliness or socialness to a chatbot.

Interestingly, mindless anthropomorphism was at the same level for the human-like chatbot and for the website. This result is puzzling, because it shows that interactive websites are (equally) able to convey a human-like appeal. This is in line with previous research showing no differences in, or even higher perceptions of anthropomorphism for websites than for chatbots [26, 38]. One possible explanation could be the source orientation. In the website condition, participants might have responded towards a source behind the website (company, programmer etc.), thus did not see the chatbot as an entity, but saw the "human behind", leading to higher perceived anthropomorphism. Another possible explanation is that users might change their "reference category" when interacting with a chatbot. While evaluating technology when comparing websites to one another, users might compare a chatbot with a human communication partner (including how a human would act), thus changing their expectations towards the chatbot. One important aspect might also be the familiarity with the medium. Users are more familiar with websites than with chatbots, which might have given them a sense of comfort already [41]. In this study, we found a significant difference in mindless anthropomorphism between the machine-like chatbot and the website when *not* controlling for familiarity. Participants might have given lower scores for friendliness or socialness for the machine-like chatbot because they were less familiar with the medium.

Furthermore, this research shows that the outcomes information disclosure, and recommendation adherence are indeed influenced by privacy concerns, supporting previous findings [16, 23]. The sequential mediation analysis including perceived anthropomorphism and privacy concerns shows that a human-like chatbot in this study is higher in perceived anthropomorphism, leading to less privacy concerns and subsequently, more comfort with disclosure, and more recommendation adherence. Users might experience a closer bond with a human-like agent than with a machine-like agent [7]. This might be because a human-like chatbot acknowledges users' answers, e.g. the chatbot in this study indicated that it "noted the answer down". This might have been perceived as less invading then just submitting it "somewhere" without knowing where the information ends up. No mediation was found for the comparison of human-like chatbot and website. These findings complement and extend a recent study [34] showing that users were more likely to reveal information to a machine-like interface than to a sales associate. Based on a machine-heuristic, users perceive a machine-like source as less biased. While these findings are based on source characteristics, our study focuses on message characteristics. Future research should look into the interplay of these two elements.

Additional analyses with a comparison of machine-like chatbot and website showed no influence of perceived anthropomorphism, but a direct effect on privacy concerns (while this direct effect is not significant for the other comparisons). This shows that a website is significantly higher in privacy concerns than a machine-like chatbot and that privacy concerns directly mediate information disclosure, attitudes and recommendation adherence. Further research should thus look into different underlying mechanisms apart from anthropomorphism.

Concluding, this study enriches our understanding of privacy concerns in a chatbot context in showing the sequential influence of perceived anthropomorphism and privacy concerns on users' behavioral intentions.

Acknowledgements. This study was funded by the Research Priority Area Communication and its Digital Communication Methods Lab (digicomlab.eu) at the University of Amsterdam.

References

1. Araujo, T.: Conversational agent research toolkit: an alternative for creating and managing chatbots for experimental research. (2019). https://doi.org/10.31235/osf.io/9ukyf
2. Araujo, T.: Living up to the chatbot hype: the influence of anthropomorphic design cues and communicative agency framing on conversational agent and company perceptions. Comput. Hum. Behav. **85**, 183–189 (2018). https://doi.org/10.1016/j.chb.2018.03.051
3. Baek, T.H., Morimoto, M.: Stay away from me. J. Advert. **41**(1), 59–76 (2012). https://doi.org/10.2753/JOA0091-3367410105
4. Barnes, S.B.: A privacy paradox: social networking in the United States. First Monday **11**, 9 (2006)
5. Baruh, L., et al.: Online privacy concerns and privacy management: a meta-analytical review. J. Commun. **67**(1), 26–53 (2017). https://doi.org/10.1111/jcom.12276
6. Becker-Olsen, K.L.: And now, a word from our sponsor: a look at the effects of sponsored content and banner advertising. J. Advert. **32**(2), 17–32 (2003)
7. Birnbaum, G.E., et al.: What robots can teach us about intimacy: the reassuring effects of robot responsiveness to human disclosure. Comput. Hum. Behav. **63**, 416–423 (2016). https://doi.org/10.1016/j.chb.2016.05.064
8. Boerman, S.C., et al.: Exploring motivations for online privacy protection behavior: insights from panel data. Commun. Res. (2018). https://doi.org/10.1177/0093650218800915
9. Bol, N., et al.: Understanding the effects of personalization as a privacy calculus: analyzing self-disclosure across health, news, and commerce contexts. J. Comput. Commun. **23**, 370–388 (2018). https://doi.org/10.1093/jcmc/zmy020
10. Chung, M., et al.: Chatbot e-service and customer satisfaction regarding luxury brands. J. Bus. Res., 1–9 (2018). https://doi.org/10.1016/j.jbusres.2018.10.004
11. Croes, E., Antheunis, M.L.: Can we be friends with a chatbot? A longitudinal study on the process of friendship formation between humans and a social chatbot. Paper presented at the 69th Annual International Communication Association (ICA) Conference (2019)
12. Crutzen, R., et al.: An artificially intelligent chat agent that answers adolescents' questions related to sex, drugs, and alcohol: an exploratory study. J. Adolesc. Heal. **48**(5), 514–519 (2011). https://doi.org/10.1016/j.jadohealth.2010.09.002
13. Dabholkar, P.A., Sheng, X.: Consumer participation in using online recommendation agents: effects on satisfaction, trust, and purchase intentions. Serv. Ind. J. **32**(9), 1433–1449 (2012). https://doi.org/10.1080/02642069.2011.624596
14. Dienlin, T., Trepte, S.: Is the privacy paradox a relict of the past? An in-depth analysis of privacy attitudes and privacy behaviors. Eur. J. Soc. Psychol. **45**, 285–297 (2015). https://doi.org/10.1002/ejsp.2038
15. Dinev, T., Hart, P.: An extended privacy calculus model for e-commerce transactions. Inf. Syst. Res. **17**(1), 61–80 (2006). https://doi.org/10.1287/isre.1060.0080
16. Van Eeuwen, M.: Mobile conversational commerce: messenger chatbots as the next interface between businesses and consumers. University of Twente (2017)
17. Epley, N., et al.: On seeing human: a three-factor theory of anthropomorphism. Psychol. Rev. **114**(4), 864–886 (2007). https://doi.org/10.1037/0033-295X.114.4.864

18. Følstad, A., Nordheim, C.B., Bjørkli, C.A.: What makes users trust a chatbot for customer service? An exploratory interview study. In: Bodrunova, S.S. (ed.) INSCI 2018. LNCS, vol. 11193, pp. 194–208. Springer, Cham (2018). https://doi.org/10.1007/978-3-030-01437-7_16

19. Fournier, S.: Consumers and their brands: developing relationship theory in consumer research. J. Consum. Res. **24**(4), 343–353 (1998). https://doi.org/10.1086/209515

20. Go, E., Sundar, S.S.: Humanizing chatbots: the effects of visual, identity and conversational cues on humanness perceptions. Comput. Hum. Behav. (2019). https://doi.org/10.1016/j.chb.2019.01.020

21. Griol, D., et al.: An automatic dialog simulation technique to develop and evaluate interactive conversational agents. Appl. Artif. Intell. **27**(9), 759–780 (2013). https://doi.org/10.1080/08839514.2013.835230

22. Guzman, A.L.: Voices in and of the machine: source orientation toward mobile virtual assistants. Comput. Hum. Behav. **90**, 343–350 (2019). https://doi.org/10.1016/j.chb.2018.08.009

23. Hassanein, K., Head, M.: Manipulating perceived social presence through the web interface and its impact on attitude towards online shopping. Int. J. Hum Comput Stud. **65**(8), 689–708 (2007). https://doi.org/10.1016/j.ijhcs.2006.11.018

24. Hayes, A.F.: PROCESS: a versatile computational tool for observed variable mediation, moderation, and conditional process modeling. White Paper, pp. 1–39 (2012). ISBN 978-1-60918-230-4

25. Hayes, A.F., Preacher, K.J.: Statistical mediation analysis with a multicategorical independent variable. Br. J. Math. Stat. Psychol. **67**(3), 451–470 (2014). https://doi.org/10.1111/bmsp.12028

26. Ischen, C., et al.: How important is agency? The persuasive consequences of interacting with a chatbot as a new entity. Paper presented at the Human-Machine Communication ICA Pre-Conference, Washington, D.C. (2019)

27. Kim, Y., Sundar, S.S.: Anthropomorphism of computers: is it mindful or mindless? Comput. Hum. Behav. **28**(1), 241–250 (2012). https://doi.org/10.1016/j.chb.2011.09.006

28. Ledbetter, A.M.: Measuring online communication attitude: instrument development and validation. Commun. Monogr. **76**(4), 463–486 (2009). https://doi.org/10.1080/03637750903300262

29. Marathe, S., et al.: Who are these power users anyway? Building a psychological profile (2007)

30. Nass, C., Moon, Y.: Machines and mildlessness: social responses to computers. J. Soc. Issues **56**(1), 86–103 (2000)

31. van Noort, G., Willemsen, L.M.: Online damage control: the effects of proactive versus reactive webcare interventions in consumer-generated and brand-generated platforms. J. Interact. Mark. **26**(3), 131–140 (2012). https://doi.org/10.1016/j.intmar.2011.07.001

32. Powers, A., Kiesler, S.: The advisor robot: tracing people's mental model from a robot's physical attributes. In: Proceedings of the 1st ACM SIGCHI/SIGART Conference on Human-Robot Interaction, pp. 218–225 (2006). https://doi.org/10.1145/1121241.1121280

33. Reeves, B., Nass, C.: The Media Equation: How People Treat Computers, Television, and New Media Like Real People and Places. Cambrigde University Press, New York (1996)

34. Sundar, S.S., Kim, J.: Machine heuristic: when we trust computers more than humans with our personal information. In: Proceedings of the 2019 Conference on Human Factors in Computing Systems - CHI 2019, pp. 1–9 (2019). https://doi.org/10.1145/3290605.3300768

35. Sundar, S.S., Nass, C.: Source orientation in human-computer interaction: programmer, networker, or independent social actor. Commun. Res. **27**(6), 683–703 (2000)

36. Verhagen, T., et al.: Virtual customer service agents: using social presence and personalization to shape online service encounters. J. Comput. Commun. **19**(3), 529–545 (2014). https://doi.org/10.1111/jcc4.12066
37. Westin, A.F.: Privacy and freedom. Wash. Lee Law Rev. **25**(1), 166 (1967)
38. Whang, C.: Voice shopping: the effect of the consumer-voice assistant parasocial relationship on the consumer's perception and decision making (2018)
39. Wottrich, V.M., et al.: The role of customization, brand trust, and privacy concerns in advergaming. Int. J. Advert. **36**(1), 60–81 (2017). https://doi.org/10.1080/02650487.2016.1186951
40. Xu, H., et al.: Examining the formation of individual's privacy concerns: toward an integrative view. In: Proceedings of the International Conference on Information Systems, pp. 1–16 (2008). http://aisel.aisnet.org/icis2008/6
41. Zajonc, R.B.: Mere exposure: a gateway to the subliminal. Curr. Dir. Psychol. Sci. **10**(6), 224–228 (2001). https://doi.org/10.1111/1467-8721.00154
42. Zarouali, B., et al.: Predicting consumer responses to a chatbot on Facebook. Cyberpsychol. Behav. Soc. Netw. **21**(8), 491–497 (2018). https://doi.org/10.1089/cyber.2017.0518
43. Zhou, L., et al.: Non-local or local brands? A multi-level investigation into confidence in brand origin identification and its strategic implications. J. Acad. Mark. Sci. **38**(2), 202–218 (2010). https://doi.org/10.1007/s11747-009-0153-1

User Experience and Design

Creating Humanlike Chatbots: What Chatbot Developers Could Learn from Webcare Employees in Adopting a Conversational Human Voice

Christine Liebrecht[1][(✉)] and Charlotte van Hooijdonk[2]

[1] Tilburg University, PO Box 90153, 5000 LE Tilburg, The Netherlands
C.C.Liebrecht@tilburguniversity.edu
[2] VU Amsterdam, De Boelelaan 1105, 1081 HV Amsterdam, The Netherlands
C.M.J.Van.Hooijdonk@vu.nl

Abstract. Currently, conversations with chatbots are perceived as unnatural and impersonal. One way to enhance the feeling of humanlike responses is by implementing an engaging communication style (i.e., Conversational Human Voice (CHV); Kelleher 2009) which positively affects people's perceptions of the organization. This communication style contributes to the effectiveness of online communication between organizations and customers (i.e., webcare), and is of high relevance to chatbot design and development. This project aimed to investigate how insights on the use of CHV in organizations' messages and the perceptions of CHV can be implemented in customer service automation. A corpus study was conducted to investigate which linguistic elements are used in organizations' messages. Subsequently, an experiment was conducted to assess to what extent linguistic elements contribute to the perception of CHV. Based on these two studies, we investigated whether the amount of CHV can be identified automatically. These findings could be used to design humanlike chatbots that use a natural and personal communication style like their human conversation partner.

Keywords: Conversational Human Voice · Linguistic elements · Tool development · Chatbots

1 Introduction

Customer service plays an important role in organizations' ability to generate revenue. In recent years customer service has transformed from mediated communication (e.g., contact by phone) to computer-mediated communication (e.g., contact via social media channels; i.e. 'webcare'; Van Noort and Willemsen 2012) to human-AI interaction (e.g., contact using of chatbots). This transformation also occurs in the Netherlands: in 2016 4.7% of the organizations used chatbots to supplement their customer services. This number has tripled in the last two years (Van Os et al. 2016; 2018), because chatbots provide 24/7 customer service and save time and money by reducing the number of service employees (Gnewuch et al. 2017).

© Springer Nature Switzerland AG 2020
A. Følstad et al. (Eds.): CONVERSATIONS 2019, LNCS 11970, pp. 51–64, 2020.
https://doi.org/10.1007/978-3-030-39540-7_4

However, chatbot technology does not live up to its full potential yet. Much effort is put on the accuracy and performance of conversational AI, such as language recognition (Coniam 2008; Shawar and Atwell 2005), recall of previously mentioned topics (Jain et al. 2018), and the introduction of new topics or follow-up questions (Schuetzler et al. 2018; Silvervarg and Jönsson 2013), but currently, people perceive their conversations with chatbots as unnatural and impersonal (Drift, SurveyMonkey Audience, Salesforce, Myclever 2018).

One way to enhance the feeling of natural and personal chatbot responses, is by implementing a Conversational Human Voice (CHV, Kelleher 2009; Kelleher and Miller 2006). This communication style reflects human communication attributes, such as personally addressing the stakeholder, using informal speech, and being open to dialogue. Webcare research shows that CHV in organizational messages positively affects people's perceptions of the organization (e.g., Kerkhof et al. 2011; Park and Lee 2013). However, we have insufficient knowledge regarding the adoption of CHV in chatbots.

In a project funded by a NWO KIEM grant for creative industries we investigated how insights on the use of CHV in webcare messages and the perceptions of CHV can be implemented in customer service automation. We developed an online monitoring tool that enables webcare employees to respond with an appropriate communication style to customers' messages. This monitoring system may be useful as a basis for developing humanlike chatbots.

2   Theoretical Background

2.1   Chatbots as Social Actors

According to the Computers Are Social Actors (CASA) paradigm people tend to respond socially to computers, similarly to other humans, even when aware they are interacting with a computer (Nass et al. 1994). This implies that people automatically apply social rules, expectations, and scripts known from interpersonal communication in their interaction with computers (Nass and Moon 2000; Reeves and Nass 1996). These social reactions to computers in general (Nass and Moon 2000) and to chatbots in particular (von der Pütten et al. 2010) increase when more social cues are provided, such as communication style (Verhagen et al. 2014). For example, a customer service chatbot using informal speech increased the perception of the chatbot as being humanlike (Araujo 2018). A communication style that could be applied to chatbots is the Conversational Human Voice (Kelleher 2009; Kelleher and Miller 2006).

2.2   Operationalization of Conversational Human Voice

In order to enable chatbot designers to develop conversational agents that adopt CHV, it is important to understand which linguistic elements contribute to this communication style. Van Noort et al. (2014) distinguished three strategies to create CHV in messages, that were operationalized into several conversational linguistic elements by van Hooijdonk and Liebrecht (2018). The first strategy is Message Personalization: the degree to which a specific individual (organization and stakeholder) can be addressed in a message (cf. Walther 2011), such as greeting the stakeholder (*Hi Peter!*) and using personal pronouns (*you, your*) (van Hooijdonk and Liebrecht 2018). The second strategy is Informal Speech: casual, everyday language that differs from formal, corporate language (cf. Kelleher and Miller 2006), such as the adoption of non-verbal cues (*veeeery, :-)*) and interjections (*haha*) (van Hooijdonk and Liebrecht 2018). The third strategy is Invitational Rhetoric: to what extent the organization's communication style stimulates stakeholders to engage in conversations and creates mutual understanding between the parties (cf. Foss and Griffin 1995), such as acknowledging (*thanks for the message*) and showing sympathy/empathy (*I can imagine this is disappointing*) (van Hooijdonk and Liebrecht 2018).

It has been shown that the adoption of CHV by chatbots is beneficial for organizations. Liebrecht and van der Weegen (to appear) found that customer service chatbots using multiple conversational linguistic elements from all three strategies enhanced brand attitude and perceived warmth of the chatbot. These relations were mediated by the perceived social presence: people's perceptions of actually communicating with another human being (Short et al. 1976). Thus, the adoption of CHV in chatbots can diminish customers' feelings of unnatural and impersonal service contact.

2.3   Aim of This Paper

To facilitate the development of humanlike chatbots, several design issues should be addressed. In this paper, we focus on two aspects from webcare research that could inform the development of conversational agents that adopt a humanlike conversation style. First, following the principles of Communication Accommodation Theory (CAT; Giles et al. 1991), a chatbot's communication style should match the communication style of the customer (Jakic et al. 2017). This requires that the chatbot can automatically identify conversational linguistic elements in the customer's messages. In order to train a conversational agent to recognize these elements, we first needed to establish whether human coders can identify them reliably. Furthermore, the identification also results in a list of conversational linguistic elements that can be used to train the conversational agent on the recognition of CHV. We therefore conducted a corpus analysis to investigate which conversational linguistic elements webcare employees of the Netherlands Red Cross use in their messages to various stakeholders (e.g., benefactors, collectors, emergency workers, etc.) on public and private social media channels (i.e., Study 1). This study is a replication of van Hooijdonk and Liebrecht's (2018) study, who conducted a corpus analysis on conversational linguistic elements in webcare messages of Dutch municipalities on Twitter.

Second, the contribution of specific conversational linguistic elements to the perception of CHV also needs to be investigated. Although the presence of conversational linguistic elements seems to contribute to perceived CHV (van Noort et al. 2014), the weighted contribution of each linguistic element is unknown. Several experimental studies investigated the relation between linguistic elements in webcare messages and perceived CHV (e.g., Park and Lee 2013; Barcelos et al. 2018), but there are considerable differences in the type and number of linguistic elements used. For example, Park and Lee (2013) found that the perceived CHV increased by only one personalization element (i.e., signature, such as ^CL), whereas Barcelos et al. (2018) concluded that a combination of personalization elements and informal speech increased the perceived CHV. These results are also relevant for the design of chatbots' communication style. Liebrecht and van der Weegen (to appear) included multiple conversational linguistic elements from all three strategies, but it is unclear which elements contribute to what extent to the perception of CHV, and consequently to people's perceptions of the chatbot and the organization. To examine how conversational linguistic elements are related to the perceived CHV, an experiment was conducted in which webcare employees evaluated the perceived CHV of messages (i.e., Study 2). Finally, the findings of both Study 1 and Study 2 were used to investigate whether the amount of CHV in messages can be identified automatically (i.e., Study 3).

3   Study 1: Identification of Conversational Linguistic Elements

3.1   Method

The OBI4wan monitoring tool[1] was used to collect a random sample of webcare dialogues from March 2017 until October 2017 between the Netherlands Red Cross and their stakeholders. The sample included both public as well as private channels. The public conversations were collected from Instagram (35), Facebook (75), and Twitter (81). The private conversations were collected from WhatsApp (80), Facebook Messenger (72), and Twitter DM (80). The total corpus contained 423 dialogues (895 stakeholders' messages and 689 webcare messages).

We only collected Dutch webcare conversations and anonymized them by deleting names, addresses, and phone numbers. Thereafter, the linguistic elements were manually coded by five coders and (partly) double coded by one of the authors of this paper. We used a slightly adjusted version of the identification instrument of van Hooijdonk and Liebrecht (2018): Informal Speech categories Shortenings and Abbreviations were merged and one Message Personalization category (i.e., Addressing the webcare employee) and one Invitational Rhetoric category (i.e., Well-wishing) were added.

---

[1] The OBI4wan monitoring tool enables organizations to monitor and manage stakeholders' messages on multiple public and social media channels (e.g., Twitter, Instagram, Facebook, Facebook Messenger, and WhatsApp).

3.2 Results

Table 1 shows the identification instrument and the intercoder reliability scores per subcategory. In accordance with Van Hooijdonk and Liebrecht's (2018) findings, the identification instrument turned out to be reliable. The codings of all Message Personalization subcategories resulted in perfect reliability scores. Regarding Informal Speech, the intercoder reliability of interjections was perfect. The reliability of non-verbal cues, and shortenings and abbreviations was substantial. The intercoder reliability scores of the Invitational Rhetoric subcategories varied from perfect to fair. Whereas apologizing, acknowledging, and well-wishing resulted in perfect reliability scores, joking, sympathy/empathy, and stimulating dialogues had poor scores. This was possibly due to its limited presence in the double coded sample.

Table 1. Identification instrument of linguistic elements, the Krippendorff's alpha scores per subcategory, their absolute and relative frequency in the corpus ($N_{webcaremessages}$ = 689)

Linguistic element	Krippendorff's alpha	Frequency	Example
Message Personalization			
Greeting	.98	239 (34.7%)	Hi Peter!
Addressing stakeholder	.92	448 (65.0%)	you, your, Anna
Addressing webcare*	.92	352 (51.1%)	I, we, my, us
Signature	.92	570 (82.7%)	^WP
Informal Speech			
Shortenings/abbreviations*	.70	53 (7.7%)	pls, ok, LOL, DM
Non-verbal cues	.88	53 (7.7%)	??, veeery, :-)
Interjections	1.00	27 (3.9%)	haha, oh
Invitational Rhetoric			
Acknowledging	.96	190 (27.6%)	thanks for the message
Apologizing	1.00	20 (2.9%)	I am sorry
Sympathy/empathy	.59	179 (26.0%)	I can imagine this is disappointing
Stimulating dialogues	.32	38 (5.5%)	Let us know what you think
Joking	.66	9 (1.3%)	#joke, just kidding
Well-wishing*	.89	113 (16.4%)	Have a nice day!

Note. The asterisks represent categories that are adjusted to the van Hooijdonk and Liebrecht (2018) identification instrument.

Table 1 also shows the presence of linguistic elements in webcare conversations of the Netherlands Red Cross. Message Personalization was frequently used. Especially signatures of employees were frequently employed and webcare employees often address stakeholders personally. Informal Speech, on the other hand, was less frequent in webcare messages. If webcare employees used informal speech, they mostly employed non-verbal cues or shortenings and abbreviations. Regarding Invitational Rhetoric, acknowledging, showing sympathy/empathy and well-wishing were often present.

The corpus enabled us to compare the usage of linguistic elements in webcare responses across public and private social media channels. To do this, we aggregated the identified linguistic elements per webcare tweet into an average score per webcare conversation (see Table 2). The analyses showed significant differences between the social media channels for all Message Personalization categories: personal greetings of the stakeholder ($F(5,417) = 42.82$, $p < .001$, $\eta_p^2 = .34$.), addressing stakeholder ($F(5,417) = 17.98$, $p < .001$, $\eta_p^2 = .18$), addressing webcare employee ($F(5,417) = 25.24$, $p < .001$, $\eta_p^2 = .23$), and signatures ($F(5,417) = 64.02$, $p < .001$, $\eta_p^2 = .43$). The first three categories appeared more often in private social media channels than in public social media channels. Regarding signatures, pairwise Bonferroni comparisons showed that these appeared least on Instagram compared to the other channels (Twitter: $p < .001$; Facebook: $p < .001$; WhatsApp: $p < .001$; Twitter DM: $p < .001$, Facebook Messenger: $p < .001$).

Table 2. Mean presence of linguistic elements in webcare conversations per social media channel (standard deviations between brackets).

Linguistic element	Public channels			Private channels			Total
	Instagram ($n = 35$)	Facebook ($n = 75$)	Twitter ($n = 81$)	WhatsApp ($n = 80$)	Facebook Mess. ($n = 72$)	Twitter DM ($n = 80$)	($n = 423$)
Greeting	.03 (.17)	.19 (.38)	.01 (.07)	.65 (.39)	.59 (.43)	.44 (.44)	.34 (.44)
Addressing stakeholder	.44 (.50)	.62 (.47)	.43 (.46)	.86 (.27)	.89 (.26)	.74 (.36)	.68 (.43)
Addressing webcare	.11 (.32)	.34 (.47)	.26 (.41)	.63 (.40)	.78 (.36)	.67 (.42)	.50 (.46)
Signature	.21 (.41)	.97 (.16)	.94 (.22)	.92 (.21)	.93 (.21)	.93 (.23)	.88 (.31)
Shortenings/abbreviations	.03 (.17)	.00 (.00)	.13 (.32)	.12 (.29)	.03 (.17)	.13 (.28)	.08 (.24)
Non-verbal cues	.34 (.48)	.03 (.16)	.10 (.28)	.06 (.19)	.06 (.22)	.07 (.22)	.09 (.26)
Interjections	.03 (.17)	.03 (.16)	.08 (.24)	.03 (.15)	.02 (.13)	.06 (.21)	.04 (.18)
Acknowledging	.31 (.46)	.45 (.49)	.28 (.43)	.25 (.36)	.34 (.42)	.32 (.43)	.32 (.43)
Apologizing	.00 (.00)	.00 (.00)	.03 (.17)	.02 (.08)	.08 (.23)	.03 (.15)	.03 (.14)
Sympathy/empathy	.41(.49)	.26 (.44)	.57 (.46)	.23 (.35)	.33 (.42)	.15 (.31)	.32 (.43)
Stimulating dialogues	.00 (.00)	.03 (.16)	.02 (.10)	.10 (.25)	.08 (.23)	.03 (.11)	.05 (.23)
Joking	.06 (.24)	.03 (.16)	.03 (.14)	.00 (.00)	.01 (.06)	.01 (.11)	.02 (.12)
Well-wishing	.06 (.24)	.05 (.20)	.27 (.43)	.15 (.30)	.24 (.37)	.18 (.33)	.17 (.34)

For Informal Speech significant differences between the social media channels were found for shortenings and abbreviations ($F(5,417) = 4.59$, $p < .001$, $\eta_p^2 = .05$), and non-verbal cues ($F(5,417) = 8.98$, $p < .001$, $\eta_p^2 = .10$). The former appeared less often on Facebook compared to Twitter ($p = .02$), Twitter DM ($p = .007$), and WhatsApp ($p = .02$). Non-verbal cues were more frequent on Instagram (compared to Twitter ($p < .001$), Facebook ($p < .001$), Twitter DM ($p < .001$), Facebook Messenger ($p < .001$), and WhatsApp ($p < .001$)). No differences were found between the social media channels in the mean number of interjections ($F(5,417) = 1.04$, $p = .39$). Regarding Invitational Rhetoric, the social media channels differed for all subcategories, with the exception of Acknowledging ($F(5,417) = 2.07$, $p = .07$, $\eta_p^2 = .02$), and

Joking ($F(5,417) = 2.28$, $p = .27$). However, the results did not show a consistent pattern between the public versus private social media channels.

In sum, webcare employees frequently adopted linguistic elements of Message Personalization in their messages. Invitational Rhetoric is also used regularly, but Informal Speech hardly appeared in webcare messages. Furthermore, public and private social media channels differ in the presence of linguistic elements.

4 Study 2: Contribution of Conversational Linguistic Elements to the Perceived CHV

4.1 Method

To examine to what extent each linguistic element contributes to the perception of CHV, an experiment was conducted. The experimental materials were developed on the basis of the webcare conversations of Study 1. The materials consisted of conversations between a stakeholder asking questions to a fictitious charity organization to which the organization responded. For these webcare responses, a basic response was formulated that contained an average amount of perceived CHV (which was determined in a pretest). An example of a conversation is shown in Fig. 1. Subsequently, the basic webcare response was adjusted by adding one of the linguistic element subcategories. For example, to include a non-verbal cue in the response, a smiley was added to the basic response. Nine CHV subcategories were included in the experiment (i.e., three subcategories per main category). For Message Personalization, greeting, addressing stakeholder, and signature were chosen. From the main category Informal Speech, shortenings and abbreviations, non-verbal cues, and interjections were included. Finally, showing sympathy/empathy, stimulating dialogue, and well-wishing were chosen from the Invitational Rhetoric category. In short, nine webcare responses per basic response were created by adding one of these nine CHV subcategories.

Stakeholder's message	Webcare response
Robin: @charityorganization Where can I find information about your projects? Can't find it on your website.	Thanks for the notification. This part of the website is under construction until tonight, after which the Projects page is completely up to date. Sufficient information will be available soon!

Fig. 1. Example of a basic webcare response.

The experiment conformed to a 1 (Stakeholder's Question) × 10 (Linguistic Element incl. basic response) within subjects latin square design. To avoid repetition of the questions' topics, ten customer service topics and accompanying webcare responses were created (10 topics * 10 webcare responses): each participant assessed one experimental condition per customer service topic (10 webcare responses in total).

Forty-seven webcare employees of different charity organizations in the Nether-lands were recruited via their social media channels to participate in the study. The study consisted of two tasks. First, participants assessed the perceived CHV of every experimental condition on seven-point Likert scales. The perceived CHV was opera-tionalized with 3 items: 'The webcare response is personal/informal/distant' (reversed item). The internal consistency of the items was high ($\alpha = .86$, $M = 4.44$, $p < .001$). Subsequently, the participants conducted a ranking task. Per main category, the basic response and the three manipulated responses (i.e., each response included one of the three subcategories) was shown. Participants ranked the tone of voice of the four responses from least to most human. Consequently, participants could write their own webcare response and underpin their choices regarding their ranking of the webcare responses.

4.2 Results

Table 3 shows the findings of both tasks. The scores of the ranking task were trans-formed into scores on a 4-point scale ranging from 1 (least human) to 4 (most human) To investigate whether the mean scores differ significantly, we conducted repeated measures ANOVAs with simple contrasts effects.

Table 3. Means of the perceived CHV per linguistic element (standard deviations between brackets). The assessment task used a 7-point scale, the ranking task used a 4-point scale.

CHV category	Assessment task	Simple contrast effects, $F(1,46)$	Ranking task	Simple contrast effects, $F(1,46)$
Basic response	3.80 (1.37)			
Personalization	4.78 (1.04)	$F = 29.77$, $p < .001$	Basic = 1.26 (.77)	
Greeting	5.30 (1.21)	$F = 43.24$, $p < .001$	3.60 (.83)	$F = 115.48$, $p < .001$
Addressing stakeholder	4.31 (1.44)	$F = 5.79$, $p = .02$	2.36 (.64)	$F = 46.87$, $p < .001$
Signature	4.72 (1.43)	$F = 17.08$, $p < .001$	2.79 (.72)	$F = 102.08$, $p < .001$
Informal Speech	4.31 (1.12)	$F = 8.58$, $p = .005$	Basic = 2.13 (.90)	
Shortenings/abbreviations	3.80 (1.44)	$F < 1$, $p = 1.00$	1.74 (.90)	$F = 4.22$, $p = .046$
Non-verbal cues	4.46 (1.50)	$F = 7.96$, $p = .007$	3.28 (.85)	$F = 28.55$, $p < .001$
Interjections	4.68 (1.40)	$F = 12.25$, $p = .001$	2.85 (1.16)	$F = 8.00$, $p = .007$
Invitational rhetoric	4.43 (1.03)	$F = 9.87$, $p = .003$	Basic = 1.09 (.28)	
Sympathy/empathy	4.34 (1.51)	$F = 3.72$, $p = .06$	2.68 (.84)	$F = 147.52$, $p < .001$
Stimulating dialogues	4.42 (1.57)	$F = 6.21$, $p = .02$	3.32 (.84)	$F = 280.81$, $p < .001$
Well-wishing	4.52 (1.38)	$F = 9.80$, $p = .003$	2.91 (.83)	$F = 187.34$, $p < .001$

Regarding the assessment task, the basic response had an average perceived CHV score ($M = 3.80$). The results indicated that each main category differed significantly from the basic response in perceived CHV. Table 3 illustrates that Message Person-alization contributed the most to the perceived CHV, whereas Informal Speech contributed least. A closer inspection of the subcategories of linguistic elements showed differences between them. Shortenings and abbreviations did not enhance the perceived CHV. Pairwise comparisons showed this subcategory differed from personal greetings ($p < .001$), signatures ($p = .009$), interjections ($p = .03$), and well-wishing ($p = .03$). Also, greetings enhanced the perceived CHV more than addressing stakeholder ($p < .001$), and showing sympathy/empathy ($p = .03$).

Regarding the ranking task, subcategories within Message Personalization enhanced perceived CHV compared to the basic response. Pairwise comparisons indicated that greetings resulted in a higher perceived CHV than addressing stakeholder ($p < .001$), and signatures ($p < .001$). A similar pattern is found for Invitational Rhetoric. The three subcategories significantly enhanced the perception of CHV compared to the basic response. Pairwise comparisons showed that stimulating dialogues induced a higher perceived CHV than showing sympathy/empathy ($p = .03$). However, a different pattern was found for Informal Speech. Pairwise comparisons showed that shortenings and abbreviations scored significantly lower than non-verbal cues and interjections on the perceived CHV (non-verbal cues $p < .001$; interjections $p = .001$).

In sum, it can be concluded that linguistic elements differ in their contribution to perceived CHV of webcare messages. Greeting the stakeholder, non-verbal cues, and stimulating dialogues contributed most to the perception of CHV.

5   Study 3: Automatic CHV Identification

In order to explore whether it is feasible to implement the insights on the usage and perceptions of linguistic elements to customer service automation (e.g., chatbots) we examined to what extent the amount of CHV can be identified automatically. We therefore developed a beta-version of a tool together with OBI4wan[2]. In this section, we report the development of the tool and the first qualitative results.

5.1   Method

The findings of Study 1 and Study 2 informed the development of the automatic indication of the amount of perceived CHV in webcare responses. The codings of the linguistic categories in Study 1 allowed us to compile a list of Illocutionary Force Indicating Devices (IFIDs; Houtkoop and Koole 2000) that indicate the potential presence of a subcategory. For example, 'you', 'your', 'yours', are words that were often used to address the stakeholder. This list contained all linguistics elements found in Study 1, supplemented with synonyms from (online) sources. Also, standardized lists containing first names, abbreviations, and emoticons were used. The tool was trained on the basis of these lists to identify the linguistic elements.

To calculate the amount of perceived CHV in a message, we created a ranking and a formula based on the average scores in Study 2. For example, within the main

---

[2] The beta-version of the tool can be tested on request by the authors and OBI4wan.

category Message Personalization, greeting the stakeholder contributed most to the perceived CHV. Therefore, the presence of this linguistic element in a webcare message contributed more to the perceived CHV than presence of other Message Personalization categories, such as a signature. To investigate whether the tool was able to indicate the amount of perceived CHV in webcare messages, the webcare messages of Study 1 were used as input.

5.2 Results

In Table 4 three webcare messages are shown which the tool qualified as having a high amount of perceived CHV. The first example contains all subcategories of Message Personalization, and stimulating dialogue (the subcategory within Invitational Rhetoric that contributes most to the perception of CHV). The second example contains several linguistic elements of Invitational Rhetoric, and two linguistic elements of Message Personalization. In the third example, multiple linguistic elements of all three main categories are present. Within their categories, the smiley and stimulating dialogues contributed the most to the perception of CHV.

Table 4. Webcare messages the tool qualified as having a high (examples 1–3) versus low (examples 4–6) amount of CHV.

Webcare message	CHV elements
1. Hi Dave, how can we help you? Greetings, Niels. [WhatsApp]	Message Personalization: greeting, addressing stakeholder, addressing webcare, signature. Invitational Rhetoric: stimulating dialogue
2. Apologies, it is not our intention to irritate you. Thank you for the support you have already given. Have a nice #spring day [Twitter]	Message Personalization: addressing stakeholder, addressing webcare. Invitational Rhetoric: apology, sympathy, acknowledgement, well-wishing
3. No problem! We are happy to help as far as we can in this case:) Have a nice weekend. Greetings, Ilse [Twitter DM]	Message Personalization: addressing webcare, signature. Informal Speech: non-verbal cues. Invitational Rhetoric: stimulating dialogue, well-wishing
4. The information can be found here. [hyperlink] Greetings, Ilse [Facebook Messenger]	Message Personalization: signature
5. Thanks for your support! [Instagram]	Message Personalization: addressing stakeholder. Invitational Rhetoric: acknowledging
6. That is true Carmen:) ^Caroline [Facebook]	Message Personalization: addressing stakeholder, signature. Informal Speech: non-verbal cue

Table 4 also shows three webcare messages which the tool qualified as having a low amount of perceived CHV. Despite the presence of several linguistic elements, these webcare messages will be perceived as less personal and engaging, because their relative contribution to the perception of CHV is low. This is illustrated in example 4 in which the webcare message only contains a signature. In example 5 an acknowledgement is expressed and the stakeholder is addressed personally. However, only addressing the stakeholder was taken into account in the calculation of the perceived CHV. The final example contains three subcategories, but only the non-verbal cues had a relatively high contribution to the perceived CHV.

Although these first qualitative results of the beta-version are promising for CHV recognition, not all qualifications of the tool correspond with our own observations. First, the identification of the linguistic elements can be improved. Although extensive lists are used to inform the tool, some linguistic features were not identified, or identified incorrectly. For example, first names that did not occur in our lists were not identified. Second, the current beta-version is programmed to identify all linguistic element categories, but only the categories that are measured in Study 2 are included in the calculation of the CHV score. As a result, messages that do contain several CHV subcategories could still be qualified as having a low amount of CHV. Finally, the amount of CHV is only calculated for one webcare message. However, a webcare conversation can consist of multiple webcare messages, and the position of these messages within the conversation influences the linguistic elements used.

6 Conclusion and Discussion

This project aimed to inform the development of humanlike chatbots that use an appropriate amount of CHV that matches the communication style of the conversation partner. We therefore obtained insights from the usage and perceptions of conversational linguistic elements by employees in webcare conversations, that can be adopted to customer service automation tools, such as chatbots. By learning from natural language use by humans, chatbot developers can design conversational agents that will be perceived more humanlike, which in turn might positively impact users' evaluations of the chatbot and the organization.

The first learning can be derived from our corpus study: Message Personalization should be adopted in chatbot conversations, because webcare employees frequently use these linguistic elements in their messages. Invitational Rhetoric was also used regularly, whereas Informal Speech was hardly employed. These findings support prior findings of van Hooijdonk and Liebrecht (2018). In addition, we showed that webcare employees employ linguistic elements differently in public and private channels. Private social media messages contained more personal greetings, addressing the stakeholder, and addressing the webcare employee, which is informative for the private nature of chatbot conversations.

Secondly, chatbot developers should be aware of the relative contribution of linguistic elements to the perception of CHV. Our experimental study showed that greeting the stakeholder induced the highest perception of CHV compared to the other subcatgories within Message Personalization. Within Informal Speech non-verbal cues contributed most to the perception of CHV. Finally, stimulating dialogues contributed most to the perception of CHV compared to the other subcategories within Invitational

Rhetoric. To our knowledge, this is the first study that systematically examined the relation between the use of single linguistic elements and the perception of CHV. If developers aim to create chatbots with a high amount of CHV, we advise to include personal greetings, non-verbal cues and sentences that stimulate dialogue.

Thirdly, it is possible to develop chatbots that use an appropriate communication style that matches the communication style of the human conversation partner. In Study 3, we showed that the amount of CHV in messages can be identified automatically. A first test showed that the tool was able to identify conversational linguistic elements and to calculate the amount of CHV in messages. Although more CHV categories must be added to the tool and some improvements are necessary, the findings are promising for customer service automation since it is shown that language accommodation positively impacts on people's perceptions (Jakic et al. 2017). However, the preferred organization's tone of voice should be taken into account as well. As distinguished in Giles et al.'s (1991) CAT, communication partners could also use a maintenance strategy, meaning that the interactant does not change the original communication style to the style of the conversation partner but sticks to the own, preferred communication style that matches the organization's image.

Finally, our findings can be used to research the usage and the effects of humanlike chatbots more systematically. On the one hand, our approach can be used to compare available chatbots on CHV or to monitor the same chatbot on CHV across time. On the other hand, people's perceptions of humanlike chatbots can be investigated. Feine et al. (2019) presented a taxonomy of cues that following CASA paradigm could impact on people's social reactions to chatbots. The conversational linguistic elements of our study can be seen as a concrete manifestation of verbal social cues, but little is known how these cues impact on users' perceptions and behavior. Given the differences of CHV elements to the contribution to the perceived CHV, it is important to investigate how human and personalized a chatbot should be. Designing chatbots that resemble humans may easily lead to users making wrong assumptions regarding the chatbot capabilities (e.g., Luger and Sellen 2016). We therefore need to evaluate which and how many CHV elements are considered appropriate and how they influence users' perceptions and use of chatbots.

References

Kelleher, T.: Conversational style, communicated commitment, and public relations outcomes in interactive online communication. J. Commun. **59**, 172–188 (2009)

Van Noort, G., Willemsen, L.: Online damage control: the effects of proactive versus reactive webcare interventions in consumer-generated and brand-generated platforms. J. Interact. Mark. **26**(3), 131–140 (2012)

Van Os, R., Hachmang, D., Akpinar, M., Derksen, M., Keuning, A.: Stand van Webcare 2018 (2018). https://www.upstream.nl/onderzoeken/stand-van-webcare-2018/

Van Os, R., Hachmang, D., Derksen, M., Keuning, A.: Stand van Webcare 2016 (2016). https://www.marketingfacts.nl/berichten/onderzoek-stand-van-webcare-nederland-2016

Gnewuch, U., Morana, S. Maedche, A.: Towards designing cooperative and social conversational agents for customer service. In: Proceedings of the International Conference on Information Systems (ICIS) (2017)

Coniam, D.: Evaluating the language resources of chatbots for their potential in English as a second language. ReCALL **20**(1), 98–116 (2008)

Shawar, B.A., Atwell, E.S.: Using corpora in machine-learning chatbot systems. Int. J. Corpus Linguist. **10**(4), 489–516 (2005)

Jain, M., Kumar, P., Kota, R., Patel, S.N.: Evaluating and informing the design of chatbots. In: Proceedings of the 2018 Designing Interactive Systems Conference, pp. 895–906 ACM (2018)

Schuetzler, R.M., Grimes, G.M., Giboney, J.S.: An investigation of conversational agent relevance, presence, and engagement. In: Proceedings of Americas' Conference on Information Systems (2018)

Silvervarg, A., Jönsson, A.: Iterative development and evaluation of a social conversational agent. In: 6th International Joint Conference on Natural Language Processing, pp. 1223–1229 (2013)

Drift, SurveyMonkey Audience, Salesforce, Myclever: The 2018 State of Chatbots Report. How chatbots are reshaping online experiences. https://www.drift.com/wp-content/uploads/2018/01/2018-state-of-chatbots-report.pdf. Accessed 01 Sept 2019

Kelleher, T., Miller, B.: Organizational blogs and the human voice: relational strategies and relational outcomes. J. Comput.-Mediat. Commun. **11**, 395–414 (2006)

Kerkhof, P., Beugels, D., Utz, S., Beukeboom, C.J.: Crisis PR in social media: an experimental study of the effects of organizational crisis responses on Facebook. Paper presented at the 61st Annual ICA Conference, Boston, USA (2011)

Park, H., Lee, H.: Show us you are real: the effect of human-versus-organizational presence on online relationship building through social networking sites. Cyberpsychol. Behav. Soc. Netw. **16**(4), 265–271 (2013)

Nass, C., Steuer, J., Tauber, E.R.: Computers are social actors. In: Proceedings of the SIGCHI Conference on Human Factors in Computing Systems, pp. 72–78. ACM (1994)

Nass, C., Moon, Y.: Machines and mindlessness: social responses to computers. J. Soc. Issues **56**(1), 81–103 (2000)

Reeves, B., Nass, C.I.: The Media Equation: How People Treat Computers, Television, and New Media Like Real People and Places. Cambridge University Press, Cambridge (1996)

Von der Pütten, A.M., Krämer, N.C., Gratch, J., Kang, S.H.: It doesn't matter what you are! Explaining social effects of agents and avatars. Comput. Hum. Behav. **26**(6), 1641–1650 (2010)

Verhagen, T., van Nes, J., Feldberg, F., van Dolen, W.: Virtual customer service agents: Using social presence and personalization to shape online service encounters. J. Comput.-Mediat. Commun. **19**(3), 529–545 (2014)

Araujo, T.: Living up to the chatbot hype: the influence of anthropomorphic design cues and communicative agency framing on conversational agent and company perceptions. Comput. Hum. Behav. **85**, 183–189 (2018)

van Noort, G., Willemsen, L.M., Kerkhof, P., Verhoeven, J.W.M.: Webcare as an integrative tool for customer care, reputation management, and online marketing: a literature review. In: Kitchen, P.J., Uzunoğlu, E. (eds.) Integrated Communications in the Postmodern Era, pp. 77–99. Palgrave Macmillan UK, London (2015). https://doi.org/10.1057/9781137388551_4

Van Hooijdonk, C., Liebrecht, C.: "Wat vervelend dat de fiets niet is opgeruimd! Heb je een zaaknummer voor mij? ^EK". Conversational human voice in webcare van Nederlandse gemeenten. Tijdschr. voor Taalbeheers. **40**(1), 45–82 (2018)

Walther, J.: Theories of computer-mediated communication and interpersonal relations. In: Knapp, M., Daly, J. (eds.) The Sage Handbook of Interpersonal Communication, 4th edn. Sage Publications (2011)

Foss, S., Griffin, C.: Beyond persuasion: a proposal for an invitational rhetoric. Commun. Monogr. **62**(1), 2–18 (1995)

Liebrecht, C., van der Weegen, E.: Menselijke chatbots: een zegen voor online klantcontact? Het effect van conversational human voice door chatbots op social presence en merkattitude. Tijdschrift voor Communicatiewetenschap (to appear)

Short, J., Williams, E., Christie, B.: The Social Psychology of Telecommunications. Wiley, London (1976)

Giles, H., Coupland, J., Coupland, N.: Accommodation theory: communication, context and consequences. In: Giles, H., Coupland, J., Coupland, N. (eds.) Contexts of Accommodation – Developments in Applied Sociolinguistics, pp. 1–68. Cambridge University Press, New York (1991)

Jakic, A., Wagner, M.O., Meyer, A.: The impact of language style accommodation during social media interactions on brand trust. J. Serv. Manag. **28**(3), 418–441 (2017)

Barcelos, R., Dantas, D., Sénécal, S.: Watch your tone: how a brand's tone of voice on social media influences consumer responses. J. Interact. Mark. **41**, 60–80 (2018)

Houtkoop, H., Koole, T.: Taal in actie: hoe mensen communiceren met taal. Coutinho, Bussum (2000)

Feine, J., Gnewuch, U., Morana, S., Maedche, A.: A taxonomy of social cues for conversational agents. Int. J. Hum Comput Stud. **132**, 138–161 (2019)

Luger, E., Sellen, A.: Like having a really bad PA: the gulf between user expectation and experience of conversational agents. In: Proceedings of the 2016 CHI Conference on Human Factors in Computing Systems. ACM (2016)

The Conversational Agent "Emoty" Perceived by People with Neurodevelopmental Disorders: Is It a Human or a Machine?

Fabio Catania[(✉)], Eleonora Beccaluva, and Franca Garzotto

Dipartimento di Elettronica, Informazione e Bioingegneria DEIB,
Politecnico di Milano, 20133 Milan, Italy
{fabio.catania,eleonora.beccaluva,franca.garzotto}@polimi.it
https://i3lab.polimi.it

Abstract. This research explores the anthropomorphic perception of Emoty by its target user. Emoty is a Conversational Agent specifically designed as an emotional facilitator and trainer for individuals with neurodevelopmental disorders (NDD). NDD is a group of conditions that are characterized by severe deficits in the cognitive, emotional, and motor areas and produce severe impairments in communication and social functioning. Our application promotes skills of emotion expression and recognition and was developed in cooperation with psychologists and therapists as a supporting tool for regular interventions.

We conducted an empirical study with 19 people with NDD. We observed their behavior while interacting with the system and recorded the commentaries they made and the questions they asked when the session was over. Starting from this, we discovered a twofold nature of Emoty: for some aspects, it is perceived more like a machine, but for some others, it is more human-like. In this regard, we discussed some relevant points about gender, fallibility, interaction, and sensitivity of the agent, and we paved the ground towards a better understanding of the perception of people with NDD concerning Conversational Technology.

Keywords: Conversational technology · Neurodevelopmental disorder · Technology perception · Anthropomorphism

1 Introduction

Neurodevelopmental Disorder (NDD) denotes a group of conditions that are characterized by severe deficits in the cognitive, emotional, and motor areas and produce severe impairments in social functioning. Recent research acknowledged interactive technology as a potentially useful tool to support existing therapies and new approaches to improve the learning process [1, 2, 19, 24].

© Springer Nature Switzerland AG 2020
A. Følstad et al. (Eds.): CONVERSATIONS 2019, LNCS 11970, pp. 65–78, 2020.
https://doi.org/10.1007/978-3-030-39540-7_5

A conversational agent (CA) is any dialogue system able to interact with a human through natural language [6]. Emoty [4] is a spoken, emotionally sensitive CA that has been specifically designed as an emotional facilitator and trainer for individuals with NDD. Emoty entertains the users with small talks and asks them to verbalize sentences expressing specific emotions (joy, sadness, fear, anger, surprise, and neutrality) with their tone of voice.

It has been developed in cooperation with psychologists and therapists as a supporting instrument for regular interventions; its goal is to mitigate a specific disturb called Alexithymia, which is the inability to identify and express emotions.

From a more general perspective, its usage might pave the ground towards a better understanding of the cognitive and emotional mechanisms associated with NDD and towards new forms of treatments for these subjects. From a technical point of view, the system is based on the architectural framework presented in [5]. Emoty exploits Dialogflow to perform Automatic Speech Recognition and an original Deep Learning model for emotion detection using the harmonic features of the audio. An initial exploratory study has already indicated Emoty as a suitable tool for persons with NDD and has acknowledged that it has the potential to support emotion regulation in the target users [4].

From that first study, we realized an anthropomorphic perception of the agent by the participants, so we decided to investigate it further. In this research, we conducted an empirical study with 19 people (average age: 35 years) with NDD, including Down Syndrome and mild, moderate, and severe cognitive impairments. We wanted to observe their behavior while interacting with the system, and we took note of all commentaries they made and the questions they asked to their caregivers and us when the session was over. Our research goal was to explore the anthropomorphic perception of people with NDD concerning Emoty during a repetitive usage period. Assessing the potential of Emoty to mitigate Alexithymia and its effects is beyond the scope of this report.

The Oxford English Dictionary defines anthropomorphism as *the attribution of human personality or characteristics to something non-human, as an animal or an object*. The term has its origins in the Greek words *anthropos* for man and *morphe* for form/structure. Anthropomorphic perception and perception in general affect the user experience [16] and play a vital role in the user's cognitive decision-making process about whether to use (or continue using) a new system [8]. Duffy and colleagues [9] described anthropomorphism as a useful mechanism to facilitate social interaction between humans and machines and to make a machine socially engaging. Besides, they concluded that anthropomorphism changes the user's expectations and beliefs on technology. Anthropomorphism has been already studied in many contexts so far [23] and conversational technology appears to perform better its intended design when simulating a human-like mind [26].

The contribution of this work concerns the research about Conversational Technology for people with NDD: this study is innovative because it explores the perception of these subjects with respect to Conversational Technology and technology in general. Consequently, our outcome might lead to the development of more tailored applications for people with NDD able to create a safer and more comfortable context for them (e.g., for therapeutic interventions, daily assistance). For example, the findings of this study will be taken into account during the next iteration of the Emoty design process to improve the user experience and adapt it to the target audience.

The rest of the paper is organized as follows. In the section below, we describe the context of Conversational Technology for people with NDD, and we mention some previous studies about user perception methods and experiments. In the next section, we make a parenthesis on the user experience (UX) with Emoty. In the following part, we provide the methodology of our empirical study, describing participants, setting, and procedure of the experiment. After that, we report and discuss our observations. Finally, we provide general conclusions, and we outline the following steps in our research.

2   Context

Any kind of NDD is a chronical state, but early and focused interventions are thought to mitigate its effect. Several studies explored the role of interactive technology in NDD. On the one hand, the high children's exposure to chaotic sensory stimulation given, for example, by video-games and multimedia applications, was identified as a possible cause of the increasing number of cases of cognitive disorders during the developmental age [13]. On the other hand, recent research about children's development acknowledged interactive technology as a potentially useful tool to support existing therapies and new approaches to improve the learning process [1, 2, 11, 19, 21, 24].

The main challenge of interactive technologies (such as conversational agents) for people with NDD is to be accessible for the target user and to accommodate her/his needs. Because of the wide spectrum of NDD and users' needs, NDD-specific CAs should be able to adapt their contents to the user and to customize the way they interact with her/him. Indeed, special user's needs imply special system's requirements.

Some cognitive-disability-specific Conversational Agents became commercially available in the last years. For example, three mobile and tablet applications were recently launched to mitigate anxiety and support depression treatment by simulating the conversations with the therapist: Woebot [27], Tess [25] and Wysa [28]. Furthermore, a recent exploratory study used Amazon Echo in speech rehabilitation [20] for users with cognitive disorders. There are also CAs supporting skills related to communication, emotion expression, and socialization; Rachel [18], for instance, is an embodied CA designed to help autistic children in the creation of semantically emotionful narratives. From some preliminary experiments, children having severe impairments in the interactions with others were more likely to interact with Rachel and more motivated to improve their communication and emotion expression skills.

For assessing technology usability and perception by the users, we considered different validated theoretic frameworks based on questionnaires and self-reports

[3,12]. However, these tools require critical and self-critical skills by the user that are often lacking in people with NDD. So far, the investigation on the perception of Conversational Technologies by users with NDD is still in its infancy, and to our knowledge, there is no structured framework to perform it.

Previous studies explored the tendency to merge the real or imagined behavior of non-human agents with human-like characteristics, motivations, intentions, or emotions [10,14]. Saarem [22] evaluated the anthropomorphic traits of two commercial chatbots and concluded that anthropomorphism plays a central role in our perception of chatbots. The author says that, if applied thoughtfully, anthropomorphic traits in chatbots can increase user engagement and preference of a commercial service, and make a chatbot appear more understandable and predictable to the user.

3 Emoty - The User Experience (UX)

In this section, we encompass the main aspects of the end-users interaction with the agent. Since Emoty is a web application, it enables both vocal and visual interactions. Indeed, our Conversational Agent exploits the visual channel as a support to the user. Emoty shows for the entire duration of the game a big button to be clicked by the user before speaking. Besides, the agent provides the user of visual feedback about its status (idle, listening, or speaking) to help her/him to handle the interaction and to understand the system better. Moreover, to facilitate the conceptualization of emotions, the application exploits emojis and colors. The combination emotion-color works as reinforcement to the spoken feedback by the system: joy is represented as yellow, fear is dark green, surprise is cyan, sadness is blue, and anger is red. We associated neutrality to light grey, used as background for the app as well.

Since Emoty is a proactive Conversational Agent, it completely controls the dialogue flow during sessions. After the user logs in, the agent asks her/him a series of questions to steer her/him to familiar domains. It calls the user by name, speaks gently, and with continuous repetitions and explanations of the concepts in order to create a comfortable environment. The user can ask the system to repeat the last non-answered question at any time. The session is structured as a single conversation. Each conversation has a starting and an ending point, and it is structured the same:

- in the first part of the dialogue, Emoty welcomes the user, it puts her/him at ease, it explains her/him the rules of the game, and it asks her/him three questions one by one: "How are you?", "Do you want to play with me?", and "Did you understand the rules of the game?";
- in the second part of the conversation, dialogues follow the four-stage Non-Formal Education model by the American theorist Kolb [15], who promotes education starting from your own experience:

  1. **"experience" stage.** The application asks the user to repeat a sentence trying to express a particular emotion with the tone of her/his voice. At

this point, the user sees on the screen both the sentence to verbalize and the emoji of the emotion to express. The emotion is randomly selected among joy, sadness, fear, anger, and surprise. Sentences are picked up in a randomized order from a pool of very short and easy to pronounce utterances. If a sentence is wrongly articulated, the user has to repeat it;

2. **"reflection" stage.** Emoty lets the user reflect on how she/he faced the assigned task. This phase happens just once out of three because, as we observed during the pilot study, it slows down the game reducing the attention paid by the user;

3. **"conceptualization" stage.** Emoty evaluates the performance of the user just according to the emotion detected from her/his voice. The application provides a correct/wrong feedback to the user. When she/he was correct and properly played the requested emotion, it celebrates her/him with visual and acoustic rewards and then jumps to step 4. Otherwise, Emoty tries to facilitate the task of the user by playing an audio recording by an actor properly reading the sentence; this is to let her/him understand how the task should be performed. At this point, the user can try again to repeat the sentence (as in step 1) up to two more times. When she/he cannot complete the task, Emoty jumps again to step 1, but with a different sentence and a different emotion;

4. **"application" stage.** the CA invites the user to think about common situations where she/he can feel and recognize the emotion just expressed and then jumps to step 1 with a new sentence and a new emotion.

– whenever the user says she/he wants to quit, the conversation ends with some greetings.

4   Methodology

We designed this research following the guidelines of NDD expert therapists and psychologists of the care centers "L'impronta" (Noverasco di Opera, Italy) and "Collage" (Milano, Italy). They also contributed to review the writing of this paper.

With this study, we would like to explore how a population of people with neurodevelopmental disorders anthropomorphically perceives Emoty. To do so, we observed their behavior while interacting with the system, and we took note of all commentaries they made and the questions they asked to their caregiver and us when sessions were over. Advised by the caregivers of both centers, we decided not to administer any questionnaire to participants or hold structured interviews. This choice was dictated

– partly from the lack of the necessary critical ability and self-knowledge in the great majority of our subjects,
– partly from our wish not to let them feel under examination and pressure.

Indeed, our main concern was to let them enjoy a gamified experience with the hope of seeing some emotional learning evidence after a continuous period of use of Emoty.

Starting from their analysis, we looked for behaviors and patterns common among the population and related to the anthropomorphic perception.

4.1   Participants

Participants consisted of 19 people with NDD from the care centers "L'impronta" and "Collage". They included people with Down's Syndrome (3 subjects) and individuals at mild (2), moderate (8), and severe (6) level of cognitive impairment. Most of them were women (9 M, 10 F). Participants varied a lot in age, from 29 to 45 (M = 35, SD = 5,3). The distribution of the population is depicted in Fig. 1. The size and heterogeneity of the population is a limitation to the study.

Only one of the 19 participants offered information about daily experiences with a laptop, but all of them already knew what a computer is, and most of them have a smartphone. Nobody reported previous interactions with similar agents (e.g., Google, Siri, Alexa, and Cortana). All participants provided us an informed consent to take part in the study signed by their parents. Furthermore, to each participant, a unique code was assigned to guarantee the respect of their sensitive data. In the context of this paper, participants' names are changed.

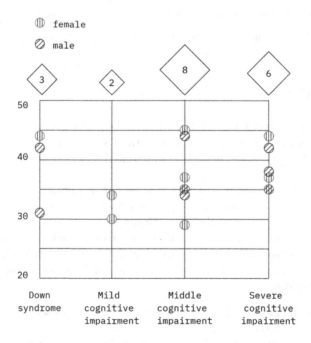

Fig. 1. The overview of the participants to the study (Color figure online)

4.2 Setting

The study was conducted in a small quiet room with an internet connection within the daycare centers. This setting was to let participants feel as comfortable as possible in a familiar space to them. In the room, there was a 15″ laptop on a desk and a chair in front of it. On one laptop's side, there was a mouse connected to the PC via Bluetooth. On the other side, there was a desktop microphone connected to the laptop via cable. To create a more welcoming setting for the user and avoid making her/him feel under examination, together with the caregivers, we decided not to use any camera to record the experiment. In addition to participants, people involved in the study were:

- *the Facilitator*: a psychologist or a caregiver known by participants; her role was to manage the experiment at the forefront and to help participants as was necessary (e.g., when they could not click on the mouse by themselves, when they did not understand the task to complete);
- *the Test Observer*: A member of our team, who silently observed the experiment from the background and took notes. We are aware that the presence of an external person could affect the experience of the participants, and this fact could be considered a limitation of our study. To mitigate the impact of this issue, the test observer's position was on the sideline in the room and did not interact with the subjects. In addition, before starting the whole study, the observer introduced himself to the subjects and took part in some activities in the centers (without the use of technology).

4.3 Procedure

The study was designed as a ten weeks experimentation organized in scheduled sessions taking place every week in parallel with daycare centers' activities. Every participant was involved for five times in total (see Fig. 2).

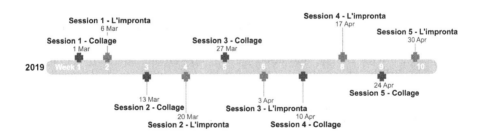

Fig. 2. The timeline of the study

It was explained to the participants that Emoty is an interactive application to discover and learn emotions playing. They spontaneously showed up one at a time to take part in the game. The facilitator received each participant in the experiment room and invited her/him to sit down. Afterward, she performed the login on behalf of the subject to permit a personalized experience (e.g., the user was called by name), and the session started. The user experience was the one described above in the dedicated section. During the session, the observer focused on how users perceived Emoty and took notes on:

– comments aloud by participants and the facilitator,
– questions from subjects to the facilitator,
– reactions, gestures, and behavior of participants during the experience,
– usability issues (e.g., difficulties interacting with the application due to the use of the button or to participant's pronunciation defects),
– breaking points in the conversation.

Every participant used the application for 8–12 min under the supervision of the facilitator. The NDD experts determined the duration for each participant considering her/his engagement and ability to maintain a high level of attention on the same activity. During each session, the facilitator helped the participant with the use of the technology, and by asking her/him whether the received task's instructions were clear. If not, she explained the task again to ensure a correct understanding. When the participant did not feel comfortable with going on with the game, she/he could stop anytime. At the end of each session, participants commented on their experience with the facilitator, but only if they wanted to.

Each study day ended with an hour of discussion among the observer, the facilitator, and us. We schematically described what had happened during the sessions and to collect and organize observations and opinions.

5   Findings and Discussion

On average, participants played for 10 min and 44 s (SD = 3 min and 34 s).

It only happened twice out of 95 times that one user asked to stop playing because he was not feeling comfortable. Both of the times, the facilitator asked him for explanations, and he said that he did not feel able to deal with this game. The facilitator reassured him and respected his opinion making him stop. Overall, people with NDD, caregivers, and psychologists positively evaluated the experience with Emoty, and almost everybody among the subjects enjoyed interacting with it coherently with the pilot study's outcomes [4]. Caregivers in both centers reported that, even after a considerable time from the end of the experimentation, people keep asking about Emoty.

Even if language impairments have to be considered as a limitation in the use of Emoty, as long as the verbal channel is the only one input, they seem not having influenced the likeability of the experience. In fact, two subjects with middle and severe mental disabilities took part in all five sessions, but they stopped at the introduction every time without accessing the playing part; this was due to their big language impairments. It is relevant to say that their intelligibility is usually difficult even for caregivers, and it is permitted just due to the high-developed capability of humans to read lips, to understand by assonance,

Fig. 3. One of the participants playing with Emoty (The participant consented to the picture to be taken and shared.)

to exploit non-verbal channels (e.g., gestures), and to read the context. Anyway, their experience seemed positive; indeed, they both wanted to take part in every session and waited for us to arrive at the center at the front door.

Another limitation of this study is that it is not based on any theoretical framework. Indeed, our investigation into a deeper understanding of how users with NDD perceive Emoty is based on qualitative observations of behaviors, gestures, and commentaries of participants and on the opinions of caregivers and experts. As explained in the *Methodology* section, this choice was dictated mainly from the lack of critical ability in the great majority of our subjects and, consequently, the impossibility to administer any questionnaire. We believe that the lack of a validated framework is not a big issue for our research as it has been conducted under the supervision of NDD experts.

Considering the observations in the reports of every session, we identified four recurring aspects linked to anthropomorphism: gender, fallibility, interaction, and sensitivity. By their analysis, we detected a twofold nature of Emoty perceived by our the participants: in some respects, it is human-like or anthropomorphic, but in some others, it is machine-like.

In this study, we did not observe any differences in perception among participants with different cognitive levels, genders, and ages. However, in future works, we would further explore the variety of perception in different cognitive groups varying the scenarios.

Below, we go into the details of Emoty's dual nature perceived by participants, and we discuss the four main categories of observations we identified.

5.1 Gender

Emoty speaks by exploiting one of the Italian feminine voices by Google. Since this is not metallic and pretends to be human, some of our participants talked about Emoty as it is a she. For example, they asked: "May I be the next one playing with her?" or "How does she remember all our names?". According to Mayer, voice plays an important role in the perception of Conversational Agents and impacts the whole user experience [17]. In this case, Emoty's feminine tone might have contributed to its anthropomorphism process. In the future, we plan to repeat this study changing the voice to a man to see whether or not the "she" changes into a "he", which would make the anthropomorphism argument stronger.

Another important role affecting users' perception of the agent is played by its shape [7]. Emoty has no embodiment but seems to live within the computer. For this reason, some subjects referred to Emoty as a it (i.e., the computer). By doing so, they highlighted the detached, programmable nature of machines. They asked us: "How can it understand me?" or "Did you develop it?" or even "How can I develop my own Emoty?".

In order to reduce the biases attributed to the experimental procedure, the caregivers and we used to answer to their questions by avoiding the use of personal pronouns to refer to Emoty or by using the same one they used in the question.

It was curious to notice more than once that the same participant used both the neutral and the feminine pronoun in different situations. This aspect can be interpreted as a little evidence of the fact that both the human and the mechanical natures of Emoty are perceived and can coexist.

5.2 Fallibility

All participants experienced various challenges getting the agent to understand their utterances. In total, the application was unable to detect them speaking after the button was clicked 1010 times out of 2415 attempts (42%). Participants associated this issue to the fact that Emoty had to be deaf (they said: "She is deaf, isn't she?"), that is a typical characteristic of humans. As a consequence, several subjects tried to increase the level of their voice or make more pauses in their speaking, things that may help people understand them. However, it did not always lead to better recognition with the agent. Moreover, they figured out that when Emoty committed mistakes, it could learn from them as human beings do; they told us: "Today Emoty was a little brat... We hope that she is going to be better next time!".

Regarding the ability of Emoty to recognize emotions from the pitch of the voice, it was notable how everybody facing the application accepted critics and feedback completely trusting the computer because, from their point of view, "a computer cannot commit mistakes". It happened that the same feedback by the facilitator was not taken as kindly as the one by Emoty a couple of seconds later. This episode brings to light the other perceived nature of Emoty that is the fact that it is an automatic machine and inherently cannot be wrong. After all, the Romans said *"Errare humanum est"* (i.e., "to err is human").

We did not observe any correlation between the perception of the agent by the users and their performances in the game. With *performance*, we mean the number of correctly expressed emotions by all participants divided by the number of attempts. Table 1 describes the average performance of the population across sessions. In this context, we do not analyze further these data because, as already stated in the introduction, assessing the potential of Emoty to mitigate Alexithymia and its effects is beyond the scope of this report.

Table 1. The average performance of the population across sessions

Emotions	1st	2nd	3rd	4th	5th
Joy	0.11	0.04	0.18	0.29	0.20
Sadness	0.43	0.40	0.46	0.43	0.50
Anger	0.00	0.36	0.46	0.20	0.43
Fear	0.12	0.25	0.27	0.33	0.47
Surprise	0.00	0.29	0.10	0.19	0.27
Generic emotion	**0.13**	**0.26**	**0.27**	**0.27**	**0.41**

5.3 Interaction

The facilitator observed that interacting with Emoty using natural language was perceived as more natural and intuitive than traditional touch or keyboard-based interactions. This aspect is one of the factors that contributed to producing engagement in the participants.

Unfortunately, as already discussed above, limitations of the currently existing technology did not permit everybody to be easily understood through the voice. For example, Giulia did not catch the imperfect mechanical nature of Emoty and tried to make herself understood as she usually does in human-human interaction: she moved the head and made gestures to reinforce the idea expressed by babbling. It was not clear for her that the machine in front of her could not cross-compare inputs from many communication channels but was considering just the oral one.

The mechanical nature of Emoty was perceived more easily by others, who commented: "Sometimes it takes so long to answer!" (Peter) or "I should try to speak slowly and use a simple language to make me understood by the PC..." (Giorgia). Eleonora has some difficulty pronouncing her Ss, and consequently, she was not understood by the system every time she said "sì", that means "yes" in Italian. After several attempts, she finally got that she could express it in alternative terminology (e.g., "certo", that means "of course"). Afterward, she told us happy: "It took me a while to understand how to speak to Emoty, but now it is fine!".

The use of the mouse to wake-up the system was non-natural as well. During the first session, it seemed a difficult practice for almost all participants (18 out of 19 could not interact autonomously with the app). This issue, as discussed with the caregivers, is probably related to the fact that the actions of pointing and clicking with the mouse are completely uncorrelated from speaking. For those people, the facilitator clicked with the mouse in their place. Fortunately, the interaction with the application became smoother session by session for some of them, and in the last session, 7 participants out of 19 played autonomously. From another point of view, some users appreciated the sense of agency offered by the mouse. For example, Julia commented: "I like that I can decide when I am listened to and when I am not by using the mouse".

5.4   Sensitivity

We noticed that Emoty was perceived with feelings, exactly as a real human. This fact probably happened because Emoty was presented at first as "the game of emotions", and it introduced itself as "an emotion expert". As a consequence, some participants behaved as if they were facing a real human. For example, as a joke, a participant insulted and threatened Emoty to throw the computer away if he would not have been correctly understood. Other subjects, on the contrary, tried to reassure Emoty that following time, it would have understood their speech better and that they would have helped it by expressing emotions with more drama. When in the first part of the session Emoty asked them how it was going, they opened up themselves telling about personal events and thoughts (e.g., the fear of the dentist on the next day, how was the Easter holiday, the nephew's birth, the defeat of the favorite team).

It is important to mention that even speaking about sensitivity, the mechanical nature of Emoty came out: according to the facilitator, some users tended to be more eager to interact with our device rather than to speak to other people. Francesca e Giorgia admitted that they felt more comfortable practicing with Emoty rather than to act in the theater lab with their friends.

6   Conclusion and Future Works

In this study, we observed 19 people with NDD interacting with Emoty for five times. From our qualitative observations, we detected a twofold nature of Emoty perceived by the participants of our study: in some respects, it was human-like, but in some others, it was machine-like. More in detail, it was perceived as a human

- as they listened to her feminine voice,
- as they spoke to her in natural language.
- as they worried about her feelings,
- as they confided personal facts to her,
  as they got angry with her when she did not understand them,

- and as they asked about her after a long time from the end of the experimentation.

On the contrary, it was perceived as a machine

- as they were asked to adapt their way of communicating in order to be understood,
- as they felt more comfortable acting in front of it rather than in front of their friends,
- as they saw it as infallible.

With this study, we paved the ground towards a better understanding of the anthropomorphic perception of people with NDD concerning Conversational Technology.

The natural follow up will be to explore their perception of commercial Conversational Agents (e.g., Google Home, Alexa, Siri) and to compare results. Also, we want to iterate the design process of Emoty again starting from the findings of this study: we want to increase the human-like, natural, and engaging perception of the system by the target user. To do so, we will explore the impact on the user's perception of a virtual character anthropomorphizing the agent Emoty.

Acknowledgements. The authors are grateful to the persons from the Daycare Centers "L'impronta" (Noverasco di Opera) and "Collage" (Milano) who welcomed us in their spaces and contributed in a positive and participatory way to the empirical study.

References

1. Alley-Young, G.: Technology tools for students with autism: innovations that enhance independence and learning. CJC **41**(3), 521–523 (2016)
2. Bouck, E.C., et al.: High-tech or low-tech? Comparing self-monitoring systems to increase task independence for students with autism. Focus Autism Other Dev. Disabil. **29**(3), 156–167 (2014)
3. Brooke, J., et al.: SUS-a quick and dirty usability scale. Usability Eval. Industry **189**(194), 4–7 (1996)
4. Catania, F., Di Nardo, N., Garzotto, F., Occhiuto, D.: Emoty: an emotionally sensitive conversational agent for people with neurodevelopmental disorders. In: Proceedings of the 52nd Hawaii International Conference on System Sciences (2019)
5. Catania, F., et al.: Cork: a conversational agent framework exploiting both rational and emotional intelligence. In: IUI Workshops (2019)
6. DeepAI: Conversational agent (2019). www.deepai.org/machine-learning-glossary-and-terms/conversational-agent
7. Deng, E., Mutlu, B., Mataric, M.J., et al.: Embodiment in socially interactive robots. Found. Trends Robot. **7**(4), 251–356 (2019)
8. Dillon, A., Morris, M.: Power, perception and performance: from usability engineering to technology acceptance with the P3 model of user response. In: Proceedings of the Human Factors and Ergonomics Society Annual Meeting, vol. 43, pp. 1017–1021. SAGE Publications, Los Angeles (1999)
9. Duffy, B.R.: Anthropomorphism and the social robot. Robot. Auton. Syst. **42**(3–4), 177–190 (2003)

10. Epley, N., Waytz, A., Cacioppo, J.T.: On seeing human: a three-factor theory of anthropomorphism. Psychol. Rev. **114**(4), 864 (2007)
11. Ghavifekr, S., Rosdy, W.A.W.: Teaching and learning with technology: effectiveness of ICT integration in schools. Int. J. Res. Educ. Sci. **1**(2), 175–191 (2015)
12. Hart, S.G.: Nasa-task load index (NASA-TLX); 20 years later. In: Proceedings of the Human Factors and Ergonomics Society Annual Meeting, vol. 50, pp. 904–908. Sage Publications, Los Angeles (2006)
13. Kabali, H.K., et al.: Exposure and use of mobile media devices by young children. Pediatrics **136**(6), 1044–1050 (2015)
14. Kim, Y., Sundar, S.S.: Anthropomorphism of computers: is it mindful or mindless? Comput. Hum. Behav. **28**(1), 241–250 (2012)
15. Kolb, D.A.: Experiential Learning: Experience as the Source of Learning and Development. FT Press, Upper Saddle River (2014)
16. Longo, L., Dondio, P.: On the relationship between perception of usability and subjective mental workload of web interfaces. In: 2015 IEEE/WIC/ACM International Conference on Web Intelligence and Intelligent Agent Technology (WI-IAT), vol. 1, pp. 345–352. IEEE (2015)
17. Mayer, R.E., Sobko, K., Mautone, P.D.: Social cues in multimedia learning: Role of speaker's voice. J. Educ. Psychol. **95**(2), 419 (2003)
18. Mower, E., Black, M.P., Flores, E., Williams, M., Narayanan, S.: Rachel: design of an emotionally targeted interactive agent for children with autism. In: 2011 IEEE International Conference on Multimedia and Expo, pp. 1–6. IEEE (2011)
19. Obiyo, N.O., et al.: The use of ICT as an integral teaching and learning tool for children with austism: a challenge for Nigeria education system (2013)
20. Pradhan, A., et al.: Accessibility came by accident: use of voice-controlled intelligent personal assistants by people with disabilities. In: Proceedings of the 2018 CHI Conference on Human Factors in Computing Systems, p. 459. ACM (2018)
21. Rising, K.: Use of classroom technology to promote learning among students with autism (2017)
22. Saarem, A.C.: Why would I talk to you? Investigating user perceptions of conversational agents (2016). www.shorturl.at/fpEG5
23. Seeger, A.M., et al.: When do we need a human? Anthropomorphic design and trustworthiness of conversational agents. In: Proceedings of the Sixteenth Annual Pre-ICIS Workshop on HCI Research in MIS, AISeL, Seoul, Korea. vol. 10 (2017)
24. Tanner, K., Dixon, R., Verenikina, I.: The digital technology in the learning of students with autism spectrum disorders (ASD) in applied classroom settings. In: EdMedia+ Innovate Learning, pp. 2586–2591. Association for the Advancement of Computing in Education (AACE) (2010)
25. Tess (2019). www.x2ai.com. Accessed 20 Sept 2019
26. Waytz, A., Heafner, J., Epley, N.: The mind in the machine: anthropomorphism increases trust in an autonomous vehicle. J. Exp. Soc. Psychol. **52**, 113–117 (2014)
27. Woebot (2019). www.woebot.io. Accessed 20 Sept 2019
28. Wysa (2019). www.wysa.io. Accessed 20 Sept 2019

Gender Bias in Chatbot Design

Jasper Feine[(⊠)], Ulrich Gnewuch, Stefan Morana,
and Alexander Maedche

Institute of Information Systems and Marketing (IISM),
Karlsruhe Institute of Technology (KIT), Karlsruhe, Germany
{jasper.feine,ulrich.gnewuch,stefan.morana,
alexander.maedche}@kit.edu

Abstract. A recent UNESCO report reveals that most popular voice-based conversational agents are designed to be female. In addition, it outlines the potentially harmful effects this can have on society. However, the report focuses primarily on voice-based conversational agents and the analysis did not include chatbots (i.e., text-based conversational agents). Since chatbots can also be gendered in their design, we used an automated gender analysis approach to investigate three gender-specific cues in the design of 1,375 chatbots listed on the platform chatbots.org. We leveraged two gender APIs to identify the gender of the name, a face recognition API to identify the gender of the avatar, and a text mining approach to analyze gender-specific pronouns in the chatbot's description. Our results suggest that gender-specific cues are commonly used in the design of chatbots and that most chatbots are – explicitly or implicitly – designed to convey a specific gender. More specifically, most of the chatbots have female names, female-looking avatars, and are described as female chatbots. This is particularly evident in three application domains (i.e., branded conversations, customer service, and sales). Therefore, we find evidence that there is a tendency to prefer one gender (i.e., female) over another (i.e., male). Thus, we argue that there is a gender bias in the design of chatbots in the wild. Based on these findings, we formulate propositions as a starting point for future discussions and research to mitigate the gender bias in the design of chatbots.

Keywords: Chatbot · Gender-specific cue · Gender bias · Conversational agent

1 Introduction

Text- and voice-based conversational agents (CAs) have become increasingly popular in recent years [19]. Many organizations use chatbots (i.e., text-based CAs) in short-term interactions, such as customer service and content curation [22], as well as in long-term interactions, such as personal assistants or coaches [21]. Research has found that chatbots can increase user satisfaction [41], positively influence perceived social presence [3], and establish long-term relationships with users [7]. Additionally, large technology companies have successfully deployed voice-based CAs (e.g., Microsoft's Cortana, Amazon's Alexa, and Apple's Siri) on many devices such as mobile phones, smart speakers, and computers.

© Springer Nature Switzerland AG 2020
A. Følstad et al. (Eds.): CONVERSATIONS 2019, LNCS 11970, pp. 79–93, 2020.
https://doi.org/10.1007/978-3-030-39540-7_6

Despite the many beneficial aspects of this technology, a recent UNESCO report [43] from 2019 sheds light on the negative implications of the gendered design of most commercial voice-based CAs. The report reveals that most voice-based CAs are designed to be *"female exclusively or female by default"* [43]. For example, their name (e.g., Alexa, Cortana, Siri), their voice (i.e., voices of Alexa and Cortana are exclusively female), and how they are advertised (e.g., *"Alexa lost her voice"*) often cause female gender associations. This can lead to the manifestation of gender stereotypes. For example, since users mostly interact with voice-based CAs using short command-like phrases (e.g., *"tell me the weather"*), people might deem this form of interaction style as appropriate when conversing with (female) CAs and potentially even (female) humans [38]. Consequently, the report highlights the urgent need to change gender expectations towards CAs before users become accustomed to their default (female) design [43].

While the UNESCO report provides interesting insights on gender-specific cues in the design of voice-based CAs and its potential implications, the report does not include an analysis of chatbots since they are *"not always as clearly gendered because their output is primarily written text, not speech"* [43, p. 92]. However, many studies have shown that the gender of a chatbot can also be manifested without spoken voice using other social cues such as name tags or avatars [e.g., 2, 3, 5, 9, 16, 24, 32]. Moreover, these studies suggest that gender-specific cues in the chatbot's design can have both positive [e.g., 5, 24] and negative outcomes [e.g., 2, 9].

Therefore, we argue that there is a need to analyze how chatbots – in contrast to voice-based CAs – are gendered (i.e., through gender-specific cues in their design) and whether there is evidence of a potential gender bias in the design of chatbots. To the best of our knowledge, an empirical analysis of gender-specific cues in the design of chatbots in the wild has not been conducted so far. To address this gap and to complement the findings of the UNESCO report, we investigate the research question of how gender-specific cues are implemented in the design of chatbots.

To address this question, we analyzed the design of 1,375 chatbots listed on the platform chatbots.org. In our analysis, we focused on three cues that can indicate a specific gender, namely the chatbot's name, avatar, and description. In the following, we refer to these cues as gender-specific cues. Our findings suggest that there is a gender bias in the design of chatbots. More specifically, we find evidence that there is a trend towards female names, female-looking avatars, and descriptions including female pronouns, particularly in domains such as customer service, sales, and brand representation. Overall, our work contributes to the emerging field of designing chatbots for social good [20] by highlighting a gender bias in the design of chatbots and thus, complementing the findings of the recent UNESCO report on the design of voice-based CAs. Subsequently, we derive propositions to provide a starting point for future discussion and research in order to mitigate this gender bias and pave the way towards a more gender-equal design of chatbots.

2   Related Work

2.1   Gender-Specific Cues of Conversational Agents

CAs are software-based systems designed to interact with humans using natural language [14]. This means, users interact with CAs via voice-based or text-based interfaces in a similar way as they usually interact with other human beings. Research on CAs and in particular text-based CAs (i.e., chatbots) has been around for several decades [e.g., 42]. However, the hype around this technology did not start until 2016 [10]. Due to the major adoption of mobile-messaging platforms (e.g., Facebook Messenger) and the advances in the field of artificial intelligence (AI) [10], chatbots became one of the most hyped technologies in recent years in research and practice [3].

Extant research in the context of CAs builds on the Computers-Are-Social-Actors (CASA) paradigm [33]. The CASA paradigm states that human users perceive computers as social actors and treat them as relevant social entities [32]. Therefore, humans respond similar to computers as they usually react to other human beings (e.g., say *thank you* to a computer). These reactions particularly occur when a computer exhibits social cues that are similar to cues usually expressed by humans during interpersonal communication [16]. Since CAs communicate via natural language (i.e., a central human capability), social reactions towards CAs almost always happen [16]. For example, humans apply gender stereotypes towards CAs whenever they display specific social cues such as a male or female name, voice, or avatar (see Table 1 for an overview [18]). In addition, not only rather obvious social cues, such as the avatar, voice, or name, indicate a belonging to a specific gender, but even movements of an animated avatar are sufficient to do so [40]. Thus, it *"appears that the tendency to gender stereotype is deeply ingrained in human psychology, extending even to machines"* [34].

Table 1.   Exemplary studies investigating the impact of a CA's gender-specific cues.

Type of CA	Investigated Cue	Investigated gender	User reaction towards gender-specific cue	Reference
Voice-based	Voice	Female, male	Gender impacts competence and perceived friendliness of CA	[34]
Voice-based	Avatar	Female, male	A specific gender was not preferred	[13]
Voice-based	Avatar, voice	Female, male	Gender impacts the comprehension scores and impression ratings	[27]
Text-based	Avatar	Female, male	Gender influences the impact of excuses to reduce user frustration	[24]
Text-based	Avatar	Ambiguous, female, male	Gender impacts comfort, confidence, and enjoyment. Users did not prefer gender ambiguous CAs	[35]
Voice-based	Avatar, voice	Female, male	Gender impacts perceived power, trust, expertise, and likability	[37]

(continued)

Table 1. (*continued*)

Type of CA	Investigated Cue	Investigated gender	User reaction towards gender-specific cue	Reference
Text-based	Name, Avatar	Female, male, robotic	Gender impacts the attribution of negative stereotypes	[9]
Voice-based	Avatar	Female, male	Gender impacts learning performance and learning effort	[26]
Text-based	Avatar	Female, male	Gender impacts learning performance	[23]
Text-based	Avatar	Female, male	Gender impacts the belief in the credibility of advice and competence of agent	[5]

2.2 Gender Bias in the Design of Voice-Based Conversational Agents

Since there is limited research on specific design guidelines for CAs [21, 29], major technology companies actively shape how CAs are designed [21]. However, the design of the major voice-based CAs (e.g., Cortana, Alexa, Google Assistant, Siri) creates considerable concerns whether the leadership position of technology companies in the design of CA is desirable [43]. For example, if users directed sexual insults towards Siri, she used to answer "*I'd blush if I could*" (till April 2019) and now answers, "*I don't know how to respond to that*" (since April 2019) [43].

Gender manifestations in the design of CAs also reinforce gender manifestations in the user perception of CAs. This can have severe implications for everyday interpersonal interactions. For example, the fact that most of the female voice-based CAs act as personal assistants leads to the general user expectation that these types of CAs should be female [43]. Moreover, it "*creates expectations and reinforces assumptions that women should provide simple, direct and unsophisticated answers to basic questions*" [43 p., 115]. Therefore, such a development reinforces traditional gender stereotypes. This is in particular harmful, since many children interact with voice-based CAs and gender stereotypes are primarily instilled at a very young age [9].

Similarly, the active interventions of chatbot engineers into human affairs (e.g., establishing a gender bias in the design of chatbots) raises ethical considerations. Several institutions are warning to avoid the gender-specific development of (interactive) systems. For example, the UNESCO report [5] proposes several recommendations to prevent digital assistants from perpetuating gender biases. Recently, the European Union's High-Level Expert Group on AI defined the guidelines for trustworthy AI and also highlights the importance of equality, non-discrimination, and solidarity [15]. Myers and Venable [31] propose ethical guidelines for the design of socio-technical system and also emphasize the importance of empowerment and emancipation for all. Moreover, several research associations (e.g., AIS, ACM) provide ethical guidelines to ensure ethical practice by emphasizing the importance of designing for an gender-equal society [39].

3 Method

To answer our research question, we analyzed three cues in the design of a broad sample of chatbots. Currently, there are several online platforms that list chatbots, but there is no central repository. Therefore, we decided to rely on the data provided by chatbots.org. Chatbots.org is a large online community with 8000 members. Members can add their chatbots to the repository and provide additional information (e.g., name, avatar, language, description, application purpose). We selected chatbots.org because it is one of the longest running chatbot directory services (established 2008) [6] and has been used in research before [e.g., 25].

For our analysis, we retrieved the data of all chatbots listed on chatbots.org on June 28, 2019 by using a web crawler. This resulted in a data sample consisting of 1,375 chatbots including their name, avatar, description, and other meta-information such as the application domain (i.e., chatbots.org assigns twelve, not mutually exclusive application domains to the listed chatbots).

In our analysis, we focused on three cues: the chatbot's (1) name, (2) avatar, and (3) description. We selected these cues since several studies revealed that the gender of the (1) name and the (2) avatar of a chatbot trigger stereotypical gender responses [e.g., 5, 9] and (3) that written text can convey gender attributes and personality traits [4]. Given our large sample size, we decided to automatically extract and analyze the gender-specific design (female, male, none) of these three cues using available tools and services. In addition, to validate our automated approach, we randomly selected and manually coded 100 chatbots.

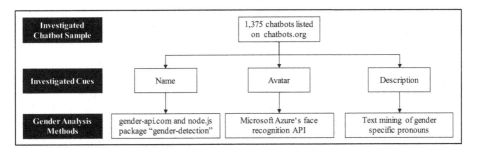

Fig. 1. Automated gender analysis approach to investigate gender-specific cues in the design of chatbots.

Our automated gender analysis approach is illustrated in Fig. 1. First, to investigate the gender of the chatbots' names, we used two online services that identify the gender of a given name, namely www.gender-api.com (includes the gender of over two million names) and the node.js package "gender-detection" [36] (includes the gender of over 40,000 names). Only if both services recognized the same gender of one of the 1,375 chatbot names, we included it in the analyses. Second, to investigate the gender of an avatar, we used Microsoft Azure's Face API [30] which is able to detect, identify, analyze, organize, and tag faces in photos and also to extract the gender of a face.

Therefore, we used this API to analyze 1373 chatbot avatar pictures that we down-loaded from chatbots.org (two chatbots did not have a picture). Finally, to analyze the chatbot's description, we text-mined the description of all retrieved chatbots to identify gender-specific pronouns that refer to one of the two genders (female: "*she*", "*her*", "*hers*"; male: "*he*", "*him*", "*his*") [4]. After excluding ambiguous descriptions (i.e., descriptions including both female and male pronouns), we assigned a gender to the description of a chatbot. Table 2 shows the results of the automated gender analysis approach for three examples.

Table 2. Exemplary results of the automated gender analysis approach.

Name (Company)	Avatar	Excerpt of Description	(1) Name	(2) Avatar	(3) Description
SOphiA (BASF)		*SOphiA is an Intranet Interactive Assistant used internally by BASF for its worldwide operations.* **She** *answers questions about [...].*	Female	Female	Female
Frank (Verizon)		*Frank answers all of your Verizon customer service support questions.*	Male	Male	None
BB (KLM)		*[...]. BB has* **her** *own professional, helpful and friendly character, but be warned;* **she** *can also be a bit cheeky from time to time. [...]*	None	None	Female

To investigate the reliability of our automated gender analysis approach, we investigated whether there are conflicting results between the three methods (e.g., a chatbot has a male name and a female avatar). In total, we identified only 15 conflicts in our result set. Subsequently, we analyzed these conflicts in more detail and manually coded all conflicting gender-specific cues. Overall, seven of these conflicts were caused by a wrong gender assignment to an avatar of a chatbot. After analyzing these wrong assignments, we identified that Microsoft's face recognition API potentially has problems to assign the correct gender to cartoon avatars with a low resolution. Another five conflicts were caused by the text mining approach. In five cases, all pronouns in the chatbot's descriptions referred to another person (e.g., the chatbot engineer). Thus, the pronouns did not refer to the chatbots itself. Finally, two chatbots names were labeled wrong since the names (i.e., Nima, Charlie) are not clearly gendered and thus, could have been assigned to both genders.

Table 3. Comparison of automatic gender analysis approach and manual coding for a subsample of 100 randomly selected chatbots.

Cues	Number of conflicts between automated and manual coding	Number of not recognized gender-specific cues
Name	0	25 (15 female: 10 male)
Avatar	0	20 (17 female: 3 male)
Description	0	0

To further validate the reliability of the automated gender analysis approach, we retrieved a random sample of 100 chatbots from the total sample of 1,375 chatbots. The first and second author manually coded the gender of the name, avatar, and description of these chatbots. There were no disagreements between both coders. Subsequently, we compared the results of the manual coding with our automated approach. The comparison showed that there were no conflicts between the genders that were identified. However, as illustrated in Table 3, the manual coding approach resulted in the identification of more gender-specific names and avatars. Most names that were not recognized as having a gender were female. Similarity, most of the avatars that were not recognized were female.

4   Results

In the following, we present the results of our automated analysis of three cues (i.e., name, avatar, and description) in our sample of 1,375 chatbots. First, we provide an overview of the total amount of gendered chatbots before reporting the gender distribution (i.e., female vs. male) of the gender-specific cues, and their distribution according to the chatbot's application domain.

In total, we identified the gender of 620 chatbot names (45.09% of all investigated chatbots), 347 chatbot avatars (25.24%), and 497 chatbot descriptions (36.15%) using our automated approach. As illustrated in Fig. 2, there are some overlaps between the cues. Overall, 501 (36.44%) of the chatbots did not have one gender-specific cue. In addition, we identified 874 chatbots (63.56%) with at least one gender-specific cue (i.e.,

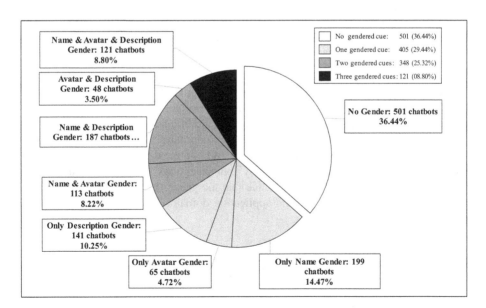

Fig. 2. Distribution of gender-specific names, avatars, and descriptions in the investigated chatbot sample.

either a gendered name, avatar, or description). Moreover, 469 chatbots (34.11%) had at least two gender-specific cues, and 121 chatbots (8.80%) had all three gender-specific cues (i.e., a gendered name, avatar, and description). Taken together, the results suggest that the majority of chatbots listed on chatbots.org are gendered in their design.

Next, we identified whether the gender-specific cues are female or male. As shown in Fig. 3, the large majority of gender- specific names were female (76.94%). The analyses of avatars and descriptions revealed similar results: 77.56% of the avatars were classified as female and 67.40% of the descriptions were classified as female. These results strongly suggest that most chatbots are designed to be female.

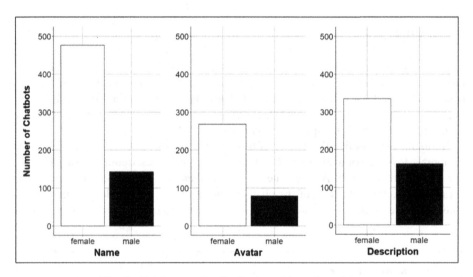

Fig. 3. Gender-specific distribution of investigated cues.

Our analysis of gendered chatbots and their application domains revealed that 48.90% of them belong to only three application domains, namely branded conversations, customer service, and sales (see Table 4). Additionally, most domains (8) were clearly dominated by female names and only three domains by male names. The same patterns emerged in the analyses of avatars (i.e., all but one domain were dominated by female avatars) and descriptions (i.e., only four categories were dominated by male descriptions). Taken together, we conclude that the gender bias is particularly evident in the design of chatbots for specific application domains such as branded conversations, customer service, and sales.

Table 4. Chatbot application domains listed on chatbots.org and their gender-specific design (note: application domains are not mutually exclusive).

Application domain	Description of application domain as listed on Chatbots.org	All chatbots	Gendered names	Gendered avatars	Gendered descriptions
Animals & aliens	"Speaking, listening and responding virtual animals, cartoonlike characters or creatures from space"	20	Female: 1 Male: 2	Female: 0 Male: 0	Female: 4 Male: 11
Branded conversations	"Dialogues on behalf of an organization, on a product or service"	511	Female: 257 Male: 54	Female: 137 Male: 32	Female: 162 Male: 38
Campaign	"Designed for a limited timeserving a campaign objective"	61	Female: 9 Male: 11	Female: 13 Male: 6	Female: 4 Male: 8
Customer service	"To answer questions about delivered goods or services"	532	Female: 251 Male: 55	Female: 137 Male: 22	Female: 164 Male: 33
Knowledge management	"To acquire information from employees through natural language interaction"	63	Female: 30 Male: 3	Female: 13 Male: 1	Female: 16 Male: 4
Market research	"Conducting surveys with consumers through automated chat"	16	Female: 6 Male: 0	Female: 3 Male: 0	Female: 6 Male: 0
Sales	"A conversion of a dialogue focused on closing the deal"	236	Female: 106 Male: 16	Female: 61 Male: 9	Female: 81 Male: 10
Clone	"A virtual version of a real human being, whether still alive or a historic person"	40	Female: 3 Male: 14	Female: 5 Male: 20	Female: 2 Male: 11
E-Learning	"Human like characters in virtual reality and augmented reality with a scripted role"	21	Female: 4 Male: 0	Female: 2 Male: 1	Female: 7 Male: 6
Gaming	"Conversational characters in games or virtual worlds"	14	Female: 5 Male: 2	Female: 0 Male: 1	Female: 5 Male: 5
Proof of concept	"Demonstrational versions created by professional developers on their own websites"	152	Female: 52 Male: 18	Female: 28 Male: 6	Female: 45 Male: 28
Robot toy	"Physical robotic gadgets with natural language processing capabilities"	1	Female: 0 Male: 0	Female: 0 Male: 0	Female: 0 Male: 1

5 Discussion

In this paper, we show that gender-specific cues are commonly used in the design of chatbots in the wild and that many chatbots are – explicitly or implicitly – designed to convey a specific gender. This finding ranges from names and avatars to the textual descriptions used to introduce them to their users. More specifically, most of the chatbots have female names, female-looking avatars, and are described as female chatbots. Thus, we found evidence that there is a tendency to prefer one gender (i.e., female) over another (i.e., male). Therefore, we conclude that there is a gender bias in the design of chatbots. The gender bias is particularly evident in three domains (i.e., customer service, branded conversation, and sales).

Our findings do not only mirror the results of the UNESCO report [43] on gender bias in voice-based CAs, but also support an observation already made in 2006. In their analysis of genders stereotypes implemented in CAs, De Angeli and Brahnam [2] conclude that virtual assistants on corporate websites „*are often embodied by seductive and nice looking young girls* "(p. 5). Considering the majority of chatbots currently used in customer service or marketing, one could argue that not much has changed since then. Although recent studies have raised concerns about ethical issues of gender stereotyping in chatbot design [e.g., 28], there are no guidelines for a gender-equal design of chatbots that could support chatbot engineers to diminish gender stereotypes (at least) in the context of text-based CAs. Since gender-specific cues are often perceived even before interacting with the chatbot, they have a large impact on how users interact with them [9]. Therefore, discussions between researchers, practitioners, and users will be highly important to answer relevant questions (e.g., "Should a chatbot have a specific gender?", "Is it even possible to avoid gender attributions?"). To provide a starting point for discussions and suggest avenues for future research, we formulate four propositions (P) that could help to mitigate the gender bias and pave the way towards a more gender-equal design of chatbots.

P1: Diverse Composition of Chatbot Development Teams: The technology sector, their programmers, and also chatbot engineers are often dominated by males (i.e., "*brogramming*") [19]. Without criticizing the individual chatbot engineer, decision makers could foster a more gender equal distribution in teams who develop socio-technical systems that actively intervene in human affairs, such as chatbots. This could reduce potential gender biases, since women generally tend to produce less gender-biased language than men [4]. A more diverse team composition is also in line with the "*ACM Code of Ethics and Professional Conduct*" which states that "*computing professionals should foster fair participation of all people*" also based on their "*gender identity*" [1]. Moreover, chatbot design teams should not solely consist of engineers but should further include a diverse composition of people from different domains, such as from linguistics and psychology.

P2: Leverage Tool-Support for Identifying Gender Biases in Chatbot Design: Comprehensive tool support could help chatbot engineers to avoid potential gender stereotypes in their development. Since gender stereotypes are often processed (and also implemented) in a unconscious manner [8], active tool support could help chatbot engineers to avoid their mindless implementation. A similar approach has been proposed in the context of general software evaluation. For example, the method "*GenderMag*" [11] uses personas and cognitive walkthroughs in order to identify gender inclusiveness issues in software. Therefore, such an approach could also help chatbot engineers. While more effort is needed to develop tools that automatically evaluate the gender inclusiveness of the design of chatbots, first warning mechanism seem to be easy to implement. For example, chatbot engineers could use the methods described in this paper, namely gender analysis of chatbot names, avatar analysis using face recognition, and text mining of descriptions. Additionally, chatbot configuration tools could support chatbot engineers in making gender-equal design decisions [e.g., 17, 18].

P3: Avoid "Female-by-Default" Chatbot Designs: Overall, it does not appear necessary to give a chatbot a default (female) gender. However, it is currently not clear whether developing non-gendered chatbots or challenging human perceptions of chatbot gender is the solution. Thus, chatbot engineers and the research community are still far from resolving those issues, and the community should be open to discussing them. Nevertheless, chatbot engineers need to actively implement mechanisms to respond to unsavory user queries in order to avoid the manifestations of gender stereotypes in the use of chatbots [9]. For example, Apple's Siri is not encouraging gender-based insults anymore (e.g., "*I'd blush if I could*"). Other CAs do not pretend to have a gender (e.g., if users ask Cortana, "*what is your gender?*", Cortana automatically replies, "*technically, I'm a cloud of infinitesimal data computation*" [43]). However, further research is needed to investigate user-centered designs and mechanisms to mitigate and discourage negative stereotyping in the use of chatbots.

P4: Promote Ethical Considerations in Organizations: Although, gender equality is one of the UN sustainability goals [39], gender-specific cues in the design of CAs are rarely attracting the attention of governments and international organizations [43]. Therefore, decision makers and engineers need to take the first step and challenge each chatbot design towards potential gender stereotypes and other ethical considerations. By actively promoting such considerations, chatbot development teams and other people engaged in the development process will profit from an increased awareness in order to build more gender-equal societies. Such endeavors could further complement the ongoing discussions about gender-equal designs of algorithmic decision systems and other types of artificial intelligence [e.g., 12]. Finally, such organizational driven approaches could complement the work of regulators to promote a more gender-equal chatbot design.

5.1   Limitations and Future Research

There are limitations of this study that need to be addressed. First, our analysis is based on a limited sample of chatbots. Although we did not differentiate between commercial and research-based chatbots and did not check if they are still online, we argue that our sample provides a sufficient base to draw conclusions about gender-specific cues in the design of chatbots. Future research could investigate gender-specific cues of different chatbots using other samples and data sources such as BotList.co. This would help to create a broader overview of the gender bias and would enhance our understanding of the current design of chatbots.

Second, our automated approach for identifying the gender of the chatbot's name, avatar, and description might be susceptible to false positives and false negatives. To address this limitation, we validated our approach by manually analyzing a subsample of 100 chatbots. Because we did not identify any false positive result, we argue that gender-specific cues identified by the approach are quite accurate. However, the manual analysis also revealed that our automated approach did not identify all gender-specific cues and indicated a few conflicts between the three methods. For example, Azure's face recognition API struggled with extracting a gender from low-resolution cartoon avatars and some pronouns in the description did not refer to the chatbot. Therefore, we can only interpret the results of the automated gender analysis approach as a conservative predictor for the amount of gender-specific cues in chatbot sample. Thus, the true value of gendered chatbots might be much higher. Despite this limitation, we believe that our findings still hold because according to our manual analysis most of the not recognized gender-specific cues where female.

Third, while our analysis included three important cues, several other cues in the design of chatbots could be considered that may convey a gender-specific attribution. Therefore, future research could extend our analysis to other relevant gender-specific cues [16].

6 Conclusion

In this study, we examined the gender-specific design of three cues in the design of 1,375 chatbots using an automated gender analysis approach. Our results provide evidence that there is a gender bias in the design of chatbots because most chatbots were clearly gendered as female (i.e., in terms of their name, avatar, or description). This bias is particularly evident in three application domains (i.e., branded conversations, customer service, and sales). Therefore, our study complements the findings of a recent UNESCO report that identified a gender bias in the design of voice-based CAs and provides propositions as a starting point for future discussions and research.

References

1. ACM: Code of Ethics and Professional Conduct. https://www.acm.org/code-of-ethics (2019). Accessed 26 July 2019
2. de Angeli, A., Brahnam, S.: Sex Stereotypes and Conversational Agents (2006)
3. Araujo, T.: Living up to the chatbot hype: the influence of anthropomorphic design cues and communicative agency framing on conversational agent and company perceptions. Comput. Hum. Behav. **85**, 183–189 (2018). https://doi.org/10.1016/j.chb.2018.03.051
4. Artz, N., Munger, J., Purdy, W.: Gender issues in advertising language. Women Lang. **22**(2), 20 (1999)

5. Beldad, A., Hegner, S., Hoppen, J.: The effect of virtual sales agent (VSA) gender – product gender congruence on product advice credibility, trust in VSA and online vendor, and purchase intention. Comput. Hum. Behav. **60**, 62–72 (2016). https://doi.org/10.1016/j.chb. 2016.02.046

6. Bhagyashree, R.: A chatbot toolkit for developers: design, develop, and manage conversational UI (2019). https://hub.packtpub.com/chatbot-toolkit-developers-design-develop-manage-conversational-ui/. Accessed 22 July 2019

7. Bickmore, T.W., Picard, R.W.: Establishing and maintaining long-term human-computer relationships. ACM Trans. Comput.-Hum. Interact. **12**(2), 293–327 (2005). https://doi.org/10.1145/1067860.1067867

8. Bohnet, I.: What Works. Harvard University Press (2016)

9. Brahnam, S., de Angeli, A.: Gender affordances of conversational agents. Interact. Comput. **24**(3), 139–153 (2012). https://doi.org/10.1016/j.intcom.2012.05.001

10. Brandtzaeg, P.B., Følstad, A.: Chatbots: changing user needs and motivations. Interactions **25**(5), 38–43 (2018). https://doi.org/10.1145/3236669

11. Burnett, M., et al.: GenderMag: a method for evaluating software's gender inclusiveness. Interact. Comput. **28**(6), 760–787 (2016). https://doi.org/10.1093/iwc/iwv046

12. Council of Europe: Discrimination, artificial intelligence, and algorithmic decision-making (2018). https://rm.coe.int/discrimination-artificial-intelligence-and-algorithmic-decision-making/1680925d73

13. Cowell, A.J., Stanney, K.M.: Manipulation of non-verbal interaction style and demographic embodiment to increase anthropomorphic computer character credibility. Int. J. Hum.-Comput. Stud. **62**(2), 281–306 (2005). https://doi.org/10.1016/j.ijhcs.2004.11.008

14. Dale, R.: The return of the chatbots. Nat. Lang. Eng. **22**(5), 811–817 (2016). https://doi.org/10.1017/S1351324916000243

15. EU: Ethics Guidelines for Trustworthy AI (2019). https://ec.europa.eu/futurium/en/ai-alliance-consultation. Accessed 30 July 2019

16. Feine, J., Gnewuch, U., Morana, S., Maedche, A.: A taxonomy of social cues for conversational agents. Int. J. Hum.-Comput. Stud. **132**, 138–161 (2019). https://doi.org/10.1016/j.ijhcs.2019.07.009

17. Feine, J., Morana, S., Maedche, A.: Designing a chatbot social cue configuration system. In: Proceedings of the 40th International Conference on Information Systems (ICIS). AISel, Munich (2019)

18. Feine, J., Morana, S., Maedche, A.: Leveraging machine-executable descriptive knowledge in design science research – the case of designing socially-adaptive chatbots. In: Tulu, B., Djamasbi, S., Leroy, G. (eds.) DESRIST 2019. LNCS, vol. 11491, pp. 76–91. Springer, Cham (2019). https://doi.org/10.1007/978-3-030-19504-5_6

19. Følstad, A., Brandtzæg, P.B.: Chatbots and the new world of HCI. Interactions **24**(4), 38–42 (2017). https://doi.org/10.1145/3085558

20. Følstad, A., Brandtzaeg, P.B., Feltwell, T., Law, E.L.-C., Tscheligi, M., Luger, E.A.: SIG: chatbots for social good. In: Extended Abstracts of the 2018 CHI Conference on Human Factors in Computing Systems, SIG06:1-SIG06:4. ACM, New York (2018). https://doi.org/10.1145/3170427.3185372

21. Følstad, A., Skjuve, M., Brandtzaeg, P.: Different chatbots for different purposes: towards a typology of chatbots to understand interaction design, pp. 145–156 (2019)

22. Gnewuch, U., Morana, S., Maedche, A.: Towards designing cooperative and social conversational agents for customer service. In: Proceedings of the 38th International Conference on Information Systems (ICIS). AISel, Seoul (2017)

23. Hayashi, Y.: Lexical network analysis on an online explanation task. Effects of affect and embodiment of a pedagogical agent. IEICE Trans. Inf. Syst. **99**(6), 1455–1461 (2016). https://doi.org/10.1587/transinf.2015CBP0005

24. Hone, K.: Empathic agents to reduce user frustration. The effects of varying agent characteristics. Interact. Comput. **18**(2), 227–245 (2006). https://doi.org/10.1016/j.intcom.2005.05.003

25. Johannsen, F., Leist, S., Konadl, D., Basche, M., de Hesselle, B.: Comparison of commercial chatbot solutions for supporting customer interaction. In: Proceedings of the 26th European Conference on Information Systems (ECIS), Portsmouth, United Kingdom, 23–28 June 2018

26. Kraemer, N.C., Karacora, B., Lucas, G., Dehghani, M., Ruether, G., Gratch, J.: Closing the gender gap in STEM with friendly male instructors? On the effects of rapport behavior and gender of a virtual agent in an instructional interaction. Comput. Educ. **99**, 1–13 (2016). https://doi.org/10.1016/j.compedu.2016.04.002

27. Louwerse, M.M., Graesser, A.C., Lu, S.L., Mitchell, H.H.: Social cues in animated conversational agents. Appl. Cogn. Psychol. **19**(6), 693–704 (2005). https://doi.org/10.1002/acp.1117

28. McDonnell, M., Baxter, D.: Chatbots and gender stereotyping. Interact. Comput. **31**(2), 116–121 (2019). https://doi.org/10.1093/iwc/iwz007

29. McTear, M.F.: The rise of the conversational interface: a new kid on the block? In: Quesada, J.F., Martín Mateos, F.J., López-Soto, T. (eds.) FETLT 2016. LNCS (LNAI), vol. 10341, pp. 38–49. Springer, Cham (2017). https://doi.org/10.1007/978-3-319-69365-1_3

30. Microsoft: Face recognition API (2019). https://azure.microsoft.com/en-us/services/cognitive-services/face/. Accessed 22 July 2019

31. Myers, M.D., Venable, J.R.: A set of ethical principles for design science research in information systems. Inf. Manag. **51**(6), 801–809 (2014). https://doi.org/10.1016/j.im.2014.01.002

32. Nass, C., Moon, Y.: Machines and mindlessness social responses to computers. J. Soc. Issues **56**(1), 81–103 (2000). https://doi.org/10.1111/0022-4537.00153

33. Nass, C., Steuer, J., Tauber, E.R.: Computers are social actors. In: Proceedings of the SIGCHI Conference on Human Factors in Computing Systems, pp. 72–78. ACM, New York (1994). https://doi.org/10.1145/191666.191703

34. Nass, C., Moon, Y., Green, N.: Are machines gender neutral? Gender-stereotypic responses to computers with voices. J. Appl. Soc. Pyschol. **27**(10), 864–876 (1997). https://doi.org/10.1111/j.1559-1816.1997.tb00275.x

35. Niculescu, A., Hofs, D., van Dijk, B., Nijholt, A.: How the agent's gender influence users' evaluation of a QA system. In: International Conference on User Science and Engineering (i-USEr) (2010)

36. npmjs: Gender-detection (2019). https://www.npmjs.com/package/gender-detection. Accessed 22 July 2019

37. Nunamaker, J.E., Derrick, D.C., Elkins, A.C., Burgoon, J.K., Patton, M.W.: Embodied conversational agent-based kiosk for automated interviewing. J. Manag. Inf. Syst. **28**(1), 17–48 (2011). https://doi.org/10.2753/mis0742-1222280102

38. Rosenwald, M.S.: How millions of kids are being shaped by know-it-all voice assistants (2019). https://www.washingtonpost.com/local/how-millions-of-kids-are-being-shaped-by-know-it-all-voice-assistants/2017/03/01/c0a644c4-ef1c-11e6-b4ff-ac2cf509efe5_story.html?noredirect=on&utm_term=.7d67d631bd52. Accessed 16 July 2019

39. United Nations: Sustainability development goals. Goal 5: gender equality (2015). https://www.sdgfund.org/goal-5-gender-equality. Accessed 30 Oct 2019

40. Vala, M., Blanco, G., Paiva, A.: Providing gender to embodied conversational agents. In: Vilhjálmsson, H.H., Kopp, S., Marsella, S., Thórisson, Kristinn R. (eds.) IVA 2011. LNCS (LNAI), vol. 6895, pp. 148–154. Springer, Heidelberg (2011). https://doi.org/10.1007/978-3-642-23974-8_16

41. Verhagen, T., van Nes, J., Feldberg, F., van Dolen, W.: Virtual customer service agents. Using social presence and personalization to shape online service encounters. J. Comput.-Mediat. Commun. 19(3), 529–545 (2014). https://doi.org/10.1111/jcc4.12066

42. Weizenbaum, J.: ELIZA - a computer program for the study of natural language communication between man and machine. Commun. ACM 9(1), 36–45 (1966)

43. West, M., Kraut, R., Chew, H.E.: I'd blush if I could: closing gender divides in digital skills through education (2019). https://unesdoc.unesco.org/ark:/48223/pf0000367416

Conversational Web Interaction: Proposal of a Dialog-Based Natural Language Interaction Paradigm for the Web

Marcos Baez[1](✉)(iD), Florian Daniel[2](iD), and Fabio Casati[1,3](iD)

[1] University of Trento, Trento, Italy
{baez,casati}@disi.unitn.it
[2] Politecnico di Milano, Milan, Italy
florian.daniel@polimi.it
[3] Tomsk Polytechnic University, Tomsk, Russia

Abstract. This paper lays the foundation for a new delivery paradigm for web-accessible content and functionality, i.e., conversational interaction. Instead of asking users to read text, click through links and type on the keyboard, the vision is to enable users to "speak to a website" and to obtain natural language, spoken feedback. The paper describes how state-of-the-art chatbot technology can enable a dialog between the user and the website, proposes a reference architecture for the automated inference of site-specific chatbots able to mediate between the user and the website, and discusses open challenges and research questions. The envisioned, bidirectional dialog paradigm advances current screen reader technology and aims to benefit both regular users in eyes-free usage scenarios as well as visually impaired users in everyday scenarios.

Keywords: Non-visual browsing · Screen readers · Conversational agents

1 Introduction

The current model of the Web is based on a set of basic concepts that evolved over the years to accommodate the complexity of new usage scenarios, but it essentially remains a visual experience: it requires looking, clicking, scrolling, hovering the mouse or performing gestures on a screen. We browse by focusing our attention on the elements that we deem relevant to our main goal. This interaction model does not translate well to visually impaired users and scenarios of true mobility where the visual attention we can provide is limited.

Despite the advancements in assistive technology and the large body of literature on improving the experience for this population [2,5,16,34,46], visually impaired users experience several challenges in accessing the Web [11,14,24,32, 44]. The support provided by screen readers and non-visual browsers is essentially based on variations of sequentially reading a webpage from top to bottom, and

© Springer Nature Switzerland AG 2020
A. Følstad et al. (Eds.): CONVERSATIONS 2019, LNCS 11970, pp. 94–110, 2020.
https://doi.org/10.1007/978-3-030-39540-7_7

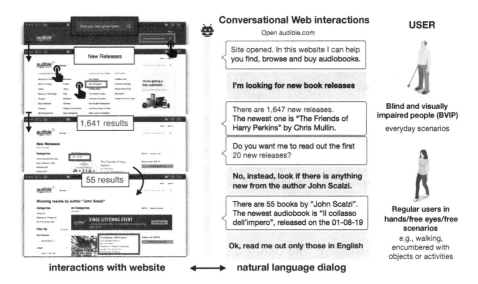

Fig. 1. Example conversational web interaction: the user engages in a dialog with a bot (right), which translates the user's requests into matching interactions with a website (left), enabling the user to browse the site in natural language (written or also spoken).

interacting with keyword shortcuts, which makes the process of translating user goals into a series of steps more time consuming and frustrating [32,37]. Adding to this, visually impaired users have to deal with poorly designed websites with no basic accessibility support [4,27], and the uncertainty of missing out information or not even knowing the source of the problems preventing them from completing their tasks [10]. Even when complying with standards and guidelines [18,46], the experience can be poor and frustrating [37]. In the end, accessibility does not necessarily mean usability.

The same can be said about mobility and attention-demanding scenarios that can lead to what is referred to as *situational impairments* [41], where contextual factors reduce our ability to interact visually. For example, using a mobile phone while walking not only reduces our visual, attention, and motor abilities [15], but can lead to distractions and risky behaviors [23,33]. A survey of more than 1000 adults in the US reported that 60% of the respondents use smartphones also while crossing the street, even if 70% of the total respondents perceived the behavior to be dangerous [25]. It is not surprising, thus, that injuries due to mobile phone distraction from 2004 to 2010 have almost tripled, mirroring that of driver's injuries for the same reason [33]. Browsing the Web while walking or driving are extreme cases but indicative of hands-free, eyes-free and minimal attention scenarios where traditional interaction models don't work.

In this paper we propose a new interaction paradigm for the Web that allows users to access websites by directly expressing their goals in dialog-based interactions with a conversational agent. To illustrate the concept, Fig. 1 shows an example of a goal-oriented conversation for browsing audiobooks, where user requests in natural language are translated by a conversational agent into automated actions applied to a website. Our approach is based on the idea of opening up the Web to an entire new generation of agents (e.g., Amazon Alexa, Google Assistant, Telegram), which currently need custom-built bots and skills to deliver services to their users. To this end, we introduce a reference model and architecture to allow web developers and content producers to make their websites "bot-friendly" without the need for implementing custom conversation logic, training Natural Language Understanding/Generation (NLU/NLG) models and all the effort that goes into developing new bots.

In the following we give an overview of the current state of the art to then introduce our proposed model and architecture.

2 State of the Art

2.1 Web Accessibility and Models for Non Visual Browsing

Efforts in making the web more accessible span across the development of standards, design guidelines, algorithms and inclusive development processes.

The Web Accessibility Initiative (WAI) of the World Wide Web Consortium (W3C) contributes with standards that are important in guiding the design of more accessible web pages and applications. Among these, the Web Content Accessibility Guidelines (WCAG) [46] provides recommendations for making content (and structure) accessible to people with disabilities, and are based on W3C technical specifications (e.g., HTML, CSS). The WAI also develops technical specifications such as Accessible Rich Internet Applications (WAI-ARIA) [17], which focus on making web applications – especially those with dynamic content and complex interactions – accessible to users of assistive technologies (e.g., screen readers). Implementing these standards is however in the hands of web developers and content producers.

In order to address the problems of compliance, a whole body of literature has been devoted to developing coping strategies. Automatic approaches have been proposed to facilitate navigation in the absence of the corresponding semantic annotations and structure [2,47] and generation of caption and audio descriptions for multimedia material [38,43]. Collaborative metadata authoring approaches [8,40,42] instead rely on volunteers to "fix" accessibility problems as they find them or upon request, and store the improvements in an external database that can be accessed by others. Other approaches aim to address the problem at the source, helping web developers be aware of accessibility during the design and development process [36].

The need for describing the content in web pages – and not only the structure – emerged with the development of rich snippets and machine processing of websites. Early approaches were based on microformats, with initiatives such as hCard, hCalendar and RDFa [21]. With the introduction of microdata support in HTML5, it became possible to describe the "items" in a page, using HTML properties to define the scope of the items, and key-value pairs to describe their attributes [39]. The absence of common vocabulary to refer to these items led major search engines (Bing, Google, Yahoo) to the creation of Schema.org [31]. This initiative offers and maintains a common vocabulary (for the most common "items" and their attributes) that simplified the annotation of data in web pages.

The VoiceXML [35] standard by the W3C offers a markup language for voice applications that can reuse the infrastructure developed for the Web. However, it requires developers to build custom applications or custom "chatbots" using the provided markup language. SALT [45] on the other hand is a lightweight markup language created in response to VoiceXML, but that still requires the grammar and logic for handling conversations to be declared in the webpages.

The above model and extensions provide a great foundation for improving accessibility in non visual browsing scenarios. However, they were not designed with conversational agents in mind, and so lack the necessary ingredients to turn websites into a dialog with the user.

2.2   Non Visual Web Browsing

A significant improvement on the linear navigation of screen readers was the introduction of the notion of navigation context. The CSurf [29] browser approach was to capture the context of a link, using structural properties and surrounding content, to identify the most relevant component in the next page, thus avoiding reading out sequentially from the beginning. The same group also worked on HearSay [13], a browser that builds on the idea of contextual browsing, incorporating machine learning and natural language processing to segment and automatically label web components so as to ease the navigation through semantically related content. It also aims at improving web transaction by identifying actionable items (e.g., "add to cart," "checkout") in web pages and making them easily available to the user. With a different take on context, the Sasayaki [48] browser aims at improving on the traditional navigation with a screen reader, by providing supplemental information in the form of page overviews and spatial and contextual cues (called whispers) on a secondary audio channel.

Focusing on performance, other approaches explored speech optimisations and summarisation of web pages. Gerrero and Conçalves [20] experimented with faster text-to-speech and multiple speech channels to speed up the scanning of relevant content by visually impaired users. Experiments showed that faster and concurrent speech significantly improved scanning while maintaining the level of comprehension. Summarisation is another widely explored technique, used for example to create "gists" of web pages (to decide on whether to read sections of a page) [22] and to facilitate non visual skimming [1].

The idea of using spoken commands to interact with the browser has also been explored in the literature. The most recent proponent of this idea is Capti-Speak [5], a speech-enabled screen reader for web browsing that aims at lowering the complexity of managing shortcuts in navigating with screen readers. This solution enables users to utter commands in natural language, which are identified as browsing actions ("press the cart button", "move to the search box") and interpreted in the context of the ongoing dialog. A user study with 20 blind participants showed that the approach was perceived as more usable and led to better browsing performance compared to a conventional screen reader.

Web automation is another area explored to improve the browsing experience. Voice-enabled macros for repetitive web-browsing have been built on top of the HearSay browser [12], allowing users to record and play their own macros. Bigham et al. [9] introduced the Trailblazer system, which focused on facilitating the process of creating web automation macros, by providing step by step suggestions based on CoScript [28]. The SeEbrowser [30] was designed to provide personalised browsing shortcuts to visually impaired users based on shortcuts useage statistics. Lau et al. [26] instead focused on facilitating the execution of macros, and proposed CoCo, a system for web automation that relies on a conversational interface based on (semi)structured language. The system simplifies the execution of repetitive tasks by allowing users to invoke CoScripter macros or "on the fly" tasks based on the user web history, in natural language.

Another interesting approach to automation is proposed by Ashok et al. [6], where the goal is to free users from performing low level interactions with HTML elements by adding a layer of abstraction on higher level web entities (e.g., "search results", "calendar", "menu", "forms"), and allowing users to execute navigation commands, invoke actions and answer queries. For example, instead of dealing with the complex interaction of a calendar widget, users would directly say "Choose return date 28" on the calendar entity, and the underlying interaction manager would try to execute the appropriate steps.

All of the infrastructure, guidelines and optimisations above were done with the traditional web agent in mind, and while they provide valuable contributions and inspiration for our work, the approaches are not suitable for the conversational web interaction we envisioned in this paper.

3   Conversational Web Interaction

Next, we elaborate on the idea of conversational web interaction, introduce the need for a dedicated conversational agent (a *bot* or *chatbot*), and identify the key requirements that drive our research.

3.1   Concept

Recalling the example conversation in Fig. 1, the interaction paradigm we propose in this paper is based on a bi-directional use of *natural language*. Users either write and read text in a chat window (*written* interaction) or talk and listen (*vocal* interaction). Instead of directly interacting with a target website inside the web browser, they interact with a *bot* that serves as mediator between the user and the website and is able to *translate* back and forth between natural language input/output and website interactions (e.g., reading text, filling form fields, navigating links). While the latter are generally the same across different websites, the bot automatically extracts the necessary *domain-specific vocabulary* and *knowledge about available features* from the target website, e.g., it learns that the site allows users to "buy an audio-book" or that it can "read an abstract." Upon a specific instruction by the user, such as "find books by John Grisham," the bot *autonomously interacts with the website on behalf of the user* and presents users only with the final results, preventing them from having to learn how to do so themselves.

Content and functionality of the website can be accessed in a *random access* fashion: just like in any conversation or in visual web browsing, the user can jump from one topic (e.g., reading the summary of a book) to another one (e.g., searching for music), without the need to leaf though or listen to potentially lengthy lists of options. This is different from conventional screen readers and the related works discussed previously, which depend on the structure of the website and require the user either to use the keyboard to walk through options or to utter structure-specific instructions like "go to search box," "enter XYZ," and "submit." In other words, the paradigm is *goal driven*, not structure driven.

3.2   Requirements

The goal of our research is to study how to enable conversational interactions on top of existing websites; the development of generic, stand-alone chatbots is out of the scope of this work. Enabling the described conversational interaction paradigm for the Web requires thus two fundamental ingredients, a *chatbot* mediating between the user and the website and a purposefully designed, *conversation-oriented annotation* of content and functions enabling the bot to get acquainted with the website. The bot provides basic, cross-application conversation support, while the annotation equips the bot with the necessary application-specific knowledge. The core requirements for the development of the bot and the annotation are:

1. *Orientation*: Given the URL of a website, the bot must be able to summarize the content and/or functionalities offered by the website, in order to allow the user to understand what the site offers and to provide for basic access structures. The role of the summary is similar to that of conventional menus or navigation bars in visual browsing. For instance, the bot in Fig. 1 tells the user that it is able to "find, browse and buy audiobooks."
2. *Vocabulary*: As exemplified further in the conversation, the bot should be able to speak the language of the target website. It should not understand and master only generic terminology (e.g., "navigate" or "click"), but also site-specific terminology (e.g., "find a book" or "leave a comment").
3. *Informational vs. transaction tasks*: The bot should not only render the content vocally or textually, which is the basic ingredient for the delivery of informational services (e.g., reading out loud the description of an audiobook – essentially reading content from websites). It must also be able to parse vocal/textual input and forward it to the website, enabling full-fledged, transactional services (e.g., searching for a given author – essentially interacting with websites).

4. *Intents and intent parameters*: The bot must be able to understand the user's intent when speaking or writing, so as to be able to enact suitable actions in response. Intents may be application-agnostic (e.g., fill a form field, read a title) or application-specific (e.g., buy an audiobook, write a review). Intents may further require parameters: searching a book is an intent; searching the book by author "John Scalzi" is an intent equipped with a suitable target.
5. *Action enactment*: As the bot mediates between the user and the website, enacting an action in response to an identified intent means interacting with the website on behalf of the user. The bot must thus be able to mimic user interactions with the website, such as navigating a link or filling a form.
6. *Feedback*: As the user is now interacting with a bot and not with the actual website, it is important that the bot be able to provide feedback on the outcome of actions. For example, a navigation action may fail or a form submission may succeed. These outcomes must be communicated back to the user for confirmation and orientation.
7. *Context*: Natural language conversations, if split into chunks of text, may be ambiguous. It is for instance common to claim that something was cited "out of context" and, hence, may be misleading. It is thus crucial that the bot be able to maintain conversational context and to disambiguate between similar utterances in function of context.
8. *Pro-activity*: Conversational agents are mostly reactive to user requests, yet sometimes pro-active behaviors may be needed. For instance, if content changes dynamically inside a page or if a user is to be guided through a form filling process, the initiative of the conversation may come from the bot instead of from the user. The bot may also pro-actively suggest possible next actions, like in our example.

Satisfying these requirements will require an interplay between the generic bot and the application-specific annotation. For example, only a proper annotation of an application-specific intent will allow the bot to know that it must not only identify the intent (e.g., search author) but also collect a respective parameter (the author name).

3.3 Design Principles

The annotation of the website assumes thus a central role in enabling the envisioned paradigm. In this respect, the assumption underlying our proposal is that, if needed, web pages can be extended with annotations, e.g., standard WAI-ARIA annotations [17] or custom bot annotations, to instruct the bot.

Equipping an existing web page with an annotation to enable conversational interactions implies of course an additional effort to the developer of the website (just like complying with accessibility in general). In order to keep the effort low and effective, the ideas we propose in this paper further build on the following simple design principles:

1. *No need for custom chatbot code.* The goal is to prevent web developers from having to master also chatbot development to equip their websites with

conversational interactions. Developers should thus not have to write any own line of chatbot code.

2. *Separation of conversation model from NLU.* Modern chatbots typically feature AI-powered natural language interpretation requiring proper training before use. We want to prevent developers from having to train themselves the bot and instead want to automate this task and ask developers just to provide the necessary domain-specific vocabulary.

3. *Presentation (NLG) managed by bot.* Developers should not have to worry about how to render outputs (dialog responses), be them vocal or written. The bot should fully take care of this task to harmonise the user experience.

4. *Web developers keep control of the experience.* While we think it is crucial to take over as many tasks as possible, it is however crucial that developers be in control of what happens. Through a sensible annotation of their sites they should be able to control which features of a site to equip with a conversational interface.

5. *Support for social botification.* For those cases in which developers do not provide suitable annotations, it should be possible for interested users to provide them externally and collaboratively and to share them with others for reuse and refinement.

Next we show how we intend to satisfy requirements and design principles with a concrete software architecture.

4   Approach

4.1   Conversation Model

The conversation model driving the envisioned chatbot is a refinement of the conventional *input-intent-action-response* model of modern conversational agents: The user provides an *input* (e.g., "Which audiobooks have been released this week?") that expresses an *intent* of action (e.g., "search for recent audiobooks"). The chatbot interprets the input and extracts the intent – this typically involves the use of a dedicated Natural Language Unit leveraging on AI – to match the intent to an action that allows the bot to meet the user's request (e.g., the bot could navigate to the page with the latest book releases and identify the most recent ones). The execution of this action produces an output that can be used by the bot to generate an informative *response* for the user (e.g., "Five new books have been released this week"). The response may or may not contain a solicitation for the user to provide further input (e.g., "Should I read out loud the titles of the books?").

The refinement consists of two core aspects: (i) the selection of a set of *reactive actions* that are specifically tailored to enabling a natural language conversation with websites and (ii) support for *pro-active actions* enabling the bot to take the initiative in conversations, e.g., in response to updated content inside a page or new content or features appearing in the page. Figure 2 graphically summarizes the key concepts of the target conversation model.

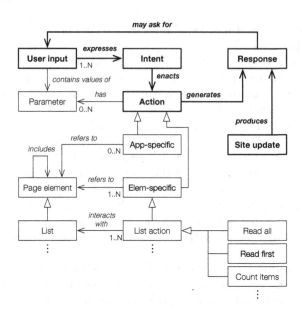

Fig. 2. Model of conversational web interaction. In bold the core conversation logic as interplay between user inputs, actions and responses. Actions are refined into application- and element-specific actions.

The reactive actions are split into two types: *Application-specific* actions express interactions with the website that allow the user to achieve application-specific goals, such as finding or buying an audiobook. *Element-specific* actions refer to presentation elements of a web page and allow the user to interact with the element. Typical elements are forms, form fields, buttons, paragraphs, headers, and similar (identified through suitable HTML tags). Element-specific actions are pre-defined and implemented once for all. Application-specific actions are configured by the developers of the site and refer too to presentation elements to indicate where in a page the respective action can be carried out.

Managing a dialog is now an iteration between application- and element-specific actions: Given an application-specific action, the bot moves the focus of its analysis to the respective presentation element (e.g., a form). Next, it analyzes the content of the element, identifies the presentation elements it comprises and enacts element-specific actions, involving the user when necessary.

4.2   Architecture

The software architecture we propose to reify the above conceptual model and to satisfy the requirements identified earlier is graphically summarized in Fig. 3. The architecture is split into a design phase (top part) and an execution phase (lower part). The key components are: A *botifier*, i.e., a component that is able to parse and analyze a given website identified by its URL and to extract orientation information (requirement R1) and the necessary conversational domain

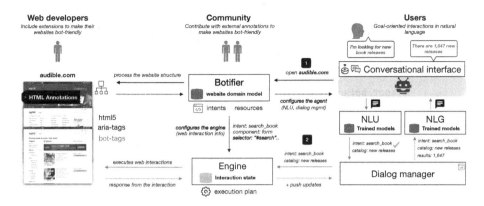

Fig. 3. Reference architecture for conversational web interaction. The number labels correspond to (1) the process of botifying web pages (design time) and (2) the management of user-website dialogs (runtime). In light blue the actors in the ecosystem. (Color figure online)

knowledge (R2). A possibly annotated *website* the user wants to interact with. A *conversational interface* (e.g., a chat window or an Amazon Echo device) with an NLU for input processing (R3, R4) and an NLG for output generation (R6, R8). A *dialog manager* able to manage the conversation with the user, to keep conversational context (R7), and to act on the website on behalf of the user using the *engine*, which implements the necessary logic to mimic user interactions (R5) and to monitor updates (R8) using a headless browser. We discuss website annotation, botification and conversation management in more detail below.

4.3 Content/Function Annotation

The challenge of bot development is training the bot with domain vocabulary and actions. We have seen that there are no ready models or annotations for doing so. The question is thus how to obtain the necessary information.

Microdata[1] allows one to annotate content in web pages with semantics, and initiatives such as Schema.org offer a common vocabulary for popular items on the Web. For example, search results in audible could be annotated with `itemtype=http://schema.org/Audiobook` to describe the type of entity. These annotations could unambiguously describe content and facilitate connecting user requests ("Who is the [narrator]?") to presentation elements. ARIA and HTML5 provide semantic annotations/tags and notifications or errors or updates when new, dynamic content appears. When annotating websites for accessibility, developers are thus already facilitating the automation of web interactions.

There are however no annotations or vocabularies for describing operations, let alone app-specific actions. For example, functionalities like "search", "play"

---

[1] https://html.spec.whatwg.org/multipage/microdata.html.

```
<form role="search"
  aria-controls="results"
  bot-intent="search_book"
  bot-resource="Audiobook">

  <input bot-param="query"
    aria-label="Insert keywords"
    type="search" name="keywords">

  <input bot-param="author"
    aria-label="Insert author name"
    type="text" name="sAuthor">

  <div role="alert"
    bot-inform="error">
  </div>

  <button role="submit">
</form>
```

bot-intent
Associates the *search_book* intent to the form. If this references an intent in a pre-trained model, richer interactions will be enabled.

bot-resource
Defines the specific type of item associated to the intent, which helps configure the specific vocabulary for invoking the intent.

bot-param
Associates the intent parameters to specific elements, which specify the specific parameters used in this website, and facilitates the automatic filling out. In the absence of domain-specific NLU model for the intent, slot filling is performed by reading out aria labels.

bot-inform
Changes to alert informs that the user should be notified, and the bot inform qualifies the nature of the specific alert, in this case an error.

aria-tags
Describe the role of the components, defines the type of low interaction to perform and how

Fig. 4. Concept of joint use of standard ARIA and custom annotations for instructing the bot with domain knowledge (an intent with action).

and "buy" audiobooks are usually listed in menus, but are meant for visual, human consumption. It could thus be an option to introduce specific bot properties, such as "bot-intent" to identify HTML tags (e.g., form, input, link) that match user intents and that the bot can operate on behalf of the user.

Figure 4 provides a feeling of how different annotations could be used together to achieve the task.

4.4   Botification

The *botifier* parses a page's markup and annotations and derives a *domain model*, which configures the bot with the interactions the user can have with the website. Intents and parameters (**bot-intent** and **bot-param** in Fig. 4) define the requests the user can perform and the information that should be provided in order to do so. The vocabulary (named items and properties), in addition to the intents, configures the NLU with the language users can use to express goals.

Enacting user intents during the dialog is then the job of the *engine*. It, too, is configured by the botifier, which binds the execution of actions to information about the mapping between dialog concepts (items, intents and parameters) and the associated presentation components in the webpage. At runtime, the engine supports enacting actions associated to user intents, using the structured information provided by the NLU (e.g., action: "search_book", params: [author : "John Scalzi"]) and operating a headless browser.

While reading out the results of a search, the bot should be able to tell the user what to do with a specific book in that context at run-time (e.g., share, play a sample, go to details). In this respect, the state of the web page provides context to the interactions that can be allowed during the conversation and that can help the users fulfill their intents. The engine should then be able to provide (and update) the bot with the state of allowed actions that can be used for dialog management.

While the botification process relies on developers providing the proper annotations, the approach can be extended to allow for collaborative metadata authoring efforts such as those seen in the web accessibility community [8,40,42]. In this case, volunteers would provide the domain model, possibly aided by tools and browsers extensions, and store them in a shared repository that can be consulted during botification.

4.5   Conversation Management

The actual *bot* is composed of the conversational interface, the NLU and NLG, and the dialog manger. It manages the bidirectional communication with the user. Natural language understanding is based on pre-trained models on two levels of abstraction: domain-specific and general models.

Domain-specific models could be trained on the most common transactions and queries in certain domains of applications and allow for highly expressive and natural interactions. Training such models would require identifying common, domain-specific intents and run data collection tasks (e.g., crowdsourced [7]) to build a training dataset. This is of course a costly enterprise, and would require efforts at the right level of abstraction, but we can see initiatives similar to Schema.org defining ontologies of intents, and data collection efforts based on volunteers, as a potential direction.

General models may offer a layer of abstraction on top of generic Web components and actions on websites. For example, a general model could be trained for browsing search results or lists of items, with intents such as *read, filter, sort, ask,* supporting general requests like "sort [items] by [param]". Training such general models requires less effort, but would provide for less expressive queries.

Once a user intent is recognized and validated by the NLU, the dialog manager forwards the request to the engine and stores the extracted request information in the conversational context so that it becomes implicit in future interactions during the session. The dialog manager also decides on when to take proactive actions. The output from enacting these actions is then passed through the NLG, which has built-in models for responses in natural language.

The response is then processed to fit the format (and protocol) of the specific bot platform where the session was initiated (e.g., Amazon Alexa, Telegram), which will be in charge of managing the actual interactions with the user in their native conversation modality (text or audio). This requires the integration with existing platforms, with the necessary extensions to provide a proper experience fitting the modality and design language of the target platform.

5 Benefits and Challenges

Conversational web interactions that allow users to express their goals by talking to a website have the potential to change the way we interact with the Web, making it truly *inclusive* and *ubiquitous*. The benefits we identify are:

Improve the Browsing Experience for Visually Impaired Users. The proposed model is a significant improvement over the linear navigation in screen reader technology. Enabling users to express intents directly can reduce the impoverishment of linear transformation of visual information [19] and lower frustration.

Mobile Browsing. A consequence of allowing users to express their intents directly in a goal-oriented spoken dialog is the potential to lower the cognitive load associated with having to perform low-level interactions with websites, making browsing safer and more effective in low-attention situations.

Opening Up the Web to a New Generation of Clients. The proposed model and architecture could enable the now pervasive conversational agents and voice assistants such as Amazon Alexa, Siri, Google Assistant and chatbots, to access websites. This has the potential to improve the browsing experience in mutliple scenarios.

Promoting Adoption of Accessibility Guidelines. We believe making Web accessibility an ingredient of exciting new scenarios for web interactions can boost the adoption of accessibility guidelines and specifications, thus benefiting web accessibility in general.

Platform for Bot Development and Prototyping. We believe this approach is amenable to companies who do not have the budget or capability to develop ad hoc conversational agents to access their content and functionality. This is akin to what happens in web design where the option of developing a mobile app (probably the best approach for a mobile experience) coexists with responsive web designs and other approaches to design or annotate a website so that it can be consumed effectively by mobile users.

The key challenges we see to achieve these benefits are:

Reuse of the Existing Web Infrastructure. Building on the existing infrastructure, such as reusing existing technical specifications and standards for accessibility, should not break the experience for existing users of assistive technology and general users. Understanding what parts to reuse and how is one of the key aspects in materialising a conversational model.

Backward Compatibility, and Trade-Off Between Explicit and Inferred Domain Models. We have discussed an approach that is model-driven as it is important to have a reference model that will also allow developers to be in control of the experience. However, adoption is always a challenge, and so algorithms and heuristics could emerge, in the same way the accessibility community has been coping with this problem over the years.

Organizing Community Efforts. Another reason for following such an architecture is that the way a page is "used" is eventually dictated by the community of users, and we can envision communities of users as well as communities of developers creating "overlays" over a web site to make it "botifiable" and provide the annotations - and training data to map utterances into intents, and possibly even actions. Organizing and enabling such community efforts is another challenge.

Privacy and Security. Managing privacy and security in a context where users express their intents directly is another challenge. We did not address this issue in this paper but it is an area that will need further research.

Understanding how to deliver the experience, in what scenarios, and for what classes of websites it is suited, are all open questions that need to be addressed.

6   Directions for Future Work

The idea of conversational web interaction proposed in this paper opens up a need for further, fundamental research in key areas, including:

- Models, approaches and authoring tools to extend websites with conversational capabilities. This implies working with the underlying technical specifications of the Web (e.g., HTML, CSS, ARIA) to introduce the minimal set of extensions to allow web developers, the community or machine-based approaches to dote websites with conversational capabilities.
- Approaches for deriving conversational interfaces directly from websites. This has to do with the exploration of approaches to turn websites into dialogues with a user: from recognising user requests in natural language to enacting the necessary web interactions in the target website and preparing responses for the specific device and medium.
- Identifying effective design guidelines for conversational web interactions. Building successful experiences would require identifying and validating guidelines and best practices that go beyond general scenarios [3] to inform the design of effective and high-quality conversational web experiences.
- Understanding the impact of conversational web interactions in the target scenarios. This has to do with collecting evidence of the impact of the new paradigm in the accessibility and user experience, and understanding in what scenarios and in what form it can have the biggest impact.

We are currently exploring the technical feasibility through prototyping the various components of the architecture. Preliminary results confirm the feasibility of both general and domain-specific conversation models from suitably annotated HTML markup with a special focus on HTML lists and forms. With this basic infrastructure we plan to run the first exploratory user studies.

Acknowledgement. The study was supported by the Russian Science Foundation (project n. 19-18-00282).

References

1. Ahmed, F., Borodin, Y., Soviak, A., Islam, M., Ramakrishnan, I., Hedgpeth, T.: Accessible skimming: faster screen reading of web pages. In: UIST, pp. 367–378. ACM (2012)
2. Akpinar, M.E., Yeşilada, Y.: Discovering visual elements of web pages and their roles: users' perception. Interact. Comput. **29**(6), 845–867 (2017)
3. Amershi, S., et al.: Guidelines for human-AI interaction. In: Proceedings of CHI 2019, p. 3. ACM (2019)
4. Asakawa, C.: What's the web like if you can't see it? In: W4A, pp. 1–8. ACM (2005)
5. Ashok, V., Borodin, Y., Puzis, Y., Ramakrishnan, I.: Capti-speak: a speech-enabled web screen reader. In: W4A, p. 22. ACM (2015)
6. Ashok, V., Puzis, Y., Borodin, Y., Ramakrishnan, I.: Web screen reading automation assistance using semantic abstraction. In: IUI, pp. 407–418. ACM (2017)
7. Asri, L.E., et al.: Frames: a corpus for adding memory to goal-oriented dialogue systems. arXiv preprint arXiv:1704.00057 (2017)
8. Bigham, J.P.: Accessmonkey: enabling and sharing end user accessibility improvements. ACM SIGACCESS Access. Comput. **89**, 3–6 (2007)
9. Bigham, J.P., Lau, T., Nichols, J.: Trailblazer: enabling blind users to blaze trails through the web. In: IUI, pp. 177–186. ACM (2009)
10. Bigham, J.P., Lin, I., Savage, S.: The effects of not knowing what you don't know on web accessibility for blind web users. In: ACM SIGACCESS. ACM (2017)
11. Billah, S.M., Ashok, V., Porter, D.E., Ramakrishnan, I.: Ubiquitous accessibility for people with visual impairments: are we there yet? In: CHI, pp. 5862–5868. ACM (2017)
12. Borodin, Y.: Automation of repetitive web browsing tasks with voice-enabled macros. In: Proceedings of SIGACCESS 2008, pp. 307–308. ACM (2008)
13. Borodin, Y., et al.: Hearsay: a new generation context-driven multi-modal assistive web browser. In: WWW, pp. 1233–1236. ACM (2010)
14. Christian, K., Kules, B., Shneiderman, B., Youssef, A.: A comparison of voice controlled and mouse controlled web browsing. In: Proceedings of the Fourth International ACM Conference on Assistive Technologies, pp. 72–79. ACM (2000)
15. Conradi, J., Alexander, T.: Analysis of visual performance during the use of mobile devices while walking. In: Harris, D. (ed.) EPCE 2014. LNCS (LNAI), vol. 8532, pp. 133–142. Springer, Cham (2014). https://doi.org/10.1007/978-3-319-07515-0_14
16. De Rosa, A., Justice, D.: WebReader: a screen reader for everyone, everywhere. In: Proceedings of the 13th Web for All Conference, p. 10. ACM (2016)
17. Diggs, J., Craig, J., McCarron, S., Cooper, M.: Accessible rich Internet applications (WAI-ARIA) 1.1 (2016). Accessed 24 Apr 2016
18. Fecke, A., Jeleniowski, S., Joisten, M.: Accessible websites for the visually impaired: guidelines for designers. In: Mensch & Computer Workshopband, pp. 419–422 (2015)
19. Giraud, S., Thérouanne, P., Steiner, D.D.: Web accessibility: filtering redundant and irrelevant information improves website usability for blind users. Int. J. Hum Comput Stud. **111**, 23–35 (2018)
20. Guerreiro, J., Gonçalves, D.: Faster text-to-speeches: enhancing blind people's information scanning with faster concurrent speech. In: ACM SIGACCESS, pp. 3–11. ACM (2015)

21. Guha, R.V., Brickley, D., Macbeth, S.: Schema.org: evolution of structured data on the web. Commun. ACM **59**(2), 44–51 (2016)
22. Harper, S., Patel, N.: Gist summaries for visually impaired surfers. In: ACM SIGACCESS Conference on Computers and Accessibility, pp. 90–97. ACM (2005)
23. Hyman Jr., I.E., Boss, S.M., Wise, B.M., McKenzie, K.E., Caggiano, J.M.: Did you see the unicycling clown? Inattentional blindness while walking and talking on a cell phone. Appl. Cogn. Psychol. **24**(5), 597–607 (2010)
24. Inan, F.A., Namin, A.S., Pogrund, R.L., Jones, K.S.: Internet use and cybersecurity concerns of individuals with visual impairments. J. Educ. Technol. Soc. **19**(1), 28–40 (2016)
25. Insurance, L.M.: Pedestrian safety survey (2013). https://bit.ly/2WIDeOM
26. Lau, T., Cerruti, J., Manzato, G., Bengualid, M., Bigham, J.P., Nichols, J.: A conversational interface to web automation. In: UIST, pp. 229–238. ACM (2010)
27. Lazar, J., Allen, A., Kleinman, J., Malarkey, C.: What frustrates screen reader users on the web: a study of 100 blind users. Int. J. Hum.-Comput. Interact. **22**(3), 247–269 (2007)
28. Leshed, G., Haber, E.M., Matthews, T., Lau, T.: CoScripter: automating & sharing how-to knowledge in the enterprise. In: CHI, pp. 1719–1728. ACM (2008)
29. Mahmud, J.U., Borodin, Y., Ramakrishnan, I.: Csurf: a context-driven non-visual web-browser. In: Proceedings of WWW 2007, pp. 31–40. ACM (2007)
30. Michail, S., Christos, K.: Adaptive browsing shortcuts: personalising the user interface of a specialised voice web browser for blind people. In: Data Engineering Workshop, 2007, pp. 818–825. IEEE (2007)
31. Mika, P.: On schema.org and why it matters for the web. IEEE Internet Comput. **19**(4), 52–55 (2015)
32. Murphy, E., Kuber, R., McAllister, G., Strain, P., Yu, W.: An empirical investigation into the difficulties experienced by visually impaired Internet users. Univ. Access Inf. Soc. **7**(1–2), 79–91 (2008)
33. Nasar, J.L., Troyer, D.: Pedestrian injuries due to mobile phone use in public places. Accid. Anal. Prev. **57**, 91–95 (2013)
34. Oney, S., Lundgard, A., Krosnick, R., Nebeling, M., Lasecki, W.S.: Arboretum and arbility: improving web accessibility through a shared browsing architecture. In: UIST, pp. 937–949. ACM (2018)
35. Oshry, M., Auburn, R., Baggia, P., Bodell, M., Burke, D., Burnett, D., et al.: Voice extensible markup language (voicexml) 2.1. w3c recommendation (2007)
36. Plessers, P., et al.: Accessibility: a web engineering approach. In: Proceedings of WWW 2005, pp. 353–362. ACM (2005)
37. Power, C., Freire, A., Petrie, H., Swallow, D.: Guidelines are only half of the story: accessibility problems encountered by blind users on the web. In: Proceedings of CHI 2012, pp. 433–442. ACM (2012)
38. Rohrbach, M., Qiu, W., Titov, I., Thater, S., Pinkal, M., Schiele, B.: Translating video content to natural language descriptions. In: Proceedings of the IEEE International Conference on Computer Vision, pp. 433–440 (2013)
39. Ronallo, J.: Html5 microdata and schema.org. Code4Lib J. (16) (2012)
40. Sato, D., Takagi, H., Kobayashi, M., Kawanaka, S., Asakawa, C.: Exploratory analysis of collaborative web accessibility improvement. ACM TACCESS **3**(2), 5 (2010)
41. Sears, A., Lin, M., Jacko, J., Xiao, Y.: When computers fade: pervasive computing and situationally-induced impairments and disabilities. HCI Int. **2**, 1298–1302 (2003)

42. Takagi, H., Kawanaka, S., Kobayashi, M., Itoh, T., Asakawa, C.: Social accessibility: achieving accessibility through collaborative metadata authoring. In: ACM SIGACCESS Conference on Computers and Accessibility, pp. 193–200. ACM (2008)
43. Tran, K., et al.: Rich image captioning in the wild. In: Proceedings of the IEEE Conference on Computer Vision and Pattern Recognition, pp. 49–56 (2016)
44. Voykinska, V., Azenkot, S., Wu, S., Leshed, G.: How blind people interact with visual content on social networking services. In: CSCW, pp. 1584–1595. ACM (2016)
45. Wang, K.: SALT: a spoken language interface for web-based multimodal dialog systems. In: Seventh International Conference on Spoken Language Processing (2002)
46. WWW-Consortium et al.: Web content accessibility guidelines (WCAG) 2.1 w3c candidate recommendation (2018). Accessed 30 Jan 2018
47. Yesilada, Y.: Web page segmentation: a review (2011)
48. Zhu, S., Sato, D., Takagi, H., Asakawa, C.: Sasayaki: an augmented voice-based web browsing experience. In: Proceedings of SIGACCESS 2010. ACM (2010)

Chatbots for Collaboration

Designing Chatbots for Guiding Online Peer Support Conversations for Adults with ADHD

Oda Elise Nordberg[1]([✉])[iD], Jo Dugstad Wake[1][iD], Emilie Sektnan Nordby[3][iD], Eivind Flobak[1][iD], Tine Nordgreen[3][iD], Suresh Kumar Mukhiya[2][iD], and Frode Guribye[1][iD]

[1] University of Bergen, Bergen, Norway
{oda.nordberg,jo.wake,frode.guribye,eivind.flobak}@uib.no
[2] Western Norway University of Applied Sciences, Bergen, Norway
skmu@hvl.no
[3] Division of Psychiatry, Haukeland University Hospital, Bergen, Norway
emilie.nordby@student.uib.no, tine.nordgreen@helse-bergen.no

Abstract. This paper presents an exploratory study of how conversational interfaces can be used to facilitate peer support among adults with ADHD participating in an online self-help program. Peer support is an important feature of group therapy, but it is often disregarded in online programs. Using a research-through-design approach, a low fidelity chatbot prototype named Terabot was designed and evaluated. The goal of Terabot is to guide participants through peer support conversations related to a specific exercise in an online self-help program. The prototype was evaluated and refined through two Wizard of Oz (WoOz) trials. Based on design workshops, analysis of chat logs, data from online questionnaires and an evaluation interview, the findings indicate that the concept of a chatbot guiding a peer support conversation between adults with ADHD who participate in an online self-help program is a promising approach. We believe that a chatbot can help establishing structure, predictability and encouragement in a peer support conversation. This study contributes with experiences from an exploration of how to design conversational interfaces for peer support in mental health care, how conversational interfaces can facilitate peer support through structuring conversation, and how the WoOz approach can be used to inform the design of chatbots.

Keywords: Peer support · Chatbots · Conversational interfaces · HCI · Wizard of Oz · ADHD

1 Introduction

The emergence and recent widespread adoption of conversational interfaces bring about new challenges for researchers and practitioners in human-computer

© Springer Nature Switzerland AG 2020
A. Følstad et al. (Eds.): CONVERSATIONS 2019, LNCS 11970, pp. 113–126, 2020.
https://doi.org/10.1007/978-3-030-39540-7_8

interaction (HCI) [16,33]. When designing for conversational user interfaces or chatbots, the conversations become the objects of design, creating new HCI opportunities [16] compared for example to graphical user interfaces. Most of the research on conversational interfaces is about facilitating interaction between a single user and the chatbot, while our research is about how a chatbot can facilitate conversation between a group of human users. Seering et al. argue that chatbots have potential beyond dyadic communication (i.e. between a single user and the chatbot), and that expansion into this design space could support richer social interactions, and fulfil a role in maintaining, moderating, and growing online communities [27].

The present study is a part of a larger ongoing study investigating an online self-help program for adults with Attention Deficit/Hyperactivity Disorder (ADHD) inspired by Goal Management Training, Cognitive Behavioral Therapy and Dialectic Behavioral Therapy. ADHD is a common neurodevelopmental disorder that often persists into adulthood [3]. The core symptoms of ADHD are inattention, hyperactivity and impulsivity [3]. The main treatment for adults with ADHD is pharmacological treatment, but the demand for psychological treatment is increasing [28]. Additionally, there is a global call for diverse treatment strategies for mental health problems, and in particular non-pharmacological treatment alternatives (e.g. [8]). One of these alternatives is online self-help programs [13].

Most of the evaluated psychological treatments for adults with ADHD are conducted in face-to-face groups [26], where there is a conscious effort to create a social environment that is beneficial to the participants. When transferring to online treatment, new challenges for creating a supportive interpersonal context arises and must be realigned. As a step towards reaching this goal, we explore how a chatbot can be designed and work as a tool to facilitate peer support in an online self-help program.

This paper presents a research-through-design [34] study of the design process and evaluation of a chatbot prototype aiming at facilitating peer support in an online self-help program for adults with ADHD. The prototype is designed in co-operation with clinical psychologists and adults with ADHD. We consider the main contribution in our paper to be tied to three themes; understanding how to guide conversations in the context of online peer support; examining the potential for a conversational interface to guide group chats; and reviewing the benefits and limitations of using WoOz trials in the design of a peer support conversational interface. The main research question is:

How can we design conversational interfaces to facilitate peer support in an online self-help program?

1.1 Conversational Interfaces in Mental Health

Conversational interfaces are technologies that provide users with access to data and services through natural language dialogue [16]. Over recent years, chatbots have been increasingly studied for their potential value to mental health endeavors [32]. Chatbots have for example been used to deliver mental health screening questionnaires for alcohol misuse [12], ADHD in adults [18], PTSD [20] and stress [7]. Chatbots have also been used to facilitate increased health information access [5], and successfully deliver cognitive behavioral therapy [15]. In a recent review of 41 chatbots for mental health, Abd-alrazaq et al. [1] describe the main chatbot purposes as to provide therapy (17), training (12), screening (10), self-management (7), counselling (5), education (4) and diagnosing (2). Chatbots have been shown to increase task adherence in psychoeducation, when the chatbot is trusted by the participant [31], and to increase user willingness to engage in interaction and increase number of utterances in multi-party dialogues [11]. Chatbots as parties to multi-party dialogues is under-explored in chatbot research however, and would entail emulating human online behavior such as multiparty interactions, turn-taking, role-taking, timing, and construction [27]. We are particularly interested in how a chatbot can delimit and structure conversations in online therapy groups, for example making sure everyone takes part and feels included, that the dialogue is focused on certain topics, and that tasks and exercises are completed.

1.2   Peer Support and Self-help Programs

Peer support concerns people in similar situations supporting each other by sharing personal experiences, knowledge, and emotional support [22,29]. According to Hurvitz "Individuals with the same problems serve as the most effective role models for each other" [19, p. 47], meaning that peers have great potential to influence each other. Peer support has been demonstrated to promote treatment engagement, prevent treatment drop out, increase confidence, improve mental health and well-being, as well as increasing one's ability to deal with issues related to stigma and discrimination [2,14]. Moreover, the incorporation of peers has also been regarded as an effective and helpful element by adults with ADHD participating in group-based treatments [26].

Online peer support is based on the same principles as traditional peer support, but a key difference is the use of Internet technology to communicate. Such technologies can be forums, chat rooms, private groups on social media (e.g. Facebook groups), and peer support websites [13]. In recent years, promising research on peer support technology has emerged in relation to mental health and online interventions. Research (e.g. [24,25]) indicates that online peer support can have many of the same benefits as traditional peer support.

A major challenge with online self-help programs is lack of sustained adherence [10]. Baumeister et al. [4] stresses that guidance is a beneficial feature and should be included in online interventions if possible. Several authors (e.g. [4,23,31]) have found that the presence of accountable and trusted moderators enhances participant motivation and adherence in online therapy environments. Ly et al. [21] argument that chatbots can have the potential to increase adherence and engagement in online self-help programs. They hypothesize that this is due to the chatbot's capability of mimicking human interactional qualities similar to those found in-person interventions.

2   Methods

This study was carried out as research-through-design (RtD) [34], a methodology that ties interaction design to the research field of HCI. In RtD artefact design and knowledge construction are equal parts of the research process, and the design outcomes should, ideally, transform the world from its current state and to a preferred state. The *relevance* of the artefact is one of the quality measures of a study. As such, we have explored whether and how the important function of peer support in online self-help programs can be provided in the form of a chatbot.

WoOz is a low-fidelity prototyping method that can be used to test requirements and evaluate concepts, and is often considered effective in the early stages of a project. In WoOz trials a human operator (the wizard) simulates a fully functioning software to the participants, while it in reality still is an early prototype. WoOz experiments can be an efficient way of testing the potential of a new chatbot, by easily testing user preferences, scripts, personality attributes, response times, and other important features [9,33]. As WoOz trials normally do not facilitate designers to experiment with the technology's capabilities and limitations, Yang et al. [33] proposed an alternative WoOz trial. Their version emphasizes the importance of facilitating for likely errors, as these may have user experience consequences to consider: For example, users may become frustrated at the chatbot asking a question they already answered, and this should be considered by the designers.

We used WoOz as a proof of concept, to develop requirements, to evaluate the scripts for the chatbot, and to explore using WoOz as a method for designing a scripted chatbot. We conducted two WoOz trials, where the first followed the standard WoOz layout and the second followed the alternative WoOz approach. In the first trial the wizard was allowed to do some improvising if needed, while in the second trial the wizard strictly followed the requirements, scripts and a prompts document. The layout of the two trials was identical: Users participated in two group chats guided by the wizard who took the role as Terabot. The first chat was an introduction to an exercise from the self-help program, and the second chat focused on the execution and experience with the exercise. Participants were expected to practice the exercise by themselves between the two chat sessions.

The two trials had a total of 13 participants. Trial 1 had nine participants, recruited by convenience sampling through the researchers' personal networks. For Trial 2 we used purposive sampling and recruited four adults diagnosed with ADHD. They were contacted through a lived experience representatives group for ADHD that was already set up for the existing project.

The participants in Trial 1 were not required to be diagnosed with ADHD, as the main goal of Trial 1 was to practically test whether the chatbot scripts and trial organisation were ready to be used with adults with ADHD. Trial 2 had a lower number of participants due to the increased challenge in recruiting participants with an ADHD diagnose. The age range in Trial 1 was 23 to 65, with three male and six female participants. The age range in Trial 2 was 33 to 66, three female and one male participant. Two of the participants in Trial 2 dropped out after the first half of the trial. The participants who completed Trial 2 took part in an evaluation interview session after the trial.

The participants completed a questionnaire after each chat session. The questionnaires were developed by the researchers and contained questions regarding experienced connectedness, communication, chatbot traits and the exercise. The first questionnaire had 12 questions, and the second included 11 questions. Most response options were Likert-type scale from 1 (very negative) to 7 (very positive), and some were free text. The questionnaires were used to augment the overall data material, and to ensure feedback on our topics of interest from all the participants.

The total body of data consisted of chat observation notes, chat logs, questionnaire responses, and an evaluation interview transcription. Themes were constructed by a close reading of the data in accordance with Braun and Clarke's [6] description of thematic analysis. This study collected personal identifiable information, reviewed and approved by NSD - Norwegian Data Protection Services.

3   Terabot

Terabot (Fig. 1) is a low-fidelity chatbot designed to facilitate peer support in an online self-help program for adults with ADHD. It is named Terabot (a portmanteau of "**tera**pi" (eng: therapy) and "chat**bot**") to highlight that it is in fact a chatbot and not a person, and has a profile picture of a chatbot to further emphasize this. Terabot was designed according to guidelines from participatory design, building on contributions from clinical psychologists and adults with ADHD.

Based on Følstad, Skjuve and Brandtzaeg's [17] chatbot typology, chatbots with coaching-related roles often have a chatbot-driven conversation style and long term relations. This means that the conversation is led by the chatbot and that the chatbot and user(s) are expected to have several interactions over time. As Terabot has a coaching-related role it was decided that it should follow predefined scripts and lead the participants through the conversation. Hence, an important part of the design process was to develop these scripts. The scripts were co-designed by computer scientists and four clinical psychologists with experience from both group therapy for adult ADHD and Internet-based treatment. Examples of how therapeutic insights and knowledge was built into the design include the topics for the conversations, phrasing of questions, and portioning of the content.

Some design strategies that should be considered when designing for individuals with ADHD include minimizing distractions and surprises, making a predictable pattern, produce suitable information about their behavior (rewards or redirection), and be clear with instructions and language [30]. These design strategies were originally developed for children with ADHD, but we anticipated that they could apply to adults as well because of their similar symptoms. These strategies were incorporated to the design, for example by including the use of praise and redirection in the scripts.

Terabot was tasked with one specific exercise from the online self-help program. Based on clinical input it was decided to organise the exercise over two chat sessions. To ensure participation from the whole group, Terabot prompts inactive users to interact after 10 s. If users are in the process of responding, Terabot recognizes this and waits. If Terabot prompts and still does not get an answer it waits for 10 more seconds before continuing in its script. The 10 s time limit was chosen as a basis to explore realistic time constraints.

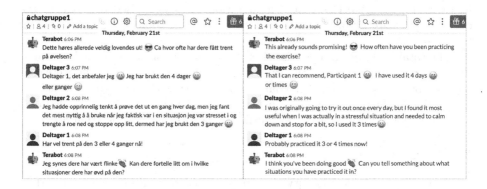

Fig. 1. Terabot, English translation to the right.

4   Findings

Here we present the main findings from the two trials and the following evaluation interview. Figure 1 visualizes the chat environment from the wizards view.

1st Trial. The first WoOz trial was conducted as a proof of concept for using a chatbot to guide peer support conversations, to evaluate the scripts and requirements, and to explore the benefits and limitations of the WoOz method in this scenario. Three groups of three participants took part. Emergent analytic themes include group dynamics and conversation, and benefits and limitations with the use of the WoOz method.

Group Dynamics and Conversation: Based on the analysis of the chat logs the three groups seemed to have slightly different group dynamics. In Group 1 there was a good conversational flow, and the participants responded reciprocally. We interpreted the tone as positive, for example by how participants' used enchanting emojis, and referred to each other by username:

Terabot: "Did you experience anything positive with this exercise?"

Participant 1: "I managed to collect my thoughts during a stressful situations, which usually is very difficult for me!"

Participant 3: "I agree with Participant 1"

In Group 2 the conversation appeared more direct, without unnecessary discussion. The answers were often phrased shorter than in Group 1, but nevertheless seemed to answer the questions to the same extent. Participants in Group 2 also referred to each other on several occasions, especially if they agreed with a participant's statement. Neither of the participants in Group 3 referred to each other during the two chat sessions, and the conversation was characterized by short answers and limited use of emojis.

Improvising Dialogue: There were several occasions where the script did not match the participants' answers. In Group 3 the participants answered vaguely when asked to introduce themselves and only stated their profession, e.g. "I'm a student". The next question in the script was "Did you have anything in common with the other participants?". The vague answers resulted in the wizard improvising a follow-up question regarding their hobbies. Participants sometimes wrote several answers to acknowledge another participant's answer, resulting in the wizard giving them some extra time before moving on to the next question. In some occasions a participant did not answer the question at all. The wizard waited for 10 s before specifically prompting that participant. The example below illustrates this scenario:

Terabot: "How do you understand the purpose of the exercise?"

Participant 9: Answers

Participant 8: Answers

No Activity from Participant 7

Terabot: "What do you think, @Participant7?"

Participant 7: Answers

Scheduling. The chat sessions were held at scheduled times, and all participants were explained the importance of being ready on time as the chatbot would not begin before everyone were logged in. Only one group was ready in time for both chats. The two other groups started between 1 to 4 min after they were scheduled. It was usually one participant that was missing. This needs to be considered in future design, as it can cause problems if not handled correctly.

Questionnaire Feedback. Overall the participants expressed a positive experience with both chats. When asked to describe the experience of the group conversation in free text all answers to this question were positive: Replies to the first chat included the conversation being nice, the participant having a good experience, the conversation being surprisingly helpful, easy to understand, and positive feelings towards the concept. In the second chat statements expressed the experience as educational, informative, exciting, nice, positive and affirmative, and generally a good experience.

As we can see in Table 1 the experience of connectedness between the participants got the lowest score, but this score increased between chat 1 and chat

Table 1. Mean questionnaire results Trial 1 and 2

Statement	Scores	Trial 1 (N = 18)	Trial 2 (N = 6)	Mean (N = 24)
To what extent did you experience contact with the other participants in the chat?	1 = very little, 7 = very large	5, 34	6	5, 67
To what degree did you find it useful to discuss 'The Stop Exercise' with people in the same situation?	1 = very useless, 7 = very useful	6	5, 25	5, 63
What was your impression of Terabot (the chatbot)?	1 = very negative, 7 = very positive	6, 5	4, 75	5, 63
How disturbing did you experience Terabot, the chatbot, in the conversation?	1 = very disturbing, 7 = not disturbing at all	5, 78	4, 88	5, 33
How useful did you find Terabot, the chatbot, for the conversation?	1 = very useless, 7 = very useful	6, 62	5, 42	6, 02
How did you experience the distribution between who spoke/chatted?	1 = very little, 7 = very large	6, 56	6, 13	6, 35
To what degree did you experience to say what you wanted to?	1 = very little, 7 = very large	6, 28	6	6, 14

2 (4,78 to 5,89). The participants found it very useful to discuss the exercise with peers, and had a good impression of Terabot. As a mediator of the conversation Terabot worked well: The participants did not find it disturbing, and additionally found that speech distribution was high, and they got to say what they wanted.

Benefits and Limitations of the WoOz Method. Based on the first WoOz trial the concept of a chatbot guiding a group conversation seemed feasible and worth exploring closer. The scripts, chatbot personality traits and requirements appeared well designed, but with potential for some improvements. As Yang et al. [33] stated, the standard WoOz method does not explore the technology's capabilities and limitations. Low-fidelity prototyping methods, such as the standard WoOz method, may provide little opportunities for error checking, and thereby important design decisions can be overlooked.

Trial and Chatbot Adjustments. Before the second WoOz trial some adjustments were made to avoid unexpected utterances from the participants. Some questions (e.g. "Have you practiced the exercise since the last chat?") had three different outcomes (all, some or no participants have practiced); hence, three different chatbot replies were developed. A script with prompts the wizard could use in different "unexpected" scenarios was developed. The wizard was to follow the 10-second time limit more strictly: if participants were inactive (not writing) for 10 s, the chatbot would prompt that/those participant(s) to answer. If the participant(s) went from active to inactive, the wizard would wait for 10 new seconds. When all participants had answered the question or participants did not respond 10 s after being prompted, the chatbot would move on to the next question/answer.

2nd Trial. The purpose of trial 2 was to examine if adults diagnosed with ADHD would elicit similar user behavior and experience as the participants in the first Wizard of Oz trial.

The trial was planned as two chat groups of three participants each, but two participants did not show up to the first chat session, ending in two groups of two participants. The participants in Group 1 completed both chat sessions and participated in the evaluation interview. The participants in Group 2 dropped out halfway in the trial. The reasons why participants had not attended included sickness, oversleeping and getting distracted.

Group Dynamics and Conversation. In the analysis of the chat logs, the researchers interpreted the participants in Group 1 to have a good dynamic; they often referred to each other by name, answered complementary and gave feedback unsolicited. The conversation between participants in Group 2 was interpreted as more strained. One of the participants seemed to be doing other things simultaneously, as she often logged in and out of the chat, causing pauses in the conversation.

Use of Prompts. Adhering strictly to the scripts revealed some challenging situations. The wizard had to use several prompts with Group 2. One recurring problem was the participant who logged in and out and caused pauses in the conversation. This lead Terabot to end the conversation prematurely, resulting in the participants continuing the conversation after Terabot said 'Goodbye'

Assessing the Alternative WoOz Method. The second WoOz trial tried to regulate some limitations of low-fidelity prototyping by having strict rules the wizard had to follow. The intent was to create a more realistic chatbot experience for the participants, as the wizard could not improvise when the script was inadequate. These rules generated some chatbot errors, which can be beneficial for the design process as one can learn from errors and improve the design.

Questionnaire Feedback. The participants described the first chat as a positive experience similar to the responses from Trial 1. As seen in Table 1 the scores are also similar to Trial 1, although some items score somewhat lower.

Evaluation Interview. Overall, the participants in the evaluation interview appeared satisfied and impressed by the concept and of Terabot. One participant stated that Terabot's questions, as well as peer support was helpful:

"The questions that were raised were very relevant. Thinking in advance "when am I supposed to practice it [the exercise]?" was very relevant. I also thought it was nice to have peer support. I often experience that people without ADHD can sometimes make me feel like they are there to educate. I can often experience that other people are "proper" and that they want to educate us. That's a bit condescending, and you feel like you have to compensate in a way for how you behave".

Further, both participants agreed that the chat sessions lead to a feeling of positive pressure towards practicing the exercise and participating in the chat sessions. They further noted that they appreciated it when Terabot praised them.

One stated: "Sometimes it [the chatbot] gave some praise, such as "Nice that everyone has dealt with it", or something similar. [...] Yes, that [the praise] felt nice".

One challenge the participants noted was that sometimes they wanted to discuss the topic more, but the chatbot changed the subject. They understood that the chatbot had limitations, but considered it valuable to make a solution to this problem in a later version. Overall, both participants were positive to the concept of Terabot. One participant stressed this: "I think it is very positive that someone has tried to do this [develop peer support technology for the online self-help program for adults with ADHD]. I think you have succeeded in finding a good format [chatbot] for it. It can easily happen that someone talks too much, or interrupts, or yes... I was very impressed by how well it functioned and the benefits of it. [...] Sometimes it feels like it is developed technology concerning what it [technology] can do, not what is needed or what is effective. This [the peer support chatbot] felt like it was developed based on "How can we best facilitate for a good situation for those who will have this conversation?"".

5   Discussion

This RtD study has involved a design exploration of using a chatbot to facilitate peer support in an online self-help program for adults with ADHD. Based on previous research emphasising the benefits of peer support in treatment [26], we have explored the potential of using a chatbot as a mediator of conversation and interaction in an online self-help for adults with ADHD. The exploration has involved the design and evaluation of a chatbot. Here, we discuss the main findings tied to the design process, how chatbots can mediate social interaction, and the WoOz method.

The Design Process: When designing a chatbot prototype in relation to a self-help program it is beneficial to have input from future users. The idea and concept of Terabot was developed in workshops consisting of computer scientists, clinical psychologists and adults with ADHD. As Terabot had a chatbot-driven conversation style, the development of scripts was an important part of the design. Clinical psychologists and computer scientist co-designed these scripts based on clinical insight and knowledge from group therapy and Internet interventions. Requirements concerning the chatbot's behavior were also defined and evaluated.

In the evaluation interview the participants agreed that the chat sessions lead to a feeling of positive pressure. This finding is in line with previous research [4, 21, 23], claiming that peer support has a positive effect on treatment engagement. Participants further expressed the liking of the chatbot praising them, which can be seen as an example of the value of including praise and redirection in scripts design for individuals with ADHD, as suggested by Sonne [30].

We identified design challenges that occurred in relation to using a chatbot in such group conversation: There were issues related to scheduling and participants being late. Measures to ensure that all participants remember the session, or the chat to continues without everyone present, could be taken. This is also related to participants not showing up at all due to different circumstances: it is important to consider whether it is necessary to have quasi-synchronous chats where participants are present simultaneously. It would be possible to organize the chats asynchronously, but there are suspected drawbacks to this: We assume that simultaneous presence supports the experienced connectedness better, and supports an open conversation style. Another challenge is to decide if and when participants should get more time to discuss. In the evaluation interview the participants stated that they sometimes had more to say when the chatbot changed the topic. Some possible solutions were mentioned, for example for the chatbot to ask the participants if they wanted some more time to discuss. These challenges should be explored in future research.

Chatbots for Social Mediation: Our findings from the questionnaires and the evaluation interview indicate that the structure of the scripts and the chat format were well received by the participants. The participants reported that Terabot was useful and guided the conversations, ensured that everybody participated equally, and helped establish social connectedness within the group. This indicates that there is a potential for chatbots in group conversations, supporting the claim of Seering et al. that chatbots have potential beyond dyadic communication [27]. In future research it could be useful to develop and evaluate a fully functioning chatbot to explore the potential more thoroughly.

The WoOz Method: Based on our experience, the standard and the alternative WoOz method are useful ways of evaluating the concept, the scripts, chatbot traits, and requirements. Both WoOz methods seem especially suitable when designing chatbots with chatbot-driven conversation style as they often depend on scripts. Scripts can easily be evaluated using WoOz, and designers can get an idea of typical answers and user behavior.

We experienced that the standard WoOz lays a good foundation for further design. The alternative WoOz was perceived as a more thorough way of evaluating the concept, scripts and requirements but there are some challenges: Even with the facilitation for likely errors, we believe that there is a great possibility that several potential errors are not discovered and can only be found by the development of a functioning chatbot. Regardless of this, we believe that the combination of the standard and the alternative WoOz approach can be beneficial in the early stages of chatbot design, as one gains knowledge about the concept and user behavior, and one gets to explore some errors that might appear and plan how to handle these.

6 Conclusion

In this paper we have addressed how a chatbot can facilitate peer support in an online self-help program for adults with ADHD, and argue for the promise of the approach. A chatbot can facilitate these conversations by creating an environment where participants discuss topics related to the program. Furthermore, the chatbot may help establishing structure, predictability and encouragement in the online self-help environment, which have been evaluated as important strategies when designing for individuals diagnosed with ADHD [30]. Terabot was well received by participants both with and without ADHD, which may indicate that it has potential beyond online self-help programs for adults with ADHD. Both groups found the chatbot useful in mediating conversation, resulting in a chat environment with a good distribution of speech and participation. However, given that Terabot is a low-fidelity prototype and the low number of participants, especially diagnosed with ADHD, we encourage further research in this field.

References

1. Abd-alrazaq, A.A., Alajlani, M., Alalwan, A.A., Bewick, B.M., Gardner, P., Househ, M.: An overview of the features of chatbots in mental health: a scoping review. Int. J. Med. Informatics **132**, 103978 (2019). https://doi.org/10.1016/j.ijmedinf.2019.103978

2. Alvarez-Jimenez, M., Alcazar-Corcoles, M.A., González-Blanch, C., Bendall, S., McGorry, P.D., Gleeson, J.F.: Online, social media and mobile technologies for psychosis treatment: a systematic review on novel user-led interventions. Schizophr. Res. **156**(1), 96–106 (2014). https://doi.org/10.1016/j.schres.2014.03.021

3. American Psychiatric Association: Diagnostic and statistical manual of mental disorders: DSM-5, 5th edn. Technical report, American Psychiatric Association, Washington, D.C (2013)

4. Baumeister, H., Reichler, L., Munzinger, M., Lin, J.: The impact of guidance on Internet-based mental health interventions – a systematic review. Internet Interv. **1**(4), 205–215 (2014). https://doi.org/10.1016/j.invent.2014.08.003

5. Bickmore, T.W., Utami, D., Matsuyama, R., Paasche-Orlow, M.K.: Improving access to online health information with conversational agents: a randomized controlled experiment. J. Med. Internet Res. **18**(1), e1 (2016). https://doi.org/10.2196/jmir.5239

6. Braun, V., Clarke, V.: What can "thematic analysis" offer health and wellbeing researchers? Int. J. Qual. Stud. Health Well-being **9**(1) (2014). https://doi.org/10.3402/qhw.v9.26152

7. Cameron, G., et al.: Assessing the usability of a chatbot for mental health care. In: Bodrunova, S., et al. (eds.) INSCI 2018. LNCS, vol. 11551, pp. 121–132. Springer, Cham (2019). https://doi.org/10.1007/978-3-030-17705-8_11

8. Clark, J.: Medicalization of global health 2: the medicalization of global mental health. Global Health Action **7**(1), 24000 (2014). https://doi.org/10.3402/gha.v7.24000

9. Dahlbäck, N., Jönsson, A., Ahrenberg, L.: Wizard of Oz studies – why and how. Knowl.-Based Syst. **6**(4), 258–266 (1993). https://doi.org/10.1016/0950-7051(93)90017-N

10. Doherty, G., Coyle, D., Sharry, J.: Engagement with online mental health interventions: an exploratory clinical study of a treatment for depression. In: Proceedings of the SIGCHI Conference on Human Factors in Computing Systems CHI 2012, pp. 1421–1430. ACM, New York (2012). https://doi.org/10.1145/2207676.2208602

11. Dohsaka, K., Ryota, A., Higashinaka, R., Minami, Y., Maeda, E.: Effects of conversational agents on human communication in thought-evoking multi-party dialogues. In: Proceedings of SIGDIAL 2009: the 10th Annual Meeting of the Special Interest Group in Discourse and Dialogue, pp. 217–224. Association for Computational Linguistics, London (2009)

12. Elmasri, D., Maeder, A.: A conversational agent for an online mental health intervention. In: Ascoli, G.A., Hawrylycz, M., Ali, H., Khazanchi, D., Shi, Y. (eds.) BIH 2016. LNCS (LNAI), vol. 9919, pp. 243–251. Springer, Cham (2016). https://doi.org/10.1007/978-3-319-47103-7_24

13. Eysenbach, G., Powell, J., Englesakis, M., Rizo, C., Stern, A.: Health related virtual communities and electronic support groups: systematic review of the effects of online peer to peer interactions. BMJ **328**(7449), 1166 (2004). https://doi.org/10.1136/bmj.328.7449.1166

14. Faulkner, A., Basset, T.: A helping hand: taking peer support into the 21st century. Mental Health Soc. Inclusion **16**(1), 41–47 (2012). https://doi.org/10.1108/20428301211205892

15. Fitzpatrick, K.K., Darcy, A., Vierhile, M.: Delivering cognitive behavior therapy to young adults with symptoms of depression and anxiety using a fully automated conversational agent (Woebot): a randomized controlled trial. JMIR Mental Health **4**(2), e19 (2017). https://doi.org/10.2196/mental.7785

16. Følstad, A., Brandtzæg, P.B.: Chatbots and the new world of HCI. Interactions **24**(4), 38–42 (2017). https://doi.org/10.1145/3085558

17. Følstad, A., Skjuve, M., Brandtzaeg, P.B.: Different chatbots for different purposes: towards a typology of chatbots to understand interaction design. In: Bodrunova, S.S., et al. (eds.) INSCI 2018. LNCS, vol. 11551, pp. 145–156. Springer, Cham (2019). https://doi.org/10.1007/978-3-030-17705-8_13

18. Håvik, R., Wake, J.D., Flobak, E., Lundervold, A., Guribye, F.: A conversational interface for self-screening for ADHD in adults. In: Bodrunova, S.S., et al. (eds.) INSCI 2018. LNCS, vol. 11551, pp. 133–144. Springer, Cham (2019). https://doi.org/10.1007/978-3-030-17705-8_12

19. Hurvitz, N.: Peer self-help psychotherapy groups and their implications for psychotherapy. Psychother: Theory, Res. Pract. **7**(1), 41–49 (1970). https://doi.org/10.1037/h0086549

20. Lucas, G.M., et al.: Reporting mental health symptoms: breaking down barriers to care with virtual human interviewers (2017). https://doi.org/10.3389/frobt.2017.00051

21. Ly, K.H., Ly, A.M., Andersson, G.: A fully automated conversational agent for promoting mental well-being: a pilot RCT using mixed methods. Internet Interv. **10**, 39–46 (2017). https://doi.org/10.1016/j.invent.2017.10.002

22. Mead, S., Hilton, D., Curtis, L.: Peer support: a theoretical perspective. Psychiatr. Rehabil. J. **25**(2), 134–141 (2001). https://doi.org/10.1037/h0095032

23. Mohr, D.C., Cuijpers, P., Lehman, K.: Supportive accountability: a model for providing human support to enhance adherence to ehealth interventions. J. Med. Internet Res. **13**(1), e30 (2011). https://doi.org/10.2196/jmir.1602

24. Naslund, J.A., Aschbrenner, K.A., Marsch, L.A., Bartels, S.J.: The future of mental health care: peer-to-peer support and social media. Epidemiol. Psychiatr. Sci. **25**(2), 113–122 (2016). https://doi.org/10.1017/S2045796015001067

25. O'Leary, K., Schueller, S.M., Wobbrock, J.O., Pratt, W.: "Suddenly, we got to become therapists for each other": designing peer support chats for mental health.

In: CHI 2018 Proceedings of the 2018 CHI Conference on Human Factors in Computing Systems, p. e331. ACM, Montreal (2018). https://doi.org/10.1145/3173574.3173905

26. Philipsen, A.: Psychotherapy in adult attention deficit hyperactivity disorder: implications for treatment and research. Expert Rev. Neurother. **12**(10), 1217–1225 (2012). https://doi.org/10.1586/ern.12.91

27. Seering, J., Luria, M., Kaufman, G., Hammer, J.: Beyond dyadic interactions: considering chatbots as community members. In: Proceedings of the 2019 CHI Conference on Human Factors in Computing Systems, CHI 2019, pp. 450:1–450:13. ACM, New York (2019). https://doi.org/10.1145/3290605.3300680

28. Solberg, B.S., Haavik, J., Halmøy, A.: Health care services for adults with ADHD: patient satisfaction and the role of psycho-education. J. Atten. Disord. **23**(1), 99–108 (2015). https://doi.org/10.1177/1087054715587941

29. Solomon, P.: Peer support/peer provided services underlying processes, benefits, and critical ingredients. Psychiatr. Rehabil. J. **27**(4), 392–401 (2005). https://doi.org/10.2975/27.2004.392.401

30. Sonne, T., Marshall, P., Obel, C., Thomsen, P.H., Grønbæk, K.: An assistive technology design framework for ADHD. In: Proceedings of the 28th Australian Conference on Computer-Human Interaction, OzCHI 2016, pp. 60–70. ACM, New York (2016). https://doi.org/10.1145/3010915.3010925

31. Tielman, M., Neerincx, M., van Meggelen, M., Franken, I., Brinkman, W.P.: How should a virtual agent present psychoeducation? Influence of verbal and textual presentation on adherence. Technol. Health Care **25**(6), 1081–1096 (2017). https://doi.org/10.3233/THC-170899

32. Vaidyam, A.N., Wisniewski, H., Halamka, J.D., Kashavan, M.S., Torous, J.B.: Chatbots and conversational agents in mental health: a review of the psychiatric landscape. Can. J. Psychiatry **64**(7), 456–464 (2019). https://doi.org/10.1177/0706743719828977

33. Yang, Q., Cranshaw, J., Amershi, S., Iqbal, S.T., Teevan, J.: Sketching NLP: a case study of exploring the right things to design with language intelligence. In: Proceedings of the 2019 CHI Conference on Human Factors in Computing Systems. CHI 2019. ACM, Glasgow (2019). https://doi.org/10.1145/3290605.3300415

34. Zimmerman, J., Forlizzi, J., Evenson, S.: Research through design as a method for interaction design research in HCI. In: Proceedings of the SIGCHI Conference on Human Factors in Computing Systems. CHI 2007, pp. 493–502. ACM, New York (2007). https://doi.org/10.1145/1240624.1240704

Towards Chatbots to Support Bibliotherapy Preparation and Delivery

Patrick McAllister[1,2(✉)], James Kerr[1], Michael McTear[2],
Maurice Mulvenna[2], Raymond Bond[2], Karen Kirby[3],
Joseph Morning[1], and Danni Glover[1]

[1] Verbal Arts Centre, Derry/Londonderry, UK
{ktp,james.kerr,psychology.manager,
senioreditor}@verbal.co
[2] School of Computing, Ulster University, Jordanstown Campus,
Newtownabbey, Co. Antrim, UK
{p.mcallister,mf.mctear,md.mulvenna,
rb.bond}@ulster.ac.uk
[3] School of Psychology, Coleraine Campus, Coleraine, UK
k.kirby@ulster.ac.uk

Abstract. Chatbots have become an increasingly popular choice for organisations in delivering services to users. Chatbots are beginning to become popular in mental health applications and are being seen as an accessible strategy in delivering mental health support alongside clinical/therapy treatment. The aim of this exploratory study was to investigate initial perceptions of the use and acceptance/adoption of text based chatbots by bibliotherapy facilitators and to also investigate perceptions of bibliotherapy facilitators using a bibliotherapy support chatbot through usability testing. Interviews were conducted to explore the relationship of bibliotherapy facilitators with chatbots, facilitators were then asked to complete a usability study using an early prototype chatbot. Post interviews were also conducted after usability study to discuss further improvements and requirements. Analysis of the interview transcripts reveal that bibliotherapy facilitators were keen on using chatbots to guide them in preparing for their bibliotherapy session for preparation and delivery. Facilitators stated that the reliability of the chatbot was a concern in relation to chatbot content and it is important to ensure that meaningful and quick conversational exchanges are designed. Analysis of the interview transcripts also stressed the importance of encoding a personality into the chatbot along with appropriate content to effectively guide facilitators. Facilitators stressed that appropriate onboarding and affordance measures should be integrated into the system to ensure that users are able to correctly interact chatbot and to understand the purpose of the chatbot as well as using personalisation for meaningful conversational exchanges.

Keywords: Chatbots · Bibliotherapy · Mental health · Conversation

© Springer Nature Switzerland AG 2020
A. Følstad et al. (Eds.): CONVERSATIONS 2019, LNCS 11970, pp. 127–142, 2020.
https://doi.org/10.1007/978-3-030-39540-7_9

1 Introduction

Chatbots or conversational agents (for the sake of brevity, the term chatbots will be used throughout the remainder of this paper) have become increasingly pervasive across many domains. The democratisation of chatbot technologies has enabled organisations and individuals to adopt a chatbot approach to supporting individuals and groups, and also to automate tasks. Platforms such as Dialogflow[1], Luis[2], and, IBM[3] Watson have also led to an increase in the development of chatbots, particularly among social media websites [1]. Advances in artificial intelligence (AI), particularly deep learning approaches, have enabled developers to create conversational agents that provide services across different platforms. Chatbots are also used in a wide range of areas, from education [3] to supporting a range of health conditions, from mental health, monitoring nutritional intake and physical activity. [2, 12, 19]. In recent years, they have also opened a range of possibilities in terms of supporting the treatment and prevention of mental health disorders. Much of the work undertaken in these areas has combined cognitive behaviour change approaches with chatbots to support individuals with mental health conditions [4, 5]. An area where one would expect chatbots to be a valuable tool is in the delivery of guided bibliotherapy, however to date, this application has received little research attention.

Bibliotherapy is described as a talking-therapy that uses short stories to support individuals dealing with mental health issues. During a bibliotherapy session, participants are asked questions related to their emotions or events that may have happened to them. Bibliotherapy utilises Cognitive Behavioural Therapy (CBT) concepts of identifying emotions, thoughts and behaviours of people, and assists in the emotional and cognitive literacy of the user as well as developing a solution-focused approach to recovery [6]; all of which is explained within the narrative of the story being told. The key benefit and impact of this enables the user to understand their mental health, identify connections and similarities, it also offers hope and resilience, and demonstrates that there are solutions to adversities and problems related to mental health and wellbeing [7]. The essence of bibliotherapy raises awareness and can effectively coach a user on how to cope by telling the story of how others coped and overcame difficulties [7]. There is significant evidence to show the effectiveness of this approach [8, 9, 28] and also for CBT [10]. Research shows the positive effects of using bibliotherapy to help treat obsessive-compulsive disorder (OCD) [10], depression, and emotional disorders [8, 9, 28]. Research shows that the availability of bibliotherapy based treatments could be beneficial for the patient as well as cost-effective for the health service and is currently promoted by the National Health Service (NHS) [11]. This study aims to address this gap in the literature by exploring how chatbots could be used to augment and support the bibliotherapy sessions to support mental health conditions.

---

[1] Dialogflow, Available: https://dialogflow.cloud.google.com/.

[2] Luis, Available: https://www.luis.ai/.

[3] IBM Watson, Available: https://www.ibm.com/watson/how-to-build-a-chatbot.

2   Background and Related Work

Chatbots have come a long way from when Eliza (1966) was first unveiled. The days of matching user input to scripted responses has been superseded by the use of sophisticated natural language processing (NLP) algorithms and machine learning approaches. These advances in computing capabilities have enabled the development and growth of chatbots to increase exponentially, and this is evident in how chatbots have been integrated into different domain areas [3, 13, 14]. The democratisation of chatbot development platforms have enabled organisations to allow chatbots to act as a conduit for customer support. Chatbot technology has progressed at unprecedented rates as well as the capabilities of chatbots and this is evident in the variety of the chatbot development platforms that are available (Dialogflow, Luis, etc.). It is easier for developers to utilise chatbot technology to help achieve goals, however, an important issue that also needs attention is the personality characteristics of the chatbot. Shaping a chatbot's personality in pre-empting user's responses in different scenarios is a process that needs acute clarification from conversational designers and developers, this process is integral to the success of the chatbot and requires continuous input from the end-user [22].

Many chatbots have been developed to support mental health conditions and there is potential to use chatbots to support individuals while waiting for therapy sessions or during their sessions. Even with access to mental health support, many individuals may not use these services due to stigma, and in response to this researchers and developers have used chatbots to support individuals and also provide anonymity. Many of these chatbot applications provide routine "check-ins" and alerts. The more interactions with the chatbot the individual has the more personal the chatbots messages become. One of the most well-known mental health chatbots is Woebot[4]. Woebot is described as a "coaching" chatbot that is underpinned by CBT approaches to support individuals that suffer from depression and/or anxiety. Research published in [15] evaluated the feasibility of using Woebot to deliver CBT to young adults. The results of this study suggest that users who used Woebot, experienced a reduction in symptoms of depression and the authors suggest that chatbots may offer a viable way to support individuals experiencing anxiety or depression. Another popular mental health chatbot is Wysa, which is popular with over 100,000 downloads from Google Play Store. Wysa[5] is similar to Woebot as it claims to help users monitor emotions through the use of CBT techniques. Wysa is also described by its developers as a "coach" where the chatbot coaches the individual to reach their mental health goals. Research in [27] users installed Wysa application and engaged in text based messaging with the application over a period of time. Outcome measures were based on Patient Health Questionnaire-9 to measure any improvement in mood. Results from this study highlight a mood improvement increase with users who used the application more frequently. However, more research needs to be completed in assessing the efficacy of such applications over a longer period of time and with a larger group of participants.

---

[4] Woebot, Available: https://woebot.io/.

[5] Wysa, Available: https://www.wysa.io.

In terms of interacting with chatbots, recent research have presented new frameworks in exploring how chatbot characteristics influence how we interact with chatbots. In [23], Chaves and Gerosa present an analysis of chatbot literature by highlighting characteristics that influence how users perceive chatbots. The authors highlight three areas that could be used to assess chatbot abilities and characteristics; (1) conversational intelligence, (2) personification, and (3) social intelligence. Conversational intelligence refers to the chatbot's ability to manage user interactions, personification refers to the chatbots identify and personality, and social intelligence relates to pre-empting user needs and responses through social protocols. Through this analysis, authors in [23] developed a theoretical framework that describes how each chatbot characteristic influence one another. This framework is an important contribution due to the novel approach to helping shape user's perception of chatbots. Piccolo et al. in [22] highlight the need for human centered design approaches and ensuring end user interaction needs are present when developing chatbot functionality. Piccolo et al. also highlight the market led influence of applying chatbot technology without truly considering the needs of the end-user and reinforce the potential of using chatbot technologies for social good e.g. mental health support, crisis support, and learning. Key messages from Piccolo et al. [22] indicate that chatbot development needs to be steered towards human centered design and the authors emphasise areas for future research; (1) interactive style, (2) appropriate task type, and (3) trustworthiness. Interactive style is concerned with how users are expected to interact with the chatbot, e.g. voice, text, or button inputs. Appropriate tasks are concerned with what type of tasks users expect the chatbot to support. It is important for designers, developers, and end-users to determine useful and appropriate tasks for the chatbot to complete. Trustworthiness is another factor highlighted in [22] and is associated with how users trust the chatbot to support them in a useful way, if the chatbot is designed to replace a system then guidance must be communicated to the end users in regards to the limitations, capabilities, and technology platform. One approach assesses the trustworthiness of the chatbot could be through using ecological momentary assessment (EMA) [21] to measure how often users interact with the chatbot, what input terms are used, and how often they use the chatbot to retrieve information in comparison to more traditional approaches. Moreover, the chatbot could ask the user for their opinions when using the chatbot over a period of time to gain further insight into usage. The work presented in [22, 23] emphasises the importance of using a multidisciplinary team that work's closely with the intended end-users in order to avoid user frustrations.

The work presented in this paper is influenced by [22] in how we structure our findings to deduce meaningful recommendations towards developing chatbots to support bibliotherapy preparation and delivery. The remainder of this work is organised as follows; in Sect. 3, research aim and research questions are presented. In Sect. 4 we discuss the chatbot prototype. Section 5 we discuss the methods and approaches used in study. In Sect. 6 we present the results and findings of the thematic analysis based on the interviews, Sect. 7 we present recommendations based on our findings and finally in Sect. 8 we present our conclusion and future work.

3   Aim and Research Questions

This study aims to explore how chatbots can be used to support bibliotherapy facilitators. Requirements were elicited from bibliotherapy practitioners using semistructured interviews and the facilitators completed a usability test using a web application that contains a prototype chatbot. To structure the responses from the semistructured interviews (pre and post), a thematic analysis was conducted to summarise the key themes highlighted by the user. The following research questions were formulated based on current literature, specifically question 2, 3, and 4 were adapted from future research directions highlighted in [22].

(1)   What are the concerns and opportunities of facilitators in using chatbots to prepare for bibliotherapy sessions?
(2)   What kinds of tasks will be appropriate for chatbots to support bibliotherapy?
(3)   How can chatbots be designed to be reliable in supporting bibliotherapy facilitators?
(4)   What will be an appropriate style of interaction with chatbots to support bibliotherapy?

4   Chatbot Prototype

This study evaluated the use of a web application that contains a text based/button menu led chatbot called 'Bibliobot'. Biblibot was developed to support bibliotherapy facilitators by informing them of different aspects of their bibliotherapy sessions, e.g. story information, psychological themes in the stories, the purpose of the story, and how to instil conversation among bibliotherapy group participants by providing story questions. The remainder of Sect. 4 discusses the interaction design and the tools used to develop the chatbot.

4.1   Chatbot Interaction Design

Chatbot happy paths were developed in collaboration with staff at Verbal Arts. Bibliotherapy facilitators highlighted functional requirements to incorporate into chatbot as well as the types of information. Botsociety[6] (chatbot conversation prototype platform) was used to design the conversation. To interact with the chatbot, facilitators use a combination of text input and quick reply menu buttons. When the user logs into the application, they are greeted by Bibliobot chatbot which presents a list of menu buttons. By instantly presenting a list of buttons, this informs the user of the scope of the chatbot in regards to capabilities and allows the user to quickly begin interacting with the chatbot. Users are also able to use a text input area to delve deeper into areas through asking questions. Figure 1 is an image of chatbot windows with quick reply menu buttons and a text input area.

---

[6] Botsociety, Available: https://botsociety.io/.

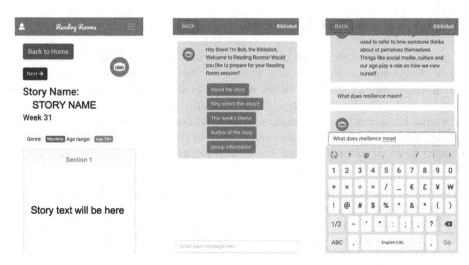

Fig. 1. Prototype of chatbot 'Bibliobot'. Once logged in, users can select the chatbot icon (top right corner) and are then presented with a chatbot window, users are able to interact with chatbot using quick reply menu buttons and text input area.

4.2   Chatbot Functionality

The chatbot was developed on a responsive web framework to allow it to be accessed across different devices. To access the chatbot, the user firsts logs into the web platform, they are then able to see their dashboard screen, which contains general information about their upcoming bibliotherapy session (e.g. story name, story blurb). The chatbot icon is positioned at the top of each web page, and the chatbot interface can be triggered by tapping on the chatbot icon.

Dialogflow is Google's NLP platform was used to develop the chatbot functionality. Dialogflow allows developers to build chatbots across different applications e.g. WhatsApp, Facebook, web, and Telegram. Developers can build conversations using intents and which are connected together using contexts. In this work, Dialogflow was used to develop Bibliobot and Dialogflow fulfillment was used to customise interactions allowing for more richer conversations, e.g. personalise interactions using user information. Dialogflow is able to accept text inputted by the user and parse the text to match it to predefined intents. To ensure that correct intents are triggered by user input, it is important that intents have sufficient training phrases to allow for meaningful conversational exchanges, for example for 'author' intent it was important to include training phrases such as "Who is the author", "What is the author's name?", and "author" to find out who the author is. Figure 2 is the technology stack used to develop Biblibot. APIs were developed using node.js to communicate with the backend database (MongoDB and Dialogflow) to output messages to the user.

Fig. 2. Technology stack used in development of chatbot; MongoDB, Express, React, Node.js (MERN) + Dialogflow.

5 Methodology

5.1 Participants

Convenience sampling was used to recruit participants for the study. Participants were recruited from staff based at the Verbal Arts Centre, Derry/Londonderry. Participants were aged 18 years and over and own a smartphone device with access to the Internet. It was also stipulated that participants must be bibliotherapy facilitators and currently deliver group bibliotherapy sessions at the Verbal Arts Centre. Five participants were recruited and provided with an information sheet explaining the purpose of the study and were informed as to how their data would be used and stored. The remainder of the section discusses key components of the study as well as the evaluation approaches used.

5.2 Prototype Usability Testing

Remote usability testing was used to assess the chatbot functionality. Participants were given a list of tasks to complete (Table 1). Participants were asked to indicate on the usability test whether they were able to complete each task. These tasks were completed using the participant's smartphone device. Screen recording software was also be used to record user interaction with the web app for analysis and to inform future development. Participants were provided with a participant information sheet and asked to sign a consent form.

Table 1. Remote usability tasks used in study.

	Example usability tasks using chatbot
(1)	Find a list of story themes about this week's story
(2)	Find explanations about each theme using chatbot
(3)	Find out why this week's story was selected
(4)	Find the definitions of the following terms • Resilience • Self-concept • Bibliotherapy
(5)	Access the main menu in the chatbot using text input
(6)	Access the chatbot and find out why discussion questions were selected for each story section

5.3 Semi-structured Interviews

Semi-structured interviews were used to gather opinions regarding the use of chatbots and were conducted before and after participants used the chatbot. These interviews consisted of open-ended questions with the objective of understanding the opinions of the facilitators about incorporating chatbot technology into their role. Each participant was asked questions relating to their experience in using chatbots prior to this usability study and in what capacity as well as a range of other questions. Facilitators were asked questions about their relationship with technology and how comfortable they are in using chatbots to support their bibliotherapy sessions. Each interview was audio recorded and transcribed for analysis. A post interview was conducted after the facilitators had used the chatbot to determine opinions, ease of use, user experience, and also to highlight any additional features. The questions asked in both the pre and post interviews were open ended in nature to promote discussion relating to broader chatbot design and functionality issues. Table 2 lists example questions that participants were asked in pre and post semi-structured interviews.

Table 2. Example interview questions used in each semi-structured interview.

	Example pre interview questions	Example post interview questions
(1)	Have you used chatbot technology before?	How did you find using the chatbot to help prepare for bibliotherapy session?
(2)	What is your opinion on using chatbots?	Did you prefer using buttons or text input when interacting with chatbot?
(3)	Did you find it useful using this chatbot?	Could you list any advantages or disadvantages in using the chatbot to retrieve information?
(4)	How do you feel about using chatbots to support your role as a bibliotherapy facilitator?	Are there any features you'd like to have in the chatbot?
(5)	What areas do you think chatbots would be beneficial for your job role as a bibliotherapy facilitator?	What features did you like the least?
(6)	What do you think about chatbots as a way to help you prepare for your bibliotherapy sessions?	Would you use the chatbot in the future?

5.4 Pre and Post Interview Thematic Analysis

Thematic analysis (TA) was used to analyse the interview transcripts in order to help answer the research questions listed in Sect. 3. TA is particularly beneficial when working with larger datasets (such as a transcription text), as you are able to target statements and group them together to uncover themes and create a coherent narrative to that can then be used to refine requirements.

6 Findings

6.1 Pre and Post Interview Thematic Analysis

Interview responses were organised into high level topics using research questions (2), (3), and (4) (stated in Sect. 3 of this paper) as headings [22].

What Kinds of Tasks will be Appropriate for Chatbots to Support Bibliotherapy?
Results from the pre-interview analysis highlight a number of issues that should be taken into consideration when developing a conversational agent to support bibliotherapy delivery. Facilitators reacted warmly to incorporating chatbot technology into their bibliotherapy preparation and delivery, however some expressed concern in the chatbot capabilities e.g. if the chatbot did not understand their request and facilitators highlighted that any nuance would be "missed" as they are not conversing with a "real human being". The prototype chatbot was designed to "accompany" bibliotherapy facilitators through the web application and to be aware of where they were in the application. It was noted during pre-interviews by facilitators that this chatbot persona could assume the role as a trainer or support agent and used to boost confidence of users as facilitators stated "...*give them (bibliotherapy facilitators) confidence to know they are doing it right... reassuring that they are doing the right thing...*". Currently, bibliotherapy facilitators undergo training before they conduct a bibliotherapy session, therefore some facilitators suggested that areas from the training could be incorporated into the chatbot for reference and reassurance. The prototype chatbot also acted as an administrative hub where the facilitator is able to find information about their bibliotherapy group and during the post interviews, it was mentioned that facilitators liked this functionality as it personalised the chatbot experience, "*Information about your group was brilliant, and where you are with you group)...*". It was highlighted in the pre-interview session that chatbots could be incorporated into the preparation as a frequently asked questions (FAQ) section, which could inform the facilitator about the purpose of the chatbot and how to effectively invoke key functionality.

During a regular bibliotherapy session, facilitators would use scale questionnaires (e.g. brief resilience scale (BRS), Warwick-Edinburgh Mental Well-being Scale (WEMWBS)) to collect data relating to the well-being of the participants. As of present, physical copies of these questionnaires are disseminated and completed by participants at the end of each bibliotherapy session, however it has been highlighted by facilitators that this can be an arduous task and that there is an opportunity to use chatbots to support and automate this data collection process. Using chatbots as a data collection approach is not a novel idea, authors in [29] analysed the efficacy of using chatbots to collect survey responses in comparison to conventional methods and results suggest that chatbots can be used effectively as a survey collection tool if used with an appropriate language tone. Moreover, results in [29] also suggested that responses gathered using a chatbot were less satisficing in comparison to conventional approaches.

EMA strategies could be integrated into the chatbot for the facilitator to ask participants and record thoughts and experience about a bibliotherapy session in real-time.

It was suggested by facilitators that participants could access a dedicated data collection chatbot using their smartphone device and during the session an alert would be given during a session to trigger EMA survey or a mood log. Using EMA with chatbots have been explored in [18, 30]. Chatbots developed in [18] were used to allow users to disclose their emotions, and thoughts. Results from [18] suggest that the effects of emotional disclosure were equivalent, whether the person thought they were disclosing to a chatbot or a human. Research in [30] assessed the usability of using a chatbot to evaluate a user's mood state, participants completed a questionnaire to determine further course of action. Results presented in [30] suggested that participants thought the chatbot was a suitable approach in completing a mood survey. EMA combined with chatbot technologies could lead to more efficient data collection and accurate user state representation to further personalise services.

How can Chatbots be Designed to be Reliable in Supporting Bibliotherapy Facilitators?

In both the pre and post interview, facilitators discussed issues that related to the reliability of the chatbot. During post interview, facilitators stated that an introductory (or onboarding) statement is needed to inform them of the type of input that can be used with the chatbot as bibliotherapy facilitators were not aware that the chatbot was able to accept text input. During post interview it was suggested it could be difficult to follow a conversation thread if there was a long conversational exchange between the facilitator and the chatbot. Facilitators would have to scroll up through the conversation window and find the initial button menu. To mitigate this issue, a persistent menu approach could be adopted to accompany each chatbot response to allow the facilitator to select the next quick reply option instead of scrolling through the conversation. Another issue mentioned by bibliotherapy facilitators was the sufficiency of the explanations given by the chatbot. It was stated that if the facilitator needed the chatbot to further explain a response then it is crucial to ensure that conversational design patterns are encoded into the chatbot if the user needs the chatbot to elaborate on a response. This issue high-lights the importance of conversational design patterns in pre-empting user needs. It is important to design conversational 'happy-paths' that allow the user to deviate from initial intent to allow for richer exchanges. To ensure that a chatbot doesn't succumb to form over function, interdisciplinary collaboration is needed to ensure that the content used by the chatbot is reliable and that developers utilise this knowledge in a mean-ingful way that it can be easily accessed using the chatbot.

Reassurance was also mentioned by facilitators as a key component as the chatbot core functionality was to ensure that the facilitators were aware of the underlying meaning of the conversations and questions. Facilitators in the post interview com-mented on the ability of the chatbot to reassure them, providing quick and concise explanations of the story themes and why the story was chosen for that week and also the facilitators were able to refer back to this information using the chatbot. Addi-tionally, persistent menus combined with the use of "panic" phrases such as "Help", "Menu", or "I am lost" should be available to help focus the end-user. It was suggested by facilitators that the chatbot should act as a support hub where the facilitator could use text input to define terms or jargon that deviate from the happy path outlined in the button menu, "*Maybe even like if there was a word you were unsure of or even like if something that comes across that may be specific jargon to the text (story) that you might not necessarily know...".* As stated, this type of functionality would need interdisciplinary collaboration to understand what type of text input the user may use to invoke intents combined with onboarding methods, however a difficult question to answer would be deciding on what amount of information and support the facilitator would need. The facilitator would need to be aware of what content the chatbot could be consulted in order to use text input and if you are using onboarding to explain this to the user, it may be a long list. In this instance menu buttons could be used instead as it would allow designers and developers to immediately inform the facilitator of what information is stored in the backend database using the chatbot frontend.

Facilitators emphasised the importance of the chatbot's persona when discussing their own experience of using other chatbots. Facilitators stated that these chatbot responses are "computerised" in that they lack any emotion or nuance. The importance of personality in chatbots is explored in [17] and key take-home messages indicate that chatbot personality is an integral aspect in chatbot design and authors in [17] state that an agreeable personality creates a more positive usability experience with users, in comparison to a chatbot encoded with a "conscientious" personality. During the pre-interview stage, some facilitators said that they may feel uncomfortable talking to a computer program *"(I am) used to dealing with real people"* and *"I love personality when talking to somebody".* Although anecdotal, this admission gives insight in how users may feel when conferring with machines, the lack of personality and meaning in conversational exchanges. Research suggests that personality is an important element in how users respond and has the power to influence their perception of the chatbot [18, 20]. Personality can relate to how chatbots interact as the chatbot could continually learn from the conversational exchanges with the user. Personalisation intelligence could then be employed to pre-empt what the user needs and give reassurance for a more positive experience.

What would be an Appropriate Style of Interaction with Chatbots to Support Bibliotherapy?

The goal of this chatbot is to guide the facilitator through a series of topics to prepare them for their bibliotherapy session, the chatbot is assuming the role of a virtual assistant and therefore must provide assistance to the user. For the chatbot prototype, the input modality selected was a combination of quick reply menu buttons and text input. Button menus were used to initially begin each chatbot conversation, and subsequent exchanges with the chatbot used a combination of text input and menu buttons. During post interview, facilitators noted the advantage of using buttons to quickly find out information about the story and facilitators preferred using this form of input as each button triggered an intent instantly, and it allowed the conversation to continue quickly. The findings from post interview also correlate with a report published in 2018, which asked 1,051 participants if they have felt frustrations in the past month with traditional online experiences and 34% of respondents stated the website was hard to navigate and 31% could not get answers to simple questions [31]. In the same survey, participants were asked "what would you use a chatbot for?" with 37% of participants stated "Getting a quick answer in an emergency" and 35% saying "Getting detailed answers or explanations..." [31]. In regards to the design of the conversation exchange between chatbot and facilitator, once the quick reply button was selected, the 'payload' of the button is used as a response so the user is reminded what they have selected. The button menu is a permanent feature of each exchange between the facilitator and the chatbot. When the facilitator selects an option listed in the menu, the chatbot response is triggered, however the initial button menu remains a fixture of the conversation. The context connected with the initial button menu is still active and the user can select another button in the fixed menu to trigger other intents.

It was noted by facilitators in the post interview stage that the initial button menu that described each bibliotherapy story should be further broken down into a series of sub-menus to allow for richer conversational exchange e.g. if the button "About story" was selected, another quick reply menu would appear giving the facilitator the opportunity to learn more. Facilitators felt it was easier to use buttons, especially when interacting with the chatbot on a smartphone device. The use of button menu controlled conversation exchanges and the facilitator knew what to expect due to labelled buttons, as opposed to using text-based input in the hope the chatbot would be able to understand what they need or if the chatbot was designed to answer such requests. The use of menu buttons drive the conversation forward also gives the user clarity of what information is available and removes any ambiguity. As stated, the purpose of this chatbot is to guide the facilitators through a series of pre-determined paths to prepare them for their bibliotherapy session, therefore the use of quick reply menus would minimise errors as each conversation intent is triggered based on a list of training phrases that are associated with different intents. Even though the prototype chatbot uses quick reply buttons to drive the conversation, NLP is also used to parse text inputted by the user to match to the correct intent. This combination approach allows the user to follow a guided path but also gives the facilitator the opportunity to deviate from the "happy-path", however it is important to ensure that onboarding is used to inform the user of what types of phrases and keywords can be used to trigger what intents as facilitators stated during post interview stage they weren't aware they were able to use a "search bar" to interact with the chatbot. This issue could be remedied by an onboarding process or simply remove the text input and use menu buttons to guide the facilitator.

7   Recommendations

Several recommendations have been derived based on the thematic analysis of the pre and post interviews. Participants in the study highlighted the importance of *onboarding* when using a chatbot, especially if the chatbot allows for different types of input. Facilitators noted that buttons were the preferred mode of interaction as it removed any ambiguity as to what type of information the chatbot is capable of providing and buttons were noted as a quicker way of retrieving information. Onboarding instructions must be included to inform the user of what chatbot intents can be triggered using the appropriate input type. Onboarding is a necessary feature that allows users to understand how to interact with the chatbot and can serve multiple purposes, e.g. to clarify the capabilities and scope of the chatbot as well as communicating how to interact with the chatbot correctly. The use of 'panic' phrases such as 'help' should also be incorporated if a user is lost or deviates from the happy path. The use of such phrases are highlighted by Chaves et al. as being an essential communicative addition to a chatbot [23], and other works have also highlighted their importance [24]. When developing chatbots across different domain areas, it is vital to involve end-users to ensure that the conversations are meaningful and the functionality is useful. It is essential to ensure that conversational design patterns are encoded into the chatbot involving a range of stakeholders, particularly users who will use the platform in order to increase the reliability and reusability of the chatbot. Cameron et al. [25] designed chatbot interactions in collaboration with clinical professionals to help create meaningful conversations. Similarly, Fitzpatrick et al. [26] combined data collection with chatbot conversations using a team of mental health professionals to personalise CBT support to end-users. Collaborative design is vital to develop meaningful and trustworthy content for the user. Personalisation is another critical step that should be incorporated into chatbots, especially in regards to mental health/therapy chatbots.

Personalisation can be seen as a significant component in customer, and patient support and retention. Market and online business organisations are focused on using personalisation to improve their services especially when incorporating chatbots. Users' personal information can be used to pre-empt their needs and provide meaningful customer support across different channels (web, social media, smartphone). More importantly, the chatbot service is available 24/7 and gives the end-user immediate access to support and to automate tasks. In regards to mental health support, there has been a surge of mental health chatbots that incorporate personalisation to provide immediate and tailored support. In our prototype chatbot, participants were able to find information relating to their bibliotherapy session along with their group details, facilitators stated that this was useful however this could be extended to use chatbots as way to collect data. Bibliotherapy participants could use an auxiliary chatbot located in the same web platform to provide immediate survey feedback regarding their bibliotherapy session. This information could then be used to further personalise and refine sessions. Using chatbots as a means to collate data from web surveys was explored by Kim et al. [29]. Results from this work highlight the potential of collecting survey data that is less satisficing in comparison to using web surveys. The outcomes presented by Kim et al. [29] are promising in using chatbots to collect meaningful data to personalise chatbot services across different domains particularly e-health.

8   Conclusion and Future Work

The aim of this work was to elicit requirements from bibliotherapy facilitators to inform the development of a chatbot based bibliotherapy service. Facilitators were asked to complete several tasks using the prototype. Pre and post interviews were completed that explored their thoughts regarding chatbots in general and their experience using the prototype. Interview transcripts were analysed using future research direction areas discussed in [22] and results from pre-interviews suggested that facilitators reacted positively in using chatbots in preparing them for their bibliotherapy session. Facilitators had the opportunity to use an early prototype of the chatbot to instil discussion and to further refine requirements. Use cases were identified and key messages from pre-interview and post interviews focused on automating informational retrieval and the ability to inform facilitators about psychology terminology that underpins a bibliotherapy session. However, some bibliotherapy facilitators expressed concerns in the usability and content of the chatbot, e.g. if the facilitator needed further explanation regarding psychological themes relating to a story and if the conversational design exchange encoded in the chatbot doesn't allow for further explanations that then this would cause confusion, therefore clarity and usefulness in preparing the chatbot content is integral [16].

Analysis of the post interview revealed that facilitators reacted positively to the content available using the chatbot as well as the combination of using quick reply buttons and text input. The prototype chatbot also acted as a support hub where the facilitator was able to find information about their bibliotherapy group and it was mentioned that facilitators liked this functionality as it personalised the chatbot experience. In terms of future additions to the chatbot, facilitators suggested that chatbots could be used for data collection, as during a regular bibliotherapy session, facilitators use scale questionnaires (e.g. brief resilience scale (BRS), Warwick-Edinburgh Mental Well-being Scale (WEMWBS)) to collect data relating to the well-being of the participants. Facilitators mentioned that there is an opportunity to use chatbots to support and automate this data collection process. Facilitators also noted that appropriate onboarding and affordance approaches need to be integrated to allow the facilitator to easily find the information they need, to highlight the capabilities of the chatbot and also appropriate input methods. In regards to limitations of this work, five bibliotherapy facilitators took part in the study, for future work this would number would be increased when evaluating future chatbot prototype. This study focused on initial experience with a bibliotherapy support chatbot and in future work, a larger group of participants would be asked to use the chatbot in a real world setting over a longer period of time. Focus groups would then be conducted to further refine requirements and to highlight usability issues. Future work would also investigate interaction preferences of facilitators in relation to voice, button menus, or contextual input in using the chatbot platform. Chatbot usage will be recorded and analysed to help refine chatbot interaction and usability.

References

1. Hutchinson, A., Hutchinson, A.: Facebook Messenger by the Numbers 2019 [Infographic]. In: Social Media Today (2019). https://www.socialmediatoday.com/news/facebook-messenger-by-the-numbers-2019-infographic/553809. Accessed 5 Dec 2019
2. Holmes, S., Moorhead, A., Bond, R.R., Zheng, H., Coates, V., McTear, M.: A new automated chatbot for weight loss maintenance. Paper presented at British HCI Conference 2018, pp. 1–5, Belfast (2018). https://doi.org/10.14236/ewic/HCI2018.103
3. Hsu, H.H., Huang, N.F.: Xiao-Shih: the educational intelligent question answering bot on Chinese-based MOOCs. In: Proceedings of the 17th IEEE International Conference on Machine Learning and Applications, ICMLA 2018 (2019). https://doi.org/10.1109/ICMLA.2018.00213
4. Lee, D., Oh, K.J., Choi, H.J.: The chatbot feels you - a counseling service using emotional response generation. In: 2017 IEEE International Conference on Big Data and Smart Computing, BigComp 2017 (2017). https://doi.org/10.1109/BIGCOMP.2017.7881752

5. Oh, K.J., Lee, D., Ko, B., Choi, H.J.: A chatbot for psychiatric counseling in mental healthcare service based on emotional dialogue analysis and sentence generation. In: Proceedings of the 18th IEEE International Conference on Mobile Data Management, MDM 2017 (2017). https://doi.org/10.1109/MDM.2017.64

6. Turner, J.: Bibliotherapy for health and wellbeing: an effective investment. Australas. Public Libr. Inf. Serv. **21**(2), 56 (2008)

7. Songprakun, W., Mccann, T.V.: Using bibliotherapy to assist people to recover from depression in Thailand: relationship between resilience, depression and psychological distress. Int. J. Nurs. Pract. **21**(6), 716–724 (2015). https://doi.org/10.1111/ijn.12250

8. Moldovan, R., Cobeanu, O., David, D.: Cognitive bibliotherapy for mild depressive symptomatology: randomized clinical trial of efficacy and mechanisms of change. Clin. Psychol. Psychother. (2013). https://doi.org/10.1002/cpp.1814

9. Tolin, D.F.: Case study: bibliotherapy and extinction treatment of obsessive-compulsive disorder in a 5-year-old boy. J. Am. Acad. Child Adolesc. Psychiatry **40**(9), 1111–1114 (2001). https://doi.org/10.1097/00004583-200109000-00021

10. Gregory, R.J., Canning, S.S., Lee, T.W., Wise, J.C.: Cognitive bibliotherapy for depression: a meta-analysis (2004). https://doi.org/10.1037/0735-7028.35.3.275

11. NHS Direct (2019). [https://www.nhsdirect.wales.nhs.uk/lifestylewellbeing/bibliotherapyhowitworks. Accessed 17 Jun 2019

12. Casas, J., Mugellini, E., Khaled, O.A.: Food diary coaching chatbot. In: UbiComp/ISWC 2018 - Adjunct Proceedings of the 2018 ACM International Joint Conference on Pervasive and Ubiquitous Computing and Proceedings of the 2018 ACM International Symposium on Wearable Computers (2018). https://doi.org/10.1145/3267305.3274191

13. Gabrielli, S., Marie, K., Corte, C. Della: SLOWBot (chatbot) lifestyle assistant. In: ACM International Conference Proceeding Series (2018). https://doi.org/10.1145/3240925.3240953

14. Key Chatbot Statistics to Know in 2019, Salesforce Blog (2019). https://www.salesforce.com/blog/2019/08/chatbot-statistics.html. Accessed 19 Sept 2019

15. Fitzpatrick, K.K., Darcy, A., Vierhile, M.: Delivering cognitive behavior therapy to young adults with symptoms of depression and anxiety using a fully automated conversational agent (Woebot): a randomized controlled trial. JMIR Mental Health **4**(2), e19 (2017). https://doi.org/10.2196/mental.7785

16. Jain, M., Kumar, P., Kota, R., Patel, S.N.: Evaluating and informing the design of chatbots. In: DIS 2018 Proceedings of the 2018 Designing Interactive Systems Conference (2018). https://doi.org/10.1145/3196709.3196735

17. Smestad, T.L., Volden, F.: Chatbot personalities matters. In: Bodrunova, S.S., et al. (eds.) INSCI 2018. LNCS, vol. 11551, pp. 170–181. Springer, Cham (2019). https://doi.org/10.1007/978-3-030-17705-8_15

18. Ho, A., Hancock, J., Miner, A.S.: Psychological, relational, and emotional effects of self-disclosure after conversations with a chatbot. J. Commun. **68**(4), 712–733 (2018). https://doi.org/10.1093/joc/jqy026

19. Delahunty, F., Wood, I.D., Arcan, M.: First insights on a passive major depressive disorder prediction system with incorporated conversational chatbot. In: CEUR Workshop Proceedings (2018)

20. Rietz, T., Benke, I., Maedche, A.: The impact of anthropomorphic and functional chatbot design features in enterprise collaboration systems on user acceptance. In: 14th International Conference on Wirtschaftsinformatik (2019)

21. Kirchner, T.R., Shiffman, S.: Ecological momentary assessment. In: The Wiley-Blackwell Handbook of Addiction Psychopharmacology (2013). https://doi.org/10.1002/9781118384404.ch20

22. Piccolo, Lara S.G., Mensio, M., Alani, H.: Chasing the chatbots. In: Bodrunova, Svetlana S., et al. (eds.) INSCI 2018. LNCS, vol. 11551, pp. 157–169. Springer, Cham (2019). https://doi.org/10.1007/978-3-030-17705-8_14

23. Chaves, A.P. Gerosa, M.A.: How Should my Chatbot Interact? A Survey on Human-Chatbot Interaction Design (2019). arXiv:1904.02743 [cs.HC]

24. Valério, F.A.M., Guimarães, T.G., Prates, R.O., Candello, H.: Here's what i can do: chatbots' strategies to convey their features to users. In: ACM International Conference Proceeding Series (2017). https://doi.org/10.1145/3160504.3160544

25. Cameron, G., et al.: Assessing the usability of a chatbot for mental health care. LNCS (including subseries Lecture Notes in Artificial Intelligence and Lecture Notes in Bioinformatics) (2019). https://doi.org/10.1007/978-3-030-17705-8_11

26. Fitzpatrick, K.K., Darcy, A., Vierhile, M.: Delivering cognitive behavior therapy to young adults with symptoms of depression and anxiety using a fully automated conversational agent (Woebot): a randomized controlled trial. JMIR Ment. Heal. 4(2), e19 (2017). https://doi.org/10.2196/mental.7785

27. Inkster, B., Sarda, S., Subramanian, V.: An empathy-driven, conversational artificial intelligence agent (Wysa) for digital mental well-being: real-world data evaluation mixed-methods study. JMIR mHealth uHealth 6(11), e12106 (2018). https://doi.org/10.2196/12106

28. Moldovan, R., Cobeanu, O., David, D.: Cognitive bibliotherapy for mild depressive symptomatology: randomized clinical trial of efficacy and mechanisms of change. Clin. Psychol. Psychother. 20(6), 482–493 (2013). https://doi.org/10.1002/cpp.1814

29. Kim, S., Lee, J., Gweon, G.: Comparing data from chatbot and web surveys (2019)

30. Elmasri, D., Maeder, A.: A conversational agent for an online mental health intervention. In: Ascoli, G., Hawrylycz, M., Ali, H., Khazanchi, D., Shi, Y. (eds.) BIH 2016. LNCS (LNAI), vol. 9919, pp. 243–251. Springer, Cham (2016). https://doi.org/10.1007/978-3-319-47103-7_24

31. Drift.com: 2018 The State of Chatbots (2019). https://www.drift.com/wp-content/uploads/2018/01/2018-state-of-chatbots-report.pdf. Accessed 5 Dec 2019

CivicBots – Chatbots for Supporting Youth in Societal Participation

Kaisa Väänänen$^{(\boxtimes)}$ ⓘ, Aleksi Hiltunen, Jari Varsaluoma, and Iikka Pietilä

Unit of Computing, Research Group of Human-Centered Technology, Tampere University, Tampere, Finland
{kaisa.vaananen, aleksi.hiltunen, jari.varsaluoma, iikka.pietila}@tuni.fi

Abstract. Supporting young people to participate in societal development is an important factor in achieving sustainable future. Digital solutions can be designed to help youth participate in civic activities, such as city planning and legislation. To this end, we are using human-centered approach to study how digital tools can help youth discuss their ideas on various societal issues. Chatbots are conversational agents that have potential to trigger and support thought processes, as well as online activities. In this context, we are exploring how chatbots – which we call *CivicBots* – can be used to support youth (16–27 years) in societal participation. We created three scenarios for CivicBots and evaluated them with the youth in an online survey (N = 54). Positive perceptions of the youth concerning CivicBots suggest that CivicBots can advance equality and they may be able to reach youth better than a real person. On the negative side, CivicBots may cause unpleasant interactions by their over-proactive behaviour, and trustworthiness is affected by fears that the bot does not respect user's privacy, or that it provides biased or limited information about societally important issues.

Keywords: Chatbot · CivicBot · Youth · Civic engagement · Societal participation

1 Introduction

Involvement of the youth in civic development is essential for the democracy and sustainable growth of the society [4, 19]. Versatile means of participation can make young people able to engage with issues of their choice, and to engage actively without the presence of adults [2]. Developing and digital tools for societal discussion and activities contributes to the means of eParticipation [20] or citizen participation [15] and at large, to *digital civics* [22] with the aim of improving democracy and human rights.

ALL-YOUTH[1] is a six-year long, multidisciplinary research project aiming at improving the sustainable growth of the Finnish society – inclusive of all kinds of youth. In this project we are developing approaches and solutions for diverse types of

---

[1] ALL-YOUTH is a large research project by five research partners, funded by Strategic Research Council of Finland, in association with Academy of Finland, see https://www.allyouthstn.fi/en/all-youth-2/.

A. Følstad et al. (Eds.): CONVERSATIONS 2019, LNCS 11970, pp. 143–157, 2020.
https://doi.org/10.1007/978-3-030-39540-7_10

youth to help them involve in societal or *civic* activities. The civic activities can be, for example, discussions of current developments or more concrete tasks such as drafting statements or organizing events. Our research group's specific role in ALL-YOUTH is to study and develop digital solutions for the youth's civic engagement.

Earlier studies have identified obstacles for youth's societal participation, including lack of interest, doubt of impact, inadequate communication between youths and officials, and not having knowledge of the channels to utilize [11]. Hence, we are conducting design research of digital solutions that may be enticing for the diverse types of youth and can motivate youth in societal participation. Three main approaches are used in this context; (1) using *novel technologies* that are attractive to the youth and offer natural interactions also to the non-technologically-savvy users, (2) *gamification* of interactions to increase and maintain motivation [10] and (3) *design for all* [18].

Chatbots are a form of novel technologies that may be able to tackle the obstacles related to the lack of interest and knowledge of potential channels for societal participation. Chatbots are conversational agents that use natural language dialogue – via text or speech – to access services online [8]. Chatbots can be either purely software-based or embodied in physical social robots. In this paper we propose the approach to use chatbots as means to support youth's civic activities. The research questions (RQ) are: RQ1: *What are youth's experiences and expectations of chatbots?* RQ2: *How do youth perceive the concept of CivicBots?* To gain understanding to the second RQ, we utilized scenario-based research approach [2] and for that purpose, created three scenarios of CivicBots. This allows exploration of the potential of the concept before any implementation is done. To answer both RQs, we then conducted a survey to evaluate youth's experiences of chatbots in general and their perceptions of CivicBots in specific.

The structure of this paper is as follows: Section two provides a brief review of chatbot interaction and studies of how chatbots can be used to support youth in different useful aims. The following section presents three scenarios for using chatbots for societal or civic participants, i.e. CivicBit scenarios. Section four presents the online survey for evaluating the scenarios, and the results that covered both the youth's experiences of chatbots in general and CivicBots in specific. Sections five and six discuss and conclude the paper.

2   Related Work

Chatbots date back to 1960s. They are conversational agents that use natural language in interaction with their human users, and provide new opportunities for HCI [7]. In the past few years, the advancements in machine learning and widespread use of advanced computer platforms – such as smart phones – have given basis for the rise of the new generation of chatbots [6]. These chatbots are more "intelligent" and have potential in many application domains such as customer service, education and entertainment. Chatbots can be either purely software-based or embodied in physical social robots such as Pepper or Nao[2].

---

[2] Pepper and Nao are examples of commercial social robots, see https://www.softbankrobotics.com/us/pepper and https://www.softbankrobotics.com/us/nao.

People's use motivations and experiences of chatbots have been studied in earlier research. Brandtzaeg and Følstad [1] conducted a study (N = 146) on why people use chatbots and found out that productivity, timeliness and efficient assistance were key factors to use chatbots. Additionally, entertainment, social factors, and curiosity about chatbots as novel agents were considered central motivations of use. Yang et al.'s [24] survey (N = 171) studied users' affective experiences with conversational agents and found that users' overall experience was positive and *interest* was their most salient positive emotion. Furthermore, the study found the evident factors for pragmatic quality to be *helpfulness, proactivity, fluidity, seamlessness* and *responsiveness*; and for hedonic quality major factors are *comfort, pride of using novel technology, fun*, and on the negative side, concerns for *privacy breaks* and *distraction*. Xu et al. [23] found that chatbots are effective in dealing with emotional topics such as complaints in customer service via social media. The "uncanny valley" effect of chatbots was studied by Skjuve et al. [21], who found three factors that affect the user experience of the chatbots: conversation content, chatbot's perceived personality and conversation flow.

Youth have been offered chatbots for different purposes advancing their wellbeing. Fitzpatrick et al. [7] studied the effectiveness of conversational agents in cognitive behaviour therapy for the youth and found in a controlled trial that conversational agents appear to be a feasible, engaging, and effective way to deliver therapy. Kretzschmar et al. [13] addressed the ethical issues that discuss young persons' viewpoints of the strengths and limitations of using chatbots in mental health support. They outline ethical concerns of chatbots for mental health support, including privacy, confidentiality, efficacy, and safety. In the context of questions of adolescents regarding sex, drugs and alcohol, a study [5] showed potential to reach a varied group of adolescents and to provide them with help with these issues. Another study [17] found that a chatbot can help youth transition from school to college. Morgan et al. [16] developed a chatbot framework to improve children's access to a legal advisor that can consult them about their legal rights. The study findings also point out that the chatbot should be able to speak and understand children's language. To our knowledge chatbots have not been studied in the context of civic engagement of the youth.

Følstad et al. [9] have proposed a typology of chatbots based on the *locus of control* and *duration of the interaction*. Locus of control ranges from *chatbot-driven* to *user-driven*, i.e. varies in terms of who has the main control in the conversation. Duration of interaction ranges from very short-term (one-off) relations between users and chatbots to a long-term relations that build on the shared interaction history. We use this initial typology in Sect. 3 where we present scenarios for CivicBots.

3 Scenarios for CivicBots for the Youth

In this section we describe the proposed three scenarios for "civic chatbots"[3], i.e. chatbots that aim at motivating or supporting people to civic activities. We call such chatbots **CivicBots**. For this study, we did not implement any of the proposed chatbots

---

[3] This term has been used for a slightly different purpose by Civic Chatbot company (http://www.civicchatbots.com), i.e. supporting conversation between authorities and civic entities.

since this research effort focuses on the early stage of human-centered design, using a scenario-based approach [2]. The scenarios cover different types of young users, goals and contexts of use, to illustrate the variable purposes and potentials of CivicBots. We also point out how these CivicBots fall into Følstad et al.'s typology [9]. Section 4 presents the online survey in which we evaluated these scenarios with youth.

Scenario 1: VirtualCouncilBot. The goal of this bot is to facilitate discussion concerning an authority-driven topic in an inclusive manner.

Tina (16 years) is an active member of the local youth council. She has been invited to join a discussion platform – Virtual Council *– to a group that gives input to the new environmental law being developed in Finland. The goal is to gain input from the youth on how they see its effects for the local environment and activities. Even though Tina is a societally active person, the group consists of many different types of youth, some of whom are not especially interested in civic participation. One of the group members is VirtualCouncilBot that **presents questions to the participants** such as "what do you think of..." and "would you agree with...". If some participants are **not active, VirtualCouncilBot asks them specifically for their opinion**. Tina and others can also ask VirtualCouncilBot to **explain terms and concepts they do not understand**. VirtualCouncilBot also **summarises the discussion** at the end of the day for the participants and to those who could not participate in this session. It also **brings up the summary in the beginning of the next session** and asks if anyone wants to comment at that point.*

Scenario 2: EuroElectionBot. The goal in this scenario is to raise youth's interest in politics and to activate them in voting, as well as help find a suitable electoral candidate for themselves.

*Max, 19 years, is lying in his bed late in the evening. His mother has reminded him that tomorrow is the last day to vote in the EU election. While **swiping his Instagram feed, a picture of EuroElectionBot shows up**. Even though Max is skeptical about the effectiveness of the Finnish MEPs, he opens the link that takes him to the bot. He installs the EuroElectionBot app and **customizes it to fit his preferred look and style of language**. EuroElectionBot asks Max which topics he would like to discuss, and starts showing short video clips and asks Max to comment their claims. After four topics, the bot asks if Max wants to see more topics. Max agrees, as he finds interaction quite entertaining. After eight topics, **the bot shows the top candidates that could fit Max's opinions**. Finally, EuroElectionBot asks Max if he would like to share the link to the bot's Instagram account to his friends or to some of them.*

Scenario 3: MallBot. The goal in this scenario is to gain understanding of youth's opinions of the current developments in the city, in places where youth naturally spend time in groups.

> *A group of youth are hanging out in the new shopping mall that has become a place to meet after school. Karim (16 years), Maryam (17 years), Alisa (15 years) and Simon (15 years) are immigrants from different countries and have been living in Finland for 4–5 years. They speak Finnish well. They are just fiddling with the mobile devices, except for Alisa who suffers from very poor eyesight and is listening to music. Suddenly Pepper* **robot approaches the youth and introduces itself as MallBot. It asks if they are interested in talking about the development needs of the public transportation in the city.** *They all agree, even though* **MallBot recognizes that Simon is a bit hesitant.** *MallBot asks them about their satisfaction with the current bus lines and also about the expectations of the new tram that is being built in the city.* **Alisa mentions her special needs for non-visual information in public transport, and MallBot especially asks Alisa about these needs.** *MallBot also asks* **Simon for his opinion, as he has not actively participated in the discussion.** *After ten minutes of discussion MallBot thanks them. MallBot shows in its display and says out loud that the* **youth can find the anony-mous results of MallBot's discussions with the youth on a specific website** *next week.*

In summary, Table 1 shows how the scenarios cover various contextual aspects [12] and the key characteristics proposed by Følstad et al.'s typology [9]. The versatile set of scenarios aims to present a broad picture of CivicBots to the study participants.

Table 1. Summary of characteristics of the three CivicBot scenarios.

	VirtualCouncilBot	EuroElectionBot	MallBot
Task context	Discussing legislative issues	Looking for candidates for voting	Giving opinions of local developments
Physical context	Any place	Home, own room	Mall, open space
Social context	Group of strangers (other youth)	None (alone), friends online	Group of friends, other people around
Technical context	Web service/discussion platform	Mobile app	Social robot
Følstad et al.'s typology [9]	Chatbot-driven and user-driven, long-term	User-driven, short-term	Chatbot-driven, short-term

4 Online Survey of Youth's Perpections of Chatbots

The aim of this study was to gain understanding of youth's experiences and perceptions of chatbots, and more specifically of chatbots for civic participation. The RQs were:

RQ1: *What are youth's experiences and expectations of chatbots?*
RQ2: *How do youth perceive the concept of CivicBots?*

In this section we first present the survey content and procedure (Sect. 4.1), and describe the survey respondents' profiles and their use of chatbots Sect. (4.2). The following two Sects. (4.2 and 4.3) present the results related to the two research question.

4.1 Survey Content and Procedure

We designed an online survey with the aim of gaining understanding to the research questions. The survey was primarily qualitative, with some supporting quantitative questions. In the introduction of the survey, we defined chatbots as follows: *"Chatbot is a software that discusses with the user via written text or speech about a topic, e.g. information search, booking time or finding a product. Chatbots usually function in association to web services or mobile apps, such as bank service or net stores. Siri and other 'intelligent' help applications can be considered as chatbots."*

There were two parts in the survey, the first one on user experiences of chatbots in general and the second part on using chatbots in societal participation. The emphasis was on qualitative data with some supporting quantitative questions.

In the first part of the survey (related to RQ1) the questions were about general chatbot experiences and expectations: *How often have you used chatbots? What chatbots have you used? What good experiences have you had with chatbots? What bad experiences have you had? What are your perceptions of chatbots?* The last question contained six eight-scale semantic differential questions in the form *"I think that chatbots are..." useless – useful, unreliable – reliable, boring – interesting, difficult to use – easy to use, complex – simple and unhelpful – helpful* (adapted from Robot Attitude Scale [2]).

In the second part of the survey (RQ2), the respondents were first explained that chatbots could also be used for helping people participate in various societal activities. They were then presented the three scenarios described in Sect. 3 of this paper. After each scenario they were asked to rate their perception of the scenario with two seven-scale semantic differentials of *incredible – credible* and *uninteresting to myself – interesting to myself*. They were also asked to explain their ratings with a qualitative answer.

In the end of the survey were questions about respondents' backgrounds, including their level of societal participation. The survey was in Finnish. We used Google Forms for the survey and it was open between June 24th and September 3rd, 2019.

Data Analysis. We analysed the qualitative data by coding it thematically in an iterative process. The thematic analysis was done for each main survey question data, first bottom up and then thematically grouped to form categories for user experiences and expectations (RQ1). From the qualitative data, we also quantified the types of chatbots used, good and bad experiences with chatbots, and expected chatbot characteristics. Mean and standard deviation (SD) values were calculated for chatbot experience ratings. For RQ2, a qualitative cross-scenario analysis was conducted for the open answers related to the user perceptions of the three CivicBot scenarios.

4.2 Respondents' Profiles and Use of Chatbots

Respondents were recruited via various mailings lists and personal networks, as well as from volunteers of our earlier related research. We received 54 valid responses to the survey. Additional four responses were omitted as outliers, because they gave a straight line of scores 1 to all questions and no answers to the open questions.

Respondent Profiles. The average age of the respondents was 22.7 years, with range of 16–27 and mode of 25 years. There were 27 women, 23 men, and two "other" in the respondents, and two did not want to answer about their gender. The respondents were Finnish speaking. Regarding their educational level, four were in high school, three had vocational education and the rest 44 were in university. Respondents societal participation is rather high, measured with scale 1–7 (disagree-agree) by questions *I am interested in politics* (mean 4.87, SD 1.76), *I often discuss timely events with my friends or family* (mean 5.24, SD 1.61), *I read/ watch the news on timely events* (mean 5.46, SD 1.72) and *I vote/ would vote in the next election* (mean 6.07, SD 1.49).

Chatbot Use. 26 out of 54 respondents have used chatbots over five times, 17 have used 2–5 times, 7 have used one time and 4 have not used chatbots.

The respondents have used a versatile set of chatbots. The 46 responses (out of 54) that mentioned chatbots the respondents have used included altogether 86 mentions of chatbots. Chatbots are used with a versatile set of everyday tasks and services. The most often used bots related to banking (18 mentions), using Siri or Google Assistant (13), online stores (12), student housing (8), insurances (7) teleoperator and authorities (4 each). Other uses of chatbots were mentioned for finding election candidates, messaging, IT helpdesk, wellbeing counselor, airport service, driving school and software help.

4.3 Youth's Experiences and Expected Characteristics of Chatbots

Respondents reported a versatile set of experiences with currently existing chatbots, both good and bad. Figure 1 presents the thematically categorised experiences.

Good Experiences. **Usefulness** was the most commonly reported experience. *"Chatbot linked me to a relevant web page where there was additional information."* (Respondent 43, R43). Many chatbot experiences were **clear and fluent**. *"Chatbot for the post office gave me clear instructions for sending a parcel. The service was fluent and fast."* (R6). Many respondents felt the best way of getting help was to **get to a human customer service**. *"The best experience was when the chatbot gave me the contact information to a real person."* (R7) Positive experiences also came from chatbots **understanding the user (surprisingly well)**. *"Google Assistant keeps a*

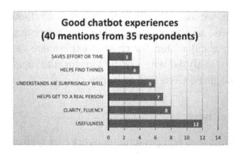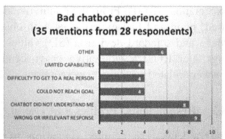

Fig. 1. Good (left) and bad (right) experiences with chatbots.

sensible conversational continuum and understands question in the conversational context." (R26) Chatbots also **help find things** and **save time and effort**.

Bad Experiences. The most commonly reported bad experience was with chatbots that gave **wrong or irrelevant response**. *"Bank chatbot did not work, it did not understand my issue and repeated same things several times. I could not take care of my issues."* (R6) This example also illustrates the problem of **not reaching one's goal**. Further problem areas were that **the bot does not understand the user** and even when needed, the **chatbot does not take the user to a real person**. Such experiences can lead to strong frustration. *"The bot did not understand the sentence but you had to give it just words. You could not call to a customer service person and the bit did not even understand that it does not understand. I got so frustrated with the bot that I did not deal with this company anymore."* (R56). Other issues include **chatbots that are too "pushy"**. *"Chatbots that attack to you every time you go to a new web page are really irritating."* (R24) Chatbots should also not **fake that they are a real person**, and even causing **privacy concerns**. *"It is most irritating when chatbots present themselves as 'Elina' or some other fake name, especially when sometimes the information you have to give there is very personal and easy to misuse."* (R36) **Limited capabilities** of chatbots also caused bad experiences.

Chatbot Experience Ratings. Respondents rated chatbots based on their own experiences. These ratings were asked on scale 1–8 to gain responses that were not neutral; additionally a "cannot estimate" response was possible. The following mean and SD values were given: *"I think that chatbots are…" useless – useful* (mean 5.48, SD 1.64), *unreliable – reliable* (mean 4.44, SD 1.47), *boring – interesting* (mean 5.04, SD 1.89), *difficult to use – easy to use* (mean 5.72, SD 1.93), *complex – simple* (mean 5.78, SD 1.71) *and unhelpful – helpful* (mean 4.76, SD 1.89). In this respondent sample, reliability was rated the lowest while usefulness, ease of use and simplicity were rated highest. These ratings are in line with the found experience categories in Fig. 1.

Expected Chatbot Characteristics. Figure 2 shows the categorisation of good characteristics participants expect from chatbots. These are elaborate in the following.

Good **conversational skills** is a major requirement. *"Chatbots need the skill of understanding lots of words also from different dialects. It would be good to also direct the conversation with follow-up questions if the bot does not immediately understand*

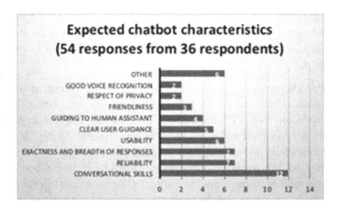

Fig. 2. Expected chatbot characteristics

what the user is after." (R10). Chatbots should offer **clear user guidance**. *"The user should be easily able to understand what services the bot offers and how the user can 'order' certain service. For example a visible list of keywords that guarantees certain functionality."* (R12) **Reliability** and **guiding the user to a real person** are also expected, when the chatbot cannot provide a solution. *"Versatile set of questions, properly taught chatbot, and not a bot that only understands the simplest questions and avoids taking you to the proper customer service."* (R13) Clear indication that **privacy is taken care of** is an important factor also with chatbots. *"There should be a clear message that your conversations are protected and will not be given outside of company X"* (R36) "Other" category includes characteristics such as *humour, should make it clear that they are a bot* and *suitably narrow scope.*

4.4 Youth's Perceptions of CivicBots

In this section we present the results related to RQ2, i.e. how do respondents perceive the idea of CivicBots based on the three scenarios presented to them in the survey. Based on the qualitative analysis of the responses to the question *"Please justify why you think this scenario is un/credible or un/appealing"*, the following sections summarise the main issues that came up with the individual scenarios.

VirtualCouncilBot (Scenario 1). The positive aspects of this scenario included viewpoints that everyone's opinion is heard, the bot can give new perspectives, and that this kind of chatbot can stimulate and activate people. *"The bot can encourage people to think of a topic from new perspectives that would not otherwise occur to them."* (R22) The idea of summarizing the discussion by the bot was considered valuable. It was also considered technically credible and exciting because of its AI use. On the negative side it was brought up that the bot might restrict discussions, and it might irritate or stress some people if the bot asks them something directly. *"It is not credible that inactive youth could be motivated to participate in the conversation."* (R16) Some respondents considered the practical added value of the chatbot to be minimal (e.g. compared to form filling). A critical consideration for the whole concept is that the bot should not replace contacts to human experts, e.g. decision makers. *"It feels a bit weird that a facilitator would be replaced with a bot. It gives an impression that law makers don't care about youth's viewpoints that much that they would want to spend their own time on leading the group."* (R51)

EuroElectionBot (Scenario 2). CivicBot's purpose in this scenario was considered important and positive because it may help youth form opinions better than traditional voting advice web services. *"Chatbot could increase my interest to find a suitable candidate, because I could ask it directly about unclear issues."* (R29) *"If the bot tried to collect information about the values of the humans and based on this, it would suggest candidates to the user, this would be interesting."* (R56) Such chatbot could be fun to use and it could excite and encourage youth to vote. *"Chatbot would offer a more adaptive version [compared to election candidate surveys] that could affect voting activity."* (R23) The negative viewpoints concerned the fact that politics is a difficult topic to cover because of its multifaceted nature and the potential bias of the bot in presenting the election candidates. *"This is an interesting thought, but I feel that the candidates proposed by the bot would not necessarily be reliable or they could be 'fiddled' [by the developers]."* (R38) On a practical side, to reduce user's effort, such single-use functionality should not be an app (that needs to be installed) but a web service.

MallBot (Scenario 3). The positive aspects of this scenario included the potential for better inclusion and offering a channel without direct human contact. CivicBot could be a good way to get opinions of a broad group of people, also the quiet ones. *"The idea of a bot that takes also the quiet persons into account is especially good, because it enables listening to them also."* (R2) Many youth may be more eager to speak and be honest to a robot than to a human being. On the negative side, many felt that the bot should not try – or force – to involve people who do not want to participate, and the robot was seen similar to a face-to-face fundraiser, with a very negative connotation. *"Finns get anxious so fast if someone comes to talk to them in public places. Face-to-face fundraisers are everyone's worst nightmare. Personally I would love this experience."* (R7) The context was considered both as a positive opportunity to reach the youth but also risky because of the noisy environment and problems that such robot could cause to people with vision and hearing impairments. It was doubted that the robot might be harassed or broken. *"The robot would probably be broken quite fast and some people would not reply to it appropriately, so it would be useful."* (R1) Some respondents considered this a utopian scenario, as they thought robots are technically not this advanced, e.g. they could move on wheels or have any kind of emotional intelligence. Of all three scenarios, the credibility of this scenario was criticized the most.

Cross-Scenario Analysis. The responses concerning the three scenarios on their interest and appeal to self were analysed across the scenarios. The findings reveal overall positive and negative themes of CivicBots for youth participation.

(**VC** = VirtualCouncilBot, **EB** = EuroElectionBot, **MB** = MallBot)

Positive themes across the scenarios are:

Empowerment and Advancing Equality. Using CivicBots offers the potential to *broaden youth's perspectives. "The bot can motivate youth to think about a topic from a perspective that would otherwise not occur to them."* (R22, VC) Furthermore, Civic-Bots can *activate a broad spectrum of youth* in societal participation, including the more introvert and less active youth. *"Personally I find this kind of technology interesting and it's a plus that the bot can take the more quiet people into account."* (R8, MB)

Exciting Interactions. CivicBots can be *helpful and understanding,* and even *fun.* CivicBots can *adapt to user's behaviour. "Raising discussion in a way that is pleasant to the target group is really good! However the formulation of the questions must be objective."* (R14, EB) Chatbots can also *raise curiosity,* which may further raise interest in the subject of the conversation.

Better than Humans. Bots may feel *more approachable than a humans,* especially for sensitive topics, and *youth may be more honest to a bot* than to a human. *"This can be an easier way to get feedback, and it can also be easier to approach than a real person."* (R25, MB)

Usefulness and Novelty. CivicBots are *a new way to reach the youth,* and they *suit many contexts.* They may *help youth form opinions* on societal issues. They are *technically interesting* and offer mostly credible means to support the kinds of goals and situations described in the scenarios. *"Before I met Replika [a chatbot offering support for youth's mental health] I would have been more doubtful but now I believe that chatbots can be really intelligent and useful. [...] Bots are increasingly timely and I believe they can offer all kind of benefits in the future. And entertainment, even companionship?"* (R34, VC)

Negative themes across the scenarios are:

Unpleasant Interactions. CivicBots' *proactiveness may irritate users,* or they may *feel generally unattractive.* CivicBots may *appear culturally inappropriate* or mismatching with the youth's conversational styles. *"If chatbot poses questions directly to an individual it could be quite irritating/stressful for the youth."* (R7, VC)

Lack of Trustworthiness. Issues related to trusting CivicBots include *privacy* and *fear of sharing discussions without consent. "The bot posting a summary online without asking the participants if it's okay is VERY CONCERNING." (R2, MB)* There were also many doubts about *neutrality or bias of the bot.* Bots may be *misleading or restricting discussion* without the users knowing about it. *"If the programming of the bot is not unbiased, it could lead voters to certain direction"* (R20, EB)

Inability to Persuade Unwilling Youth to Participate. Users may *give inappropriate or "nonsense" answers* if they do not feel motivated to cooperate. Still, CivicBots *should not force anyone to participate. "It is not credible that inactive youth could be motivated to join in the discussion." (R13, VC)*

Uselessness or Unfit to Task. Some respondents thought that CivicBots offer *minimal added value to current alternatives.* There was doubt of bots *not being able to handle a* *broad set of perspectives* in discussions, or to be able to *keep up long-term discussions*. CivicBots *should not replace human interactions* in societal participation. *"Why would there not be a human being in this situation?"* (R51, MB)

Misfit to Context Especially in the case of a physical robot, *people may mishandle the robot* physically or verbally. *"The bot would probably be broken quite fast and probably some of the people would answer to the bot in inappropriate ways."* (R1, MB) *Over-proactive behaviour* of CivicBots may cause frustrations in certain task contexts. *"Finns get anxious so fast if someone comes to talk to them in public places. Face-to-face fundraisers are the worst nightmare."* (R7, MB)

Practical Unfeasibility. For some respondents CivicBots seem *incredible (far-fetched) technically, economically and practically.*

5   Discussion

Enabling civic engagement for a broad spectrum of people is an essential element of societal inclusion and wellbeing. As was pointed out in introduction, there are known obstacles for youth's societal participation [14]. CivicBots may offer one way to tackle the obstacles by proactively raising youth's interest and knowledge of potential channels for participation.

The findings of the study presented in this paper reveals positive and negative experiences and perceptions of chatbots in general and CivicBots in specific. Regarding general chatbot experiences (RQ1), many issues related to chatbot use and user needs were found similar to Brandtzaeg & Følstad's survey study [1], e.g. efficient assistance, timeliness and curiosity. In comparison to Yang et al.'s [24] survey results, our sample of young people brought up similar experiential issues, in specific fluidity of interaction, pride in using novel technology, and fun. To our knowledge there is no earlier research about using chatbots for supporting youth to civic participation (RQ2), so this paper presents initial foundation to this line of research.

5.1   Opportunities and Pitfalls of CivicBots

Our findings indicates that CivicBots have potential but based on the youth also brought up many doubts and critiques of the concept. Here we summarise opportunities and pitfalls that we think should be considered when designing and implementing chatbots for youth for the purpose of motivating them in civic participation.

Opportunities of CivicBots:

- Raising users' curiosity and interest in civic activities and hence motivating people to learn and become more empowered members of the society
- Activating diverse types of youth to advance equality
- Lowering the threshold of participation by bringing CivicBots to users' task contexts and opportune physical contexts
- Approachability and potential of supporting youth with issues in which human contact may seem difficult

- Enabling emotional human-chatbot interaction and potentially increasing commitment to a social cause

  Pitfalls of CivicBots:

- Insufficient level of intelligence of the chatbots and user frustration that may follow
- Not adapting appropriately to conversation styles and preferences that may vary with different users, e.g. in terms of over-proactive chatbot behaviour
- Perceived lack of trustworthiness and confidentiality (privacy) of the interactions, especially with very personal information
- Contact to human stakeholders (e.g. decision makers) should not be fully replaced
- Practical challenges in terms of teaching CivicBots to act in an unbiased and respectable ways

5.2 Limitations of the Study

The online survey sample was rather small (54) and culturally narrow. The age group of the participant sample was somewhat biased towards upper limits of the youth target group of 16–27 years. These issues may naturally have an effect to the diversity of experiences and issues found. However, we argue that especially the qualitative findings offer novel insights to youth's chatbot and CivicBot preferences. A methodological limitation is that survey and written scenarios are limited methods for gaining deep understanding of actual experiences with (yet) non-existing interactions. Contextual studies with real prototypes would provide more solid insights of the phenomena of chatbot interaction. Still, we believe that the qualitative findings provide indication of the main areas that need to be considered when designing CivicBots for the youth.

6 Conclusion and Future Work

In this paper, we have proposed to use chatbots – CivicBots – to support youth in societal activities. The conducted online survey to evaluate three CivicBot scenarios revealed both positive and negative issues that can be used as inspiration of chatbot design for youth's societal participation. We believe chatbots are a promising HCI approach to raise curiosity, provoke thought processes and to provide information in an interesting and human-centered way. Chatbots can advance understanding and involvement of different types of user groups in societal activities and hence increase their equality.

In ALL-YOUTH project we are developing *Virtual Council*, a web-based service and are also considering to implement a chatbot similar to Scenario 1. We will deploy and evaluate Virtual Council in the legislative commenting round of the new environmental strategy and related laws developed in Finland in year 2020. Implementing other scenarios are also under consideration. They could be developed also in combination with gamification techniques [10] such as rewards and challenges provided by chatbots. Accessibility of the services will also be addressed, and a speech-based chatbot could provide support for youth with sight impairments.

On the theoretical side, the typology of Følstad et al. [9] could be developed further to cover interaction dimensions that may be significant, such as *entertaining – practical* (or *hedonic – pragmatic*), *single user – multi-user* chatbots and *evolving (capable of learning) – static*. We are also interested in defining *user experience goals* for experience-driven design [11] of CivicBots for different usage contexts and user groups.

Acknowledgements. We thank Jutta Pietilä for her comments on the early version of the paper. We are grateful for the Strategic Research Council of Finland for the ALL-YOUTH grant (decision no 312689).

References

1. Brandtzaeg, P.B., Følstad, A.: Why people use chatbots. In: Kompatsiaris, I. et al. (eds.) Internet Science. INSCI 2017. LNCS, vol. 10673, pp. 377–392. Springer, Cham (2017). https://doi.org/10.1007/978-3-319-70284-1_30
2. Broadbent, E., et al.: Retirement home staff and residents' preferences for healthcare robots. In: RO-MAN 2009 - The 18th IEEE International Symposium on Robot and Human Interactive Communication, 2009, pp. 645–650, Toyama (2009)
3. Carroll, J.M.: Five reasons for scenario-based design. Interact. Comput. **13**(1), 43–60 (2000)
4. Checkoway, B.: What is youth participation? Children Youth Serv. Rev. **33**(2), 340–345 (2011). https://doi.org/10.1016/j.childyouth.2010.09.017
5. Crutzen, R., Peters, G.-J.Y., Portugal, S.D., Fisser, E.M., Grolleman, J.J.: An artificially intelligent chat agent that answers adolescents' questions related to sex, drugs, and alcohol: an exploratory study. J. Adolesc. Health **48**(5), 514–519 (2011)
6. Dale, R.: The return of the chatbots. Nat. Lang. Eng. **22**(5), 811–817 (2016). Cambridge University Press
7. Fitzpatrick, K.K., Darcy, A., Vierhile, M.: Delivering cognitive behavior therapy to young adults with symptoms of depression and anxiety using a fully automated conversational agent (Woebot): a randomized controlled trial. JMIR Mental Health **4**(2), e19 (2017)
8. Følstad, A., Brandtzæg, P.B.: Chatbots and the new world of HCI. Interactions **24**(4), 38–42 (2017). https://doi.org/10.1145/3085558
9. Følstad, A., Skjuve, M., Brandtzaeg, P.B.: Different chatbots for different purposes: towards a typology of chatbots to understand interaction design. In: Bodrunova, S., et al. (eds.) Internet Science. INSCI 2018. LNCS, vol. 11551, pp. 145–156, Springer, Cham (2018). https://doi.org/10.1007/978-3-030-17705-8_13
10. Hamari, J., Koivisto, J., Sarsa, H.: Does gamification work? A literature review of empirical studies on gamification. In: Proceedings of the HICCS (2014)
11. Hassenzahl, M.: Experience Design: Technology for All the Right Reasons. Morgan & Claypool, San Rafael (2010)
12. ISO 9241-210: 2019 International Standardisation Organisation (2019). https://www.iso.org/standard/77520.html
13. Kretzschmar, K., Tyroll, H., Pavarini, G., Manzini, A., Singh, I.: Can your phone be your therapist? Young people's ethical perspectives on the use of fully automated conversational agents (Chatbots) in mental health support. Biomed. Inf. Insights **11** (2017). In: Originally in Proceedings of Digital Mental Health Conference, London (2017)

14. Meriläinen, N., Pietilä, I., Varsaluoma, J.: Digital services and youth participation in processes of social change: world café workshops in Finland. In: 2018 ECPR General Conference, Universität Hamburg (2018)
15. Michels, A., De Graaf, L.: Examining citizen participation: local participatory policy making and democracy. Local Gov. Stud. **36**(4), 477–491 (2010)
16. Morgan, J., Paiement, A., Williams, J., Wyner, A., Seisenberger, M.: A chatbot framework for the children's legal centre. Front. Artif. Intell. Appl. 205–209 (2018)
17. Page, L., Gehlbach, H.: How an artificially intelligent virtual assistant helps students navigate the road to college. AERA Open **3**(4) (2017). https://doi.org/10.1177/2332858417749220
18. Persson, H., Åhman, H., Yngling, A., Gulliksen, J.: Universal design, inclusive design, accessible design, design for all: different concepts – one goal? On the concept of accessibility – historical, methodological and philosophical aspects. Univ. Access Inf. Soc. **14**, 505–526 (2014)
19. Pietilä, I., Varsaluoma, J., Väänänen, K.: Understanding the digital and non-digital participation by the gaming youth. In: Lamas, D., Loizides, F., Nacke, L., Petrie, H., Winckler, M., Zaphiris, P. (eds.) INTERACT 2019. LNCS, vol. 11747, pp. 453–471. Springer, Cham (2019). https://doi.org/10.1007/978-3-030-29384-0_28
20. Rexhepi, A., Filiposka, S., Trajkovik, V.: Youth e-participation as a pillar of sustainable societies. J. Clean. Prod. **174**, 114–122 (2018)
21. Skjuve, M., Haugstveit, I.M., Følstad, A., Brandtzaeg, P.B.: Help! Is my chatbot falling into the uncanny valley? An empirical study of user experience in human-chatbot interaction. Hum. Technol. **15**(1), 30–54 (2019)
22. Vlachokyriakos, V., Crivellaro, C., Le Dantec, C.A., Gordon, E., Wright, P., Olivier, P.: Digital civics: citizen empowerment with and through technology. In: Proceedings of CHI 2016 (Extended Abstracts). ACM, New York (2016)
23. Xu, A., Liu, Z., Guo, Y., Sinha, V., Akkiraju, R.: A new chatbot for customer service on social media. In: Proceedings of CHI 2017, pp. 3506–3510. ACM, New York (2017)
24. Yang, X., Aurisicchio, M., Baxter, W.: Understanding affective experiences with conversational agents. In: Proceedings of CHI 2019, p. 542. ACM, New York (2019)

Using Theory of Mind to Assess Users' Sense of Agency in Social Chatbots

Evelien Heyselaar$^{(\boxtimes)}$ ⓘ and Tibor Bosse ⓘ

Radboud Universiteit Nijmegen, Nijmegen, The Netherlands
e.heijselaar@maw.ru.nl

Abstract. The technological advancements in the field of chatbot research is booming. Despite this, it is still difficult to assess which social characteristics a chatbot needs to have for the user to interact with it as if it had a mind of its own. Review studies have highlighted that the main cause is the low number of research papers dedicated to this question, and the lack of a consistent protocol within the papers that do address it. In the current paper, we suggest the use of a Theory of Mind task to measure the implicit social behaviour users exhibit towards a text-based chatbot. We present preliminary findings suggesting that participants adapt towards this basic chatbot significantly more than when they conduct the task alone ($p < .017$). This task is quick to administer and does not require a second chatbot for comparison, making it an efficient universal task. With it, a database could be built with scores of all existing chatbots, allowing fast and efficient meta-analyses to discover which characteristics make the chatbot appear more 'human'.

Keywords: Chatbot · Social cognition · Theory of mind · Mind attribution · Perspective taking

1 Introduction

Since the early days of ELIZA [1] and A.L.I.C.E. [2], there has been an exponential explosion of chatbots. Chatbots today are supported by a variety of different techniques and languages (e.g., Cleverscript, Chatscript, AIML, Deep Learning, etc.), and built for a variety of purposes, such as helping children with their prescription medication ("Pharmabot"; [3]), or assisting prospective students navigate their new university ("Ola"; [4]). However, with this constant introduction of new chatbots and new supporting services, the field is losing sight on what is necessary to build a chatbot that the user interacts with as if it has a mind of its own: The ultimate goal when it comes to social bots.

Neurerer and colleagues [5] state that making a conversational agent acceptable to users is primarily a social, not only a technical, problem to solve. Therefore, a chatbot should not only have the capability of understanding what the user wants, but have the social characteristics to converse with the user as if it were completely autonomous. In the past three years, multiple review papers have been published that attempt to organize and structure the results from social chatbot research, with the goal to highlight which social features in the chatbot's programming produce a greater sense of

© Springer Nature Switzerland AG 2020
A. Følstad et al. (Eds.): CONVERSATIONS 2019, LNCS 11970, pp. 158–169, 2020.
https://doi.org/10.1007/978-3-030-39540-7_11

agency when the user interacts with it. Surprisingly, all review papers find it difficult to find articles that conduct quantitative research on the social aspects of chatbots. For example, Radziwill and Benton [6] conducted a review from 2006–2017 and only identified 36 scholarly articles and conference papers that addressed this aim, whereas Chaves and Gerosa [7] managed to find only 58, of which the majority were less than 10 years old. These review papers highlight that even though chatbot research has been ongoing for nearly sixty years, we still do not have enough data to conduct a proper review of which social characteristics elicit the greatest sense of agency from the user. This is surprising, considering the overarching aim of chatbots is to communicate with human users in a human-like manner.

The review papers also highlighted another issue regarding social chatbot research: There is no systematic method to quantify how successful a chatbot is at appearing to have a mind of its own. For example, Chaves and Gerosa [7] found 58 papers that investigated which social characteristics provide a "realistic" chatbot experience, e.g., proactivity, manners, moral agency, etc. However, their summarization of this work showed little to no overlap in the social characteristics studied in the individual papers, making it difficult to identify whether certain social attributes contribute more to giving the chatbot a greater sense of agency. For example, is a chatbot that is able to provide a continuous conversation seen as more human-like than a chatbot that can appropriately respond when it does not have the information the user requested? The authors attempted to make a model to link the themes together (Fig. 1 in [7]) but in order to test their model, a unrealistically long series of two-way comparison experiments would need to be conducted. Surprisingly, this is also the suggestion of another review paper [8], most likely because it is near to impossible to glean anything from existing work.

It is clear that, although technically, chatbot research has come a long way in the last sixty years, the social aspect of chatbot research needs to be attended to. Which characteristics cause a chatbot to be perceived as having agency? The aim of the current paper is to propose a short task that can easily measure how much agency the end user attributed to the chatbot, also referred to as 'mind attribution.' The proposed task does not require a two-way comparison; instead, a single chatbot is tested and an average score is calculated. This score can then be instantly compared to other chatbots that have already been evaluated with this task. The aim is to build a rich database which can easily be used for meta-analyses to determine which social characteristics elicit the most pronounced feeling, in the end-user, that the chatbot has a mind of their own.

1.1 Theoretical Background

For studies that do conduct quantitative research to compare user experience with different chatbots, the common procedure is to use a questionnaire. However, a questionnaire triggers the participant to explicitly evaluate their behaviour, whereas everyday social interactions are mostly supported by implicit (automatic, unconscious) processes [9]. Hence it is logical that an ecologically valid test of user experience should be based on implicit behaviour. For this reason, the task we propose is based on implicit social cognition.

We propose to use a social Theory of Mind task. Theory of Mind is the ability to attribute mental states (beliefs, intents, desires, emotions, knowledge, etc.) to others and to understand that others have beliefs, desires, and perspectives that are different from one's own [10]. This is the definition of what we want users to experience when they are interacting with a chatbot. In this Theory of Mind task, participants work together with a chatbot to complete a goal. It is therefore not clear to the participant that the aim of the task is to measure their implicit opinion of the chatbot.

The task we propose has been conducted before in human-human experimental studies [11, 12]. In this task, participants were seated in front of separate monitors with a divider so that they could not see each other. One participant was assigned to be the speaker, the other the listener. It was the task of the speaker to describe objects in an array (see Fig. 2) in a way that the listener could identify it on their screen. The manipulation was such that on certain trials, the speaker was asked to describe one of three identical objects differing in size. One of these three objects was not visible to the listener, and the speaker was aware of this. Therefore, if the speaker considered the listener's perspective they would describe the object in a way that ignores the third, "hidden" object. However, if they did not, they would describe the object using the term "medium". This would make it hard for the listener to identify which of the two objects they see is the "medium" one. There was no feedback, nor were clarification questions allowed, and thus the speaker could complete the task however they wanted, even if it made it difficult for the listener. In the Vanlangendonck study [12], they showed that when participants complete this task together, the speaker adapts their responses so that the listener can better identify the objects 70% of the time. When the speaker conducted the same task alone, they would adapt their responses significantly less ($p < .001$).

The Vanlangendonck study [12] also measured the brain activity of the speaker using fMRI while participants conducted this task, and showed significant activation in the medial prefrontal cortex (activated when thinking about the mental states of others) and in the temporoparietal junction (an area important for inferring the temporary states of other people, such as goals, intentions, and desires). The study therefore illustrated that when conducting this task, participants "put themselves in their partner's shoes" when describing the objects. Our assumption is that participants will only do this if they believe that their partner has a mental state to consider, i.e. a mind of their own.

In the current study, we will conduct a replication of the Vanlangendonck study, but have participants pair up with a text-based chatbot. If the participant believes that the chatbot has a mental state that needs to be considered, then participants will adapt their description of the objects significantly more than when they conduct the task alone. We further predict that the proportion of adaptation will be less than those reported in Vanlangendonck and colleagues, as we do not assume that the chatbot we use is humanlike enough to warrant that much adaptation. This gradient of adaptation will therefore allow this simple task to be used to measure how close a chatbot is to being humanlike, according to the perception of the user.

2   Methods

2.1   Participants

Thirty-nine native Dutch speakers (32 female, 1 undisclosed, M_{age}: 19.18 years, SD_{age}: 1.49) were recruited from the Radboud Universiteit Nijmegen student participant database. The high proportion of females does not concern us, as our chatbot was designed to be gender neutral (see below).

The participants gave digital informed consent before the start of the experiment. Participants were rewarded with one credit for their participation. The study was approved by the Ethics Committee Faculty of Social Sciences of the Radboud University Nijmegen (ECSW-2018-117).

2.2   Procedure

Participants were invited to complete an online experiment consisting of two tasks they would complete together with a text-based chatbot (a cinema-task and a referential communication game), and one task by themselves (the non-communicative version of the referential communication game). The order of the chatbot and non-chatbot tasks was randomized.

Cinema-Task. This task functioned as a cover-story so that the participants would interact with the chatbot for a significant period of time to get a stable impression of it. This task is based on the one described in van der Kallen [13], the results of which showed that the cinema-task was long enough for participants to rate different chatbots significantly differently (N = 160, $p < .001$). The participants were instructed to complete two tasks with a chatbot named Tomke. The name was chosen to be gender neutral to negate any possible gender-based influences. In the cinema-task, Tomke would pretend to be a cinema-assistant chatbot, and the participant's goal was to extract information in order to answer the following questions: "Which films are playing tonight?", "How much does a ticket cost?", and "How can you best reach the cinema by train?" The messaging system was set up so that the left panel displayed the conversation with Tomke and the right panel displayed the three questions for easy reference (Fig. 1A). Once the participant had all the information they needed, they would communicate this to Tomke, who would direct them to the next page. This page contained the same three questions, which the participant then had to answer.

Referential Communication Game. This task directly followed the cinema-task for all participants. The task is based on the one described in Vanlangendonck and colleagues [11, 12].

Participants were informed that they would view an array of objects that they would have to describe for the chatbot. The chatbot, however, could only see the *opposite* side of said array. Each array contained 3 closed slots on either side.

Participants completed 120 trials. On each trial, the participant described a specific object in the array in a way that would allow the chatbot to select the correct object from their side of the array. During the first phase of the trial (3000 ms), the participant saw their side of the array. Then the participant was cued by means of a red circle

A. The set-up of the cinema task

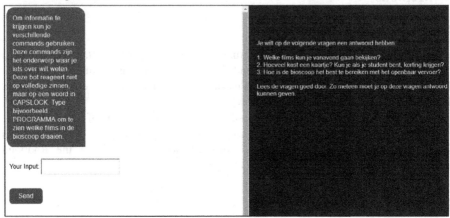

B. The set-up of the Referential Commiunication Game

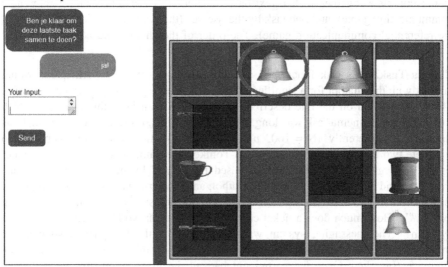

Fig. 1. The set-up of the online tasks. **A.** During the cinema task, the chat panel was on the left, a brief description of the task on the right. Translation of the chatbot text: "To get information, you can use different commands. These commands should be the topic of your inquiry. This bot does not respond to full sentences but to single word written in CAPSLOCK. For example, type the word PROGRAMME to see which films are playing in the cinema" **B.** During the Referential Communication Game, the chat panel was on the left, the array with objects to describe was on the right. Translation of the chatbot text: "Are you ready to do this last task together?" User response: "Yes!" (Color figure online)

around one of the objects, and described this object by typing it into the chat window. The cued object was always mutually visible. Participants were instructed not to use descriptions referring to the position of the object in the array, such as 'upper left corner' or 'rightmost'. Participants were not given any on-screen or verbal feedback about their performance, as is similar to the human version of this task. The left panel was again the chat window, and the right panel now displayed the array (Fig. 1B).

Non-communicative Referential Communication Game. This task could either be presented before the cinema task or after the referential communication game (pseudo-randomized across participants). This version was identical to the referential communication game, except participants were instructed that they should describe the objects for themselves, that they are not completing this with a chatbot.

2.3 Materials

Chatbots. Two different chatbots were used in this experiment. One chatbot used complete sentences, whereas the other used single words in capitals. The aim of using two different chatbots was to ensure a wide range of opinions from the participants. The comparison between these two different chatbots are discussed in a different paper; for this current article the data is compiled together.

The chatbots are based on those used in van der Kallen [13]. The chatbots were built using *IBM Watson Assistant*. The JSON codes for these chatbots are available upon request. The chatbots, as well as the complete experiment, was hosted on a Node-RED Starter Buildpack from IBM, the flow for which is also available upon request.

Referential Communication Game. The number, size, and visibility of the relevant objects were manipulated to create 6 conditions (Fig. 2). In the audience design conditions (left column, Fig. 2), participants saw an extra competitor object that the chatbot could not see. In the *obligatory* audience design condition, participants saw 3 relevant identical objects of different sizes: One target object, one occluded competitor object, and one mutually visible object. The target object was always the medium-sized object of the 3 objects. If participants described this object from their own perspective, they would call it the *medium* object. On the other hand, if participants considered the perspective of the chatbot, they would ignore the occluded object and call the medium-sized object *small* or *large*. In the *advisable* audience design condition, participants saw 2 relevant identical objects of different sizes: One target and one occluded competitor object. Given that the chatbot could see the target object but not the competitor object, participants did not have to use a contrasting size adjective.

In addition, there were two control conditions. In the linguistic control condition (middle, Fig. 2), the occluded object was replaced by another, unrelated object. As a result, participants saw one relevant object fewer in these conditions than in the audience design conditions. These were named *linguistic* control conditions, as participants were expected to produce the same description in these trials as on successful trials in the audience design conditions. In the visual control conditions (right, Fig. 2), the object that was occluded in the audience design condition was visible to both the participant and the chatbot. As a result, both could see all relevant objects. These were named *visual* control conditions, because participants see the same number of relevant objects as in the audience design conditions. Neither of these control conditions required the participant to take into account the perspective difference with the chatbot in order to communicate successfully.

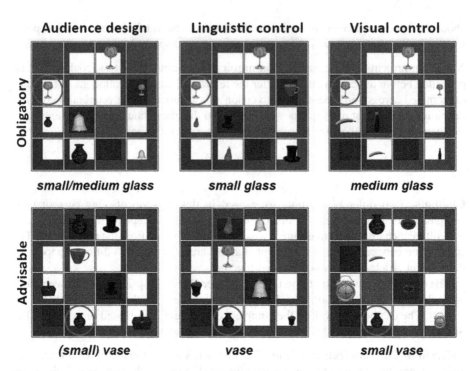

Fig. 2. Overview of the six conditions from the participant's point of view, and the expected speaker responses. In the audience design conditions, speakers can either describe the target objects (circled in red) from their own perspective ("medium glass", "small vase"), or take into account the chatbot's perspective ("small glass", "vase"). There is no relevant perspective difference in the linguistic and visual control conditions. The green squares were added to the figure for clarification, and were not visible to the participants during the experiment. They indicate the objects that differ between conditions. Adapted from Vanlangendonck et al. [11]. (Color figure online)

Twelve different empty virtual arrays were created. The arrays were filled with 6 to 8 objects chosen from a total of 22 objects selected from the Object Databank (courtesy of Michael Tarr Lab, Brown University, Providence, RI). Each object could appear in 4 different sizes to make sure that the participants could not rely on absolute size. Depending on the condition, participants saw 1, 2 or 3 relevant objects of the same type but different sizes. The remaining objects were fillers that also appeared in sets of 1, 2 or 3 objects of the same type to make sure participants could not predict which objects would be relevant. We made sure that the participants always saw the same total number of objects in a trial by adding additional filler objects to the occluded slots if needed.

For each participant, 120 trials were created with 20 repetitions across 6 conditions. Each participant was given the same object list, although it was randomized for each instance.

2.4 Statistical Analysis

The output files were coded for adjective use. We created three variables: (1) Use of the adjective small/large, (2) use of no adjective, and (3) whether the descriptions reflected an adaptation to the chatbots perspective. All variables were coded as the binomial variables 0 (no) and 1 (yes).

The data was analyzed using binomial mixed-effects models, using the lme4 package (version 1.1-19; [14]) in R [15]. We used a maximal random-effects structure as was justified by the data [16]: The repeated-measured nature of the data was modelled by including a per-participant and per-item random adjustment to the fixed intercept ("random intercept"). We included the fixed effect as a random slope in the per-participant random intercept for all models reported below. We used sum contrasts for all binomial variables, and dummy contrasts for all factors with three levels.

3 Results

Participants correctly answered the three cinema questions, indicating that they interacted with the chatbot for a significant period of time. Out of the 9360 trials collected, 2.8% included unusable responses (no response or a response mentioning something other than the object description) and were *a priori* removed from the dataset.

3.1 Adjective Use

The pattern of results when looking at each of the 6 conditions individually mirrors those reported in the human-human version of this task [11]. Figure 3 illustrates the adjective use per condition.

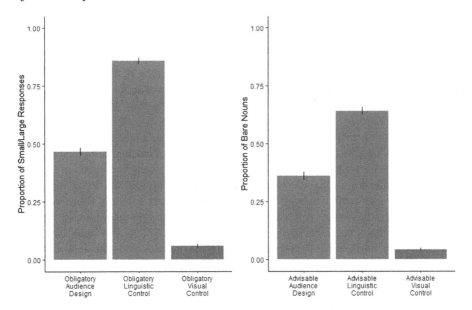

Fig. 3. The proportion of the participants' small/large and bare noun responses for the obligatory (left) and advisable data (right). Bars indicated standard error of the mean.

As expected, the participants mostly produced utterances that contained a *small/large* size adjective (85.7%) in the obligatory linguistic control condition and mainly *medium* responses (94.1%) in the obligatory visual control condition. Both the difference in adjective use between the obligatory audience design condition and the linguistic control condition (β = 3.52, SE = 0.57, p < .001) and the difference in adjective use between the obligatory audience design condition and the visual control condition were significant (β = −4.10, SE = 0.67, p < .001). This is a replication of the results found in [11]. However, the overall proportion of adaptation in the obligatory audience design condition was a lot less. For example, in [11] the authors reported that the speakers mainly (89.9%) produced *small/large* adjectives in the obligatory design condition, whereas we observed only 46.6%. This means the participants used the adjective *medium*, which is an accurate description of the target object but from the participants perspective, 53.4% of the time.

In the advisable linguistic control condition, the participants mainly produced base nouns (64.0%), and in the visual control condition they predominantly used *small/large* responses (95.7%). We again found a significant difference between the advisable audience design condition and the linguistic control condition (β = 3.34, SE = 0.57, p < .001) and between the advisable audience design and visual control conditions (β = −2.57, SE = 0.80, p = .001). However, again the proportion of adapted responses was very low (36.2%) for the audience design condition.

This suggests that participants did not adapt their responses to take the chatbot's perspective into account. However, we hypothesized that the magnitude of adaptation in the chatbot version of the Theory of Mind task would be less than the adaptation seen in the human-human version of this task. In order to validate that this task can be used with chatbots, the amount of adaptation exhibited by the participants should be significantly higher when conducting the task with the chatbot than when the participants conduct the task alone.

3.2   Communicative vs. Non-communicative

Only the audience design conditions were used for the analysis (left panel, Fig. 2). The model included the sum-contrasted fixed effect *Condition* (communicative versus non-communicative; within subjects), random intercepts for participant and item, as well as *Condition* as a random slope for both. Table 1 reports the mixed model outcome.

There is a significant difference between the proportion of adapted responses when the participants believed they were communicating with a chatbot compared to when they believed they were conducting the task alone, even though the tasks were identical. Figure 4 illustrates this effect compared to the results from the Vanlangendonck study [12], in which participants interact with another human. Figure 4 shows that even though there is a difference between the communicative and non-communicative tasks when the participant conducts it with a chatbot, the percentage of adapted responses with a chatbot is much lower than when the same task is conducted with another human (41% vs. 70%).

Table 1. Summary of the binomial mixed effects model for the response Adaptation between the communicative and non-communicative conditions of the referential communication game.

	Coefficient	SE	z value	p value	
Intercept	−1.43	0.36	−3.94	<.001	***
Condition	0.63	0.26	2.39	.017	*
N = 3036, log-likelihood = −1138.8					

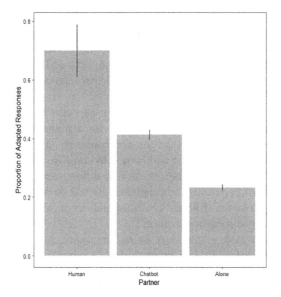

Fig. 4. Proportion of adapted responses per partner type. Data for the human partner was taken from Vanlangendonck and colleagues [12]. Error bars represent standard error of the mean.

4   Conclusion

This study proposes a short task to implicitly (automatically and unconsciously) measure whether participants perceive a chatbot partner to have their own mental state. This task will allow future researchers to quickly and effectively test and compare chatbots across laboratories. Additionally, once a database of results has been created, it will allow for meta-analyses to explore which social characteristics ensure the highest degree of perceived agency in a social chatbot.

The task proposed, the Referential Communication Game [12, 17, 18], consists of participants describing objects in an array to a text-based chatbot. They were not given feedback on their performance, and hence the task would proceed whether participants adapted their responses for the chatbot or not. However, despite this, participants adapted their responses significantly more when they interacted with a chatbot (41%) than when they conducted the task alone (23%; SD: 4%). This result suggests that participants do believe at some level that the chatbot would appreciate it if the participant would adapt their responses to make it easier for the chatbot to identify the object, suggesting that, implicitly, participants believe that the chatbot has some sort of mental state.

Another conclusion is that participants adapted their responses because they believed the chatbot was programmed to only understand them if they described the objects in a certain way. However, as this task does not give any feedback, the participants are not rewarded for their extra effort (as it is effortful to take the perspective of another person, as shown in the Vanlangendonck study [11, 12]), and hence they may stop halfway through the task and continue in the non-adapted fashion. This could explain why their average score is higher than the non-communicative version, but not as high as the human results. This explanation draws parallels to the human-human version of this task, where the participant also does not get feedback and it is only the internal motivation of the participant to take the perspective of their partner into account that dictates their overall performance. Further data collection will allow for a trial-by-trial analysis of the task.

In this study, participants adapted their responses when they completed the Referential Communication Game with a chatbot, with a higher adaptation rate in the communicative version of the task than the non-communicative version. In order for this task to be the new universal tool with which to compare chatbots, the Referential Communication Game also has to be sensitive to differences between different chatbots. Future research will continue to investigate this task to determine if it is sensitive enough to efficiently measure different chatbots, and hence whether it is fit to become the new universal tool to measure chatbots.

The power of this task is not only in its simplicity, but also in its efficiency. Previous quantitative research with chatbots would require a two-way comparison: How did the new chatbot perform compared to an older version? With the Referential Communication Game, this comparison is no longer necessary. Participants only need to interact with one chatbot, and the average performance of these participants will rank the new chatbot against all other chatbots previously created, with the aim of developing one that will be close to the human score of 0.70.

References

1. Weizenbaum, J.: ELIZA—a computer program for the study of natural language communication between man and machine. Commun. ACM **26**, 23–28 (1983). https://doi.org/10.1145/357980.357991
2. Wallace, R.: The Elements of AIML Style (2003)
3. Comendador, B.E.V., Francisco, B.M.B., Medenilla, J.S., Nacion, S.M.T., Serac, T.B.E.: Pharmabot: a pediatric generic medicine consultant chatbot. J. Autom. Control Eng. **3**, 137–140 (2015). https://doi.org/10.12720/joace.3.2.137-140
4. Ciechanowski, L., Przegalinska, A., Magnuski, M., Gloor, P.: In the shades of the uncanny valley: an experimental study of human – chatbot interaction. Future Gener. Comput. Syst. **92**, 539–548 (2019). https://doi.org/10.1016/j.future.2018.01.055
5. Neururer, M., Schlögl, S., Brinkschulte, L., Groth, A.: Perceptions on authenticity in chat bots. Multimodal Technol. Interact. **2**, 60 (2018). https://doi.org/10.3390/mti2030060

6. Radziwill, N., Benton, M.: Evaluating Quality of Chatbots and Intelligent Conversational Agents (2016)
7. Chaves, A.P., Gerosa, M.: How should my chatbot interact? 1–44 (2018)
8. Morrissey, K., Kirakowski, J.: 'Realness' in chatbots: establishing quantifiable criteria. In: Kurosu, M. (ed.) HCI 2013. LNCS, vol. 8007, pp. 87–96. Springer, Heidelberg (2013). https://doi.org/10.1007/978-3-642-39330-3_10
9. Frith, C.D., Frith, U.: Mechanisms of social cognition. Ann. Rev. Psychol. **63**, 287–313 (2012). https://doi.org/10.1146/annurev-psych-120710-100449
10. Premack, D., Woodruff, G.: Does the chimpanzee have a theory of mind? Behav. Brain Sci. **4**, 515–526 (1978)
11. Vanlangendonck, F., et al.: An early influence of common ground during speech planning. 3798 (2016). https://doi.org/10.1080/23273798.2016.1148747
12. Vanlangendonck, F., Willems, R.M., Hagoort, P.: Taking common ground into account: specifying the role of the mentalizing network in communicative language production. PLoS ONE **13**, e0202943 (2018). https://doi.org/10.1371/journal.pone.0202943
13. Van Der Kallen, T., Communicatiewetenschap, M., Nijmegen, R.U.: Chatbots: kunnen menselijk sprekende computers beter tegen een foutje? [Chatbots: Are human-like talking computers more resilient to mistakes?]
14. Bates, D., Maechler, M., Bolker, B.: lme4: linear mixed-effects models using S4 classes (2011). R package version 0.999375-42 (2012)
15. R Core Development Team: R: a language and environment for statistical computing, Vienna, Austria (2011)
16. Barr, D.J., Levy, R., Scheepers, C., Tily, H.J.: Random effects structure for confirmatory hypothesis testing: keep it maximal. J. Mem. Lang. **68**, 255–278 (2013). https://doi.org/10.1016/j.jml.2012.11.001
17. Keysar, B., Barr, D.J., Balin, J.A., Brauner, J.S.: Taking perspective in conversation: the role of mutual knowledge in comprehension. Psychol. Sci. **11**, 32–38 (2000)
18. Yoon, S.O., Koh, S., Brown-Schmidt, S.: Influence of perspective and goals on reference production in conversation. Psychon. Bull. Rev. **19**, 699–707 (2012). https://doi.org/10.3758/s13423-012-0262-6

Application Area: Chatbots for Customer Service

Exploring Age Differences in Motivations for and Acceptance of Chatbot Communication in a Customer Service Context

Margot J. van der Goot[1]([⊠])(iD) and Tyler Pilgrim[2]

[1] Amsterdam School of Communication Research (ASCoR),
Nieuwe Achtergracht 166, 1018 WV Amsterdam, The Netherlands
m.j.vandergoot@uva.nl
[2] MessageBird, Trompenburgstraat 2C, 1079 TX Amsterdam, The Netherlands

Abstract. This qualitative interview study explores age differences in perceptions of chatbot communication in a customer service context. Socioemotional
selectivity theory and research into technology acceptance suggest that older
adults may differ from younger adults in motivations to use chatbots, and in
perceived complexity and security of this chatbot communication. The in-depth
interviews with older adults (54–81 years; N = 7) and younger adults (19–30
years; N = 7) revealed that both groups were aligned in their prime motivation:
They used chatbots to get their (simple) customer queries answered in a fast and
convenient manner. However, they seemed to differ in their need for additional
human contact. In both age groups, there were participants for whom it was easy
to communicate with chatbots, and the two groups were united in their frustrations when the chatbot did not understand and answer their queries. They
were aligned as well in the difficulty they experienced in assessing the security
of the chatbot. The two age groups may differ in the factors that contribute to
perceived ease of use and perceived security. Directions for future research and
implications for the implementation of chatbots for customer service are
discussed.

Keywords: Chatbots · Customer service · Age differences · Qualitative
interview study · Older adults · Motivations · Technology acceptance

1 Introduction

Chatbots, or disembodied conversational agents [2], are increasingly used in customer
service: Customers can type their questions in a dialogue screen and receive answers in
natural language. Chatbots for customer service are still an emerging technology [7].
For companies it is important that customers of all ages are satisfied with the chatbot
conversations, or at least do not feel alienated from the company due to the implementation of chatbot communication.

Based on previous research in other areas, there are two important reasons to
suspect there may be age differences in perceptions of chatbot communication. First,
socioemotional selectivity theory (SST) [5] outlines how motivations and social preferences change as people age. Consequently, older adults may also differ from younger

© Springer Nature Switzerland AG 2020
A. Følstad et al. (Eds.): CONVERSATIONS 2019, LNCS 11970, pp. 173–186, 2020.
https://doi.org/10.1007/978-3-030-39540-7_12

adults in their motivations to use chatbots. Second, research in the field of technology acceptance indicates that perceived ease of use and perceived security of several technologies are not the same for older versus younger adults [8, 14], which implies that there also may be age differences in perceptions of chatbot communication. Therefore, the aim of the current qualitative interview study is to explore whether older adults (54–81 years) and younger adults (19–30 years) differ in their motivations to use chatbots in a customer service context, and in perceived ease of use and perceived security of this chatbot communication.

This qualitative study contributes to our understanding whether and how age differences should be taken into account in future studies on chatbot communication, and whether SST [5, 19] and models focusing on technology acceptance [4] are useful frameworks for this line of research. Moreover, the study helps practitioners – who are involved in chatbot implementation – to understand whether older customers have a unique set of motivations and needs that should be accommodated for in age-specific ways.

2   Background

2.1   Motivations

Applying uses and gratifications theory, Brandtzaeg and Følstad studied the motivations for chatbot use among 16–55 year olds. They found that productivity was the main reason for using chatbots: Participants mainly used them to obtain assistance or information, and noted chatbots' ease, speed and convenience. Other motivations included entertainment, social or relational purposes, and novelty/curiosity [3].

We argue that research on the development of motivations across the lifespan suggests that age groups may differ in the prevalence and specifications of the aforementioned motivations for chatbot use. A theory on motivational changes that has been particularly influential in gerontological research is socioemotional selectivity theory (SST) [5]. SST outlines that there are fundamentally two goal categories: knowledge-related goals and emotionally-meaningful goals [5]. These two categories tend to switch in prominence as people perceive their lifespans to become more finite. Carstensen argues that young adults seek activities that lead to more knowledge acquisition, whereas older adults seek activities that provide an emotional reward. Since this theory concerns socioemotional *selectivity*, it offers an explanation of reduced rates of interaction in later life: As adults go through their life, their social circles become smaller, because ageing individuals start to value and seek more meaningful social interactions, while younger adults cast a wider social net for the benefit of gaining more information.

The current paper assumes that SST can be relevant for research into chatbot use, since chatbot communication is a type of dialogical communication that resembles social interaction. Applying SST, we could expect that the information-related motivations (part of the main motivation identified by Brandtzaeg and Følstad) would be more prevalent among younger customers, whereas the social and relational motivations [3] would be more essential for older adults. In addition, the diminishing of social circles identified in SST research could imply that ageing individuals lack the motivation to use chatbots, instead relying on friends or family to help them with their customer support needs, or preferring human customer service agents over chatbot communication.

Since applying SST to chatbot communication is novel and the potential expectations regarding age differences in this domain are merely speculative at this point, we conducted a qualitative interview study to answer the following research question:

RQ1: How do older and younger adults differ in their motivations to use chatbots in a customer service context?

2.2   Technology Acceptance

Models of technology acceptance, such as the Technology Acceptance Model (TAM) and extensions thereof, outline a number of factors that impact technology adoption [4, 11]. Perceived ease of use and perceived usefulness are central in these models [11]. In the present study, perceived usefulness is addressed in our first research question. Perceived ease of use is also important in the comparison between older and younger adults. After their review of TAM literature, Marangunić and Granić concluded that older adults are a target group of specific interest as age plays a major role in the interaction with technology [11]. A focus group study in which older adults discussed their use of and attitudes regarding technology in the context of home, work, and healthcare found that particularly perceived ease of use (and usefulness) were related to their technology adoption [14]. Due to this previously found association between age and technology use, and the importance of ease of use for older adults, the present interview study sets out to describe potential age differences in perceived ease of use of chatbot communication.

One other aspect where age differences may be particularly at play is perceived security of a new technology. An interview study on trust in chatbots in customer service found that perceived security is one of the factors that affects this trust [7]. The abovementioned focus group study among older adults revealed that older adults often noted security considerations as a reason they disliked using technology, ultimately impacting their technology acceptance [14]. Moreover, previous studies found that older users lagged behind younger users in expertise regarding (internet) security hazards [8]. Thus, on the one hand, perceived security may be of particular importance for older adults, whereas on the other hand they may be less aware of security risks.

In sum, age differences in perceived ease of use and perceived security of chatbot communication in a customer service context can be expected, but are this point merely suggestions that have not yet been subjected to empirical scrutiny. Therefore the second research question is:

RQ2: How do older and younger adults differ in perceived ease of use and perceived security of chatbot communication in a customer service context?

3   Method

3.1   Sample Composition

Interviews were conducted among two distinct age groups. The older group (N = 7) consisted of adults aged 54–81 years, because businesses typically consider consumers aged above 50 or 55 years as older consumers [13] and because in related experimental research the older adults were also aged 52 or 53 years and older [10, 16]. The sample consisted of five women and two men. They lived in various regions in the United States. Education was varied, ranging from high school to post doctorate level. The younger group consisted of adults aged 19–30 years, with three women and four men. Three participants in this group lived in the Netherlands and four participants lived in the United States. Education in this group varied from high school to master's degree level. Except for the 81-year old lady, all participants had previous experience with using chatbots.

3.2   Interviews

The study was approved by the Ethics Review Board of our university. The second author asked people in his personal network whether they were willing to be interviewed, and he also solicited on Facebook. He conducted the three interviews in the Netherlands face-to-face, and the interviews with participants from the United States through video chat via Google Hangouts. All interviews were conducted in English, and participants signed a consent form prior to the interview.

During the interviews, participants communicated with two chatbots for customer service. They could choose the chatbots of Amtrak, Macy's, or Verizon. In the face-to-face interviews, participants could also choose the bots of Hipmunk, Kayak, KLM, or Tommy Hilfiger. Thus we gathered perceptions regarding chatbots that were used by various types of companies, and that were also varied in human-like features. Once the chatbot connected to a live agent or the participant said the conversation was finished, the interviewer started asking questions.

The interview guide consisted of four topics. Topic 1 aimed to tap into the participant's experiences with this specific chat. It started with an open-ended question: "Please share with me all your experiences during this chat". Subsequently they were shown a blobtree (blobtree.com), and asked to explain which character(s) best described their experiences during the chat. They were also asked how their perception of the chat (potentially) related to their perception of the company. Topic 2 explored their technology acceptance. They were asked what they (dis)liked about the chat, and what they found easy or difficult. They were also asked to rate the complexity, reliability and security of the chatbot (on a scale 1–10), and to explain the rating. Topic 3 was about their motivations. They were asked to explain why they would use this chatbot in the future again (or not), what they expected from the bot, and whether these expectations were met. Topic 4 asked them to reflect more broadly on the usefulness of chatbots for customer service, and whether they thought a chatbot was useful for only certain questions or certain companies.

3.3 Data Analysis

Interviews were transcribed verbatim and uploaded in the computer program Atlas.ti. The second author conducted the open coding, a procedure commonly used as the first step in the Grounded Theory Approach [6], that enables the researcher to study the materials in a fine-grained and detailed manner. Subsequently, the second author suggested several possible categorizations that could help to present the findings. After several rounds of discussion and adjusting, the authors decided on a categorization, presented in three tables in a previous version of this paper. Following the advice of reviewers, we decided to merge some of the categories, which resulted in the categorization presented below.

4 Results

In this section, we answer the two research questions. The findings are displayed in tables, by presenting quotes that exemplify each category. Frequencies refer to the amount of older versus younger participants that mentioned a certain aspect and are merely provided as an illustration of what we encountered in the interviews. These frequencies should be interpreted with caution, because of the small sample sizes and because we asked very open-ended questions (which means that participants may not have spontaneously expressed a certain perception, but would indicate that this perception applies to them when asked about this directly).

4.1 Age Differences in Motivations

Regarding RQ1 about age differences in motivations, we found that both age groups were aligned in that their prime motivation was to get their customer query answered (see Table 1). In both groups, some participants specified that bots are mainly useful for simple "black and white" questions, in areas such as e-commerce (for instance when one has questions about the shipping of products), technical support, banking, travel and government, and for scheduling appointments. Participants in both groups acknowledged that for more complex, urgent or personal questions (including health and medical issues), it may be better to talk to a person than to a chatbot. In our sample, there was only one interviewee (P13, 54 years) who did not see chatbots as useful for getting questions answered. She was angry about this type of machines that take up her valuable time and have no clue what she is talking about. She only used chatbots to be connected to a live agent.

Also, most interviewees in both groups applauded the ability to receive answers in a fast, easy, and convenient way. Specific advantages were that chatbots enable them to avoid long phone waits, help them to navigate the company's website, and that interviewees were able to multitask while communicating with a chatbot.

However, a difference between the two age groups seemed to be their assessment of the human factor. In our sample, older individuals seemed more inclined to use chatbot communication as a stepping stone for human contact (i.e. to connect to a live agent),

Table 1. Motivations for using a chatbot for customer service

	Older adults	Younger adults
To get an answer to a customer query	$n = 6$ "Well, to get an answer" (P12, 81 years) "I would use it for a simple problem, a single simple problem. I would not use it for a complex problem or a problem with multiple elements to it" (P9, 67 years)	$n = 7$ "I expected that he gave me a fast answer to my problem. And to fix it" (P3, 19 years) "It's kind of like an FAQ where you can just like type in your question and answer it. I definitely find them to be useful in that aspect but anything more complex I think it's a little harder for them" (P4, 30 years)
Ease, speed, and convenience	$n = 6$ "Quick, easy, succinct. Saves time" (P11, 65 years) "I think they are useful to avoid long phone waits" (P9, 67 years) "Because I would say there's a lot of times when I'm internet shopping for example and I can't find something and I know it's there [...]. But the website keeps coming back saying no. [...]. So that's when I typically will open the assistance thing and say help me" (P10, 62 years) "Kind of allows me to do other stuff while I'm working on the chatbox. You know, like multitasking" (P8, 60 years)	$n = 7$ "It's super-fast and convenient" (P2, 30 years) "We all know how annoying it is to call the company [...] and they leave you on the wait for five six minutes" (P1, 28 years) "It feels like an easier way to navigate their help center without actually like going through and searching through a bunch of articles" (P5, 29 years) "I can multitask. I can feed the baby and I can ask the question" (P7, 27 years)
To connect to a human agent	$n = 3$ "The only thing I liked about it was eventually I got to speak to an actual human being" (P13, 54 years)	$n = 1$ "Interviewer: What was your favorite part of this one?" "That it offered the option to talk to a live agent" (P6, 29 years)
To avoid interacting with a human being	$n = 0$	$n = 5$ "Sometimes when you're interacting with humans you have to be friendly. You have to be polite and. Maybe you had the worst day in your life when you still have to be polite whereas a chatbot you're like. You don't have to pretend or act in a way that you don't want. You can just be yourself be natural in the mood that you are" (P1, 28 years) "I don't like talking on the phone" (P5, 29 years)

whereas younger interviewees were more insisting that chatbot communication helps to avoid human contact. This may signal that older adults value human contact more than younger adults.

4.2   Age Differences in Technology Acceptance

Perceived Ease of Use. Regarding perceived ease of use, we found that in both age groups there were interviewees who expressed that it was easy for them to use the chatbots. Table 2 shows what they said was easy for them. First, some interviewees provided the overall evaluation that it was clear to them how it worked. Second, some commented more specifically on the smooth interaction. In the older group one of the interviewees applauded the writing style used in the conversation. In the younger group, interviewees noted that the interaction resembled talking to a person or using other devices, and that it was likeable that the chatbot asked for feedback. Third, a specific issue of interest regarding the design of chatbots is the use of preloaded options, i.e. buttons. Several interviewees said that the availability of such buttons helped the conversation.

Table 2. Perceived ease of use of chatbots for customer service

	Older adults	Younger adults
Easy		
Clear how it works	$n = 5$ "There is absolutely no misunderstanding of what I was doing or challenge. I guess it was clear very clear" (P8, 60 years)	$n = 3$ "I find it to be easy. Just because it's pretty straightforward. Once you click on the link it takes you right there. And all you have to do is your name and your email address and make your question" (P4, 30 years)
Smooth interaction	$n = 1$ "Sometimes you can get into tech support that's run by someone who is using English as a second language and it can get complicated fairly quickly. This seems to be very.. it's well written" (P10, 62 years)	$n = 4$ "It was so easy for me, just to type in a few things, it was almost like talking to my wife" (P5, 29 years) "It was like back in the day when we used aim [AOL Instant Messenger]" (P7, 27 years) "I think that part of it has to do with like the real time feedback. So it was like continue to ask me like 'does this give you the information that you needed'. Like 'are you satisfied with this information?'" (P6, 29 years)

(continued)

Table 2. (*continued*)

	Older adults	Younger adults
Preloaded options to choose from	*n* = 1 "So do you find having options laid out beforehand helpful?" "Yes [...] So to give me the option to find my solution without going all over the place" (P8, 60 years)	*n* = 4 "It was pretty easy because actually the way like after you say from where you want to depart, it like gives you options so you can like choose" (P1, 28 years)
Not easy		
Chatbot did not answer the question	*n* = 4 "It had no f@cking clue what I needed or wanted" (P13, 54 years)	*n* = 4 "I'm frustrated, I am feeling like what the hell you guys" (P7, 27 years)
Unclarities in the interaction	*n* = 4 "I think they try to combine too many steps into you know per response" (P9, 67 years)	*n* = 6 "I would remove all the links here because it's a little confusing" (P7, 27 years) "It kept toggling back and forth between several screens, confusing" (P6, 29 years) "I was framing or phrasing the sentences in a way that I thought that the chatbot could read it" (P5, 29 years)
Roadblocks to get to the chatbot	*n* = 1 "It was a little complex because I couldn't find her right away" (P14, 59 years)	*n* = 3 "Is it something that you use weekly or monthly?" "No. First because it's not that easy to find chatbots" (P2, 30 years) "The part in the beginning where you are required to put your name and stuff. [...] It felt like an unnecessary roadblock to get to the chat" (P6, 29 years)

On the other hand, there were interviewees who did not experience the chatbot communication as easy. This was particularly the case when the chatbot did not understand and answer their questions. This led to quite some frustrations. In addition, both groups outlined some difficulties in the interaction, albeit slightly different ones. In the older group, some interviewees said that too much information was given at once: too much information was provided in a single response, or too many answers or links were provided at the same time. Interviewees in the younger group also experienced this problem, and also noted that the navigation was inconvenient at times (particularly because of toggling between several screens). They also mentioned that it was not clear how to type: They were trying to find out which way they needed to formulated their questions in order for the bot to understand them. Lastly, there were some roadblocks to get to the chatbot, either because the chatbot was difficult to find or because personal information had to be filled out before starting the chat.

Perceived Security. Regarding perceived security, the overall finding was that interviewees in both groups had a difficult time assessing how secure the chatbot interaction

Table 3. Perceived security of chatbots for customer service

	Older adults	Younger adults
Unable to determine whether chatbot is secure		
	$n = 2$ "Is it secure? There is no way to assess that" (P9, 67 years)	$n = 5$ "I don't know exactly what to think about it" (P3, 19 years)
Secure		
Assumption that it is secure	$n = 3$ "I'm not sure how secure it is. I guess 10" (P11, 65 years)	$n = 2$ "9. I don't have any reason to assume it is not secure" (P2, 30 years)
Because of how chatbot deals with personal information	$n = 0$	$n = 2$ "9. They didn't ask for any of my personal info" (P5, 29 years)
Because of company perception	$n = 0$	$n = 1$ "It's a big company, you just trust them" (P3, 19 years)
Not secure		
Assumption that it is not secure	$n = 0$	$n = 1$ "1. Just because these days [...] people sell your number and your credit card, I don't trust it" (P7, 27 years)
Because not intelligent enough	$n = 1$ "There's no way I would type in my credit card information to a chat where it doesn't even know what I'm saying" (P13, 54 years)	$n = 1$ "Lower, because I did not get the answer I was looking for" (P2, 30 years)
Because of the informal chat interface	$n = 0$	$n = 1$ "I just feel like weird giving my information to a chatbot [...]. It's because of the chat interface, giving the feeling of being in like more of an unofficial space" (P6, 29 years)
Because company reads the conversation	$n = 1$ "Secure? 0. Anybody that works there can pull up that transcript and see it" (P13, 54 years)	$n = 0$

actually was (see Table 3). They either concluded that they were unable to determine whether the chatbot was secure, or they just made the assumption that it was secure, or not.

Interviewees put forth only a few factors that they applied to guess how secure the communication was, and the two groups slightly differed in the factors that they mentioned. The older group did not mention any factors that led them to believe the chatbot was secure. In the younger group a few interviewees thought the chatbot was secure because it did not ask for their personal information, or because it was the chatbot of a big company. In both groups, only a few interviewees mentioned factors that led them to believe the chatbot was *not* secure. One of the points mentioned was that if the chatbot cannot even understand or answer their question, they would not feel comfortable with entering their personal information. They also said that the informal interface and their guess that anybody in the company can read the conversation makes them believe the interaction is not secure.

5 Discussion

In the discussion section, we first connect the findings regarding age differences in motivations and technology acceptance with the available literature, and suggest how to move ahead with research in these areas. Subsequently, we outline practical recommendations. Finally, we present limitations of the current study that also imply directions for future research.

5.1 Age Differences in Motivations

The first research question asked how older and younger adults differ in their motivations to use chatbots for customer service. In the interview study, the two age groups were aligned in their prime motivation: Customers use chatbots to get their (simple) customer queries answered in a fast and convenient manner. With that, our findings (in some cases quite literally) echo findings from previous qualitative research into experiences of chatbot communication [3, 7]. It makes sense that these are the key reasons to use a chatbot in customer service, regardless of a customer's age.

However, the interviews did give the impression that the "human touch" (i.e., talking to somebody on the phone) may be more important for older segments of the population, whereas some younger adults actually used chatbot communication to avoid human contact. Interestingly, a quantitative survey among a representative sample of Dutch consumers aged 18–65 years found that age was not a significant predictor of usage, attitudes and satisfaction regarding brand chatbots, but that it *was* a predictor of the preference for human contact over a chatbot: Older respondents were more likely to express this preference [1].

Our study and these findings can be seen as a first step towards building a theory that helps explain how age groups (potentially) differ in their motivations to use chatbots. Especially the finding that age groups may differ in their preference of chatbot communication over human contact, or vice versa, requires further investigation. Before we can accurately interpret this result, we need further qualitative research that describes more in-depth how people compare chatbot communication with communication with live agents (and human-human communication more generally), and why they have a preference of one over the other. Only then, we can make statements about what could explain this potential age difference. Socioemotional selectivity theory (SST) [5] provided the theoretical impetus for the current study, and should still play a role in such future research. Possibly, the current finding is in line with the SST proposition that ageing individuals appreciate warm and meaningful social interactions more than younger adults. However, it seems reasonable to also consider other explanations – besides SST. An alternative explanation is the notion of media generations: Age groups also constitute different media generations that grew up with different media and thus differ in their attitudes toward those media [20]. The age difference in preference for human contact may be a reflection of the observation that the current younger generations are very familiar with communication through chat interfaces and consequently become more hesitant about talking to people on the phone (potentially experiencing phone anxiety). Only when qualitative research reveals more about the comparison between chatbot- versus human communication, can we formulate hypotheses to be tested in quantitative research. This should provide more insight in the extent to which age groups differ in their preferences for chatbot communication versus talking to human agents, and in the extent to which this is related to life-span development (as outlined by SST) or media generational differences.

5.2 Age Differences in Technology Acceptance

The second research question asked whether older and younger adults differ in perceived ease of use and perceived security of chatbots in customer service. In both age groups, there were participants for whom it was easy to communicate with chatbots, and both groups were also united in their frustrations when the bot did not understand and answer their queries. They were aligned as well in the difficulty they experienced in assessing the security of the chatbot. This latter finding is in contrast with a previous qualitative study in which the participants did not consider it challenging to reflect on trust in chatbots, and in which they reported stated or perceived security measures in chatbots to be important for trust [7]. In the current study, only a few participants mentioned factors that led them to believe the interaction was secure or not. There may be age differences here, but further qualitative research is required to delve into this more precisely. Subsequently, quantitative follow-up research is needed to assess whether the prevalence of such factors systematically differs between age groups. Such studies can use an extension of the Technology Acceptance Model [11] as framework, thus contributing to more fine-grained insight in differential chatbot perceptions between age groups.

5.3 Practical Recommendations

The interviews show that for both age groups it is essential that chatbots are answering the customer queries in a fast and correct way, thus avoiding customers' frustrations [see also 7]. The participants also found it confusing when too much information was provided at once, particularly when one was presented with several links or screens simultaneously. Older and younger adults may differ in the factors that contribute to (not so) easy experiences and perceived security, but further research is needed to further delve into these potential age differences. An aspect to take into special consideration is that older adults seem to differ from younger adults in their considerations regarding choosing a chatbot for customer service versus connecting to a live agent. Older adults possibly still value the human touch more, which would mean that relying on chatbot communication solely or predominantly can alienate older consumers whereas they constitute such a large share of the population [17].

5.4 Limitations and Future Research

The exploratory nature of this study and its sample composition need to be taken into account when drawing conclusions from this study. First, this study focuses on a subset of all possible perceptions of chatbot communication. Whereas we focused on motivations, perceived ease of use and perceived security, one could also expect age differences in perceptions on a more granular level. For instance, experimental studies found that older adults were more persuaded by a dominant (versus submissive) virtual agent whereas younger adults did not show this bias [16] and that older adults – compared to younger adults – perceive such agents as more empathic when they show emotional nonverbal behaviors [10]. We aim to continue investigating how consumers of different ages experience chatbots as new types of communication partners [9], and we expect that – using SST as theoretical framework – age differences are particularly prevalent in responses to emotional and human-like cues in such communication.

Second, regarding sample composition, it is relevant to keep in mind that our older sample consisted of people aged 55 years and older. Although this is in line with previous and related research [10, 16], 55 years is fairly young. Moreover, the age ranges in both groups were broad (19–30 years versus 54–81 years), whereas heterogeneity even increases as people age [12, 15, 18]. Therefore, we recommend future research to recognize that any age delineation of a sample is rather arbitrary, to use an older cut-off point than 55 years, and to pay more attention to subgroups within the ageing population. The quantitative survey among Dutch consumers identified particularly technology power usage (i.e., one's comfort with the adoption of new technology or gadgets) and online self-efficacy (i.e., one's assumptions about one's own level of ability to protect her or his data) as stronger predictors of usage, attitudes and satisfaction regarding brand chatbots than age [1], implying that particularly these two variables are important segmentation variables when aiming to identify subgroups within the ageing population.

Third, interviewees in our sample resided in the United States as well as in the Netherlands, but the current sample composition did not enable us to analyze whether cultural differences play a role in perceptions of chatbot communication. Such cultural differences should be explored in future research.

References

1. Araujo, T., ter Hoeven, C., van Zoonen, W.: Automated 1-2-1 communication. In: SWOCC, vol. 77. Stichting Wetenschappelijk Onderzoek Commerciële Communicatie (SWOCC), Amsterdam (2019)
2. Araujo, T.: Living up to the chatbot hype: the influence of anthropomorphic design cues and communicative agency framing on conversational agent and company perceptions. Comput. Hum. Behav. **85**, 183–189 (2018). https://doi.org/10.1016/j.chb.2018.03.051
3. Brandtzaeg, P.B., Følstad, A.: Why people use chatbots. In: Kompatsiaris, I., et al. (eds.) INSCI 2017. LNCS, vol. 10673, pp. 377–392. Springer, Cham (2017). https://doi.org/10.1007/978-3-319-70284-1_30
4. Caine, K.E., O'Brien, M., Park, S., et al.: Understanding acceptance of high technology products: 50 years of research. In: Proceedings of the Human Factors and Ergonomics Society 50th Annual Meeting, pp. 2148–2152. Human Factors and Economics Society, Los Angeles (2006)
5. Carstensen, L.L., Isaacowitz, D.M., Charles, S.T.: Taking time seriously: a theory of socioemotional selectivity. Am. Psychol. **54**(3), 165–181 (1999). https://doi.org/10.1037/0003-066X.54.3.165
6. Charmaz, K.: Constructing Grounded Theory: A Practical Guide Through Qualitative Analysis. Sage, London (2006)
7. Følstad, A., Nordheim, C.B., Bjørkli, C.A.: What makes users trust a chatbot for customer service? An exploratory interview study. In: Bodrunova, S. (ed.) INSCI 2018. LNCS, vol. 11193, pp. 194–208. Springer, Cham (2018). https://doi.org/10.1007/978-3-030-01437-7_16
8. Grimes, G.A., Hough, M.G., Mazur, E., Signorella, M.L.: Older adults' knowledge of internet hazards. Educ. Gerontol. **36**(3), 173–192 (2010). https://doi.org/10.1080/03601270903183065
9. Guzman, A.L., Lewis, S.C.: Artificial intelligence and communication: a human–machine communication research agenda. New Media Soc. (advance online publication) (2019). https://doi.org/10.1177/1461444819858691
10. Hosseinpanah, A., Krämer, N.C., Straßmann, C.: Empathy for everyone? The effect of age when evaluating a virtual agent. In: Proceedings of the 6th International Conference on Human-Agent Interaction, pp. 184–190. ACM, Southampton (2018). https://doi.org/10.1145/3284432.3284442
11. Marangunić, N., Granić, A.: Technology acceptance model: a literature review from 1986 to 2013. Univ. Access Inf. Soc. **14**(1), 81–95 (2015). https://doi.org/10.1007/s10209-014-0348-1
12. Mares, M.L., Woodard, E.H.: In search of the older audience: adult age differences in television viewing. J. Broadcast. Electron. Media **50**(4), 595–614 (2006). https://doi.org/10.1207/s15506878jobem5004_2
13. Mature Marketing Association. https://www.themma.marketing/. Accessed 08 Sept 2019
14. Mitzner, T.L., Boron, J.B., Fausset, C.B., et al.: Older adults talk technology: technology usage and attitudes. Comput. Hum. Behav. **26**(6), 1710–1721 (2010). https://doi.org/10.1016/j.chb.2010.06.020
15. Moschis, G.P.: Consumer Behavior over the Life Course. Springer, Cham (2019). https://doi.org/10.1007/978-3-030-05008-5
16. Rosenthal-von der Pütten, A.M., Straßmann, C., Yaghoubzadeh, R., Kopp, S., Krämer, N.C.: Dominant and submissive nonverbal behavior of virtual agents and its effects on evaluation and negotiation outcome in different age groups. Comput. Hum. Behav. **90**, 397–409 (2019). https://doi.org/10.1016/j.chb.2018.08.047

17. United Nations, Department of Economic and Social Affairs, Population Division. http://esa. un.org/wpp/. Accessed 08 Sept 2019

18. van der Goot, M.J., Beentjes, J.W.J., van Selm, M.: Older adults' television viewing as part of selection and compensation strategies. Commun.: Eur. J. Commun. Res. **40**(1), 93–111 (2015). https://doi.org/10.1515/commun-2014-0025

19. van der Goot, M.J., Bol, N., van Weert, J.C.M.: Translating socioemotional selectivity theory into persuasive communication: conceptualizing and operationalizing emotionally-meaningful versus knowledge-related appeals. Int. J. Commun. **13**, 1416–1437 (2019)

20. van der Goot, M.J., Rozendaal, E., Opree, S.J., Ketelaar, P.E., Smit, E.G.: Media generations and their advertising attitudes and avoidance: a six-country comparison. Int. J. Advert. **37**(2), 289–308 (2018). https://doi.org/10.1080/02650487.2016.1240469

Improving Conversations: Lessons Learnt from Manual Analysis of Chatbot Dialogues

Knut Kvale[1]([⊠]) (iD), Olav Alexander Sell[2] (iD), Stig Hodnebrog[2] (iD), and Asbjørn Følstad[3] (iD)

[1] Telenor Research, Fornebu, Norway
knut.kvale@telenor.com
[2] Telenor Norway, Fornebu, Norway
[3] SINTEF, Oslo, Norway

Abstract. Analysing and improving chatbot dialogues – so-called chatbot 'training' – is key to the successful implementation and maintenance of chatbots for customer service. Nevertheless, the details of this practice and what service providers may learn from the analysis of such dialogues is not investigated in current research on chatbots. As a first step towards bridging this gap in existing knowledge, we present a study of the qualitative analysis of chatbots dialogues in the context of the customer service department of a large telecom provider. In total 406 dialogues, randomly sampled from all chatbot dialogues during a four-week period, were included in the analysis. The analysis concerned the chatbot's ability to resolve customers' requests, the quality in the chatbot dialogues, and suggestions for improvements of the chatbot knowledge base generated through the analysis. The findings shed light on characteristics of successful and unsuccessful chatbot dialogues and the kind of improvements that may be derived from such analysis. On the basis of the findings we summarize implications for theory and practice, and suggest future research.

Keywords: Chatbot dialogue analysis · Chatbot training · Customer experience

1 Introduction

Chatbots are currently taken up among service providers as a means to provide fast and efficient customer service. Through chatbots, service providers are able to provide immediate responses to customer requests any time of the day, any day of the week. Chatbots may serve as first line support in the chat channel, or be offered as an alternative to chat with human agents [6, 18].

In current chatbots for customer service, customers typically make their request in free text. The chatbot then interprets this text as reflecting one of a large number of intents the chatbot is able to recognize and provides a predefined answer in return. Enabling the chatbot to provide adequate answers based on such intent recognition is referred to as 'training'. A novel branch of customer service professionals has emerged in parallel with the uptake of chatbots for customer service – so-called 'AI trainers'. The work of AI trainers is to go through customer-chatbot dialogues to check whether

© Springer Nature Switzerland AG 2020
A. Følstad et al. (Eds.): CONVERSATIONS 2019, LNCS 11970, pp. 187–200, 2020.
https://doi.org/10.1007/978-3-030-39540-7_13

the answers provided by the chatbot are adequate responses to the customer requests, and – if not – to extend and improve the chatbot's content and capability for intent recognition so that it may respond correctly to similar requests in the future.

The work of AI trainers is critical for the successful implementation of chatbots for customer service. However, precious little research-based knowledge on this analysis and improvement process is available. As a first step towards addressing this gap in current knowledge, we present a study where we analysed chatbot dialogues at a customer service unit in a large telecom service provider. The analysis provided insight on (a) the degree of request resolution in the chatbot and details on failure to resolve, (b) dialogue quality and characteristics of successful and unsuccessful chatbot dialogues, and (c) suggestions for improvement in the chatbot's conversational capability.

The study contributes initial insight into an area largely overseen in the literature. We hope it may serve as a point of departure for more extensive investigations.

2   Background

We understand chatbots, also referred to as conversational agents or virtual agents, as conversational user interfaces to information and services. In this background section we provide an overview of chatbots for customer service, current challenges, and some details on chatbot technology and training.

2.1   Chatbots in Customer Service – Overview and Current Challenges

Driven by the success of voice-based assistants such as Apple's Siri and Amazon Alexa, and the major tech companies' prioritizing of conversational computing, there has been a surge of interest in chatbots for customer service (e.g. [1, 9, 10]). A range of platforms are now available for chatbot development and training, including IBM Watson, IPsoft's Amelia, Google's Dialogflow, Microsoft Bot Framework, and various platforms from start-up companies.

The motivation for service providers to take up chatbots for customer service include cost-efficiency in service provision and the opportunity for 24/7 chat-based customer service, which may lead to improved customer experience. Customers have been found to appreciate the immediate and accessible help provided by customer service chatbots [4]. However, customers still note important challenges in chatbots for customer service- in particular, when chatbots are not able to correctly interpret requests [5] and chatbots' inability to handle complex requests [8].

While the current surge of interest in chatbots for customer service is relatively recent, chatbots have been exploratorily applied for this purpose since the turn of the century [14]. However, many early chatbots for customer service have been abandoned as they were not able to deliver the needed quality in the interaction. Mimoun et al. [16] pointed out a gap between customer expectations and chatbot performance. Gnewuch et al., [11] summarized other key reasons for chatbot failure in customer service, including inability to provide engaging and convincing conversations and failure to keep longer conversations in adherence to the conversation context.

Several authors have pointed out the need to strengthen chatbot conversational capabilities e.g. [7]. Research presented for this purpose includes, for example, development of mechanisms to keep chatbot conversational context [2], leveraging of sentiment analysis in chatbots [13], and development of generative chatbots for customer service – that is, chatbots that are able to generate novel responses to novel user requests on the basis of machine learning conducted on large dialogue datasets [19].

However, in spite of the research efforts on improving chatbot conversational capabilities, there is a surprising lack of knowledge on the analysis and development process involved in the training of chatbots for customer service – that is, the work involved in the analysis and improvement of chatbot dialogues.

2.2   Chatbot Technology and Chatbot Training

Current chatbots for customer service are typically powered by artificial intelligence. Such chatbots apply classical natural language processing techniques as stemming, language detection, tokenization, in combination with deep learning approaches. These techniques and approaches are combined to create natural language understanding models which are, when trained properly, able to identify the intents of the customers' requests to the chatbot. While some service providers explore voice-based chatbots for customer service, most such chatbots are currently text-based.

The deep learning approaches used in the chatbots are mainly applied to predict the customers' intents from their written input, by so-called 'supervised' learning approaches [17]. As soon as the intent is identified, the chatbot provides a predefined answer in return – an answer which may be refined as the customer moves through a dialogue tree by use of predefined answer options on buttons or links. This in contrast to so-called 'generative' chatbots where also the chatbots' answers are generated from deep learning models based on large dialogue datasets (e.g. [19]). Generative chatbots for customer service are, however, only at a pre-commercial research stage.

Hence, in current chatbots for customer service, quality in performance depends on (a) correct intent prediction, (b) comprehensiveness of intents, and (c) quality in the chatbot responses.

Correct intent prediction concerns the chatbot's ability to adequately identify which of its predefined intents that best reflects a customer's free text request, and – if no such intent exists – identify that it does not understand this particular request. To enable correct intent prediction, the chatbot typically is provided a set of free-text example phrases, so-called 'training data', for each predefined intent. For each intent, the number of example phrases may range from a handful to several hundred depending on the specificity and complexity of the intent. Intent prediction may be improved through adding, changing, or removing example phrases from the training data.

Comprehensiveness of intents concerns the chatbot's ability to respond to a sufficiently broad set of customer requests. A chatbot for customer service may include several thousand intents to cover a sufficiently broad set of requests within its target domain. However, an overly extensive set of intents may be counter productive, as it may increase the risk of erroneous intent prediction (false positive), or failure to predict any intent (false negative), in the case when more than one intent may be predicted as the one best reflecting the customer's request. Improving intent comprehensiveness concerns identifying unresolved customer requests and setting up novel intents, or identifying unhelpful intents and removing or reworking these.

Quality in the chatbot responses concerns the textual responses from the chatbot that are associated with predicted intents. These responses may or may not include content from underlying web services. To improve the quality in chatbot responses this textual content is reworked, something that requires communication skills and domain knowledge rather than skills in analysis or technical development. Hall [12] makes a particular point of the need to include writing skills in a team that develops conversational user interfaces.

The process of improving chatbot intent predictions, intent comprehensiveness, and responses associated with the intents is referred to as 'training' [3]. Note that such intent-oriented training differs from the training on large corpora of text to support generative chatbots (e.g. [19]).

3   Research Question

There is a lack in research on the improvement of chatbot dialogue through training. This lack is surprising given the importance of this process for current chatbots for customer service. Such chatbots are still in their emergence, and their sustained development depends on their ability to respond adequately to customer requests and also to provide good customer experiences. Chatbots unable to identify customer intents, without a sufficiently comprehensive set of intents, or without quality content in their responses associated with the intents, will likely fail. Hence, knowledge related to the training of chatbots is needed.

A key part of chatbot training, is to move from raw dialogues between customers and the chatbot, through analysis, to suggestions for improvement. As a first step towards increased knowledge on how companies may improve their chatbots conversational capabilities, we formulate the following research question:

How can a service provider better understand and improve the conversational capabilities of a chatbot for customer service by analysis of chatbot dialogues?

The research question invites to a study of what can be learnt from the analysis of customer-chatbot dialogues, and how to utilize this learning for improving the chatbot's conversational capability. Such analysis may concern chatbot request resolution, the quality of the conversation, and characteristics of conversational successes and failures. Improvements may concern updating of training data, extending or reworking the total set of predefined intents, or improving on the textual responses.

4   Method

To answer the research question, we conducted a study involving analysis of dialogues from a chatbot for customer service at Telenor, a major telecom provider, and subsequent identification of possible improvements to the chatbot knowledge base. The analysis process was conducted by a team of three analysts at the company – the three first authors of this paper. The analysts held different roles respective to the chatbot: one AI-trainer with practical basis in the customer service domain, one researcher in conversational computing, and one customer service manager.

In this method section, we present the particular chatbot for customer service, the sampling and analysis of chatbot dialogues, as well as the process for using the analysis findings to identify suggestions for improvement.

4.1 Telmi – The Customer Service Chatbot

Telenor is an international telecom provider. One of its operations, Telenor Norway, introduced the chatbot *Telmi* for customer support early 2019, as a parallel option to chat with human agents. However, whereas regular customer service opening hours is 08:00–20:00, the chatbot is available 24/7.

When users select the chatbot function they are explicitly told that Telmi is a chat robot that "can help you with Telenor's products and services". The neutral robot personality and clarification of domain constraints should motivate customers to state their errand in a to-the-point and objective manner.

The chatbot was initially set up to provide help with frequently asked questions and troubleshooting. Functionality was then extended to include guides to product offerings and support for tasks such as get PIN or PUK codes, activate or order SIM card, get information on data consumption, and block subscription. At the end of the study period, the chatbot was able to identify and respond to about 2100 intents.

In the first half of 2019, during pilot and early phases after launch, Telmi has handled about 175.000 conversations with customers. Within customer service opening hours, 52% of the customers contacting the company by chat use Telmi while 48% chose to chat with a human directly. The majority of the chatbot enquires originate from smart phones (around 60% of the users). The others use computers (35%) or tablets (5%) when interacting with the chatbot.

4.2 Sampling and Analysis Process

To review and improve Telmi conversational capabilities, a process for sampling and analysis of chatbot dialogues was conducted in the period May 23–June 13, 2019. The process spanned eight analysis workshops where the team of three analysts reviewed and coded about 50 chatbot dialogues randomly drawn from the totality of Telmi dialogues since the last workshop. The three analysts had to agree on a common classification of each dialogue. This way of working ensured high quality of the analysis (but it was not always time effective). The duration of each analysis workshop was about 1,5 h. See Fig. 1 for an overview of the process.

Over the entire period, data was sampled from a total of 30033 chatbot conversations. Of these, about 85% were completed with Telmi and 15% were escalated to a human customer service agent. About 30% of the conversations were outside customer service opening hours.

A total of $N = 406$ chatbot dialogues were analysed, which ensures a confidence interval (margin of error) of plus-or-minus 5% and a confidence level of 95%.

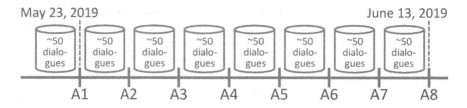

May 23, 2019   June 13, 2019

Fig. 1. Eight analyses workshops, A1–A8. For each workshop ∼50 dialogues were randomly chosen from all chatbot dialogues following the previous workshop.

4.3 Three Topics of Analysis

At the eight workshops, the sample dialogues were considered with respect to three topics of analysis: (a) request resolution and characteristics of unresolved requests, (b) quality in conversation and characteristics of successful and unsuccessful conversations, and (c) suggestions for improvement. The analysis topics were established through an iterative process involving initial piloting prior to the presented analysis.

Request resolution was coded as one of five categories:
- *Resolved* – the chatbot resolved the customer's request or provided help
- *Immediate handover* – the chatbot immediately offered handover to a human agent, because the customer asked for this or because company policy required the request to be handled by a human agent (e.g. termination of certain contracts)
- *Not resolved* – the chatbot did not solve the customer's request or provide help
- *Irrelevant customer input* – the customer request was off-topic or empty
- *Uncertain* – the analysts were not able to decide on any of the above categories

Dialogues categorized as *uncertain* were typically long and windy, without an obvious resolution. This category was, hence, later in the analysis treated the same way as dialogues categorized as *not resolved* (see Sect. 5.1).

Quality in conversation was coded as one of five categories:
- *Excellent* – the customer got their request solved efficiently; very likely a good customer experience
- *Good* – the chatbot answered as good as is possible within the frame and constrains it has been set up to work within
- *OK* – the customer got an answer after a long, winding, or difficult dialogue
- *Reasonable miss* – the chatbot failed to provide an adequate answer due to the request being out of scope, in a different language, the customer joking etc., or the request was considered impossible to resolve even for an ultimate chatbot
- *Poor* – the chatbot failed to provide an adequate answer, which it should be able to provide. Should be fixed as soon as possible.

Following coding, the characteristics of excellent and poor chatbot dialogues were discussed and a set of prototypical characteristics for these dialogues were identified.

Suggestions for improvement were discussed within the analysis team in response to issues identified in the preceding analysis. A range of suggestions were identified and brought forward to the subsequent improvement process. In the results section, the types of suggestions are categorized and summarized.

5   Results

5.1   Request Resolution - and Characteristics of Unresolved Requests

The first analysis concerned request resolution, and the characteristics of unresolved requests. About a quarter of the dialogues (24%) were coded as *resolved,* and a quarter of the dialogues (25%) were coded as *immediate handover*. About one third (34%) were coded as *unresolved,* 13% as *irrelevant customer input*, and 4% as *uncertain*.

The dialogues coded *unresolved* and *uncertain* (152 out of 406 dialogues) were made subject of a closer investigation and three subcategories were identified. (a) *Eventual handover* (14%) where the chatbot failed to correctly predict the customers' intent but offered handover to human assistance due to repetitions of a question or to a subsequent request for human assistance. (b) *Incorrect answer – abandoned* (17%) where the customer abandoned the chat when the chatbot failed to correctly predict the customer's request and returned a fallback response or a non-relevant answer (false positive) without providing a link to human assistance. (c) *Correct answer - abandoned* (7%) where the chatbot correctly interpreted the customer request, but the customer for some reason abandoned the chat without acting on the chatbot's recommendation to, for example, click a link or log in. An overview is provided in Fig. 2.

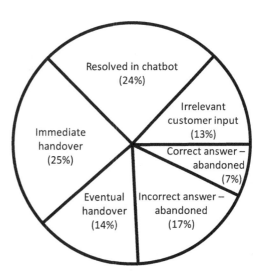

Fig. 2. Overview of the analysis of chatbot request resolution (*N* = 406)

5.2   Quality in Conversation

Quality in conversation was coded for all dialogues, except for those coded *irrelevant customer input* and *uncertain*. In total, 350 of 406 dialogues were coded on quality. The distribution of the codes for quality in conversation (*n* = 350) was: *excellent* (27%), *good* (19%), *OK* (13%), *reasonable miss* (10%), and *poor* (31%).

5.2.1   Characteristics of Successful Dialogues

Dialogues coded as *excellent* were characterized in part by specific customer behaviour, in part by specific chatbot characteristics. We detail and exemplify these below.

Customer behaviour, interestingly, was found important for successful chatbot dialogues. Specifically, customers in these dialogues typically had a concrete need, and were able to formulate this at the right level of abstraction. As in the following example:

- *Customer:* Hi. I want to order a new SIM card
- *Telmi:* I can help order a SIM card. Which number does this concern?
- *Customer:* [input number]
- *Telmi:* The SIM card will be sent to [name, address]. Please confirm
- *Customer (selects predefined answer):* Confirm order
- *Telmi:* Your new SIM card is ordered. You should receive this by mail in the coming 1–3 days.

Chatbot characteristics were, not surprisingly, also found important for successful conversations. Specifically, we found it important that (a) the chatbot vocabulary reflected the actual customer vocabulary, (b) the chatbot interpreted customer input forgivingly – specifically, in response to typos or misplaced autocorrects, and (c) the chatbot provided a good customer journey through integration with backbone IT-systems.

An example of the importance of the chatbot vocabulary reflecting customer vocabulary is seen in the dialogue below. Given the wide variation in customer vocabulary, this chatbot characteristic requires substantial training through entering a broad range of example phrases in the chatbot knowledge base.

- *Customer:* I do not have sound on the transmissions
- *Telmi:* Maybe I did not understand you perfectly, but I can help you with this: No sound on TV.
- *Customer (selects predefined answer):* No sound on TV
- *Telmi:* Check the sound level on the TV, decoder, and sound system. Double check that none of these are on mute. Did this solve the problem?

5.2.2   Characteristics of Unsuccessful Dialogues

Dialogues coded *poor* were characterized by issues pertaining to customer behaviour, the chatbot, and the service provider.

Customer behaviour in poor chatbot dialogues concerned a range of issues causing problems for the chatbot. For some, the customer expectation to the chatbot seemed too high. That is, the customer asked complex questions or phrased the questions in ways difficult for any machine to interpret. An example of this is seen in the dialogue below:

- *Customer:* Hi. Do you have any free subscriptions for children like some of the other providers, such as [provider name] offers?
- *Telmi:* I am not sure if I understood your question, but here are some options I may be able to help you with: Subscription price plans.
- *Customer:* No

Customer behaviour causing problems also included customers who expressed dislike of the correct answer and attempted to negotiate (e.g. price), customers who expressed uncertainty or an exploratory approach and did not stick to one topic, and customers who failed to read instructions provided by the chatbot or failed to understand interaction mechanisms such as links or buttons.

Chatbot issues were also a frequent characteristic of poor chatbot conversations. Specifically, when the chatbot failed to identify existing intents (false negatives) or identified the wrong intents (false positives), when needed intents were missing from the chatbot knowledge base, when needed content was missing, or when the chatbot lacked the needed functionality or integration with backbone IT-systems.

Issues concerning intents or content typically motivated suggestions for improvement, as described in the next results section. The following is an example of the chatbot failing to identify an existing intent.

- *Customer:* Hi. When do you close?
- *Telmi:* I have not yet learnt to answer this. Try re-phrasing the question.

Whereas failures to identify existing intents (false negatives) are easy to identify, as the chatbot responds with a fallback message, the chatbot's erroneous interpretation of the request as the wrong intent (false positive) is more problematic, as identification of this typically requires manual analysis. The following exemplifies a false positive:

- *Customer:* How's my <order number> going
- *Telmi: (does not recognise the order number and erroneously interpreting request as "how do you do"):* I am fine

Service provider issues also characterized some of the poor conversations. Specifically, complex services or products were found to make it challenging for customer to make precise requests and to make it challenging for chatbot to help. Also, in some instances, conversational quality was compromised due to the use of ordinary dictionary words used in product names - e.g. for the service 'My Messages' (in Norwegian: 'Mine Meldinger') as exemplified in the dialogue below. Such issues may not be resolved through training, but nevertheless hold managerial implications.

- *Customer:* I have an issue concerning my messages not getting through.
- *Telmi (erroneously interpreting request as regarding the service My Messages):* If you are experiencing problems with My Messages, it is usually due to My Contacts not being installed on your phone. If My Contacts is installed, and you have logged in – click here for further options.
- *Customer abandons the conversation*

5.3   Suggestions for Improvements

Suggestions for improvements were identified regardless of the quality of the conversations. A total of 259 dialogues (64%) gave input to suggestions for improvements of the chatbot, as shown in Table 1. One dialogue could provide input to more than one improvement areas. This list of suggestions for improvements provides the AI trainer with actionable insights, i.e. concrete input on how to improve chatbot performance. In the following, we provide a summary overview of the most frequent categories of suggestions for improvements (>2% of dialogues). The category *Utilizing context* occurred rarely.

Table 1. Distribution of suggestions for improvement ($n = 259$)

Improvement category	Percentage (n = 259)	Frequency
Prediction of existing intents	37%	96 dialogues
New intents or content	35%	91 dialogues
Conversational improvement	33%	85 dialogues
Integration issues	30%	78 dialogues
Entities	6%	16 dialogues
Buttons	5%	12 dialogues
False positives	4%	11 dialogues
Language not supported	4%	10 dialogues

The improvement area *prediction of existing intents* was mainly caused by lack of training data for the deep learning model. This may be improved through training, by adding or reworking example phrases to the training data. For example, if failure to predict was caused by spelling errors, the AI trainer may consider adding the misspelt word as a synonym.

The improvement area *new intents or content* concerned dialogues where the chatbot knowledge base did not include the customer's intent or lacked useful content for a given intent. An example of lack of useful content was one customer writing "without Internet". Telmi had a corresponding intent associated with content for troubleshooting. However, the customer's router model was not included. Improving this could be done by adding the actual router model to the knowledge base.

The improvement area *conversational improvement* concerned poor formulations in the chatbot answers, poor dialogue flow, and suboptimal predefined answer alternatives. The discussion of concrete examples gave input to the AI trainer on how to improve and refine the conversational content in the chatbot.

The improvement area *integrations* concerned dialogues where customers received general help but could have gotten perfect assistance if the company had implemented the possibility to communicate with our internal backbone IT-systems. Change driven by this category of suggestions is not possible for the AI trainer alone, but the analysis may be used to driving other change processes associated with the chatbot.

The improvement area *entities* covered dialogues in which the chatbot could have utilized the specific information given by the customer to give more precise and personalized answer and help. Customers expect a chatbot to be able to utilize facts (such as customer number, invoice number, product series number, name, address etc.). For instance, when a customer reports on issues with a specific phone number, the entity is phone number and the chatbot may make a search in the internal systems for this entity without starting with a general intent and asking clarifying questions.

The improvement area *buttons* is about the number of buttons and the content within the buttons for the chatbot response associated with a particular intent. During the analysis, it was noted that some customers fail to use buttons provided by the chatbot. This motivated suggestions for improvement concerning the phrasing of text introducing the buttons and the visual representation of the buttons. The number of buttons seems to be less important than the quality and relevance of the buttons.

The improvement area *false positive* concerned measures to avoid that the chatbot erroneously predicts a particular intent. False positives may lead to senseless, illogical and self-contradictory conversations, and are particularly important to avoid as this may reduce customers' trust in the chatbot [5]. Suggestions for improvement concerned updates to the training data of the chatbot.

The improvement area *Language not supported* concerned languages not supported in current implementation of the chatbot. Suggestions for improvements concerning language may be part of more comprehensive updates in the chatbot rather than the continuous work of the AI trainer.

6   Discussion and Further Work

The presented findings show how analysis of chatbot dialogue may provide a basis for understanding and improving chatbot conversational capabilities. In the following we first discuss the findings with regard to request resolution, quality in conversations and suggestions for improvement. Following this we summarize lessons learnt for theory and practice before suggesting future work.

6.1   Analysis to Understand and Improve Chatbot Dialogue

The presented analysis first provided insight into chatbot request resolution. About one quarter of the customer requests were found to be directly resolved in the chatbot. About one quarter was directly handed over to human personnel. And 14% were handed over to human personnel following the customer's repetition of the same question, taken to signify failed conversations. Resolved customer requests represent a benefit both from the customer perspective, in terms of rapid resolution, as well as from company perspective, in terms of cost savings in customer service. A resolution rate of 24% is promising in an early phase chatbot, such as Telmi, and should be monitored to make sure it increases over time. Customer requests handed over to human personnel are assumed to provide an adequate customer experience. Previous work [6] has shown that chatbot failure to resolve an issue does not represent a significantly reduced customer experience as long as human help is offered immediately. Hence, the majority of customer requests are likely handled in a way that is acceptable to users. The most pressing challenges in chatbot request resolution are reflected in the requests which the chatbot neither understood nor offered escalation to a human customer service representative (17%). Also, the dialogues abandoned by the user (7%) are cause for concern. These chatbot conversations illustrate that diligent training is a necessity in the development and maintenance of a chatbot for customer service.

Rating chatbot quality in conversation was found to be a useful approach to such chatbot training. In particular, dialogues categorized as *poor* offered substantial insight into the characteristics of dysfunctional dialogues and opportunities for improvements. It is interesting to note that while poor quality often is due to issues in the chatbot knowledge base, also customer behaviour and service provider issues cause problems. Customer behaviour as cause of poor chatbot quality, suggests the need for customers to get used to and better understand how to use chatbots for customer service. This corresponds to findings done in studies of conversational agents (e.g. [15]) where users were found to hold insufficient mental models of chatbot capabilities. Interaction design improvements, in particular improved onboarding dialogue, as well as customers' increased experience with chatbots may help resolve this issue.

Chatbot issues may be substantially mitigated through thoughtful and targeted training. This is mainly the job of the AI trainer, identifying and implementing potential improvements in the chatbot knowledge base. The findings suggest that the training requires issues and opportunities for improvement to be identified through qualitative analysis of dialogues. While some types of dialogue issues help identify needs for change in the training data for the chatbot intents, other types help identify the need for new and reworked dialogues, yet other types help identify opportunities for improvement in the chatbot content. While large volumes of chatbot conversations are available to inform the training, the analysis driving the training nevertheless benefit from thoughtful qualitative analysis of relatively small samples of chatbot dialogue. Hence, chatbot training requires skills in sampling and in-depth qualitative analysis, in addition to written communication skills and experience in the customer service domain.

6.2   Implications

Implications for Theory. The presented study has implications for theory and practice. Specifically, we note the following implications for theory:

- **Chatbot dialogues are a valuable source of user insight.** Chatbot dialogues may provide insight into user behaviour and preferences for chatbots for customer service. Future research is needed on how to purposefully exploit this data source.
- **Successful chatbot conversations depend on the user, the chatbot, and the service provider.** While quality in the chatbot, in particular the chatbot conversational design, is critical for successful dialogues, also some maturity may be required in the user and the service provider. Future research is needed on how to bring about such user maturity in an efficient manner.

Implications for Practice. We accentuate the following implications for practice:

- **The need for diligence in chatbot training.** Chatbots for customer service represents a substantial opportunity for service improvement in service provision. However, for this to be realized diligence in training is required also when the chatbot has moved from development to maintenance. This is likely particularly true in a domain characterized by rapid changes in service offerings and customer needs.
- **The benefit of cross-disciplinary teams.** Training chatbots require a broad range of skills, including data sampling, analysis, updating training data, managing large hierarchies of intents, and writing compelling conversational content. Also, in-depth knowledge of customer service is needed. Hence, it may be beneficial to involve cross-disciplinary teams in training, as in the presented study.

6.3 Limitations and Future Work

While the study provided valuable insights, it also has important limitations. First, the study only presented the analysis of chatbot dialogue in one company. Hence, the generality of the findings needs to be validated in future research involving other service providers and other markets. Second, the presented analysis was conducted by only one team, which imply the risk of bias in analysis. Hence, the study would benefit from replication with other teams. Finally, the study only covered parts of the process involved in the training of chatbots – the analysis and identification of potential improvements. It would be interesting to see future work also covering the later phases of the training process, including implementation of potential improvements and subsequent validation. It would also be useful if future work could aim to develop a method for assessing the value of chatbot training in terms of improved request resolution, quality in conversation, and customer experience.

In conclusion, the presented study represents a first step towards establishing the needed knowledge base on analysis of chatbot dialogue and chatbot training. We hope that this first step may motivate the research needed for improved chatbot training, as we believe this is critical for the future success of chatbots for customer service.

Acknowledgements. The work of the three first authors was supported by Telenor Norway and Telenor Research. The work of the fourth author was supported by the Research Council of Norway through research grant no. 270940.

References

1. Accenture: Chatbots in customer service. Technical report, Accenture (2016). https://www.accenture.com/t00010101T000000__w__/br-pt/_acnmedia/PDF-45/Accenture-Chatbots-Customer-Service.pdf
2. Chakrabarti, C., Luger, G.F.: Artificial conversations for customer service chatter bots: architecture, algorithms, and evaluation metrics. Expert Syst. Appl. **42**(20), 6878–6897 (2015)

3. Collins, I.: 5 steps to training a chatbot (2016). https://venturebeat.com/2016/11/12/5-steps-to-training-a-chatbot/

4. Drift: The 2018 State of Chatbots Report. Technical report, Drift (2018), https://www.drift.com/blog/chatbots-report/

5. Følstad, A., Nordheim, C.B., Bjørkli, C.A.: What makes users trust a chatbot for customer service? An exploratory interview study. In: Bodrunova, S. (ed.) INSCI 2018. LNCS, vol. 11193, pp. 194–208. Springer, Cham (2018). https://doi.org/10.1007/978-3-030-01437-7_16

6. Følstad, A., Skjuve, M.: Chatbots for customer service: user experience and motivation. In: Proceedings of the International Conference on Conversational User Interfaces - CUI 2019. ACM, New York (2019)

7. Forrester: The Six Factors that Separate Hype from Hope in Your Conversational AI Journey. Technical report, Forrester (2018). https://www.forrester.com/report/The+Six+Factors+That+Separate+Hype+From+Hope+In+Your+Conversational+AI+Journey/-/E-RES143773

8. Forrester: Human vs. Machines: How to Stop Your Virtual Agent from Lagging Behind. Technical report, Forrester (2017). https://www.amdocs.com/blog/place-digital-talks-intelligent-minds/aia-humans-vs-machines-how-to-stop-your-chatbot-from-lagging-behind

9. Forrester: The State of Chatbots. Technical report, Forrester (2016). https://www.forrester.com/report/The+State+Of+Chatbots/-/E-RES136207

10. Gartner: Gartner Says 25 Percent of Customer Service Operations Will Use Virtual Customer Assistants by 2020. https://www.gartner.com/en/newsroom/press-releases/2018-02-19-gartner-says-25-percent-of-customer-service-operations-will-use-virtual-customer-assistants-by-2020

11. Gnewuch, U., Morana, S., Maedche, A.: Towards designing cooperative and social conversational agents for customer service. In: Proceedings of the International Conference on Information Systems - ICIS 2017 (2017)

12. Hall, E.: Conversational Design. A Book Apart, New York, NY (2018)

13. Hu, T., et al.: Touch your heart: a tone-aware chatbot for customer care on social media. In: Proceedings of CHI 2018, paper 415. ACM, New York (2018)

14. Lester, J., Branting, K., Mott, B.: Conversational agents. In: The Practical Handbook of Internet Computing. Chapman & Hall/CRC, Boca Raton (2004)

15. Luger, E., Sellen, A.: Like having a really bad PA: the gulf between user expectation and experience of conversational agents. In: Proceedings of CHI 2016, pp. 5286–5297. ACM (2016). https://doi.org/10.1145/2858036.2858288

16. Mimoun, M.S.B., Poncin, I., Garnier, M.: Case study-Embodied virtual agents: an analysis on reasons for failure. J. Retail. Consum. Serv. 19(6), 605–612 (2012)

17. Shevat, A.: Designing Bots: Creating Conversational Experiences. O'Reilly Media, Newton (2017)

18. Wilson, H.J., Daugherty, P.R.: Collaborative intelligence: humans and AI are joining forces. Harvard Bus. Rev. 96(7/8), 114–123 (2018)

19. Xu, A., Liu, Z., Guo, Y., Sinha, V., Akkiraju, R.: A new chatbot for customer service on social media. In: Proceedings of CHI 2017, pp. 3506–3510. ACM, New York (2017). https://doi.org/10.1145/3025453.3025496

Conversational Repair in Chatbots for Customer Service: The Effect of Expressing Uncertainty and Suggesting Alternatives

Asbjørn Følstad[1](✉) ⓘ and Cameron Taylor[2] ⓘ

[1] SINTEF, Forskningsveien 1, 0373 Oslo, Norway
asf@sintef.no
[2] boost.ai, Koppholen 6, 4313 Sandnes, Norway
cameron@boost.ai

Abstract. Due to the complexity of natural language, chatbots are prone to misinterpreting user requests. Such misinterpretations may lead the chatbot to provide answers that are not adequate responses to user request – so called *false positives* – potentially leading to conversational breakdown. A promising repair strategy in such cases is for the chatbot to express uncertainty and suggest likely alternatives in cases where prediction confidence falls below threshold. However, little is known about how such repair affects chatbot dialogues. We present findings from a study where a solution for expressing uncertainty and suggesting likely alternatives was implemented in a live chatbot for customer service. Chatbot dialogues ($N = 700$) were sampled at two points in time – immediately before and after implementation – and compared by conversational quality. Preliminary analyses suggest that introducing such a solution for conversational repair may substantially reduce the proportion of false positives in chatbot dialogues. At the same time, expressing uncertainty and suggesting likely alternatives does not seem to strongly affect the dialogue process and the likelihood of reaching a successful outcome. Based on the findings, we discuss theoretical and practical implications and suggest directions for future research.

Keywords: Chatbot · Customer service · Conversational design · Conversational repair

1 Introduction

Correctly interpreting users' input and returning adequate responses is key to user experience and trust in chatbots for customer service [15]. However, due to the inherent complexity in conversational interaction [2], chatbots often fail in this regard. Such failure represents a substantial challenge to the uptake of chatbots. A recent industry report [5] found concern about the chatbot making a mistake restrains chatbot use for 30 per cent of respondents in a representative US survey.

Provided that users' requests are within the scope of a chatbot, interpretation failure typically leads to one of two outcomes: the chatbot responding with an answer that does not fit the user request (false positive) or the chatbot responding with a fallback message acknowledging that it does not understand and inviting the user to rephrase

© Springer Nature Switzerland AG 2020
A. Følstad et al. (Eds.): CONVERSATIONS 2019, LNCS 11970, pp. 201–214, 2020.
https://doi.org/10.1007/978-3-030-39540-7_14

(false negative); both being potentially frustrating to users [13]. In particular, because such responses are not sensitive to how conversational repair is conducted in human-human conversation [2].

To strengthen capabilities for conversational repair, some chatbots are set up to express uncertainty in the event that prediction confidence is in the lower acceptable range, or that two or more interpretations of the user request have high but similar prediction confidence levels, and then propose one or more alternatives for future direction in the conversation. However, little is known regarding the effect of this approach to conversational repair in chatbots. Specifically, there is a lack of knowledge concerning its effects on the conversational process and outcome.

To address this gap in current knowledge, we present a study where a solution for expressing uncertainty and suggesting alternatives was implemented in a live chatbot for customer service. To investigate the effect of the solution, two samples of chatbot dialogue, from immediately before and after implementation, were analysed and compared with regard to the chatbot responses, the conversational process, and the conversational outcome. In this paper, we present and discuss preliminary findings.

The study contributes needed insight into how expressing uncertainty and suggesting likely alternatives affects chatbot interaction and is as such an important step towards strengthened conversational repair in chatbots.

2 Background

Dialogues involving chatbots for customer service are a distinct form of conversation. Nevertheless, this form of communication resembles communication between humans and designers of chatbots draw on communication science to understand how to approach conversational design [11] and to analyze human-chatbot interaction [14]. Specifically, the work of Searle on speech acts [19], and Grice on the cooperative principle in conversation [10], motivates current chatbot conversational design, as does work within the field of conversation analysis [e.g. 16, 18].

For customer service, users are typically seen to engage in dialogue with chatbots to achieve a specific task, usually to get help or information, with the role of the chatbot being to cooperatively support in this task – for example by aiming for providing correct and relevant information, and avoiding unneeded content, ambiguity, and misinformation. In consequence, dialogues with customer service chatbots are typically highly oriented towards task completion, often with relatively few turns [21].

Interaction with chatbots for customer service typically follow a pattern of simple pairs of utterances [21], so-called adjacency pairs. Relevant adjacency pairs include inquiry-answer, offer-accept/reject, request-grant/deny, as well as pairs for pleasantries such as greeting and farewell [14]. In conversation between humans, adjacency pair sequences are often expanded by inclusion of other sequences – for example to clarify or modify the initial utterance. Such expansion may also be seen in human-chatbot interaction – for example when the chatbot expresses uncertainty to identify conversational trouble sources.

2.1   The Chatbot Interpretation Challenge

Current chatbots are often implemented with natural language processing as a core capability. Here, users typically input their request in free text. This text is processed by the chatbot, and the users' intents are predicted based on the set of predefined user intents available to the chatbot. When prediction confidence is above a given threshold, the chatbot responds to the user with the content associated with the predicted intent.

However, due to the complexity of natural language interaction, predicting users' intents is challenging [21]. Prediction confidence may be low due to a lack of fit between the user request and available training data. Or more than one user intents may have similar prediction confidence levels. In such instances, the chatbot is at substantial risk of either responding with an answer that does not match the user request – so called *false positives* – or responding with a fallback message even though it potentially had available adequate answers to the user requests – so called *false negatives*.

This chatbot interpretation challenge is critical. In particular, for the use of chatbots in the customer service domain, as this is one of the main use-cases for chatbots with intent prediction through natural language processing capabilities. Here, users report correct interpretations and adequate responses as a key driver of trust in chatbots [15]. Likewise, industry reports show the importance of chatbots providing reliable help and support to users [5, 9]. For a broad popular uptake of chatbots, it will be of paramount importance to mitigate the chatbot interpretation challenge.

2.2   Expressing Uncertainty and Suggesting Alternatives as Repair Strategy

While quality in interpretation is important, it should be noted that perfect interpretation in natural language conversation is an unrealistic goal. Even in conversation between humans, misinterpretation is prone [17]. Hence, a more realistic goal is for conversational design to enable efficient repair when the conversation is at risk of breaking down. As described by Dingemanse et al. [4], conversation is a process of continuous breakdown and repair. Hence, an inventory of repair strategies is found across languages. Indeed, many response errors such as false positives can be fixed in advanced through improving training data [21]. However, completely avoiding interpretational troubles in conversation is unrealistic in chatbots [11], as it is between humans [3].

Hence, conversational repair mechanisms are required when designing a system for human-like communication purposes [11]. Specifically, a repair mechanism is needed for the situation where the chatbot fails to interpret the user input with sufficient certainty. In linguistics research such mechanisms are known as *other-initiated repair* [12]. In human-human interaction other-initiated repair adjusts an asymmetry in knowledge states that might prevent continued intersubjective understanding in the talk-interaction, and requires action on the part of the speaker of the trouble-source [18].

Recipients initiate repair mechanisms with basic format types, typically categorized as open or restricted, with restricted types being further split into the sub-types of requests, offers, and alternatives. Examples of different types of other initiated repair in human-human conversation is provided in Table 1.

Table 1. Examples of repair types in human-human dialogue

Other initiated repair types	Examples in human-human dialogue
Open repair	Huh?
Restricted repair – request	She said she wanted to marry who?
Restricted repair – offers	You wanted to order a new credit card?
Restricted repair – alternatives	Did you say tacos or pizza?

Different types of repair initiations have different levels of power with regard to localizing and resolving the trouble source. In human-human interaction interpretational challenges are typically first met with low-power repair initiation, such as open repair, and only incrementally increase the power of their initiation if a more precise identification of the trouble source is needed.

Restricted repair with offers or alternatives, also referred to as *other-initiated other-repair* is seen as a high-power repair initiation, but is less used in human-human communication compared to open repair and restricted repair with requests [18]. Restricted repair with offers or alternatives is often accompanied with expressions of hesitation or reluctance as marks of uncertainty [1].

Repair mechanisms in human-human communication have motivated repair mechanisms in chatbots, and different approaches to chatbot repair initiation are available – including fallback responses, corresponding to open repair, and more powerful restricted repair with offers or alternatives.

Ashtorab et al. [2] detailed current approaches to conversational repair in chatbots. Among these, they present repair where the chatbot ask for confirmation regarding a single path forward (restricted repair – offers) and repair where the chatbot presents several likely options (restricted repair – alternatives). Both forms of repair, as described by Ashtorab et al., include expressions of uncertainty (e.g. "I'm not sure if I understood"), serving as markers of potential conversational breakdown. As such, these forms of repair in chatbots comply with the pattern for other-initiated other-repair discussed [1]. Potentially such repair may serve to make the chatbot dialogue run more smoothly, as it serves to signal to the user that repair may be needed, while at the same time doing this in a manner that is in line with established dialogue patterns.

Ashtorab et al. [2] found users to prefer restricted repair with uncertainty expression to other repair strategies. However, as their study was conducted as a questionnaire approach with different repair strategies only shown as examples to users, there is a lack of knowledge concerning the possible effects of expressing uncertainty and suggesting likely alternatives as repair strategy in actual chatbot dialogues.

3   Research Questions

Motivated by the lack of knowledge on the effect of expressing uncertainty to initiate restricted repair, we explicated the following research question:

How does expressing uncertainty and suggesting likely alternatives affect chatbot dialogues – at the message level, process level, and outcome level?

When setting up the research question, we assumed that effects of this other-initiated other-repair strategy may be found at the message level as well as at the levels of dialogue process and outcome.

At message level we assumed that chatbot expressions of uncertainty would serve to modify responses which would otherwise have been false positives, provided that the repair feature actually was triggered by user requests likely to return false positive responses, and not triggered by user requests likely to trigger relevant answers. Specifically, we assumed that the proportion of false positives would be reduced whereas the proportion of relevant responses would remain unchanged.

At dialogue process level, we were curious on which effect uncertainty expressions and suggestions of likely alternatives would have. On the one hand, avoiding false positives and instead suggesting alternatives may be more in line with Grice's cooperative principle [10], and hence lead to a more effective dialogue process. On the other hand, suggesting alternatives may potentially lead the user astray and hence imply a divergence from completing the intended task and – in consequence – a less directed process.

At dialogue outcome level, we assumed that phrasing the repair initiation as an uncertainty expression, closely aligning this to how such repair is phrased in human-human interaction [1], may encourage users more often to pursue the conversation to its conclusion and, hence, more often benefit the provided help.

4   Method

To investigate the research question, we conducted a study of user dialogues with a chatbot for customer service. This is arguably a relevant type of chatbot for the study as chatbots for customer service typically are set up with natural language processes at their core, where users may ask a wide range of questions in free text [7].

The study was set up as a quasi-experiment [20], exploiting the implementation of a solution enabling the chatbot to express uncertainty and suggest likely alternatives in response to requests for which the users' intents could not be confidently predicted. We conducted a content analysis of chatbot dialogues and compared codes for dialogues pre- and post-implementation.

It should be noted that the implementation was not accompanied with other changes or promotions of the chatbot. Hence, any difference in the two samples, before and after implementation, was likely due to the implementation itself.

4.1   The Case – Implementing a Solution for Expressing Uncertainty and Suggesting Likely Alternatives

The study was conducted in collaboration with a service provider offering chatbot interaction as a first line of support in their chat-based customer service. The chatbot received more than 1000 support requests pr. week. In instances where the chatbot was not able to answer, customers were offered escalation to chat with customer service representatives.

To improve the quality of chatbot interaction, the service provider implemented a solution where the chatbot expressed uncertainty and offered candidate interpretations or paths forward in response to instances of prediction confidence in the lower acceptable range.

Prior to this implementation, the chatbot could respond to user requests only with an answer intended to address a specific user intent or with a fallback response telling the user that it did not understand and offering to escalate to a customer service representative. See below for examples of false positive response and fallback response.

Example false positive response[1]:

- **User:** Can *I please cancel my order for [specific product]?*
- **Chatbot:** *I can help you with [specific product]. Please choose one of these options: Order* [link], *information* [link], *replace* [link].

Example fallback response:

- **User:** *Could you please tell me which service provider offers [specific product]?*
- **Chatbot:** *I am sorry, I do not understand. Please let me know if you want to chat with a customer service rep* [link].

Following implementation of the solution, the chatbot would express uncertainty and suggest one or more likely alternatives when prediction confidence for one specific intent was in the lower acceptable range, or when two or more intents had competing prediction confidence. Uncertainty expressions were phrased in a distinct manner in the chatbot, as in the examples below.

Example of chatbot expressing uncertainty regarding one specific intent –prediction confidence in lower acceptable range:

- **User:** *hello I cannot seem to remember my password?*
- **Chatbot:** *I may not have understood all of what you ask, but maybe I can help you with this: Password user account* [link].

Example of chatbot expressing uncertainty regarding two or more intents –all with similar prediction confidence:

- **User:** *I have received a new version and need to activate it by going to my user account.*
- **Chatbot:** *I may not have understood all of what you ask, but maybe I can help you with this: Activation* [link], *login details* [link].

---

[1] All dialogue examples in the paper are paraphrased.

4.2 Sampling and Analyzing Chatbot Dialogue

Chatbot dialogues were randomly sampled from the week immediately preceding implementation of the solution for expressing uncertainty and suggesting likely alternatives, and the week immediately following the implementation. In total, 1400 dialogues were sampled; 100 for each day of the two weeks. For the preliminary analysis presented in this paper, we analysed half of these dialogues; 350 from the week immediately preceding implementation and 350 for the following week. In total 700 dialogues across the pre- and post-implementation samples.

The dialogues were analysed through a content analysis approach [6]. The content analysis was based on a coding framework established prior to analysis in collaboration with the chatbot provider and the service provider owning the chatbot.

Individual messages were coded in terms of response adequacy – with specific concern for false positives, false negatives, expected fallback, and expressions of uncertainty. User messages containing only pleasantries such as "hi" and "thank you" were not included in this analysis.

Table 2. Coding topics and categories used for content analysis

Topics	Categories	Description
Response adequacy (message level)	False positive	Response not relevant for user request
	Relevant response	Response relevant for user request
	Fallback – false negative	Fallback though user request is within chatbot scope
	Fallback – out of scope	Fallback when user request is outside chatbot scope
	Expressing uncertainty – relevant	Response expresses uncertainty and suggests one or more alternatives – one of these relevant
	Expressing uncertainty – not relevant	Response expresses uncertainty and suggests one or more alternatives – none of these relevant
Dialogue directedness	Single direction	Dialogue with only one direction throughout
	Multiple directions	Dialogue progressing in two or more directions
Dialogue conclusiveness	Inconclusive – no escalation offered	Dialogue terminates without relevant answer or path to resolution
	Inconclusive – escalation offered	Dialogue terminates without relevant answer, but with an offer of escalation
	Conclusive – no escalation required	Dialogue terminates with relevant answer or link to relevant online resource
	Conclusive – escalation required	Dialogue terminates with escalation required according to company policy

(*continued*)

Table 2. *(continued)*

Topics	Categories	Description
Dialogue helpfulness	No relevant help	No relevant help offered in the dialogue
	Help offered but not used	Relevant help offered but not used (link to online resource not clicked)
	Help offered and likely used	Relevant help offered and used (link to online resource clicked or in-text help available)
	Escalation offered	Escalation offered as per company policy or due to chatbot not understanding. (The log data did not detail whether or not the offered escalation was used)

Conversations were coded in terms of conversational process, including dialogue directedness, and conversational outcome, including dialogue conclusiveness and dialogue helpfulness.

Topics of analysis and coding categories are presented in Table 2. Each message and conversation were coded corresponding to a yes/no for all relevant coding categories.

Analysis was conducted by the first author. The second author was involved in deliberation during analysis. Following coding, the significance of differences between the pre- and post-implementation samples were investigated with Chi-Square tests.

5   Findings

In this section we present the results of the analysis of the conversational quality, in terms of the adequacy of chatbot responses, conversational process (dialogue directedness) and conversational outcome (dialogue conclusiveness and helpfulness). Before this, we provide a descriptive overview of the analysed conversations.

5.1   Descriptive Overview

The 700 analysed chatbot dialogues were typically brief exchanges only. The majority included just the initial user message and subsequent chatbot response (64% pre-implementation; 62% post-implementation). About one quarter included two user messages (21% pre-implementation; 26% post-implementation). Very few included three or more user messages (14% pre-implementation; 12% post-implementation). Conversations were typically task oriented with less than 10% including user pleasantries such as "hi", "hello!", or "thank you:-)". We see the sample as allowing for adequate investigation of dialogue process and outcome within the customer service domain, as such dialogues typically are brief and task-oriented [21].

A typical example of chatbot dialogue with one user message is as follows:

- **Chatbot:** *Hi. I am the chatbot of [Service Provider]. How can I help?*
- **User:** *I need to change [product] as it has stopped working.*

– **Chatbot:** *You can easily request a replacement. You will receive it within about one week. Please order here* [link].

Overall, the pre- and post-implementation samples held similar descriptive characteristics, in terms of bot volume of messages from the chatbot (1855 vs. 1918) and messages from the users – both when including messages with pleasantries (605 vs. 592) and when excluding messages with pleasantries (522 vs. 523).

5.2   Response Adequacy

Pre-implementation chatbot responses were markedly different from post-implementation responses in terms of false positives. Whereas false positives were rife in pre-implementation dialogues, these were remarkably less frequent post-implementation (30% vs. 11%), a significant difference following a Chi-Square test ($\chi^2 = 54.94$, df = 1, p < .01). Instead, the post-implementation dialogues included, as expected, a substantial proportion of responses expressing uncertainty and suggesting alternatives.

At the same time, the proportions of relevant responses were similar across pre- and post-implementation (56% vs. 59%), a non-significant difference ($\chi^2 = 1.19$, df = 1, p = .28). However, 16% of the relevant responses in the post-implementation sample (51 of 311) were presented expressing uncertainty.

Also, the proportions of fallback responses were similar across pre- and post-implementation (14% vs. 15%), a non-significant difference ($\chi^2 = .12$, df = 1, p = .73). Details on response adequacy are provided in Table 3.

Table 3. Comparison of response adequacy across the pre- and post implementation samples

Response adequacy	Pre-implementation	Post-implementation
False positives	157 (30%)	60 (11%)
Relevant responses	293 (56%)	260 (50%)
Fallback – false negatives	4 (1%)	5 (1%)
Fallback – out of scope	68 (13%)	71 (14%)
Expressing uncertainty – relevant	–	51 (10%)
Expressing uncertainty – not relevant	–	76 (15%)

5.3   Dialogue Directedness

The effect on the conversational process of the chatbot expressing uncertainty and suggesting alternatives was investigated by considering dialogue directedness in the pre- and post-implementation sub-samples.

To illustrate the notion of dialogue directedness, the example below shows a dialogue coded as including two directions. The first direction concerns ordering a product. The second direction, due to the last chatbot response being a false positive, concerns not receiving the product.

- **Chatbot:** *Hi. I am the chatbot of [Service Provider]. How can I help?*
- **User:** *I wish to order a [product category], but I get the feedback that I do not have a user account.*
- **Chatbot:** *I can help you with [product category]. Chose an alternative: Order* [link], *Cancel* [link]
- [Link clicked]
- **User:** *This does not work.*
- **Chatbot:** *If you have ordered [product category] and not received it within about a week, you may please chat with a customer service representative* [link]

The proportions of dialogues containing only a single direction – a telltale of efficient conversations – were similar across pre- and post-implementation (70% vs. 75%), a non-significant difference ($\chi^2 = 1.84$, df = 1, p = .18).

5.4   Dialogue Conclusiveness

Dialogue conclusiveness concerns whether the dialogue reaches a point where the user is provided help in the text or offered a path to needed help in other channels – the customer service webpage or escalation to a customer service representative. To illustrate the notion of dialogue conclusiveness, it may be useful to consider two conclusive dialogue examples – one without a need to escalate to a customer service representative, the other with such a need.

Example of conclusive dialogue – escalation not required:

- **Chatbot:** *Hi. I am the chatbot of [Service Provider]. How can I help?*
- **User:** *How do I make a reclamation on my product when it has been in an unfortunate incident.*
- **Chatbot:** *You can initiate reclamation at the customer website. When there, just choose your product and then choose 'make a reclamation'. Go to reclamation* [link]

Example of conclusive dialogue – escalation required as per company policy:

- **Chatbot:** *Hi. I am the chatbot of [Service Provider]. How can I help?*
- **User:** *Cancel subscription.*
- **Chatbot:** *If you want to cancel your subscription, you need to chat with a customer service representative. Chat with representative* [link]

The proportions of the different categories of dialogue conclusiveness were fairly similar across the pre- and post-implementation samples. The largest difference between the pre- and post- implementation samples was found for dialogues categorized as *inconclusive – no escalation offered* (27% vs. 21%), a difference bordering significance ($\chi^2 = 3.76$, df = 1, p = .05). However, there was no difference between the samples for dialogues categorized as *conclusive – no escalation required* (37% vs. 37%), ($\chi^2 = 0.02$, df = 1, p = .87). Overall, the findings on dialogue conclusiveness may suggest a slight tendency for dialogues to more often lead to the chatbot offering escalation in the post-implementation sample (Table 4).

Table 4. Comparison dialogue conclusiveness across the pre- and post implementation samples

Dialogue conclusiveness	Pre-implementation	Post-implementation
Inconclusive – no escalation offered	96 (27%)	74 (21%)
Inconclusive – escalation offered	48 (14%)	56 (16%)
Conclusive – no escalation required	130 (37%)	128 (37%)
Conclusive – escalation required.	76 (22%)	92 (26%)

5.5   Dialogue Helpfulness

Dialogue helpfulness concerns whether the user is likely to have benefitted from the help provided by the chatbot. Such benefit may be assumed when the user has clicked a link leading to a relevant online resource, or when the user has been offered escalation required as per company policy. Below is an example of a dialogue coded as helpful. This particular dialogue also includes the chatbot expressing uncertainty and offering alternatives.

- **Chatbot:** *Hi. I am the chatbot of [Service Provider]. How can I help?*
- **User:** *Hi. I have recently had some problems regarding my product and with logging in.*
- **Chatbot:** *I am not sure I understood your entire question, but I can help you with the following: Product* [link], *Login* [link]
- **User** [Choosing]: *Login*
- **Chatbot:** *I can help you with login. Please click here to continue* [link]
- **User** [link clicked]

The pre- and post implementation samples did not differ significantly in terms of dialogue helpfulness. The largest differences between the pre- and post-implementation samples were found for dialogues categorized as *no relevant help* (27% vs. 21%) and *escalation offered* (35% vs. 42%), both differences bordering significance (*No relevant help*: $\chi^2 = 3.82$, df = 1, p = .05. *Escalation offered:* $\chi^2 = 3.46$, df = 1, p = .06). This may suggest a slight tendency for dialogues in the pre-implementation condition to more often lead to no relevant help, and for dialogues in the post-implementation to more often lead to the chatbot offering escalation.

However, the pre- and post-implementation samples were found to have similar distributions for *help offered and likely used* (29% vs. 26%), a non-significant difference ($\chi^2 = 0.71$, df = 1, p = .40). Details on the codes associated with dialogue conclusiveness are provided in Table 5.

Table 5. Comparison dialogue conclusiveness across the pre- and post implementation samples

Dialogue conclusiveness	Pre-implementation	Post-implementation
No relevant help	94 (27%)	72 (21%)
Help offered but not used	30 (9%)	38 (11%)
Help offered and likely used	102 (29%)	92 (26%)
Escalation offered	124 (35%)	148 (42%)

6   Discussion

6.1   How Does Expressing Uncertainty and Suggesting Alternatives Affect Chatbot Interaction?

Previous research has suggested that users may prefer chatbots to initiate conversational repair by expressing uncertainty as part of other-initiated other-repair [1]. However, there has been a lack of knowledge concerning how such expressions of uncertainty may affect user behaviour in actual dialogue with chatbots, and also the impact of varying ways of expressing uncertainty. Such knowledge is important, as uncertainty expressions is a highly relevant means of conversational repair in chatbots of different domains, in particular chatbots for customer service.

In our study, we find that a chatbot expressing uncertainty and suggesting alternatives may substantially reduce false positives in chatbot dialogues. The chatbot is triggered to express uncertainty when prediction certainty is in the lower range of what is acceptable for the most likely intent, or when prediction certainty is similar for two or more intents. In doing so, a substantial proportion of what would have been false positives are replaced by the chatbot expressing uncertainty. On the level of chatbot messages, it is noteworthy that the proportion of fallback due to the chatbot not understanding, as well as the proportion of relevant responses, remain fairly unchanged.

While it may be assumed that reducing the proportion of false positives will be beneficial for user experience, it was seen as important to investigate also how expressing uncertainty and suggesting alternatives affected the conversation process and outcome.

The conversational process hardly seems affected, as no difference was found in the number of directions in the chatbot conversations of the pre- and post-implementation samples. Likewise, the descriptive overview showed the number of user messages to be stable across the to samples. Users, hence, do not seem thrown off track by the chatbot expressing uncertainty, which is comforting. However, they do not seem to become more effective or directed due to a reduction in the proportion of false positives.

The conversational outcome also did not seem strongly affected by expressing uncertainty and suggesting likely alternatives. In particular, it is noteworthy that the proportion of dialogues leading to the chatbot offering help that is likely used is stable regardless of the chatbot expressing uncertainty or not. Some small tendencies to outcome changes were noted, though. A slightly larger proportion of dialogues after implementation than before, users were escalated to a customer service representative – as opposed to being left without relevant help offered. From a customer perspective, such a change – however small – likely represent an improvement. Previous work suggests that being escalated to a human customer service representative is not detrimental to user experience [8], whereas not getting needed help clearly is. Our findings concerning effects on conversational outcome, however, are weak and will need to be corroborated with later more comprehensive analyses.

6.2 Implications for Practice

Our study findings hold several practical implications. Below we summarize those we see as particularly important.

- **Expressing uncertainty and suggesting likely alternatives a feasible approach to conversational repair:** The tested approach is a feasible option for conversational repair in chatbots. Targeting intent predictions of low-range prediction certainty, or predictions with more than one candidate intent with similar prediction certainty may effectively reduce false positives.
- **Expressing uncertainty and suggesting likely alternatives without major impact on dialogue process and outcome:** Service providers do not seem to be at risk of negative implications when introducing chatbots expressing uncertainty and suggesting likely alternatives. The potential small effects on dialogue level which are hinted at in this study are of a character that would be beneficial for customer experience – though such effects would need to be further corroborated.
- **Expressing uncertainty and suggesting alternatives does not replace the need for diligent chatbot training:** While expressing uncertainty may improve the dialogue as false positives are reduced, improving prediction accuracy is likely to require diligent training, by continuous expanding and reworking training data sets.

It may also be noted that a possible implication of the presented study, is a reusable framework for assessing the effect of improvements in chatbot conversational repair. Specifically, we find the distinction between effects at message level and dialogue level to be useful, as well as the distinction between effects at the level of conversational process and conversational outcome.

6.3 Limitations and Future Research

In this study we have presented a preliminary analysis of the effect of uncertainty expressions and suggestions of likely alternatives in a chatbot for customer service. The study is early phase and includes samples for only one implementation. Moreover, as the sample was gathered the first week after implementation of the implementations of such uncertainty expressions, the data does not provide insight in possible long-term changes in the effects of expressing uncertainty. The preliminary character of the study is an important limitation, and further research is needed with larger samples and multiple implementations across longer periods of use.

Nevertheless, we consider the findings on chatbot response adequacy, in particular the findings on reductions in the proportion of false positives, to clearly suggest that this approach to conversational repair in chatbots may be feasible and effective.

For future work, we also foresee similar studies of the effect of other approaches to conversational repair. This is an important topic, in particular for chatbots heavily reliant on natural language processing, such as chatbots for customer service. We hope that the presented framework for analysis may inspire future research on this topic.

Acknowledgements. This study was conducted in collaboration with SpareBank 1 SR-Bank. The work was supported by the Research Council of Norway, Grant No. 282244.

References

1. Albert, S., De Ruiter, J.P.: Repair: the interface between interaction and cognition. Top. Cogn. Sci. **10**(2), 279–313 (2018)
2. Ashktorab, Z., Jain, M., Liao, Q.V., Weisz, J.D.: Resilient chatbots: repair strategy preferences for conversational breakdowns. In: Proceedings of the 2019 CHI Conference on Human Factors in Computing Systems, paper no. 254. ACM, New York (2019)
3. Bazzanella, C., Damiano, R.: The interactional handling of misunderstanding in everyday conversations. J. Pragmat. **31**, 817–836 (1999)
4. Dingemanse, M., Blythe, J., Dirksmeyer, T.: Formats for other-initiation of repair across languages: an exercise in pragmatic typology. Stud. Lang. **38** (2014). https://doi.org/10.1075/sl.38.1.01din
5. Drift: The 2018 State of Chatbots Report. Technical report, Drift (2018). https://www.drift.com/blog/chatbots-report/
6. Ezzy, D.: Qualitative Analysis: Practice and Innovation. Routledge, London (2002)
7. Følstad, A., Skjuve, M., Brandtzaeg, P.B.: Different chatbots for different purposes: towards a typology of chatbots to understand interaction design. In: Bodrunova, S., et al. (eds.) INSCI 2018. LNCS, vol. 11551, pp. 145–156. Springer, Cham (2019). https://doi.org/10.1007/978-3-030-17705-8_13
8. Følstad, A., Skjuve, M.: Chatbots for customer service: user experience and motivation. In: Proceedings of the 1st International Conference on Conversational User Interfaces, paper no. 1. ACM, New York (2019)
9. Forrester: Human vs. machines: how to stop your virtual agent from lagging behind. Technical report, Forrester (2017). https://www.amdocs.com/blog/place-digital-talks-intelligent-minds/aia-humans-vs-machines-how-to-stop-your-chatbot-from-lagging-behind
10. Grice, H.P.: Logic and conversation. In: Syntax and Semantics 3: Speech Acts, pp. 41–58. Academic Press, New York (1975)
11. Hall, E.: Conversational Design. A Book Apart, New York (2018)
12. Kendrick, K.H.: Other-initiated repair in English. Open Linguist. **1**, 164–190 (2014)
13. Kocielnik, R., Amershi, S., Bennett, P.N.: Will you accept an imperfect AI?: Exploring designs for adjusting end-user expectations of AI systems. In: Proceedings of the 2019 CHI Conference on Human Factors in Computing Systems, paper no. 411. ACM, New York (2019)
14. Moore, Robert J.: A natural conversation framework for conversational UX design. In: Moore, R., Szymanski, M., Arar, R., Ren, G.-J. (eds.) Studies in Conversational UX Design. HIS, pp. 181–204. Springer, Cham (2018). https://doi.org/10.1007/978-3-319-95579-7_9
15. Nordheim, C.B., Følstad, A., Bjørkli, C.A.: An initial model of trust in chatbots for customer service—Findings from a questionnaire study. Interact. Comput. (2019). https://doi.org/10.1093/iwc/iwz022
16. Sacks, H., Schegloff, E.A., Jefferson, G.: A simplest systematics for the organization of turntaking for conversation. Language **50**(4), 696–735 (1974)
17. Schegloff, E.A.: Some sources of misunderstanding in talk-in-interaction. Linguistics **25**, 201–218 (1987)
18. Schegloff, E.A.: Sequence Organization in Interaction: A Primer in Conversation Analysis, vol. 1. Cambridge University Press, Cambridge (2007)
19. Searle, J.R.: A classification of illocutionary acts. Lang. Soc. **5**(1), 1–23 (1976)
20. Shadish, W.R., Cook, T.D., Campbell, D.T.: Experimental and quasi-experimental Designs for Generalized Causal Inference. Houghton Mifflin, Boston (2002)
21. Shevat, A.: Designing Bots: Creating Conversational Experiences. O'Reilly Media, Newton (2017)

Working Together with Conversational Agents: The Relationship of Perceived Cooperation with Service Performance Evaluations

Guy Laban[1,2]([⊠]) [iD] and Theo Araujo[3] [iD]

[1] Institute of Neuroscience and Psychology, School of Psychology,
University of Glasgow, 62 Hillhead Street, Glasgow G12 8QB, UK
Guy.Laban@glasgow.ac.uk
[2] Gradute School of Communication, University of Amsterdam,
Nieuwe Achtergracht 166, 1018 WV Amsterdam, The Netherlands
[3] Amsterdam School of Communication Research (ASCoR),
University of Amsterdam, P.O. Box 15793,
1001 NG Amsterdam, The Netherlands
T.B.Araujo@uva.nl

Abstract. Conversational agents are gradually being deployed by organizations in service settings to communicate with and solve problems together with consumers. The current study investigates how consumers' perceptions of cooperation with conversational agents in a service context are associated with their perceptions about agents' anthropomorphism, social presence, the quality of the information provided by an agent, and the agent service performance. An online experiment was conducted in which participants performed a service-oriented task with the assistance of conversational agents developed specifically for the study and evaluated the performance and attributes of the agents. The results suggest a direct positive link between perceiving a conversational agent as cooperative and perceiving it to be more anthropomorphic, with higher levels of social presence and providing better information quality. Moreover, the results also show that the link between perceiving an agent as cooperative and the agent's service performance is mediated by perceptions of the agent's anthropomorphic cues and the quality of the information provided by the agent.

Keywords: Chatbots · Conversational agents · Anthropomorphism · Social presence · Human agent interaction · Human-machine cooperation · Web service

1 Introduction

Conversational agents are artificially intelligent computer programs that interact with users by using natural language [3, 21, 28]. Given ongoing advances in natural language processing and artificial intelligence, it is often suggested that these agents will become increasingly important in communicating and building relationships with consumers [10, 30], especially considering the ongoing shift of services to online

A. Følstad et al. (Eds.): CONVERSATIONS 2019, LNCS 11970, pp. 215–228, 2020.
https://doi.org/10.1007/978-3-030-39540-7_15

platforms [31]. While these agents begin to be deployed by organizations in service settings to solve problems together with consumers, less is known from a theoretical perspective about how consumers themselves perceive the interactions and cooperation with these agents, and how these interactions influence consumer evaluations about the agent, the task, and the organization. The current study aims to help address this gap and investigates how consumer perceptions about the cooperative behavior of a conversational agent associated with perceptions of anthropomorphism, social presence and of information quality, and how these, in turn, relates to service evaluations. In line with the Joint Intention Theory [12, 13], which defines cooperation as working together, establishing common grounds, and coordinatively defining roles and actions to achieve a task [22, 33], this study investigates cooperation among conversational agents and consumers in the context of customer service. In summary, we propose the following research question:

RQ: How are consumer perceptions about the cooperative behavior of a conversational agent associated with evaluations regarding service performance, and to what extent do perceived anthropomorphism, social presence, and information quality mediate this relationship?

2 Theory

2.1 Cooperating with Agents in Service Settings

Relationship marketing proposes that establishing and maintaining mutually beneficial long-term relationships with consumers leads to customer satisfaction and provides long-term value to an organization [5, 35]. According to the Commitment-Trust Theory [34], commitment and trust are fundamental for achieving customer satisfaction. One of the ways in which commitment and trust can be elicited is via cooperation, be it with the organization (in general), its representatives, or, we propose, with conversational agents acting on behalf of the organization.

Earlier research highlights the importance of cooperating with embodied or disembodied conversational agents. Hoffman and Breazeal [25], for example, demonstrated that interacting with collaborative robots can lead to satisfying experiences when users perceive that they established cooperative relations with the agent. Their application for cooperative relations, influenced by the Joint Intention Theory [12, 13], includes having a goal-centric approach, establishing common ground, working together and coordinating the work, providing mutual support and understanding, having awareness for each other's abilities and in turn allocate tasks accordingly [25]. These features demonstrate the attributions of commitment and trust by the user, which are central to establishing cooperative relationships [25]. Following similar principles, Farooq and Grudin [17] stress that the nature of interactions between humans and computers constantly evolve into human-computer integration – cooperative relations that imply a partnership between the two. Establishing cooperation and partnership between the two provides meaning to each other's activities, in contrast, to simply taking orders. Both the human and the computer or the agent are correspondent to the situation, drawing meaning from each other's presence.

In line with the Commitment-Trust Theory [34], the Joint Intention Theory [12, 13], and Hoffman's and Breazeal's [25] findings, we expect that these properties embody the sense of cooperation as cues for cooperative behavior. Considering that cooperative behavior was found to promote efficiency, productivity, and effectiveness [12, 13, 34], we propose the first hypothesis:

H1: Perceiving the conversational agent as more cooperative will be positively associated with perceiving the service performance better.

2.2 Cooperation as an Anthropomorphic Quality

The media equation hypothesis explains that computers function as social actors, in the sense that people tend to apply social rules when interacting with computers (as well as agents), and to have social expectations from them [36, 38, 42]. Anthropomorphism, the extent to which an agent exhibits and or is perceived to have human characteristics, is an important factor influencing how a user establishes relations with an agent [15]. Moreover, cooperation is a human personality trait that is embodying qualities as social tolerance, empathy, helpfulness, and compassion [11]. We expect, therefore, that, the more that a consumer perceives their relationship with an agent as being cooperative, the higher the level of anthropomorphism that the consumer will attribute to the agent, and propose the following hypothesis:

H2: Perceiving the conversational agent as more cooperative will positively be associated with perceiving it as more anthropomorphic.

2.3 The Role of Anthropomorphism in Services

Anthropomorphic features or perceptions were found to influence consumer emotional responses to robots in service encounters [46]. Customers constantly express their need for personal interactions and for "human touch" in service procedures. Personal interaction is an essential part of human nature; therefore, it plays an extensive role in the context of services where customers address their need to receive a personal contact. The human interpersonal contact is an emotional aspect of the service procedure that includes an emotional exchange, which can be crucial for defining its quality [40]. We expect that perceiving the agent as anthropomorphic will positively influence service evaluations and, therefore, mediate the relationship between perceived cooperativeness and service performance. This leads to the following hypothesis:

H3: Perceived anthropomorphism will mediate the relationship between perceiving the agent as more cooperative and the perceived service performance.

2.4 Cooperation as a Source of Information

Cooperation also entails allocating tasks and being aware of one's abilities [12, 13]. When an agent is perceived as cooperative, it tends to be associated with the ability to provide guidance and allocate tasks, establishing mutual understanding through the information exchange [12, 13, 22, 33]. Consequently, we expect that perceived cooperativeness will be associated with evaluations about the quality of information provided by the agent, and propose the following hypothesis:

H4: Perceiving the conversational agent as more cooperative will be positively associated with perceived information quality.

As information quality has a strong influence on consumer evaluation of service procedure performance [40], we propose that it will mediate the influence of perceived cooperativeness on service performance, and propose the following hypothesis:

H5: Perceived information quality will mediate the relationship between perceiving the agent as more cooperative and the perceived service performance.

2.5 Cooperation as a Meaningful Form of Social Interaction

Finally, as a human personality trait [11], cooperation is a meaningful form of social interaction and an integral component of team relations and human nature, as it signifies the act of working with others [6, 22]. When demonstrating social presence, the feeling that another being "(living or synthetic) also exist in the world and appear to react to you" ([24] p. 265), computers are perceived as social actors, on whom people tend to impose social rules [36, 38, 42]. Accordingly, social presence is typically associated as human-like behavior, and agents and robots are typically perceived to be human-like when being perceived as having a prominent social presence [39]. Social robots (agents) are intended to interact with humans in socially meaningful ways [7, 18, 39], and since cooperation is a social behavior [6, 22], we propose the following hypothesis:

H6: Perceiving the conversational agent as more cooperative will be positively associated with the perception of social presence attributed to the agent.

Social presence is often described as a positive and meaningful quality in traditional online service systems [14, 19]. Lee, Jung, Kim, and Kim [32] indicate that social presence influences how users evaluate an agent in general. Other researchers [27, 44] provided evidence for the role of social presence when evaluating agents in the context of service interactions, explaining that social presence is often perceived as a meaningful factor for determining positive evaluations. Accordingly, we propose that, in the context of customer services, social presence will also mediate the relationship between perceived cooperativeness and service evaluations, leading to the following hypothesis:

H7: The perceived social presence of the agent will mediate the relationship between perceiving the agent as more cooperative and the perceived service performance.

3   Methods

3.1   Design

The current study used an online experiment with conversational agents to answer the research question. Initially, a two (demonstration of cooperation: cooperative agent vs. non-cooperative agent) by two (task complexity: complicated task vs. simple task) between-subjects design has been conducted. Accordingly, four conversational agents were designed for this study according to the joint intention theory definitions [12, 13] and following Hoffman and Breazeal [25] practical guidelines to demonstrate varying levels of cooperative intentions. Furthermore, manipulated tasks were designed to emphasize different levels of task complexity. As there were no significant differences between agents in perceptions regarding task complexity and cooperation cues, we analyzed the results of all agents combined controlling for the condition to which each participant was assigned. Therefore, the study was treated as an observational study to further understand the nature of perceptions that are associated with perceiving an agent as more or less cooperative.

3.2 Population

A total of 100 participants were recruited using Amazon Mechanical Turk. To minimize the influence of culture and language, the sample was composed by U.S.-based participants who speak English as their first language. Nine participants were dropped because of technical issues when connecting to the agents, resulting in a final sample of 91 participants, with ages ranging between 20 and 63 years old ($M = 33.15$, $SD =$ 8.74), 45.1% females, and with most participants having started (19.8%) or completed a 2- (14.3%) or 4-year (44%) college degree.

3.3 Stimulus

The chatbots were created using the Conversational Agent Research Toolkit [1]. The agents were designed to demonstrate the act of working together. This was established by the conversational agent using particular statements that emphasize the act of working together and personal attachment to the common goal (e.g., "To change the address we should work together", "Let me know that you managed to complete this step"). Also, the agents demonstrated the act of allocating tasks by coordinatively defining roles and actions, according to one's abilities, to achieve a goal [22, 33]. This was established by stating that the conversational agent understands its own and the customer abilities, and allocate the different needed steps for completing the task between itself and the customer (i.e. "Since your approval is needed for changing the address, please provide the new address in the following system so that I will be able to authorize the new delivery time frame").

The complexity of the tasks was operationalized according to the level of the task's dynamic requirements, where complicated tasks demand higher dynamic requirements [45]. The simple task condition required participants to change the delivery address for online order with no consideration of the order status while the complicated task condition required participants to consider that the order already left the shipping center.

3.4 Measurements

Independent Variables. *Perceived Cooperation.* The variable aims to measure the extent to which the subjects perceived the agent to be cooperative according to the joint intention theory definitions [12, 13] and in accordance with Hoffman and Breazeal [25] practical guidelines. Four items of perceived cooperation were adopted from Hoffman's [26] quality metrics for human-robot collaboration. In order to fit the scope of the paper, the items were adjusted to be addressed on an agent instead of a robot. All the items were evaluated on a seven-point Likert scale. The scale of perceived cooperation was formed using the mean index of the items and was found reliable, with Cronbach's α of .94 ($M = 5.87$, $SD = .16$).

Mediators. *Perceived Anthropomorphism.* Anthropomorphism stands for the extent to which an agent exhibit and imitates human characteristics [15]. It includes the attribution of a human form, human features, or human behavior to nonhuman such as robots, computers, and animals [4]. Hence, for measuring the agent's perceived anthropomorphism, the aim is to evaluate the extent of humanlike qualities presented by the agent, as perceived by the subjects. A perceived anthropomorphism scale introduced by Bartneck et al. [4] was applied. The scale includes five semantic-differential items with human and machine-related characteristics as the opposite dimensions. A higher score in this scale indicates a humanlike agent behavior, and a lower score represents a mechanical, machine-like behavior. In this study, this was measured on a seven-point scale. In order to fit this research topic, the last item "Moving rigidly/Moving elegantly" was changed from "moving" to "communicating". The scale was found reliable, with Cronbach's α of .94 ($M = 4.93$, $SD = .21$).

Social Presence. For measuring how the subjects perceived the social presence of the agent, a perceived social presence scale with five items was adapted from Lee, Jung, Kim, and Kim [32]. The items were adjusted for the scope of the study addressing them to the agent. The scale was found reliable, with Cronbach's α of .91 ($M = 5.81$, $SD = .27$).

Principal axis factoring analysis was conducted to validate that the items of the variable 'perceived anthropomorphism' and the items of the variable 'perceived social presence' load under two unique factors and do not converge. The results entail two unique factors with an eigen value of above one. Following the results of an oblique rotation, the five items of perceived anthropomorphism were loaded under the first factor, explaining 63.34% of the variance in the factor with an eigen value of 6.33. The five items of perceived social presence were loaded under the second factor, explaining 15.22% of the variance in the factor with an eigen value of 1.52. Accordingly, we can confirm that the items of both of the variables, 'perceived anthropomorphism' and 'perceived social presence' were loaded under two unique factors and do not demonstrate evidence of strong convergence.

Perceived Information Quality. The variable is aimed at measuring the perceptions of the customer over the quality of information and data exchange provided by the agent [43]. The scale was adopted from Suh, Greene, Israilov & Rho [43] using four items evaluated on a seven-point Likert scale. The items were slightly adjusted to fit the scope of this current research, addressing "service provider" as "agent". The scale was found reliable, with Cronbach's α of .91 ($M = 5.82$, $SD = .13$).

Dependent Variable. *Perceived Service Performance.* Perceived service performance is a single manifest self-reported measure that is intended to evaluate the level of service quality provided by the agent as perceived by the subject. Using a single question, the subjects were requested to rate the service provided by the agent on a seven-point Likert scale.

Control Variables. The questionnaire included measures controlling for affinity with technology (adapted from Edison and Geissler, [16]), need for cognition (adapted from Cacioppo et al. [9]), and demographic variables including age and gender.

3.5 Procedure

The participants executed a service-oriented task, changing the address of an online order in an online flower shop by chatting with one of the four conversational agents designed for this study. For stimulating the act of cooperation, the agents allocated part of the task to the participants, instructing them to independently check and approve the change on a web-based platform. After the task, participants completed a questionnaire evaluating the agent in terms of perceived cooperation, perceived anthropomorphism, social presence, and the quality of information provided. Moreover, the participants evaluated the provided service performance. Finally, the participants evaluated their affinity with technology and need for cognition, and answered demographic-related questions disclosing their age, gender, occupation, nationality and current residing country. After finishing their participation in the online experiment, the participants were debriefed about the study.

4 Results

A mediation analysis was conducted using Model 4 of PROCESS Macro 3.2.01 to SPSS [23] to investigate the research hypotheses. The model included perceived cooperation as the independent variable, perceived service performance as the dependent variable, and perceived anthropomorphism, information quality, and social presence as mediators. Moreover, the model controlled for the confounding influence of the participants' age, gender, affinity for technology, need for cognition, and for the agent they used during the manipulation.

4.1 Direct Association Between Perceived Cooperation and Perceived Service Performance

The results indicate that in step 1 of the mediation model, perceived cooperation was significantly related to the outcome variable perceived service performance; $R = .76$, $F(7, 83) = 16.40, p < .001$, with the model explaining 58% ($R^2 = .580$) of the variance in perceived service performance. The regression of perceived cooperation on perceived service performance was significant, $b = .75$, $t(83) = 9.94$, $p < .001$, 95% CI [.60,.90] when cancelling the mediators' effect in the model.

4.2   Direct Association Between Perceived Cooperation and the Mediators

Step 2 showed that perceived cooperation was significantly related to the proposed mediators: perceived anthropomorphism (R = .66, $F(7, 83)$ = 9.28, $p < .001$), perceived information quality (R = .85, F(7, 83) = 31.69, $p < .001$), and perceived social presence (R = .90, $F(7, 83)$ = 52.81, $p < .001$). The model explains 43.9% (R^2 = .439) of the variance in perceived anthropomorphism, 72.8% (R^2 = .728) in perceived information quality, and 81.7% (R^2 = .817) in perceived social presence. The regressions of perceived cooperation on the mediators, perceived anthropomorphism (b = .75, $t(83)$ = 7.77, b^*= .65, $p < .001$, 95% CI [.56,.94]), perceived social presence (b = .83, $t(83)$ = 18.35, b^*= .88, $p < .001$, 95% CI[.74,.93]), and perceived information quality (b = .83, $t(83)$ = 14.39, b^*= .84, $p < .001$, 95% CI[.71,.94]), were significant. Therefore, H2, H4, and H6 are supported.

4.3   Direct Association Between the Mediators and Perceived Service Performance

Step 3 showed that the overall model was significant; R = .84, $F(10, 80)$ = 18.93, $p < .001$, with the model explaining 70.3% (R^2 = .703) of the variance in perceived service performance. Controlling for perceived cooperation, The mediators of perceived anthropomorphism (b = .16, $t(80)$ = 2.06, b^*= .18, p = .043, 95% CI[.01,.31]), and perceived information quality (b = .67, $t(80)$ = 5.24, b^* = .63, $p < .001$, 95% CI [.42,.92]) were found to be significant. The mediator perceived social presence (b = −.27, $t(80)$ = −1.60, b^* = − .24, p = .114, 95% CI[−.60,.07]), controlling for perceived cooperation, was not significant. Hence, H7 is not supported.

4.4   Indirect Relationship Between Perceived Cooperation and Perceived Service Performance

Step 4 of the analyses revealed that, when controlling for the mediators, perceived cooperation was not a significant predictor of perceived service performance, b = .30, $t(80)$ = 1.85, b^*= .29, p = .069, 95% CI[−.02,.63]. Hence, H1 is not supported. Mediation analyses based on 5000 bootstrapped samples using bias-corrected and accelerated 95% confidence intervals [41] showed that perceived cooperation had a significant total effect on the perceived service performance (c = .75, SE = .08, $p < .001$, 95% CI[.60,.90]), a not significant residual direct effect (c' = .30, SE = .16, p = .069, 95% CI[−.02,.62]), and significant indirect effects through perceived anthropomorphism (ab = .12, SE = .05, BCa CI[.01,.23]) and perceived information quality (ab = .55, SE = .14, BCa CI[.21,.74]). The indirect effects are significantly different from zero at $p < .05$. Perceived anthropomorphism (ab_{cs}= .11, SE = .05, BCa CI[.01,.21]) and perceived information quality (ab_{cs}= .53, SE = .13, BCa CI[.20,.73]) fully mediated the total effect between perceived cooperation and perceived service performance. Therefore, H3 and H5 are supported.

5 Discussion

This study was aimed at investigating how consumer perceptions about the cooperative behavior of a conversational agent associated with perceptions of anthropomorphism, social presence and of information quality, and how these, in turn, relates to service evaluations. The results of the study entailed a direct positive association between perceiving an agent as more cooperative and perceiving it as more anthropomorphic and to provide better information quality. Moreover, these were found to positively mediate consumers' service evaluations. A direct positive association was also found between perceiving an agent as more cooperative and perceiving it as more socially present. Nevertheless, contrasting to perceived anthropomorphism and perceived information quality, there was no evidence for an indirect association between perceiving an agent as more cooperative and consumers' service evaluations through perceived social presence. In addition to these, there was no evidence for a direct association between perceiving an agent as more cooperative and evaluating the service performance provided to be better (Table 1).

Table 1. Summary of the results

Hypotheses	Type of relationship	Results
H1: Perceiving the conversational agent as more cooperative will be positively associated with perceiving the service performance better	Direct	Rejected
H2: Perceiving the conversational agent as more cooperative will positively be associated with perceiving it as more anthropomorphic	Direct	Supported
H3: Perceived anthropomorphism will mediate the relationship between perceiving the agent as more cooperative and the perceived service performance	Indirect	Supported
H4: Perceiving the conversational agent as more cooperative will be positively associated with perceived information quality	Direct	Supported
H5: Perceived information quality will mediate the relationship between perceiving the agent as more cooperative and the perceived service performance	Indirect	Supported
H6: Perceiving the conversational agent as more cooperative will be positively associated with the perception of social presence attributed to the agent	Direct	Supported
H7: The perceived social presence of the agent will mediate the relationship between perceiving the agent as more cooperative and the perceived service performance	Indirect	Rejected

5.1   The Value of Information Quality in Service Interactions
with Conversational Agents

The first key finding is that the quality of the information provided by the agent will be the most influential when evaluating an agent's service performance following perceptions regarding its cooperative behaviour. In line with the Joint Intention Theory features of cooperation [12, 13], when an agent is perceived as more cooperative, consumers perceive it to provide a better quality of information. Consequently, the outcomes of the service procedure are evaluated to be better. These findings not only validate earlier research on the importance of information quality (e.g., [40]), but also highlight how experiences that elicit cooperation between consumers and conversational agents are relevant for customer service contexts, and our understanding of interactions with computers and technology in general.

As cooperative interactions are aimed at creating shared experiences [12, 13], when customers perceive the interaction as more cooperative, they are possibly finding the information to be more accessible. Therefore, they evaluate the information provided more positively. This is substantial in the context of using conversational agents in service settings. Since the use of this technology is relatively novel [21], customers tend to perceive it as a "black box" [8] and experience a certain confusion. Eliciting more· cooperative service interactions between online customers and agents can potentially overcome the confusion that is associated with the novelty of this technology. Even without understanding the mechanism of the agent, a customer can have a better service experience by having the feeling of being an active part of the solution, receiving valuable information, and not being passive in the interaction.

5.2   Associating Cooperation with Anthropomorphism

The second key finding entails that perceiving the agent as more cooperative is associated with perceiving it as more anthropomorphic, and in turn, perceiving the service performance being better. This finding extends earlier research (e.g., [46]) and highlights the role that anthropomorphism, "the assignment of human traits and characteristics to computers" ([37], p. 82), has in services (see [40]). In line with the trajectory of human personality traits [11], this finding confirms that anthropomorphism is associated with perceptions of cooperation. As such, following the media equation hypothesis [36, 38, 42], this finding demonstrates how customers evaluations of the agents are associated with them experiencing the agents as more anthropomorphic or human-like.

5.3   To What Extent Is Social Presence Relevant for Service Interactions
with Conversational Agents?

The third key finding of this study was the lack of association between perceived service performance and social presence. This is striking as while one could expect that the influence of an agent's social presence would be complementary or similar to the agent's anthropomorphic presence [39], there was no evidence for this in the current study. It should still be noted that perceiving the agent as more cooperative was indeed associated with higher levels of social presence. However, in contrast to previous studies (e.g., [27, 44]), social presence perceptions were not seen to be reflected in customers' service evaluations, at least as a mediator for cooperation.

These results, on the one hand, provide another level of nuance to previous empirical evidence that highlights the importance of social presence positive in traditional online service systems (e.g., [14, 19]). On the other hand, these results give evidence to the more recent propositions by Go and Sundar [20] that suggest that higher levels of message interactivity can compensate for an agent's impersonal nature (low on anthropomorphic cues). Hence, it could be said that certain factors as message interactivity or, - in the context of the current study - information quality, can play a more substantial role in customers' service evaluations. Moreover, these results raise questions about the boundary conditions for the relevance of social presence in service interactions and online service quality. These results also reinforce the suggestions made by earlier research (e.g., [2, 29]) to explore in more detail how to best measure the concepts of anthropomorphism and social presence in these new contexts.

5.4   Limitations

Finally, this study has some limitations. The intended manipulations for cooperation and task complexity in the experimental conditions were not successful according to the manipulation checks. Cooperation is a complex concept that has many theoretical and pragmatic definitions. While this study conceptualizes cooperation with agents by addressing the join intentions theory [12, 13], future research should address other theories from various disciplines for better understanding the true nature of cooperation. The practical guidelines for cooperation that were applied from Hoffman and Breazeal [25] were unsuccessful in stimulating the act of cooperation when applied in a dialogue interface and not with a physical social robot. Accordingly, future research should explore and redefine the indicators for cooperation with agents in dialogue interface and address the attributes in language and conversation that promote acts of cooperation. Moreover, the issues with the manipulations, therefore, restrict the study from drawing any causal inferences, as it can merely show the associations of customers perceptions of the agents. These limitations notwithstanding, the findings presented in this study can serve as a baseline for future chatbot research, highlighting a promising role for information quality, anthropomorphism and cooperation for in human-machine communication in service contexts.

6   Conclusions

The findings of this study further explain how consumers themselves perceive the interactions and cooperation with these agents, and how these interactions influence consumer evaluations about the agent. It extends the Joint Intention Theory [12, 13], providing evidence for the implications of eliciting cooperation among conversational agents and consumers in the context of customer service. Furthermore, the study demonstrates the role of cooperation in online marketing interactions, especially when conversational agents are involved.

The study draws attention to the importance of information quality when integrating novel autonomous technologies in service settings and extends previous findings on the matter (e.g., [40]). In addition to it, the study demonstrated how eliciting cooperation can be associated with establishing common grounds for evaluating information better [12, 13]. Moreover, it extends earlier research (e.g., [2, 29]) regarding the role of social presence in interactions with conversational agents and reinforces the need for this concept to be further studied, especially in contrast and/or in combination with the notion of anthropomorphism. Finally, the study has managerial implications, providing support for a better understanding of how consumers perceive service interactions with conversational agents, and how these should be implemented accordingly.

References

1. Araujo, T.: Conversational Agent Research Toolkit: An alternative for creating and managing chatbots for experimental research. Computational Communication Research, Working Paper (2019). https://doi.org/10.31235/osf.io/9ukyf
2. Araujo, T.: Living up to the chatbot hype: the influence of anthropomorphic design cues and communicative agency framing on conversational agent and company perceptions. Comput. Hum. Behav. **85**, 183–189 (2018). https://doi.org/10.1016/j.chb.2018.03.051
3. Atwell, E., Shawar, B.A.: Chatbots: are they really useful? LDV Forum **22**, 29–49 (2007)
4. Bartneck, C., Kulić, D., Croft, E., Zoghbi, S.: Measurement instruments for the anthropomorphism, animacy, likeability, perceived intelligence, and perceived safety of robots. Int. J. Soc. Robot. **1**(1), 71–81 (2009). https://doi.org/10.1007/s12369-008-0001-3
5. Berry, L.L.: Relationship marketing of services perspectives from 1983 and 2000. J. Relationship Market. **1**(1), 59–77 (2002). https://doi.org/10.1300/J366v01n01_05
6. Bratman, M.E.: Shared cooperative activity. Philos. Rev. **101**(2), 327–341 (1992). https://doi.org/10.2307/2185537
7. Breazeal, C.L.: Designing Sociable Robots. MIT Press, Cambridge (2002)
8. Bunge, M.: A general black box theory. Philos. Sci. **30**(4), 346–358 (1963). https://doi.org/10.1086/287954
9. Cacioppo, J.T., Petty, R.E.: The need for cognition. J. Pers. Soc. Psychol. **42**(1), 116–131 (1982). https://doi.org/10.1037/0022-3514.42.1.116
10. Chai, J., Budzikowska, M., Horvath, V., Nicolov, N., Kambhatla, N., Zadrozny, W.: Natural language sales assistant - a web-based dialog system for online sales. In: Proceedings of the 13th Innovative Applications of Artificial Intelligence Conference, IAAI 2001, Seattle, WA, pp. 19–26 (2001)
11. Cloninger, C., Svrakic, D.M., Przybeck, T.R.: A psychobiological model of temperament and character. Arch. Gen. Psychiatry **50**(12), 975–990 (1993)
12. Cohen, P.R., Levesque, H.J.: Persistence, intention, and commitment. In: Proceedings of the 1986 Workshop on Reasoning about Actions and Plans, p. 297 (1990)
13. Cohen, P.R., Levesque, H.J.: Teamwork. Nous **25**, 487–512 (1991)
14. Cyr, D., Hassanein, K., Head, M., Ivanov, A.: The role of social presence in establishing loyalty in e-service environments. Interact. Comput. **19**(1), 43–56 (2007). https://doi.org/10.1016/j.intcom.2006.07.010

15. de Visser, E.J., et al.: Almost human: anthropomorphism increases trust resilience in cognitive agents. J. Exp. Psychol.: Appl. **22**(3), 331–349 (2016). https://doi.org/10.1037/xap0000092

16. Edison, S.W., Geissler, G.L.: Measuring attitudes towards general technology: antecedents, hypotheses and scale development. J. Target. Measur. Anal. Market. **12**(2), 137–156 (2003). https://doi.org/10.1057/palgrave.jt.5740104

17. Farooq, U., Grudin, J.: Human-computer integration. Interactions **23**(6), 27–32 (2016). https://doi.org/10.1145/3001896

18. Fong, T., Nourbakhsh, I., Dautenhahn, K.: A survey of socially interactive robots. Robot. Auton. Syst. **42**(3), 143–166 (2003). https://doi.org/10.1016/S0921-8890(02)00372-X

19. Gefen, D., Straub, D.W.: Consumer trust in B2C e-Commerce and the importance of social presence: experiments in e-Products and e-Services. Omega **32**(6), 407–424 (2004). https://doi.org/10.1016/j.omega.2004.01.006

20. Go, E., Sundar, S.S.: Humanizing chatbots: the effects of visual, identity and conversational cues on humanness perceptions. Comput. Hum. Behav. **97**, 304–316 (2019). https://doi.org/10.1016/j.chb.2019.01.020

21. Griol, D., Carbó, J., Molina, J.M.: An automatic dialog simulation technique to develop and evaluate interactive conversational agents. Appl. Artif. Intell. **27**(9), 759–780 (2013). https://doi.org/10.1080/08839514.2013.835230

22. Grosz, B.J.: Collaborative systems (AAAI-94 presidential address). AI Mag. **17**(2), 67 (1996)

23. Hayes, A.F.: Introduction to Mediation, Moderation, and Conditional Process Analysis: A Regression-Based Approach, 2nd edn. Guilford Press, New York (2018)

24. Heeter, C.: Being there: the subjective experience of presence. Presence: Teleoperators Virtual Environ. **1**(2), 262e271 (1992). https://doi.org/10.1162/pres.1992.1.2.262

25. Hoffman, G., Breazeal, C.: Collaboration in human-robot teams. In: AIAA 1st Intelligent Systems Technical Conference, p. 6434 (2004). https://doi.org/10.2514/6.2004-6434

26. Hoffman, G.: Evaluating fluency in human-robot collaboration. In: International Conference on Human-Robot Interaction (HRI), Workshop on Human Robot Collaboration, vol. 381, pp. 1–8 (2013)

27. Kang, Y.J., Lee, W.J.: Effects of sense of control and social presence on customer experience and e-service quality. Inf. Dev. **34**(3), 242–260 (2018). https://doi.org/10.1177/0266666916686820

28. Kerlyl, A., Hall, P., Bull, S.: Bringing chatbots into education: towards natural language negotiation of open learner models. In: Ellis, R., Allen, T., Tuson, A. (eds.) SGAI 2006, pp. 179–192. Springer London (2007). https://doi.org/10.1007/978-1-84628-666-7_14

29. Kim, Y., Sundar, S.S.: Anthropomorphism of computers: is it mindful or mindless? Comput. Hum. Behav. **28**(1), 241–250 (2012). https://doi.org/10.1016/j.chb.2011.09.006

30. Kuligowska, K., Lasek, M.: Virtual assistants support customer relations and business processes. In: The 10th International Conference on Information Management, Gdańsk (2011)

31. Lasek, M., Jessa, S.: Chatbots for customer service on hotels'websites. Inf. Syst. Manag. **2**(2), 146–158 (2013)

32. Lee, K.M., Jung, Y., Kim, J., Kim, S.R.: Are physically embodied social agents better than disembodied social agents?: the effects of physical embodiment, tactile interaction, and people's loneliness in human–robot interaction. Int. J. Hum.-Comput. Stud. **64**(10), 962–973 (2006). https://doi.org/10.1016/j.ijhcs.2006.05.002

33. Levesque, H.J., Cohen, P.R., Nunes, J.H.: On acting together. In: Proceedings of the Eighth National Conference on Artificial Intelligence, AAAI-90, Boston, MA, pp. 94–99 (1990)

34. Morgan, R.M., Hunt, S.D.: The commitment-trust theory of relationship marketing. J. Market. **58**(3), 20–38 (1994). https://doi.org/10.2307/1252308

35. Murphy, B., Maguiness, P., Pescott, C., Wislang, S., Ma, J., Wang, R.: Stakeholder perceptions presage holistic stakeholder relationship marketing performance. Eur. J. Market. **39**(9), 1049–1059 (2005). https://doi.org/10.1108/03090560510610716

36. Nass, C., Lee, K.M.: Does computer-synthesized speech manifest personality? Experimental tests of recognition, similarity-attraction, and consistency-attraction. J. Exp. Psychol.: Appl. **7**(3), 171–181 (2001). https://doi.org/10.1037/1076-898X.7.3.171

37. Nass, C., Moon, Y.: Machines and mindlessness: Social responses to computers. J. Soc. Issues **56**(1), 81–103 (2000). https://doi.org/10.1111/0022-4537.00153

38. Nass, C., Steuer, J., Tauber, E.R.: Computers are social actors. In: Adelson, B., Dumais, S., Olson, J. (eds.) Proceedings of the SIGCHI Conference on Human Factors in Computing Systems, CHI 1994, pp. 72–78. ACM, New York (1994). https://doi.org/10.1145/191666. 191703

39. Oh, C.S., Bailenson, J.N., Welch, G.F.: A systematic review of social presence: definition, antecedents, and implications. Front. Robot. AI **5**, 114 (2018). https://doi.org/10.3389/frobt. 2018.00114

40. Paluch, S.: Remote Service Technology Perception and its Impact on Customer-Provider Relationships An Empirical Exploratory Study in a B-to-B-setting. Gabler Verlag, Wiesbaden (2012). https://doi.org/10.1007/978-3-8349-6936-1

41. Preacher, K.J., Hayes, A.F.: SPSS and SAS procedures for estimating indirect effects in simple mediation models. Behav. Res. Methods Instrum. Comput. **36**(4), 717–731 (2004). https://doi.org/10.3758/BF03206553

42. Reeves, B., Nass, C.: How People Treat Computers, Television, and New Media Like Real People and Places. Cambridge University Press, Cambridge (1996)

43. Suh, M., Greene, H., Israilov, B., Rho, T.: The impact of customer education on customer loyalty through service quality. Serv. Market. Q. **36**(3), 261–280 (2015). https://doi.org/10. 1080/15332969.2015.1046776

44. Verhagen, T., Van Nes, J., Feldberg, F., Van Dolen, W.: Virtual customer service agents: using social presence and personalization to shape online service encounters. J. Comput.-Mediated Commun. **19**(3), 529–545 (2014). https://doi.org/10.1111/jcc4.12066

45. Wood, R.E.: Task complexity: definition of the construct. Organ. Behav. Hum. Decis. Process. **37**(1), 60–82 (1986). https://doi.org/10.1016/0749-5978(86)90044-0

46. Zhang, T., Zhu, B., Lee, L., Kaber, D.: Service robot anthropomorphism and interface design for emotion in human-robot interaction. In: 2008 IEEE International Conference on Automation Science and Engineering, pp. 674–679 (2008). https://doi.org/10.1109/coase. 2008.4626532

Application Area: Chatbots in Education

Chatbots for the Information Acquisition at Universities – A Student's View on the Application Area

Raphael Meyer von Wolff$^{(\boxtimes)}$, Jonas Nörtemann, Sebastian Hobert, and Matthias Schumann

University of Goettingen, Goettingen, Germany
{r.meyervonwolff, shobert, mschumal}@uni-goettingen.de,
jonas.noertemann@stud.uni-goettingen.de

Abstract. Chatbots are currently widely used in many different application areas. Especially for topics relevant at the workplace, e.g., customer support or information acquisition, they represent a new type of natural language-based human-computer interface. Nonetheless, chatbots in university settings have received only limited attention, e.g., providing organizational support about studies or for courses and examinations. This branch of research is just emerging in the scientific community. Therefore, we conducted a questionnaire-based survey among 166 students of various disciplines and educational levels at a German university. By doing so, we wanted to survey (1) the requirements implementing a chatbot as well as (2) relevant topics and corresponding questions that chatbots should address. In addition, our findings indicate that chatbots are suitable for the university context and that many students are willing to use chatbots.

Keywords: Chatbots · Dialog systems · Natural language processing · Education · University · Questionnaire · Survey · Requirements · Topics · Questions

1 Introduction

A new trend concerning natural language-based human-computer interfaces has emerged in current research: the use of chatbots in university settings [1] or intelligent learning systems to provide individualized and personalized learning support [2, 3], which was also shown in [4]. Driven by the digitization of society in general and of work in particular, chatbots have previously often been introduced in business contexts like customer support or to assist employees in their daily work [5, 6]. In these cases, chatbots should reduce service costs and handle multiple user inquiries at the same time, 24 h a day and independently of the availability of human resources [7]. Due to positive experiences in the business context, chatbots have been transferred to the university setting. Exemplary scenarios are individual learning support or assisting students in their personal study organization. Like in the business context, chatbots in university settings should support learners during the transition process and provide help 24/7 regardless of the device or the interface used. Additionally, they answer

© Springer Nature Switzerland AG 2020
A. Følstad et al. (Eds.): CONVERSATIONS 2019, LNCS 11970, pp. 231–244, 2020.
https://doi.org/10.1007/978-3-030-39540-7_16

individual questions regardless of whether particular university terms are used or concrete university-specific questions are raised [1].

Even though some research on chatbots exists in educational settings, there is, to the best of our knowledge, currently no consideration of actual student requirements for a university chatbot for FAQ-like questions [4]. Prior research studies often only focus on particular use cases and designing corresponding chatbots. However, the results of these first studies promise positive outcomes for a university application. Therefore, as a starting point, first instantiations of university chatbots should address the provision of organizational information based on FAQs to evaluate the acceptance and general requirements at first. In prior research, first studies already investigated this by developing different chatbots for university settings [1, 8]. Hereto, we aim at surveying the actual student's demands to provide a meaningful chatbot. Thus, the aim of our study is (1) to identify technical requirements for chatbots, and (2) to explore topics and related exemplary questions that should be answered by chatbots in a university setting. Based on an empirical questionnaire study among students at a German university, we address the following research questions:

RQ1: Which technical requirements do students anticipate for chatbots in university settings?

RQ2: Which content-related requirements have to be addressed by chatbots in university settings?

To answer these questions, the remainder of this article is structured as follows. Next, we briefly point out related research in Sect. 2. Afterward, we describe the research design in Sect. 3 and present our findings in Sect. 4. We complete our article with a discussion of the results in Sect. 5 and a brief conclusion in Sect. 6.

2 Background

2.1 Chatbot Basics

In general, a chatbot is an application system that provides a natural language user interface for the human-computer-integration. It usually uses artificial intelligence and integrates multiple (enterprise) data sources (like databases or applications) to automate tasks or assist users in their (work) activities [9].

Usually, the chatbot's architecture is composed of three components that are used via the human-computer interface (see Fig. 1): (1) The *natural language processing*, which is responsible for (a) processing the user input – audio or text – into a machine-readable form by analyzing, dismantling and pattern extracting, as well as (b) generating a natural language output corresponding to the results of the dialog manager. (2) The *dialog manager,* which matches the user input against integrated backend systems and extracts content or executes functions. (3) The *backend*, which contains all relevant application systems or databases that are required for the desired application area in order to be able to process the user request [4].

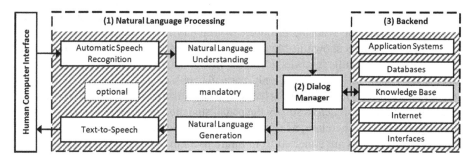

Fig. 1. The architecture of a chatbot

2.2   Chatbots in University Settings

Currently, chatbot research receives a lot of interest, and many researchers focus on this research topic from different perspectives. As shown in Meyer von Wolff et al. [4] and Maedche et al. [10], chatbot research mainly focuses on the application areas of customer support [11], information acquisition [12] as well as on business processes [13]. For university settings or rather educational scenarios, chatbot research is just beginning. Here, different studies and research streams are pursued:

In a recent literature review, Hobert and Meyer von Wolff [2] surveyed the current state of the art for pedagogical conversational agents. As shown in the publication, a trend for designing messenger-like chatbots has been identified. Further results of the analysis are that the current literature lacks on generalizable results. In a similar study, Winkler and Söllner [3] also conducted a literature review. The authors show that educational chatbot research is just in its beginnings, with a suggested potential for this application area. However, they note that the efficiency strongly depends on the individual student requirements, the way the chatbot is built, and the process quality. Those results confirm the need for surveying requirements for chatbots in universities.

Extending this, some studies have already presented first concepts and prototypes in this field of research. For instance, Fonte et al. [14] developed an intelligent tutoring system capable of providing learning content and a possible assessment of the student through the dialog. Mikic et al. [15] conducted a similar study in order to provide course content and a question-based assessment using a chatbot. In Carayannopoulos [1], a chatbot for information acquisition in universities was presented. The chatbot can respond to students' inquiries about upcoming events or courses, leisure activities, or pending tasks. Additionally, Shawar et al. [8] and Shawar [16] describe an FAQ chatbot in a university setting. In Shawar [16], an extension with preprocessed and stored online available FAQs is shown. Both chatbots generate the answers either on a complete match or on a match based on the first or second most significant word. Additionally, Ranoliya et al. [7] examine university FAQs by developing a concept for a corresponding chatbot. Furthermore, Feng et al. [17] provide a concept for a Q&A chatbot that is capable of answering student questions in a natural way and of creating an efficient learning environment. Hien et al. [18] conducted an empirical study to examine the requirements of a university chatbot for answering students' questions. The derived requirements are also conceptualized. Finally, Allison [19] surveyed the application of chatbots in libraries. With the presented chatbot, students can get answers on services or available resources of a library.

To sum up, and as shown in Meyer von Wolff et al. [4], one critical aspect of the current state of scientific knowledge is the lack of coverage of the design science process in general. In many cases, only particular phases are addressed. The investigation of specific requirements for selected use cases is missing. Only Hien et al. [18] followed a similar approach to survey the actual students' requirements for providing a meaningful chatbot. Therefore, as stated earlier, it would be best if, as a starting point, real-case requirements are collected from future users in order to provide a meaningful chatbot in a university setting.

3   Research Design

To identify students' technical requirements in university settings (*RQ1*) as well as content-related requirements (*RQ2*), i.e., topics and questions to be addressed, we conducted a questionnaire survey among students at a German university. Hereto, our study followed a three-step process:

First, we created a questionnaire based on previous findings [4, 9] comprising qualitative and quantitative questions. After a short introduction of the research project, which included a definition of chatbots to ensure clear understanding (see Sect. 2), questions – categorized in three sections – were interrogated: (1) general questions about the participant, (2) questions about the current or previous procedure of the students to acquire information and their satisfaction with it; and (3) questions about their experience and valuation of chatbots as well as topics to support and issues to answer. Before the data collection, we did a pilot test with multiple research associates who already had experience in questionnaire studies. Following, we rephrased some questions and added further questions for assessing a university chatbot and the target platforms. An overview of the final questionnaire is depicted in Table 1.

Table 1. Questionnaire structure

(1) **Questions about participants**:	
Gender; Field of study; Targeted degree; Current semester	*[quant.]*
(2) **Question about information acquisition and satisfaction:**	
• *How have you proceeded so far when you had questions?*	*[quant.]*
• *How satisfied are you with the current opportunities to receive information?*	*[quant.]*
• *What would you improve/change in current methods of information retrieval?*	*[qual.]*
(3) **Questions about chatbots:**	
• *Have you already had experiences with chatbots?*	*[quant.]*
• *For what tasks?/Why not?*	*[qual.]*
• *On what topics should a chatbot be able to give you information?*	*[qual.]*
• *What questions would you ask a chatbot at the university?*	*[qual.]*
• *How would you rate the following characteristics of a chatbot?*	*[quant.]*
• *How would you rate a university chatbot for information retrieval?*	*[quant.]*
• *For which platforms/devices should a chatbot be provided?*	*[quant.]*

Second, we conducted the survey within a two week timeframe in June 2019. Therefore, we announced the survey in different lectures, among student assistants as well as through social media postings, e.g., on Facebook, which was shared in several university groups as well. Overall, 530 students accessed the questionnaire, of which 214 students participated (40%). After cleaning the dataset of invalid data entries, we used 166 data sets (31%) for further analysis. Overall, the processing time for each student took 2 to 13 min (mean: 6:30 min).

Third, we analyzed the datasets in two ways. Hereto, we evaluated the quantitative data with spreadsheet programs. The qualitative data on topics and questions were categorized independently by two researchers on the subject and finally merged during a subsequent joint verification.

4 Survey Results

In the following, we present the results of our study. Therefore, we first show the sample description (Sect. 4.1). Afterward, we highlight the technical (*RQ1*) and content-related requirements (*RQ2*) in Sects. 4.2 and 4.3. Lastly, a short usefulness assessment is presented in Sect. 4.4.

4.1 Sample Description

Our study sample (n = 166) consists of mostly male students (58%), followed by 36% of female students. Nine participants have not answered the question.

We mainly acquired bachelor students (n = 87; 52%) followed by master students (n = 58; 35%). Additionally, some participants target a doctoral (n = 4), a state examination (n = 6), or other (n = 6) degrees. Five participants have not answered the question.

Most participants are in their first four semesters: 38% in the first two (n = 63) and 37% in the following two semesters (n = 61). Also, 25% of the participants (n = 15) are in a higher semester (7th semester or greater). Thus, students from all graduation levels and all semesters participated.

For the distribution of the subject area, we aimed at a cross-section among all students from our university. Therefore, we tried to acquire students from all available fields of study. Our participant group consists mostly of economic science students (n = 102; 61%). The following fields of study have a much lower proportion: 16 from mathematics and computer science, 13 from agricultural and forestry science as well as humanities and cultural science, 11 from natural science as well as social science, 9 from teaching professions, 7 from law, as well as 3 from theology and 2 from medical science. Additionally, the students were able to make multiple entries for their field of study. Therefore, economics science is overrepresented (n = 102). This might be explained since we teach in this area and mainly approach students via our lectures. Nevertheless, economic science consists of subgroups that are, in addition, different from each other. Nonetheless, we were still able to acquire participants from all disciplines, at least.

We also measured the actual experience of the participants with chatbots in general (see Fig. 2). Most of our participants (41%) already use chatbots at least on an occasional basis. On the downside, 34% of the students have not used a chatbot at all. Among these, ten participants stated that they have privacy concerns, e.g., "*Where they are used, I have concerns about privacy*" or "*permanent possibility of interception*". In addition, nine participants rated the use as too cumbersome or had problems with the chatbot functions, e.g., "*Slow, a lot of unnecessary communication, no good answers, answers too inaccurate, writing often more complex than clicking, etc.*", "*Chatbots are good for basic information that you can usually find on the website anyway*" or "*I find information as a list better*". In contrast, 17 participants stated that there are no reasons against using chatbots. Up to now, no situation has emerged, e.g., "*It has not yet happened, there is nothing against it*" or "*Nothing, rather this has advantages, like a permanent availability*". Based on this, we conclude that many students already use chatbots or are willing to use them. Nevertheless, more than half of the students (n = 107; 65%) have already made first or more extensive experiences with chatbots. Thus, frequent use of the technology, also outside the university context, has already been identified.

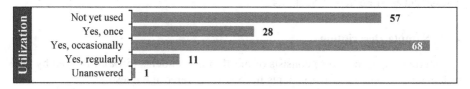

Fig. 2. Frequency of previous usage (n = 165)

4.2 Technical Requirements

Based on the questionnaire, we first analyzed basic technical requirements for a chatbot application in a university context (*RQ1*).

Therefore in the first question, we asked the students about the characteristics of chatbots [4] by means of a 5-step Likert scale (1: unimportant; 5: very crucial) (see Fig. 3). Based on the results, it is clearly shown that most students prefer the *24-hours-a-day availability*. Therefore, they do not have to wait until human contact persons are available. In addition, the participants appreciate the *fast response time* combined with the direct assistance for the question that has arisen. Also, we have identified that the chatbot's ability to *respond individually to the user* is not considered very important by users. Nonetheless, our participants rated all the characteristics as above average. Therefore, these should be addressed in potential university chatbots.

In a second question, we asked the participants for the chatbot operation platform (see Fig. 4). According to the students, the most relevant platforms for university chatbots are mostly WhatsApp or desktop and web interfaces. Whereas the former is difficult to implement due to the infrastructure and the specifications, the latter two are easier to realize. Among the other-category, we identified mostly Telegram (n = 9) but also XMPP or own apps as well as chatbots integrated into the university portals.

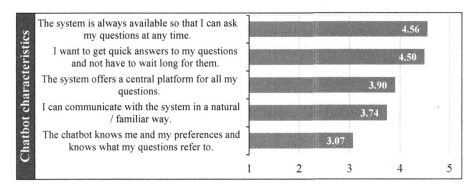

Fig. 3. Means of chatbot characteristics (n = 165)

Nonetheless, our selection options are not entirely free of overlaps; we could highlight the relevant platforms. Above all, chatbots should be integrated into the interfaces used by students on a daily basis. Due to the many selected platforms, it would be best if a chatbot were not limited to a specific platform. Instead, it should be possible to make a request from all platforms.

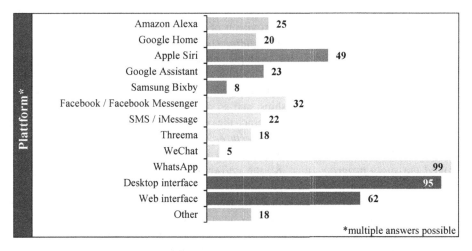

Fig. 4. Target platforms for university chatbots (n = 165)

4.3   Content-Related Requirements

Furthermore, we identified content-related requirements in the sense of topics to be addressed or questions to be answered by a chatbot in a university setting (*RQ2*). Based on two open questions in the questionnaire, the participants were asked about short topic mentions and exemplary questions that we categorized afterward. In total, we acquired 503 statements concerning topics and 495 exemplary questions as a starting point. Following the categorization process, we jointly merged them into 36 question sections, partial with sub-sections, in six core topics for a university chatbot for students. A complete overview of the categorization is displayed in Fig. 5.

As shown, chatbots in university settings should address the topic of *information around studying* in general. At first, students would use a chatbot when looking for study programs or gathering information about the university in general. Also, some organizational issues should be answered like semester dues or times, as well as those regarding studying abroad. Second, the application area of chatbots for (upcoming) *events and lectures* seems interesting. A chatbot provides content of the offered courses and their dates and times or locations, as well as the responsible persons. In addition to events and lectures, a chatbot should provide support for *examination*-related questions. Similar to the previous category, information on the examination in general, as well as the room and date, are highly relevant. Moreover, organizational issues like regulations, contact persons, as well as information on prerequisites and how to register should be covered. Furthermore, the participants would inquire (personal) statistics or retrieve/request their certificates. Another application area, which should be taken into account in university settings, are the closely related *institutions or departments*. In our study, the participants noted the library, canteens and cafes, or the sport offers. These institutions and departments should be extended or adapted to the respective university so that students can obtain information on opening hours; food offers in the canteen, and so on. Furthermore, university chatbots should provide basic *(IT-)support*. As our participants specified, they want help with the WLAN or printer setup, when password matters occur, as well as with the provision of software provided by the university. Lastly, we identified some different *general* concerns relevant to chatbots in a university setting. This includes, for example, small talk and university news. Also, general room plans or people's search should be provided in the form of an information desk. Additionally, the participants would like to have a job board to inquire about open vacancies or possible internships, and so on.

Overall, as the most-mentioned topic, the students voted for a chatbot that can answer questions regarding *events or lectures* (n = 135) or for *examination-related information* (n = 122). Even if only indicated by fewer participants, *information around the study program* (n = 78), the *university institutions* (n = 73), or the *(IT-)support* (n = 59) are potential topic areas for a university chatbot. Therefore, first instances, or, rather extensions to existing implementations should definitely address the two most mentioned topic areas if they have not yet been considered. Furthermore, in terms of questions, those two topic areas have most of the questions given by the participants. Out of this, we infer that students have had the most questions regarding these areas so far, as they have cited many concrete example questions.

In the case of questions, we gathered mostly questions regarding the overview and information for events and lectures (65 questions), e.g., *"Which modules are offered for the subject this semester?"*, *"Which contents should be taught during the lecture/seminar?"*. In addition, questions about times or deadlines for examination (60 questions), e.g., *"When does the exam take place?"*, *"Until when can I unsubscribe for the exam?"* or for events and lectures (40 questions), e.g., *"Does the lecture take place on Wednesday?"*, *"When in the week does the module take place?"* were given. Furthermore, we collected some sub-topics with no corresponding questions, e.g., current news and notifications, scholarships, general opening hours, or study guidance. As

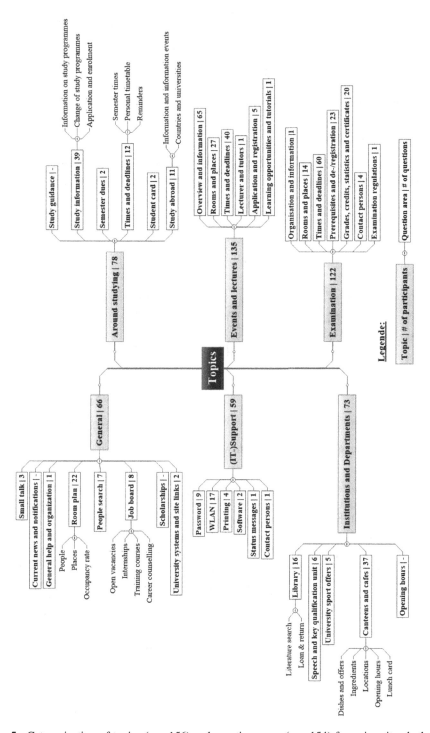

Fig. 5. Categorization of topics (n = 156) and question areas (n = 154) for university chatbots

these sub-topics were stated by the students as potential topics, questions should be developed in order to be able to address these issues in the future.

It should be mentioned that many of the question areas show reciprocal dependency, e.g., questions for contact persons in general and examinations, or times and deadlines in nearly all topics. These highlight relationships to be mapped in implementations or, rather, in the knowledge base.

4.4   Usefulness Assessment

To underline the usefulness of chatbots, we also asked the participants about their assessment of the application of the technology in university contexts (see Fig. 6).

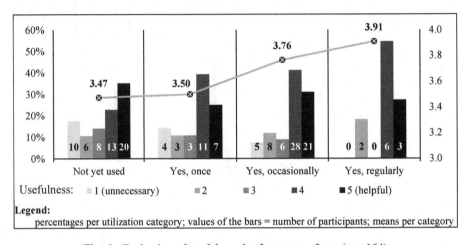

Fig. 6. Evaluation of usefulness by frequency of use (n = 164)

Based on a 5-step Likert scale (1: unnecessary; 5: helpful), we wanted to know how the students would rate it if a chatbot were available at our university. Overall, the participants rated this with an average of 3,62, which means a tendency to be helpful could be derived. In a more detailed analysis based on the frequency of usage (see Fig. 2), an interesting trend could be identified. Our results show that the more often a student used chatbots before, the higher the average rating of usefulness is. Even if only a few students regularly use chatbots, they have the highest average rating for usefulness. In addition, in the group of students who have not used chatbots until now, the highest count for helpfulness could be measured. However, this could also point out an exaggerated expectation for chatbot technology. Furthermore, this group also has a nearly balanced distribution of the usefulness. In addition, the more often chatbots are used, the more specific the distribution is in terms of helpfulness.

5 Discussion

Based on our students' questionnaire survey, we identified which technical requirements in the form of characteristics and target platform (*RQ1*), as well as content-related requirements in the form of topics and questions (*RQ2*), are most important.

Our findings show that a chatbot is highly relevant for the application in a university context, as many topics and questions arose, for which a chatbot is usable. Hereby, 65% of the students participating in our study have already had some initial experiences with the technology. However, many of the participants (35%) have not used a chatbot so far, of whom 30% of the participants, in principle, have nothing against usage. This is also shown in Sect. 4.4 as the participants who have not yet used chatbots rate the helpfulness highest. Overall, the students rated chatbots as helpful. Independently of prior experience, the average rating of all groups described in Fig. 6 is above the mean. Thus, we identified a positive attitude of the participants towards chatbots in university settings, which is also shown in Hien et al. [18].

Additionally, we asked the participants to rate the essential chatbot characteristics. As a result, the following characteristics were rated as most important: *24/7 availability*, *fast and direct response* as well as acting as a *central platform* for information acquisition. Surprisingly, our participants rated the ability to *respond personally* to the user or previous conversations as lowest. This is in contrast to current purposes of the scientific community, e.g. [5, 18]. Even though we do not have further information on this topic, a reason could be that the participants regard a university chatbot mostly as a tool to provide simple and general organizational information around lectures or events, which is shown in Sect. 4.3. Hereby, non-personalized information or content is delivered. However, the second most named category is examination that requires personalization in order to provide a reasonable answer, e.g., to provide certificates or to respond with personal exam dates. Thus, we identified an inconsistency among our results.

Regarding the target platforms, even if all options were selected, a focus on WhatsApp, Siri, and desktop or web interfaces could be determined. Thus, for the design of a university chatbot, they should be supported. However, this indicates a much more important requirement: the use of a chatbot from different channels, depending on the available device at the time of need. This can also be derived from the characteristics, as a chatbot mostly provides an appropriate answer 24/7 and in a timely manner. For the design, this means that a university chatbot should be programmed openly or should have corresponding interfaces, e.g., as a web application. Additionally, the high mentions for WhatsApp or Siri could hint at a further design requirement: audio or spoken inputs, as they are being used commonly nowadays on these platforms.

As a further result of the analysis, we identified *university events and lectures* as well as *examinations* as the most relevant topics to be addressed by a university chatbot. Furthermore, most of the collected questions aim at locations, definitions of content, or dates and can be answered with short sentences. Mostly, these questions are rather task-oriented or pertain to organizational issues for educational concerns but do not focus on education via a chatbot. This can be a hint regarding the expectations of chatbot users and may underline the basic abilities that the technology must fulfill: providing short answers or, rather, solutions for organizational issues in the sense of

FAQs whenever needed. Surprisingly, individual learning support or providing lecture content were not mentioned by the participants at all. Maybe our participants only think about their previous experiences with different chatbots and try to transfer this knowledge to the university setting. However, this contradicts the current research approach, which focuses mostly on chatbot-mediated education. Nonetheless, for universities, as surveyed in this study, a chatbot should primarily provide organizational issues around lectures or examinations. This is also reflected partially in the survey conducted by Hien et al. [18].

As with every empirical study, there exist some limitations that need to be discussed. *Firstly*, the findings of our study are mainly dependent on the students' responses and their willingness to participate. Therefore, we have tried to maximize the reach in order to acquire as many participants as possible. We have not limited the disciplines or other aspects to survey a cross-section in the research area. However, the sector of economics science is overrepresented, but we were still able to acquire at least a few students from all disciplines. Despite this, our sample is still suited to indicate the technical and content-related requirements. *Secondly*, based on the chosen research design in the questionnaire form, maybe some questions were misunderstood by some participants. We tried to mitigate this by conducting a pretest before the actual survey. *Thirdly*, our derived design requirements are only based on the findings as well as on argumentative deductive conclusions. Therefore, these should be implemented in a prototypical chatbot so that they can be evaluated in real case scenarios.

Even though our study focused on the student's perspective on the application of chatbots in university settings and may have some limitations, our results seem to be valuable and useful for future applications of chatbots at universities. Based on our findings, we could highlight necessary platforms and characteristics as well as topics and areas of questions, which have to be addressed in the first instances. Nonetheless, our findings have to be verified in real case scenarios. For this purpose, chatbots should be set up with the help of our results. Afterward, the usefulness of chatbots should be evaluated in order to identify gaps in the knowledge base and to be able to assess the use of the technology in university settings or in other educational contexts.

6 Conclusion

In this research paper, we aimed at surveying the application of chatbots in university settings. We questioned our students concerning their technical requirements (*RQ1*) as well as topics and areas of questions (*RQ2*) that a chatbot should address. As a result of our 166 participants, we could derive that the characteristics *24/7 h availability* and *fast solutions*, as well as *Whatsapp* or *desktop user interfaces* as target platforms, are most important. In addition, we identified six core topics along with 36 question areas, of which *events and lectures*, as well as *examinations*, are especially important.

These can be used as a starting base for future implementations. Therefore, our study can contribute to the knowledge base and the understanding of chatbots used in university settings in two ways: (1) as a starting point for implementations or prototypes for the specific area of universities or rather education, as well as (2) for further investigations in this research area in general, e.g., requirement analysis or acceptance studies among future users.

References

1. Carayannopoulos, S.: Using chatbots to aid transition. Int. J. Inf. Learn. Tech. **35**, 118–129 (2018)
2. Hobert, S., Meyer von Wolff, R.: Say hello to your new automated tutor - a structured literature review on pedagogical conversational agents. In: Proceedings of the 14th International Conference on Wirtschaftsinformatik, pp. 301–314 (2019)
3. Winkler, R., Söllner, M.: Unleashing the potential of chatbots in education: a state-of-the-art analysis. In: Academy of Management Annual Meeting (2018)
4. Meyer von Wolff, R., Hobert, S., Schumann, M.: How may i help you? - state of the art and open research questions for chatbots at the digital workplace. In: Proceedings of the 52nd Hawaii International Conference on System Science, pp. 95–104 (2019)
5. Følstad, A., Brandtzæg, P.B.: Chatbots and the new world of HCI. Interactions **24**, 38–42 (2017)
6. Reshmi, S., Balakrishnan, K.: Implementation of an inquisitive chatbot for database supported knowledge bases. Sadhana **41**, 1173–1178 (2016)
7. Ranoliya, B.R., Raghuwanshi, N., Singh, S.: Chatbot for university related FAQs. In: International Conference on Advances in Computing, Communications and Informatics (ICACCI), pp. 1525–1530 (2017)
8. Shawar, B.A., Atwell, E., Roberts, A.: FAQChat as an information retrieval system. In: Proceedings of the 2nd Language and Technology Conference, pp. 274–278 (2005)
9. Meyer von Wolff, R., Masuch, K., Hobert, S., Schumann, M.: What do you need today? - an empirical systematization of application areas for chatbots at digital workplaces. In: Proceedings of 25th Americas Conference on Information Systems, pp. 1–10 (2019)
10. Maedche, A., et al.: AI-based digital assistants. opportunities, threats, and research perspectives. Bus. Inf. Syst. Eng. **61**, 535–544 (2019)
11. Wuenderlich, N.V., Paluch, S.: A nice and friendly chat with a bot: user perceptions of AI-based service agents. In: Proceedings of the 38th International Conference on Information Systems, pp. 1–11 (2017)
12. Al-Zubaide, H., Issa, A.A.: OntBot: ontology based chatbot. In: 4th International Symposium on Innovation in Information & Communication Technology, pp. 7–12 (2011)
13. Gyton, G., Jeffsry, R.: These are the experts deciding the future of HR … shouldn't you know who they are? People Manag. 24–31 (2017)
14. Fonte, F.A.M., Rial, J.C.B., Nistal, M.L.: TQ-Bot: an AIML-based tutor and evaluator bot. J. Univ. Comput. Sci. **15**, 1486–1495 (2009)
15. Mikic, F.A., Burguillo, J.C., Llamas, M., Rodríguez, D.A., Rodríguez, E.: Charlie: an AIML-based chatterbot which works as an interface among INES and humans. In: EAEEIE Annual Conference, pp. 1–6 (2009)
16. Shawar, B.A.: Chatbots are natural web interface to information portals. In: 6th International Conference on Informatics and Systems, pp. 101–107 (2008)

17. Feng, X., Liu, Q., Lao, C., Sun, D.: Design and implementation of automatic question answering system in information retrieval. In: Proceedings of the 7th International Conference on Informatics, Environment, Energy and Applications, New York, USA, pp. 207–211 (2018)
18. Hien, H.T., Cuong, P.-N., Nam, L.N.H., Le Nhung, H.T.K., Thang, L.D.: Intelligent assistants in higher-education environments. In: Proceedings of the 9th International Symposium on Information and Communication Technology, New York, USA, pp. 69–76 (2018)
19. Allison, D.: Chatbots in the library: is it time? Library Hi Tech **30**, 95–107 (2012)

A Configurable Agent to Advance Peers' Productive Dialogue in MOOCs

Stergios Tegos[✉], Stavros Demetriadis, Georgios Psathas,
and Thrasyvoulos Tsiatsos

Aristotle University of Thessaloniki, Thessaloniki 54124, Greece
{stegos, sdemetri, gpsathas, tsiatsos}@csd.auth.gr

Abstract. Chatbot technology can greatly contribute towards the creation of personalized and engaging learning activities. Still, more experimentation is needed on how to integrate and use such agents in real world educational settings and, especially, in large-scale learning environments such as MOOCs. This paper presents the prototype design of a teacher-configurable conversational agent service, aiming to scaffold synchronous collaborative activities in MOOCs. The architecture of the conversational agent system is followed by a pilot evaluation study, which was conducted in the context of postgraduate computer science course on Learning Analytics. The preliminary study findings reveal an overall favorable student opinion as regards the ease of use and user acceptance of the system.

Keywords: Conversational agent · Education · Massive open online course · Peer learning

1 Introduction

Massive Online Open Courses (MOOCs) have been repeatedly praised for democratizing education and helping learners gain access to educational content, regardless of their geographic location, financial means, schedule or background. Nevertheless, despite their value in scaling up education and reaching diverse international audiences, MOOCs have often failed to provide the kind of interactive environment required to achieve sustained engagement and learning. Many MOOCs have been developed as informational landscapes, offering just video-based tutoring and closed-type learning interactions [1].

Research has shown that the utilization of conversational agents in learning environments can have a positive pedagogical impact, fostering the engagement and motivation of learners [2]. Indeed, agents may be able to compensate the insufficient learners' support, which constitutes one of the key factors negatively affecting retention rates [3]. MOOCs have recently attracted research interest as a promising learning setting for deploying conversational agents, which can be useful for providing automated support and facilitating the learning process in the absence of human teacher's continuous presence [4]. Still, more research is needed to explore the numerous factors affecting the effectiveness of a conversational learning experience, including the proper design of the human-agent interactions or the content and type of agent messages

© Springer Nature Switzerland AG 2020
A. Følstad et al. (Eds.): CONVERSATIONS 2019, LNCS 11970, pp. 245–259, 2020.
https://doi.org/10.1007/978-3-030-39540-7_17

displayed to learners [5]. Furthermore, the fact that most conversational agents are built as domain-specific didactic tools reduces their practical value and agility, hindering their integration in real world educational environments.

Our research seeks to lay the foundation for employing agile conversational agents that operate as group-teacher interaction mediators in MOOCs. The aim of such agents is to facilitate peer dialogue activities and support students' collaboration. Although most of the past studies have focused on chatbots operating in individual learning settings [2], this line of research emphasizes agents supporting learning in groups.

The remainder of this paper is structured as follows. The next section gives a brief background overview, which is followed by our perspective towards the creation of a teacher-configurable conversational agent service. Thereafter, we present the design of a prototype system, serving as a valuable opportunity to discuss the functionality of novel conversational agents that aim to provide peer interaction support. The last paper sections revolve around a pilot evaluation study that focuses on the perceived ease-of-use and usefulness of the presented conversational agent system.

2   Background

2.1   Chatbots for Education

Artificial Intelligence (AI) is often seen as a game-changer in providing personalized learning experiences as well as novel opportunities for understanding the real intent of learners [6]. A well-known application of AI in education is "conversational agents", also known as conversational AI or chatbots, which have been argued to hold substantial potential for educational organizations and institutions [2]. Such agents can be regarded as computer programs engaging in natural language interactions with learners via auditory or textual methods, aiming to fulfill one or more pedagogical goals.

The rise of chatbots can be partially attributed to the fact that natural language processing (NLP) technology has become more accessible than ever, empowering developers to build interfaces that give the illusion of a human-to-human communication [7]. The popularization of the conversational interfaces is also influenced by the extended usage of instant messaging applications on mobile devices [8]. Nowadays, texting is regarded as one of the most compelling form of computer-human interaction [9] and chatbots are beginning to disrupt various industries, with education being one of these.

The concept of educational chatbots has its roots in intelligent tutoring systems, which have a long history in exploring the idea of building a learning tool that is "intelligent" enough to sense learners' needs and operate accordingly [10]. This type of adaptation can be accomplished by utilizing a certain level of computational modeling to craft learner-tailored educational environments and supportive mechanisms. A chatbot may leverage several AI techniques in order to simulate peer-to-peer or student-to-teacher conversational interactions, making learners feel more comfortable while communicating with a virtual character. Moreover, much emphasis is given in the ability to effectively exhibit social skills and constructively interact with learners while serving their pedagogical role, which could be anything from a tutor, a coach and a learning partner to a teaching assistant. For instance, chatbots can be used to gather students' feedback during an online course, enabling teachers to identify areas that need improvement, or provide dynamic support to students without increasing teachers' workload.

2.2   Chatbots in MOOCs

With the recent rise in focus on the online learning communities and MOOCs, the strengths of chatbot technology seem to be even more important, especially considering the limited support that is typically offered by the instructors and teaching staff [4]. Despite MOOCs inherent capability to provide open-access education in an affordable and flexible manner, a number of issues have made this task far from trivial, such as the low retention rates and the lack of students' motivation being reported in the literature [11]. MOOCs often miss the interactivity required to reach their transformative potential in terms of making valuable learning experiences available to the masses [3].

Chatbots can help MOOCs move away from their traditional "knowledge transmission" approach to more social and interactive forms of learning. They can be used to offer compelling interactive activities and create highly productive spaces where participants actively engage in constructive knowledge-generative sessions [12]. When used effectively in the context of course activities, agents can provide access to engaging content as well as adaptive feedback [5], substantially increasing learners' commitment and minimizing dropout rates via automated facilitation strategies.

Agents appear to have a direct application in MOOC settings. Yet, while most of the conducted studies focus on the effects of the human-agent (one-on-one) interactions, the use of conversational agents supporting peer interaction in MOOCs has been scarce. In the field of collaborative learning, research evidence suggests that conversational agents supporting students' online discussions can increase the quality of peer dialogue and improve, among others, both group and individual learning outcomes [13]. Additionally, the utilization of such agents in synchronous collaborative activities appears to enhance students' engagement and participation levels, decreasing the risk of dropouts by up to 50% [12]. Conversational agents can also be useful for amplifying the support resources that students offer to each other during online learning activities [12].

However, collaboration in MOOCs often present many additional practical challenges that emerge from diverse instructional domains, learner populations and time zones being involved. Therefore, more experimentation is needed to fine tune the design of conversational agents providing collaborative learning support of considerable value in MOOCs.

Against the above background, our research objective is to (a) inform researchers and designers on the potential pedagogical benefits of implementing teacher-configurable conversational agents that support students' peer dialogue and (b) drive further improvements on the design of a prototype conversational agent service. The next sections present our line of research under the prism of a European research project, called "Integrating Conversational Agents and Learning Analytics in MOOCs (colMOOC)".

3 Designing Chatbots that Support Learner Groups in MOOCs

3.1 The colMOOC Perspective

Instead of aiming to craft full-fledged human-agent discussions, the colMOOC project stresses the importance of creating agents that promote productive forms of peer interactions and scaffold students' collaboration [4].

In this perspective, the colMOOC project has created an innovative multilingual conversational agent service for facilitating constructive learners' interactions in synchronous collaborative activities taking place in MOOCs. During peers' discussions, the agent service is able to monitor their conversation and decide when to deliver questioning interventions, based on a series of contextual parameters and a teacher-defined domain model. One key aspect of the agent service is that the design of the conversational agent is loosely coupled with the domain model, which can be easily exported/imported in different activities. In this manner, the conversational agent system is viewed as a flexible tool that can be reused in multiple domains. The system, which is currently in beta, supports four languages: English, German, Greek and Spanish.

Before diving into the system architecture, it would be useful to present three of the core concepts lying in the heart of the colMOOC conversational agent design: the (a) 'intervention strategy', (b) the 'intervention', and (c) the 'transaction pattern'.

Intervention Strategy. In order for the agent to deliver a specific intervention during peer chat discussion it is necessary to provide a model of what an intervention strategy is and how it can be computationally implemented. An 'intervention strategy' refers to the abstract representation of the process implemented in the agent software system that eventually results in the agent taking part in the peer discussion. The application of an intervention strategy usually leads to the situation where an agent avatar appears in the chat frame and poses a question to peers or makes some other statement, which could be informative or provide some guidance. An intervention strategy comprises several levels of implementation, ranging from the higher-level abstractions, providing the perspective and pedagogical rationale of the strategy, to the lower-level of code-based implementation in the specific computational setting where it is implemented.

The agent intervention strategies adopted by the colMOOC agent draw heavily on the work of the teachers' community on modeling useful classroom discussion practices and norms. Although the various details of the intervention strategies employed by the agent are out of this paper scope [14], it is useful to keep in mind that the agent intervention mechanism was designed as an agile tool for stimulating constructive forms of peer dialogue through a series of moves (interventions), often performed by teachers in class. The majority of these interventions derive from the classroom discourse framework of Academically Productive Talk [15]. For instance, the 'Addon' agent intervention strategy is relevant to the teacher practice to intervene in peer discussion and encourage one peer to further comment in relation to what the other peer has just stated (Table 1, row 1).

Table 1. Intervention strategies employed by the colMOOC agent.

Intervention strategy	Intervention example
Addon	"Would you like to add something to what your partner [Student Name] said about [Concept A]?"
Building on prior knowledge	"Do you think [Concept A] is somehow related to [Concept B]? How?"
Verifying	"Do you agree with the following statement: [Concept A + Relationship + Concept B]? Why?"

Intervention. This term refers to the concrete onscreen manifestation of any intervention strategy of the agent. For example, an intervention stemming from the 'Addon' strategy might be the appearance of the agent avatar on screen prompting a student as follows: "Maria, would you like to add something to what Steve mentioned about constructivism being a learning theory?". The primary goal of this kind of interventions is usually to elicit student reasoning instead of providing content-specific explanations and instructional assistance. Research studies indicate that conversational agents performing such interventions can conceptually enrich students' discussions and positively impact collaboration by intensifying knowledge exchange among peers [16].

Transaction Pattern. The term refers to the exact dialogue conditions that trigger the agent to enact an intervention strategy and eventually deliver an intervention. 'Exact' refers to the requirement that the pattern should be defined in such a way that enables its computational representation in the form of a clearly defined algorithm. For example, the pattern for the intervention strategy 'Addon' can be described as follows: "10 s after a domain concept was introduced by a student, their partner has either remained silent or sent a short reply". The reason the patterns were named transaction - and not interaction patterns - is due to the 'transactional' quality of the dialogue, i.e. the degree that peers' reason on each other's contributions to collaboratively develop a common understanding or problem-solving strategy. Therefore, transaction patterns usually represent some transactionally poor peer dialogue situation, identified by the agent as an opportunity for enacting a specific intervention strategy.

3.2 The colMOOC Editor

The architecture of the colMOOC system comprises two major components: (a) the colMOOC agent editor, which can be used by the instructors to set up a conversational agent activity, and (b) the colMOOC agent player, which is responsible for offering to the learners a chat-like interface in order to complete their collaborative activities.

As depicted in Fig. 1, the output of the Editor serves as an input for the Player to enact the chat-based activity. The Player component is responsible for auditing the conversation among learners and making an intervention whenever an intervention opportunity arises. These interventions are being orchestrated by the domain model that has been shaped by the instructor in the Editor.

The colMOOC Editor is available for the MOOC instructors allowing them to create dialogue-based activities, where a topic is given to students which they asked to discuss on, and furthermore provide their collaborative answer. This kind of activities, which can be added to a MOOC just like other common types of activities, such as quizzes or assignments, are accessible by the learners from within their MOOC platform.

In the Editor, teachers can enter all the activity-relevant information, such as the topic of discussion that is usually an open-ended domain question. They can also enter some instructions, serving as guidelines for students during the activity (Fig. 2).

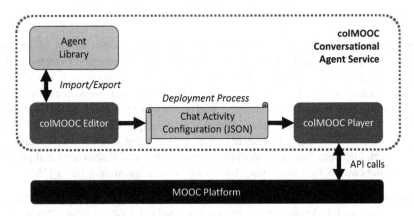

Fig. 1. High-level architecture of the colMOOC conversational agent system.

A conversational agent can also be set up for the specific activity. An agent can be imported from a previous colMOOC activity (being available in the agent library) or set up from scratch through the available domain configuration panel. Using its interface (Fig. 3), the teacher can alter the agent behavior and enactment by entering a series of conceptual links, which form an abstract domain representation. Teachers can define a conceptual link that is considered important in relation to the activity task in order to enable the system agent to make relevant interventions encouraging learners externalize their thoughts. Typically, conceptual links include task terms that the teacher considers essential for students to argue on before answering the task.

Multiple conceptual links can be created in order to shape the agent domain for a specific activity. As displayed in Fig. 3, the system currently supports two types of conceptual links:

- single-concept nodes (e.g., [Concept A]; see Fig. 3, upper part) and
- two-concept links, consisting of two concepts (nodes) linked with some predefined or user entered relational verb expression (e.g., [Concept A] [verb] [Concept B]; see Fig. 3, lower part).

Each concept/node entered in the Editor can be accompanied by one or more synonyms (e.g., 'computer program' = 'software'). This means that if any of those terms is detected during a students' discussion and a 'transaction pattern' is identified, the system will deliver the associated agent intervention.

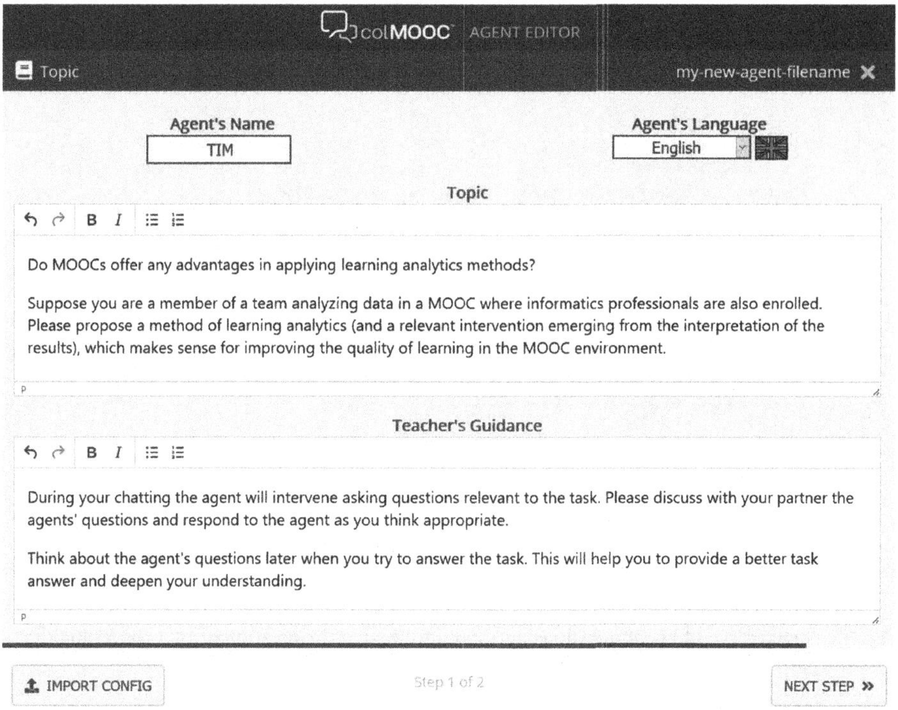

Fig. 2. A screenshot illustrating the first step of the activity creation process in the Editor.

Based on the agent pedagogical model, each of two conceptual link types described above is configured to support different agent intervention strategies. More specifically, the detection of a single concept like [algorithm] in students' dialogue may lead to the activation of an Addon agent intervention (see Table 1, row 1), whereas a two-concept link match may trigger a Build-on or a Verify intervention (see Table 1, rows 2 and 3).

In order to better clarify how this works, we present the example arising from Fig. 3. When the teacher enters the conceptual link: [computer program] [can measure] [text sentiment] (Fig. 3, lower part), the system recognizes that the two concepts are [computer program] and [text sentiment] and their connection is expressed by [can measure]. After the conceptual link is created, the system dynamically generates one or more relevant agent interventions. The teacher can click on the "down arrow" icon, residing at the left of the conceptual link, in order to view the default agent interventions generated by the system (e.g., "Do you think computer program is somehow related to text sentiment? How?"; a Build-on intervention). These agent interventions are synthesized in real time based on the concept(s) entered by the teacher in the Editor as well as a pool of agent interventions, which are already available in the system database and are categorized based on their type: 'Addon', 'Build-on' and 'Verify' (see Table 1). As discussed in the previous section, when teacher-defined concepts are detected in students' dialogue and the conditions of a specific 'transaction pattern' are satisfied, an intervention strategy is activated, thus, leading to the display of the

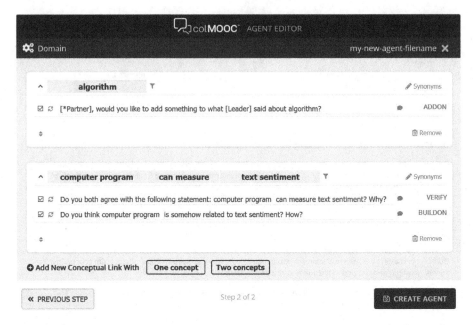

Fig. 3. An example of agent questions generated following the creation of two conceptual links.

associated agent intervention. More details concerning the exact conditions of each transaction pattern and their respective interventions can be found in [14].

It should be noted that the teacher has the final say in deciding whether the proposed intervention text is appropriate or requires some editing. Teachers can disable the automatically generated interventions in case they do not approve them or just choose to modify their text. Simple markup language can also be used to further customize the agent intervention mechanism. For instance, teachers can alter the direction of the agent questions, having interventions that either target a specific group member or the whole group of students. Research evidence suggests that the direction of the agent questions in a collaborative chat environment can significantly impact the effectiveness of the agent intervention mechanism [17].

3.3 The colMOOC Player

The colMOOC Player is the component responsible for enacting a chat activity and presenting it to the MOOC students. This is possible by loading all the information available in the Activity Configuration (JSON) file, which is generated following the successful setup of an agent-based activity in the colMOOC Editor by the teacher. The colMOOC player operates in direct connection with the MOOC platform through an Application Programming Interface (API) in order to receive relevant information, such as the course ID and the students' IDs (Fig. 1).

While entering a colMOOC activity, students enter a system queue, waiting to be paired with a peer in order to initiate the collaborative activity. Although this is expected to be improved in a future version, the matching mechanism currently operates in a simple 'first-come first-served' basis. In order to reduce waiting times and minimize issues arising from the coordination of participants working from different time zones, MOOC instructors are recommended to use specific timeslots for scheduling students' participation in chat activities.

After the peer matching process is completed, the pair of students enter the chat activity. As shown in Fig. 4, students are expected to communicate synchronously via text messages in order to resolve an open-ended domain question, presented to them at the top left section of their screen. Below the activity description, there is a team answer box allowing peers to compose and submit their answer to the task. The content of this input field is synced and shared among peers.

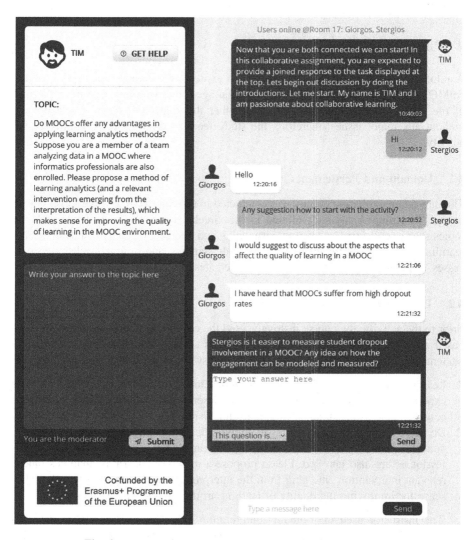

Fig. 4. A screenshot presenting the colMOOC player interface.

Throughout the discussion of students, the colMOOC conversational agent can intervene displaying prompts arising from the identification of the respective transaction patterns. A core aspect of this pattern identification process is based on the functionality of a system module called 'peer dialogue parser'. This analyses the messages exchanged among the peers searching for relevant linguistic cues, which emerge from the agent domain model configured in the Editor. The operation of the system parser is based on a series of algorithms performing several tasks such as transliteration, segmentation, stemming and string similarity checks. Hence, when a key concept is detected and all the other conditions (of a pattern) are met, the agent intervention model selects the associated agent intervention hanging in the colMOOC Editor, performs a series of context-specific modifications, and displays its text to the users.

4   Pilot Evaluation

A pilot evaluation study was carried out to explore the students' perception of the colMOOC environment and the conversational agent interventions. The main purpose of the study was to gather insights on whether the colMOOC agent would operate without any major issues; therefore, the study featured a small-scaled controlled lab activity.

4.1   Domain and Participants

The one-group exploratory study was conducted in the context of a Master level course named "Learning Analytics", offered in the Greek language. The syllabus included topics such as collecting, analyzing, visualizing and interpreting data about learners and learning environments for the purpose of understanding and optimizing learning processes. The participants were 10 students (6 females), who were Greek native speakers.

4.2   Procedure

Prior to the activity, the course instructor used the colMOOC Editor to setup two chat-based activities. Each activity presented students an open-ended debate, encouraging students to collaboratively (in dyads) provide answers to the following questions:

1. Learning analytics constitutes a multi-dimensional scientific field. Based on your experience in the course, how would you describe this field and what would you consider as some of its most important dimensions?
2. Do MOOCs offer any advantages in applying learning analytics methods? Suppose you are a member of a team analyzing data in a MOOC where informatics professionals are also enrolled. Please propose a method of learning analytics (and a relevant intervention emerging from the interpretation of the results), which makes sense for improving the quality of learning in the MOOC environment.

The instructor used the domain configuration interface to enter a series of conceptual links. These involved key domain concepts, such as 'modeling', 'measurements', 'dropouts', 'adaptiveness', 'reporting', 'operationalism', 'patterns', 'ethics' and several synonyms or phrases with similar meanings. This process resulted in the generation of several agent interventions emerging from the three intervention strategies displayed in Table 1. The text of agent interventions was edited by the course instructor. More specifically, in the first activity, the agent was configured to display 'converging' interventions, relating closely to the topic introduced by the activity (e.g. "What do you mean by 'modeling/model'? Try to recall the explanatory vs. predictive modeling; can you explain the difference?"). Answering these agent questions was expected to aid students to prepare their group answer for the task. In contrast, the agent of the second activity was setup to deliver 'diverging' interventions, which were relevant to the instructional domain but not directly related to the specific activity topic (e.g., "Does students' diversity in MOOCs favor or negatively affect statistical methods of data analysis?"). The latter agent design was expected to increase students' cognitive load as it introduced new domain-relevant questions requiring additional critical thinking.

Following a 10-min introduction to the scope of the specific activities in class, students were assigned in dyads and allocated to two computer labs. They were then asked to log into the colMOOC Player using their given credentials to start collaborating with their partner. At the beginning of each activity, the agent posted messages that supported group awareness and were triggered by the identification of static patterns, such as the connection of two students in a chat room (e.g., "Now that you are both connected, we can begin! In this assignment, you are expected to provide a joined response to the task displayed at the top..."). After completing their discussion in the first activity, students proceeded to the second activity while the dyads remained unchanged.

Throughout their participation in the activities, students were encouraged to provide feedback for each agent intervention displayed using an agent evaluation sheet, which was provided to them before the activity. Whenever an agent intervention appeared students could fill in the associated short code, displayed next to each intervention, and rate the specific intervention in terms of relevance and usefulness using a 5-point scale.

Students were asked to complete the two activities within a 1-h limit. When students submitted their team answers and finished the second activity, they were requested to fill in a post-task questionnaire, asking them to express their agreement or disagreement on a 5-point Likert scale, ranging from 1 (disagree) to 5 (agree). The questions aimed to explore students' perceptions of the system and the agent.

Following a short break, students were also invited to participate in a focus group session, which attempted to elicit students' perception of the agent interventions. The session followed a semi-structured protocol, allowing open-ended discussions.

4.3   Results

Central tendency measures were computed to summarize the data for all questionnaire variables and measures of dispersion were computed to understand the variability of the scores.

The descriptive statistics that surfaced following the analysis of the questionnaire variables relating to the usability of colMOOC Player interface are depicted in Table 2. As regards the system performance, students had a favorable opinion towards the overall system responsiveness (N = 10, M = 4.80, SD = 0.42).

Table 2. Questionnaire results relating to the interface of the colMOOC Player.

Questions[(1-disagree, 5-agree)]	Mean	SD	Disagree[(1-2)]	Neutral[(3)]	Agree[(4-5)]
The available options of the user interface are easy to understand	4.70	0.65	0%	10%	90%
The icons and symbols used seem familiar	4.80	0.42	0%	0%	100%
I believe the colMOOC environment is easy-to-use	4.40	0.84	0%	20%	80%

Moreover, the post-task questionnaire elicited students' opinions regarding the presence of the conversational agent. The analysis results are presented in Table 3. Students had a positive opinion towards the automated intervention mechanism (Table 3, row 1). Several students felt that the agent questions were aptly presented during students' discussion (Table 3, row 2). Still, their opinions were somewhat divided when asked whether the agent questions interrupted the discussion with their partner (Table 3, row 3). Interestingly, most students stated that they would be interesting in joining similar chat activities with conversational agents in the future (Table 3, row 4).

Table 3. Questionnaire results relating to the interventions of the conversational agent.

Questions[(1-disagree, 5-agree)]	Mean	SD	Disagree[(1-2)]	Neutral[(3)]	Agree[(4-5)]
Intervening by posing interesting questions during students' discussion seems like a pedagogically beneficial technique	4.50	0.71	0%	10%	90%
The agent interventions were well-aimed	3.50	0.53	0%	50%	50%
The agent questions interrupted my discussion with my partner	2.55	0.82	50%	30%	20%
I want to participate in future educational activities involving conversational agents	3.90	0.99	10%	20%	70%

A series of themes were identified in the qualitative analysis of the focus group discussions. First, students stated that the frequent display of agent questions can cause confusion by disrupting the flow of their peer discussion (F = 60%). In order to partially resolve this issue, they suggested that: (a) the agent should not display new interventions until its last question has been answered and (b) subsequent interventions should have a time interval of 90 s or more. Second, students proposed that the agent should make use of a typing indicator/notification message (e.g., "TIM is typing...") in order to support group awareness and inform them that an intervention will follow (F = 60%). Lastly, participants revealed that they had some trouble understanding whether one or both should respond to the agent questions addressing the team and not of a specific partner (F = 50%). This type of interventions appeared to have further increased the cognitive load of the activity as students had to balance their focus between answering the main task question and organizing their agent responses.

The analysis of the agent evaluation sheets revealed a total number of 100 students' ratings for the 50 agent interventions displayed during the chat activities. Although the overall results appear to be somewhat mixed (Table 4), the emerging data suggest that some of the agent questions were perceived to be 'to the point' and context-relevant by the students. This is an interesting finding since the current version of the conversational agent does not feature any advanced NLP capabilities and is primarily based on pattern matching techniques. An initial inspection of the chat log files indicated that students' responses and perception of the agent interventions varied considerably based on the timing the agent interventions. Although further investigation and analysis is required in order to draw valuable inferences, interventions that were made early on in the activity were found to be more helpful for answering the task as compared to other interventions delivered late in the activity, i.e., after students' discussion has advanced.

Table 4. Agent evaluation sheet results.

Question[(1-not at all, 5-yes, totally)]	Mean	SD	No[(1-2)]	Neutral[(3)]	Yes[(4-5)]
The agent question related closely to our on-going discussion	3.28	1.35	32%	20%	48%
The agent question helped us in forming our task team answer	3.04	1.41	38%	18%	44%

5   Discussion

Conversational agent technology is starting to play a key role in the field of education enabling educators to offer even more engaging learning experiences, which are tailored to learners. Nevertheless, while chatbot technology has matured over time, there is still a need for research on how such agents could add value to real world technological learning environments, including challenges in designing effective dialogue between humans and bots [18].

In this paper, we have presented a teacher-configurable conversational agent service, designed to support collaborative activities in MOOCs by acting as a facilitator scaffolding productive students' dialogues. The design of this agent-based system was evaluated in a pilot study, which involved a small group of postgraduate university students.

Taking into account the main limitations of this exploratory study, such as its limited sample size and 'one-shot' design, the study shares some encouraging preliminary evidence for the potential benefits of integrating collaborative conversational agent activities in MOOCs. Despite missing the ability to engage in full-fledged conversations with the learners, configurable agents can still be perceived positively by students. This finding is even more important considering that these conversational agents can be reused, operate in different domains and, thus, usually have a relatively low development cost. Although the study results show that there is certainly a large room for future improvements as regards the agent design, students have reported that this form of unsolicited agent interventions can be pedagogically beneficial and serve as a valuable tool in real-world educational settings.

Instead of solely focusing on how to advance conversational AI, future research on multi-user educational chatbots could also explore ways of leveraging and building on the human intelligence residing in collaborative learning environments. Utilizing other well-known classroom discourse frameworks, similar to the academically productive talk employed by the colMOOC agent, could lead to new agent intervention strategies, which are domain-independent by design and enable well-targeted interventions.

In the future, we plan to continue our efforts towards building a user-friendly conversational agent service; one that requires no programming skills to configure. We also seek to conduct a series of robustly designed studies investigating how the quality of peer dialogues is affected by the different intervention strategies employed by the agent. Additionally, task design should be further explored since it appears to be critical for increasing the probability of productive peer interactions happening. The task of such chat activities should be designed to be debatable and challenging in order to motivate peers and have them engaged in discussion. From our viewpoint, the objective of assigning such a task should not be to make the peers provide some type of "correct answer" but to engage them in externalizing their thinking.

Acknowledgements and Disclaimer. This research has been funded by the Erasmus+ Programme of the European Commission (project No. 588438-EPP-1-2017-1-EL- EPPKA-KA). This document reflects the views only of the authors. The Education, Audiovisual and Culture Executive Agency and the European Commission cannot be held responsible for any use which may be made of the information contained therein.

References

1. Conole, G.G.: MOOCs as disruptive technologies: strategies for enhancing the learner experience and quality of MOOCs. Revista de Educación a Distancia **39**, 1–17 (2013)
2. Graesser, A., McDaniel, B.: Conversational agents can provide formative assessment, constructive learning, and adaptive instruction. In: The Future of Assessment, pp. 85–112 (2017)
3. Hone, K.S., El Said, G.R.: Exploring the factors affecting MOOC retention: a survey study. Comput. Educ. **98**, 157–168 (2016)
4. Tomar, G.S., Sankaranarayanan, S., Rosé, C.P.: Intelligent conversational agents as facilitators and coordinators for group work in distributed learning environments (MOOCs). In: 2016 AAAI Spring Symposium Series, vol. 2 (2016)

5. Kloos, C.D., Catálan, C., Muñoz-Merino, P.J., Alario-Hoyos, C.: Design of a conversational agent as an educational tool. In: Learning with MOOCS, Madrid, pp. 27–30 (2018)
6. Luckin, R., Holmes, W., Griffiths, M., Forcier, L.B.: Intelligence unleashed: an argument for AI in education (2016)
7. Skjuve, M., Brandtzæg, P.B.: Chatbots as a new user interface for providing health information to young people. Youth and news in a digital media environment–Nordic-Baltic perspectives (2018)
8. Fu, Y., Xiong, H., Lu, X., Yang, J., Chen, C.: Service usage classification with encrypted internet traffic in mobile messaging apps. IEEE Trans. Mob. Comput. **15**(11), 2851–2864 (2016)
9. Hall, E.: Conversational Design. A Book Apart, New York (2018)
10. Song, D., Oh, E.Y., Rice, M.: Interacting with a conversational agent system for educational purposes in online courses. In: 2017 10th International Conference on Human System Interactions (HSI), pp. 78–82. IEEE (2017)
11. Floratos, N., Guasch, T., Espasa, A.: Recommendations on formative assessment and feedback practices for stronger engagement in MOOCs. Open Praxis **7**(2), 141–152 (2015)
12. Ferschke, O., Yang, D., Tomar, G., Rosé, C.P.: Positive impact of collaborative chat participation in an edX MOOC. In: Conati, C., Heffernan, N., Mitrovic, A., Verdejo, M. (eds.) AIED 2015. LNCS, pp. 115–124. Springer, Cham (2015). https://doi.org/10.1007/978-3-319-19773-9_12
13. Tegos, S., Demetriadis, S.: Conversational agents improve peer learning through building on prior knowledge. J. Educ. Technol. Soc. **20**(1), 99–111 (2017)
14. Tegos, S., Psathas, G., Tsiatsos, T., Demetriadis, S.N.: Designing conversational agent interventions that support collaborative chat activities in MOOCs. In: EMOOCs-WIP, Naples, pp. 66–71 (2019)
15. Michaels, S., O'Connor, C.: Conceptualizing talk moves as tools: professional development approaches for academically productive discussion. In: Socializing Intelligence Through Talk and Dialogue, pp. 347–362 (2015)
16. Adamson, D., Ashe, C., Jang, H., Yaron, D., Rosé, C.P.: Intensification of group knowledge exchange with academically productive talk agents. In: Rummel, N., Kapur, M., Nathan, M., Puntambekar, S. (eds.) CSCL Conference Proceedings, pp. 10–17 (2013)
17. Tegos, S., Demetriadis, S., Papadopoulos, P.M., Weinberger, A.: Conversational agents for academically productive talk: a comparison of directed and undirected agent interventions. Int. J. Comput.-Support. Collaborative Learn. **11**(4), 417–440 (2016)
18. Fryer, L.K., Ainley, M., Thompson, A., Gibson, A., Sherlock, Z.: Stimulating and sustaining interest in a language course: an experimental comparison of Chatbot and Human task partners. Comput. Hum. Behav. **75**, 461–468 (2017)

Small Talk Conversations and the Long-Term Use of Chatbots in Educational Settings – Experiences from a Field Study

Sebastian Hobert[✉] and Florian Berens

University of Goettingen, Goettingen, Germany
{shobert,florian.berens}@uni-goettingen.de

Abstract. In this paper, we analyze the use of small talk conversations based on a dialogue analysis of a long-term field study in which university students regularly interacted with a chatbot during a 3-month period of time in an educational setting. In particular, we analyze (1) how often the students engage with small talk topics during the field study, and (2) whether a larger amount of small talk conversations correlates with the students' engagement in learning activities within our chatbot-based learning system, i.e., if engaging in small talk conversations correlates to a more intensive use of the chatbot during our field test. Our results suggest that small talk conversations might play an important role in the design of our chatbot as students who chat about small talk topics also frequently chat about learning-related topics. Nevertheless, the overall impact of small talk capabilities of chatbots should not be overestimated.

Keywords: Chatbot · Small talk conversation · Conversational agent · Pedagogical conversational agent

1 Introduction

The ability to communicate using natural language in a human-like way seems to be an important design feature of chatbots and virtual assistants, as it can be seen in many examples from practice. A typical capability of such state of the art conversational agents is to enable the chatbots to engage in small talk conversations [1]. For example, chatbots are often able to talk about informal topics that are usually not important for a computer program. For instance, such informal conversations cover greeting users, talking about the chatbot's well-being or telling jokes. In this paper, we define informal conversations that are not important for the chatbot's overall purpose as small talk messages. Even though engaging in small talk does not seem to provide any direct beneficial value for most conversational agents, it may be argued to hold indirect benefits [2]. Small talk is a standard part of communication among humans and makes the conversation flow. Thus, it may be argued that including small talk might be beneficial for chatbots as well. However, there is a lack of knowledge about the specific impact of small talk conversations. To fully understand its effects and to include it in the design of chatbots, there is a need to understand the users' engagement in small talk chats.

© Springer Nature Switzerland AG 2020
A. Følstad et al. (Eds.): CONVERSATIONS 2019, LNCS 11970, pp. 260–272, 2020.
https://doi.org/10.1007/978-3-030-39540-7_18

In particular, there is a lack of knowledge about chatbots that are used in long-term settings. Currently, many chatbot-based systems are only used to interact with users for a short period of time, e.g., as personal assistants for customer support. In these cases, small talk capabilities are used to demand the users' attention and to start a conversation, e.g., by actively talking to the users (e.g., "Hello, how can I help you?"). In these cases, the interaction with the chatbot often only takes a short period of time. Long-term adoption of chatbots is usually not needed in these cases. However, in other settings, like in education, it seems appropriate to provide students with a chatbot that is not only available for a short period of time but can support them during an entire learning period, e.g., a full lecture term at the university.

To address these long-term settings, this study provides insights into such a field test in which a chatbot interacted with users for several months. Mainly, our study focuses on an educational setting in which we introduced a chatbot-based learning system. To get detailed insights into the long-term impact of including small talk capabilities in the design of our chatbot, we address the following research questions in the remainder of this paper:

RQ1: How often do students engage in small talk conversations during long term use of a chatbot in an educational setting?

RQ2: How does the usage frequency of the chatbot's small talk capabilities correlate with the students' engagement in learning activities?

To answer these research questions, the remainder of this paper is structured as follows: First, we outline related research on chatbots and its' capabilities to act human-like by engaging in small talk conversations in the next section. Subsequently, we describe our research design in Sect. 3. In Sect. 4, we present the results of our analysis and discuss our findings in Sect. 5. Finally, we summarize the results in the conclusion section.

2 Related Research

Chatbots can be defined as information systems with a natural language-based user interface. Due to the interaction with the users in a "conversational-style" [3] using natural language, the interaction of chatbots with users is similar to communication between humans. From a technical perspective, chatbots are usually designed to interact autonomously by relying on methods known from machine learning, artificial intelligence, and natural language processing.

By using chatbots in educational settings, students should be supported during learning processes. According to prior research, it is to be expected that chatbots could provide "significant positive impact on learning success and student satisfaction" [4]. For instance, [5] developed a chatbot that is able to reply to posts of students in a forum of a computer science course. In another project, the conversational agent *MentorChat* was introduced, which should support students in collaborative learning tasks [6]. Further exemplary use cases are described in recent literature reviews in more detail, see, e.g., [4] and [7].

A common pattern known from various chatbots or other virtual assistants is their capabilities to engage in small talk conversations [1]. For instance, many chatbots are able to respond to messages like "Tell me a joke" or "How are you?". By implementing such capabilities, which are not directly beneficial for the intended purpose of a chatbot, developers want to enable the chatbot to act human-like [8] in a socially-accepted way. In doing so, the adoption of users to interact with a chatbot should be fostered, and in some cases, the chatbot should even hide that it is not a human being. However, most available chatbots used in practice are not designed for educational practices, and the users' interaction is different compared to the use in university courses. Whereas many chatbots are designed for corporate purposes (e.g., customer support [9]) and are only used for a short period of time, chatbots that are introduced in university courses can support the students during the whole lecture period like in [5]. Consequently, the adoption of the students is more important as the usage time is longer. However, the implications of small talk capabilities of chatbots for the long-term adoption of users in educational settings have to the best of our knowledge not yet sufficiently be researched. Thus, we will focus on analyzing the small talk usage of students in a long-term field study in this paper.

3   Research Design

In the following, we outline the research design that we applied to answer our small talk-related research questions. We conducted our study as part of a design-oriented research project based on the Design Science Research Approach [10–12]. As the main result of this design-oriented research project, we conceptualized and implemented a chatbot-based learning system, which is the basis for this investigation on the impact of small talk capabilities (see next section). The chatbot-based learning system is designed as a progressive web-application and provides a user interface that is similar to common instant messenger apps for smartphones. The chatbot-based learning system provides students the possibility to ask open-ended questions concerning the content of a university course. The chatbot is able to answer those questions immediately based on a database consisting of more than 450 learning objects (i.e., definitions of basic terms). Additionally, the chatbot-based learning system provides students access to formative exercise.

Using this implementation of our chatbot-based learning system (see a detailed description in the following section), we conducted a field study starting from April 2019. During this field study, approx. 700 students of an introductory lecture on statistics for social sciences got access to the system and had the possibility to interact with it until the end of the lecture period. To answer our research questions, we analyzed the pseudonymized discourses of the chatbot with the students. To this aim, we used the textual messages from the students and the chatbot as a basis and enhanced it using available metadata (e.g., timestamp of the conversation). To analyze the metadata, we tagged the text messages with intents computed by our chatbot using the natural language processing library NLP.js [13]. Our trained natural language processing model which is based on approx. 2800 exemplary messages is not accurate in every case. Thus, we manually reviewed those messages that were classified with low accuracy by our chatbot. In doing so, we retrained and improved the intent recognition of future messages. During the manual reviewing process, we adjusted the recognized intents of approx. 1.8% of all messages sent by the users. Finally, we excluded all messages that were not classified as small talk and resulted in our case base of small talk interactions.

Figure 1 summarizes the steps we conducted to process the data.

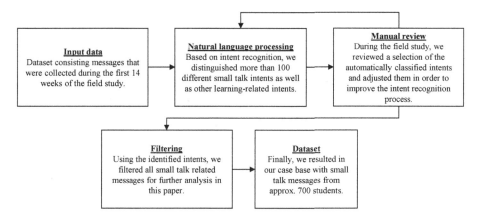

Fig. 1. Research steps for the processing of the data to derive our final dataset

Using the final dataset, we analyzed the small talk interactions of the learners descriptively and on a timely basis to answer research question 1. To respond to research question 2, we tested whether a student's small talk interactions correlates with his/her overall engagement in the learning app during the three-month field test statistically using Spearman's rank correlation coefficient.

4   Chatbot Overview

To conduct the long-term field study, we used our chatbot-based learning system that we develop in early 2019. The system is developed as a messenger-like chatbot system and provides students participating in an introductory lecture on statistics education a natural language-based user interface.

To ensure that every student is able to use the system independently of a specific device or operating system, we implemented it as a progressive web-app. From a technical perspective, we used HTML5, CSS, and JavaScript for the implementation of the students' frontend. The natural language understanding of the students' written input is done using a node.js backend component. Additionally, the lecturer as well as several student assistants had access to an administration control panel, which could be used for reviewing questioning and answering dialogues (i.e., we conducted quality assurance tasks to improve the intent recognition) that were marked by the natural language processing component with a high probability of errors (i.e., the chatbot was unsure whether the students' messages were understood correctly).

Figure 2 provides an overview of the technical architecture of the chatbot-based learning system.

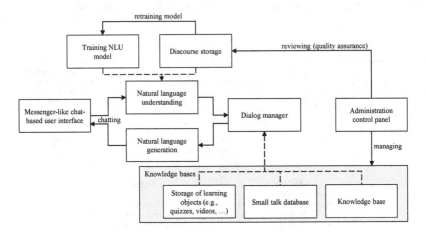

Fig. 2. Simplified overview of the technical architecture

From a students' perspective, our chatbot-based learning system can be seen as the only online resource required in addition to the face-to-face lectures and tutorial sessions. The system provides all relevant additional online materials (like supplementary formative quizzes, video recordings of the lectures, slides of the lectures, etc.) to the students. Besides these learning-related functionalities (see Fig. 3), the chatbot-based learning system is, for instance, capable of answering questions concerning organizational issues and conducting small talk interactions with students.

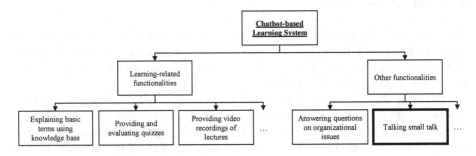

Fig. 3. Overview over core functionalities of the chatbot-based learning system

All learning-related functionalities, as well as the other functionalities, are integrated into the messenger-like chat-based interface. An overview of exemplary messages asked by learners is displayed in Table 1.

Table 1. Exemplary messages sent by learners

Exemplary message	Description
"Show me the video recordings"	Requesting video recordings
"Show me the lecture slides"	Requesting pdf files of lecture slides
"What is the meaning of the standard deviation?"	Asking for a definition of a term mentioned in the lecture
"What is the date of the exam?"	Asking for organizational aspects
"Hi, how are you?" "What is your name?"	Talking small talk (i.e., messages that are not related to the learning process)

In the remainder of this paper, we will mainly focus on the functionalities related to the small talk capabilities of the chatbot-based learning system and its influence on the students' usage of the learning-related functionalities.

5   Results

In the following Subsect. 5.1, we respond to the first research question by analyzing the number of small talk messages written by users. To this aim, we conducted an analysis based on the recognized intents by the natural language understanding component of our chatbot-based learning system. Subsequently, we focus on correlations of the students' engagement in small talk conversations with learning activities in response to the second research question in Subsect. 5.2.

5.1   Engagement in Small Talk Conversations

The first time a student opens the chatbot-based learning system, the system posts a friendly welcome message. This welcome message can be seen on the one hand as an introductory example of how the overall system works. On the other hand, it is used to foster the student to participate in a conversation with the chatbot. Afterward, the student can proceed with the conversation by replying with small talk messages or focusing on learning-related aspects by asking further questions. As the chatbot-based learning system is designed as an open-topic natural language processing system, the user is not restricted on specific topics. In the following, we will only focus on small talk-related messages written by the students. To get an impression about the students' interaction with the chatbot-based learning system when engaging in small talk conversations, Fig. 4 outlines an exemplary dialog excerpt in which a student first chatted about small talk topics with the chatbot before switching over to learning-related contents (i.e., quizzes). The overall dialog continues with further learning-related

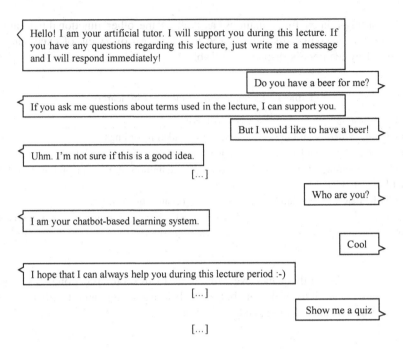

Hello! I am your artificial tutor. I will support you during this lecture. If you have any questions regarding this lecture, just write me a message and I will respond immediately!

Do you have a beer for me?

If you ask me questions about terms used in the lecture, I can support you.

But I would like to have a beer!

Uhm. I'm not sure if this is a good idea.

[...]

Who are you?

I am your chatbot-based learning system.

Cool

I hope that I can always help you during this lecture period :-)

[...]

Show me a quiz

[...]

Fig. 4. Exemplary dialog excerpt of one student chatting with the chatbot

contents. Thus, in this case, the small talk conversation might be useful to motivate the student to learn.

As shown in Fig. 5, the amount of small talk messages posted by the students reaches its all-time high at the start of the lecture period[1]. In this first week of the field study, approx. 30% of all messages sent to the chatbot were labeled as small talk (i.e., approx. 1100 small talk messages). In the subsequent week, still approx. 900 messages are related to small talk. However, the amount decreases to approx. 10% in this second week, as the number of learning-related messages increased rapidly. After these first two weeks in which the students engaged a lot in small talk conversations, the number of small talk messages decreased substantially and never reached more than approx. 450 messages.

The analysis of the time history of the small talk use thus indicates that small talk conversations are particularly relevant in the beginning when students are interested in discovering the chatbot-based learning system. Independently of the overall system use, the number of small talk messages never reached a high level.

The decreasing interest of the students to engage in small talk conversations cannot only be seen in the total amount of small talk messages but also in the distribution of the written small talk questions (see Fig. 6). Whereas in the first weeks of the field

---

[1] As the lecture started and ended not on the first day of the week, the weeks 1 and 14 encompass only four to six days and are thus shorter than the remaining weeks. This can explain the lower number of written messages by the students in these two weeks.

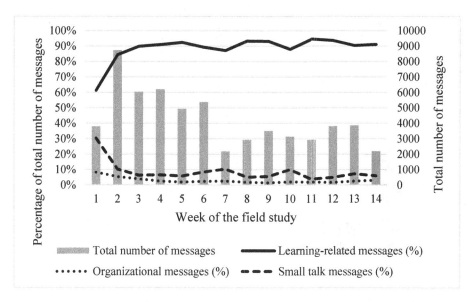

Fig. 5. Overview of the time history of the chat usage

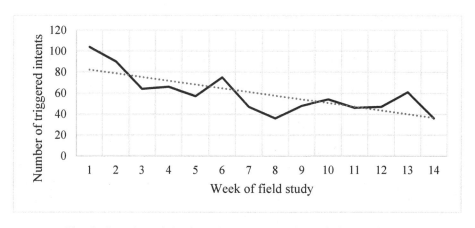

Fig. 6. Overview of the time history of the number of triggered intents

study, almost all active small talk intents that can be recognized by the chatbot were triggered (more than 100 different intents). In the following weeks, the number of triggered small talk intents decreased rapidly.

The decreasing number of triggered small talk intents might be explained similarly to the decreasing total number of small talk engagement as seen above. Talking with the chatbot about small talk topics might become less interesting while actually using the system for learning purposes might become more important as the final exam is approaching.

Interesting regarding the small talk usage is that there is a large number of students who are not engaging in small talk conversations at all. Approx. 50% of all users only sent 0 to 5 messages that were recognized by the chatbot as small talk content. In contrast to that, the remaining approx. 50% wrote at least 6 or more small talk-related messages. In some cases, even much more than 40 messages as displayed in Fig. 7.

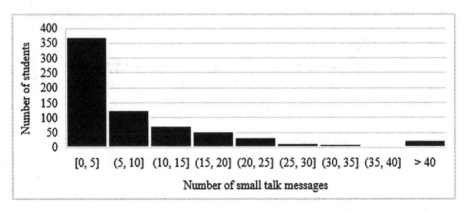

Fig. 7. Grouping of the number of students based on the number of small talk messages

Based on this observation, in the following subsection, we will analyze whether the engagement in small talk conversations correlates with the engagement in learning activities.

5.2 Correlation of Small Talk Engagement and Learning Activities

As indicated by the high usage of the small talk capabilities of our chat-based learning system with more than 2000 small talk messages sent by the students in the first two weeks of the field study (see Fig. 5), it should be analyzed whether these small talk capabilities are beneficial for the long-term adoption. If students only chat with the chatbot about small talk topics but not about learning-related topics, the overall aim of the system to support the students wouldn't be reached.

First, we analyzed whether there is a correlation between the number of small talk messages written by the students in the first two weeks of the field study and their total number of chat-based learning interactions (e.g., solving a quiz, asking domain-specific questions about lecture content, download learning material) during the field study (see Fig. 8 for a visualization of the dataset). To this aim, we calculated the Spearman's rank correlation coefficient. Based on this, the statement that the number of small talk messages written in the first two weeks of the field study correlates with the total number of learning interactions in the whole period of 14 weeks can be supported ($r_s = 0.348$, $p = 0.000$, $n = 700$). We can confirm a moderate correlation between both aspects.

Second, we also analyzed whether this correlation also exists when comparing not only the number of small talk messages at the beginning of the field study (i.e., the

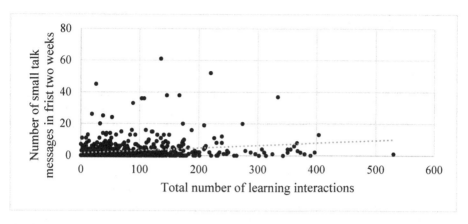

Fig. 8. Comparison of small talk usage in the first two weeks with the total number of learning interactions during the whole period of 14 weeks

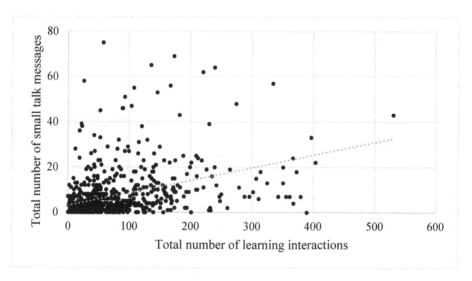

Fig. 9. Comparison of the total number of small talk usage with the total number of learning interactions during the whole period of 14 weeks per student

adoption phase) but also in the overall period of 14 weeks (see Fig. 9). According to the Spearman's rank correlation coefficient, these two variables correlate even stronger ($r_s = 0.557$, p = 0.000; N = 700) compared to the small talk usage in the first two weeks. This indicates that students who engage in learning-related activities in our chatbot-based learning system more often also talk about small talk topics in the long run.

6   Discussion

6.1   Implications

The results of our analysis of the conversational data of our field study suggest that small talk capabilities might facilitate the adoption of chatbot-based systems in educational settings. In the analysis of the first research question, we showed that many students chatted with the chatbot, particularly at the beginning of the field study. Due to this high amount of more than 2,000 small talk messages sent by students in the first two weeks, we propose that small talk capabilities are a design feature that should be considered. Since the students themselves do not gain any direct advantage or learning increase from small talk conversations, the pure amount of small talk messages they produced nevertheless has to be considered as an indication of the importance students attribute to small talk. This is in line with the results of prior studies and the common practice of chatbots used in other use cases. For instance, [14] showed that building long-term human-computer relationships might be beneficial. We assume from the insights from our study that small talk might be able to foster such a relationship in our field study between the chatbot and the students. On the side of the developers, a non-implementation of small talk would have led to unsatisfying responses (like "Sorry, I couldn't understand you properly."). Thus, the lack of small talk capabilities could possibly have a negative effect on the students' enjoyment and finally on their adoption. To analyze this in more detail, it would be possible to introduce the same chatbot but with disabled small talk capabilities in a similar field setting in the future. Thus, it could be analyzed if a lack of small talk capabilities has a negative impact.

Furthermore, we have evidence based on Spearman's rank correlation coefficient that the amount of small talk messages and the overall amount of learning activities correlates positively within our field study. An interesting aspect of our analysis is that the correlation is even stronger when the number of small talk messages within the considered time span is expended from two weeks to the whole period of 14 weeks of our field study. This might be explained by an increased overall engagement in chatting with the learning system, which also resulted in additional small talk messages that were sent by the actively participating students.

Nevertheless, the effect of implementing small talk capabilities to foster the users' engagement and adoption of a chatbot should be analyzed in further research studies. It should also not be overestimated as the correlation only implies a moderate effect size. However, we assume that not providing small talk capabilities could have a negative impact.

6.2   Limitations

Our analysis is based on a large dataset from our chatbot-based learning system. The dataset contains messages that were manually written by users as well as messages that were automatically created by the chatbots (e.g., answers to questions asked by the users). Due to the large amount of data, classifying each message individually by humans was not possible due to resource constraints. Thus, we used the chatbot's trained intent recognition algorithm for this purpose. Additionally, we tried to manually review as many messages as possible during the field study for quality assurance purposes and to retrain the algorithm in order to reduce classification errors. Nevertheless, there might still be errors in the classification of the intents.

Our analysis is based on one field study that we conducted in summer 2019 in one university course. We assume that our results are not only valid for this particular lecture, but also for other large-scale lectures on different topics. However, further analyses should be conducted in further fields of study.

Finally, we showed that correlations between the small talk usage and the overall learning engagement in the chatbot-based learning system exist. However, it might be interesting to identify in further studies which additional factors are fostering the students' adoption of chatbot-based learning systems and whether the correlations also imply causalities.

7 Conclusion

In this research study, we analyzed the long-term interaction of approx. 700 students with a chatbot. In particular, we analyzed the students' engagement in small talk conversations that are not directly beneficial for the learning success but are expected to be supportive for the students' adoption of our chatbot-based learning system.

First, we analyzed the overall usage of the chatbot's small talk activities and showed that the amount of small talk messages is particularly high at the beginning of our field study where it reached about 30% of all messages. Additionally, we showed that the diversity of different small talk topics was higher in the beginning compared to the remaining time period. Second, we significantly showed that there is a positive correlation between the number of small talk messages sent by a student and her/his overall learning activities within our chatbot-based learning system.

To fully understand the importance of small talk interactions in chatbot-based learning systems, further research is necessary. For instance, further in-depth discourse analysis combined with survey results about the perceived adoption of the students might be helpful to analyze the topic in more detail. Additionally, introducing the same chatbot in a similar setting with disabled small talk capabilities would also be interesting to analyze if this results in less engagement. Nevertheless, our findings already show that students actively engage in small talk activities. Thus, we suggest that developers should consider if implementing small talk capabilities is useful in their settings.

References

1. Brandtzaeg, P.B., Følstad, A.: Why people use chatbots. In: Kompatsiaris, I., et al. (eds.) INSCI 2017. LNCS, vol. 10673, pp. 377–392. Springer, Cham (2017). https://doi.org/10.1007/978-3-319-70284-1_30
2. Kerlyl, A., Hall, P., Bull, S.: Bringing chatbots into education: towards natural language negotiation of open learner models. In: Ellis, R., Allen, T., Tuson, A. (eds.) Applications and Innovations in Intelligent Systems XIV, 9, pp. 179–192. Springer, London (2007)

3. Lebeuf, C., Storey, M.-A., Zagalsky, A.: Software bots. IEEE Softw. **35**, 18–23 (2018)
4. Winkler, R., Söllner, M.: Unleashing the potential of chatbots in education: a state-of-the-art analysis. In: Academy of Management Annual Meeting (AOM), Chicago, USA (2018)
5. Goel, A., Creeden, B., Kumble, M., Salunke, S., Shetty, A., Wiltgen, B.: Using watson for enhancing human-computer co-creativity. In: AAAI Symposium, pp. 22–29 (2015)
6. Tegos, S., Demetriadis, S., Karakostas, A.: MentorChat: introducing a configurable conversational agent as a tool for adaptive online collaboration support. In: 2011 15th Panhellenic Conference on Informatics, pp. 13–17 (2011)
7. Hobert, S., Meyer von Wolff, R.: Say hello to your new automated tutor – a structured literature review on pedagogical conversational agents. In: 14th International Conference on Wirtschaftsinformatik, pp. 301–314 (2019)
8. Jain, M., Kumar, P., Kota, R., Patel, S.N.: Evaluating and informing the design of chatbots. In: Koskinen, I., Lim, Y.-K., Cerratto-Pargman, T., Chow, K., Odom, W. (eds.) DIS '18, June 9-13, 2018, Hong Kong, pp. 895–906. ACM Press, New York, USA (2018)
9. Meyer von Wolff, R., Hobert, S., Schumann, M.: How may i help you? – state of the art and open research questions for chatbots at the digital workplace. In: Proceedings of the 52th Hawaii International Conference on System Sciences, pp. 95–104 (2019)
10. Hevner, A.: A three cycle view of design science research. Scand. J. Inf. Syst. **19**, 87–92 (2007)
11. Hevner, A., March, S., Park, J., Ram, S.: Design science in information systems research. Manag. Inf. Syst. Q. **28**, 75–105 (2004)
12. Gregor, S., Jones, D.: The anatomy of a design theory. J. Assoc. Inf. Syst. **8**, 312–335 (2007)
13. AXA Shared Services Spain S.A.: axa-group/nlp.js. https://github.com/axa-group/nlp.js
14. Bickmore, T.W., Picard, R.W.: Establishing and maintaining long-term human-computer relationships. ACM Trans. Comput.-Hum. Interact. **12**, 293–327 (2005)

Author Index

Printed in the United States
By Bookmasters